RACING DATES

Classic Moments from the Sport of Kings

RACING DATES

Classic Moments from the Sport of Kings

Graham Sharpe

First published in Great Britain in 1993 by
Virgin Books
an imprint of Virgin Publishing Ltd
332 Ladbroke Grove
London W10 5AH

ISBN 0 86369 756 9

Typeset by TW Typesetting, Plymouth, Devon
Printed and bound in Great Britain by
The Guernsey Press Co. Ltd, Guernsey, CI

Acknowledgements

This book would have been far less accurate than it now is had it not been for the generous offices of Roger Plummer, part of the *Daily Mirror's* Spotform team, who cast an expert eye over the proofs, picking up many little errors which might otherwise have crept through. Damien Snee, a member of the William Hill Odds Compiling Department, rummaged through dusty form books to confirm or condemn items of information which required verification – and I thank him for that.

There may still be an inaccuracy or two – for these I apologise. Every date herein has been checked and double-checked where possible, but as memories, both written and verbal, can let the owner down on occasion, there is always the possibility that an error is perpetrated. If you spot one (or more!), feel free to notify me via the publishers so that it can be corrected in any future edition.

I owe a note of thanks to Sally Holloway at Virgin Publishing for her enthusiasm for the idea of the book; to Ríona MacNamara, also of Virgin, for the work and encouragement she has put into its production; and to my boss at William Hill, David Hickling, for backing the project.

Dedication

To Sheila, Steeven and Paul – you can have the breakfast
table back now!

1 JANUARY

1831 Jockey JOHN MANGLE died aged 81. He was known as 'Crying Jackie' because of his tendency to burst into tears after being beaten in a race. Racing's early equivalent of Gazza perhaps. Rode 5 St Leger winners and later became a trainer.

1834 Racehorses at Newmarket began to celebrate their 'official' birthdays on this date. The rest of the country followed suit in 1858.

1859 Seldom mentioned when nominations are made for the title 'best jockey ever', ISAAC MURPHY (originally Burns) was born in Kentucky. He went on to ride 628 winners from 1,412 rides - an incredible winning percentage of 44 for the black rider, who was paid a $10,000 per year retainer to ride for owner Lucky Baldwin. Died of pneumonia, aged 37.

1920 GORDON RICHARDS arrived at Foxhill, Wiltshire, to start his first job in racing - as stable lad to Martin Hartigan. He was fifteen.

1925 EASTER HERO, who was to go on to win two Cheltenham Gold Cups, raced for the first time, finishing unplaced in the Killeston Plate at Baldoyle, Ireland.

1940 Aussie jockey GEORGE MOORE rode his first winner, Eagle Farm, at Ascot in Brisbane.

1951 Lambourn trainer DUNCAN SASSE born. Trained 28-1 shot Roland Gardens to win the 1978 2,000 Guineas. Went on to train in Italy.

1955 Jockey STEPHEN PERKS born. Champion Apprentice 1973.

1960 Jockey KELLY MARKS born. She also became an actress, appearing in the films *Champions* and *A View To a Kill*. Rode in England, California, Holland and Belgium.

1972 Trainer DERMOT WELD rode his first winner on the flat - Chevy Chase at Baldoyle. Later, on the same card, he sent out his first jump winner when Peter Russell rode Spanner to victory.

1973 CHARMIAN HILL, subsequently to own Champion Hurdle-Cheltenham Gold Cup heroine DAWN RUN, became the first lady rider to compete against men in Ireland. She finished 3rd in a National Hunt race at Fairyhouse.

1990 Jockey MAREE LYNDON became the first woman to win the 3,200-metre Auckland Cup in New Zealand, riding Miss Stanima.

1991 For the first time ever a husband and wife finished 1st and 2nd in a Group Race when JIM COLLETT rode Star Harvest (46-1) to win the $400,000 Auckland Cup in New Zealand while his wife TRUDY rode Shugar to be 2nd just 3/4 length behind.

1992 The Queen Mother's FURRY KNOWE (ridden by Ben de Haan) won at Devon to become her first Cath Walwyn-trained winner.

2 JANUARY

1920 Owner of Arc runner-up Park Top and 8 times hurdles winner Gay George, the DUKE OF DEVONSHIRE born. Colours: straw.

1939 ARTHUR 'FIDDLER' GOODWILL rode Khordad to win the Charlton Handicap Hurdle for Tom Leader's stable at Manchester.

1946 *Timeform* Director GEOFF GREETHAM born.

1946 EDWARD OWEN JR, Welsh trainer of Monte Ceco and Rupertino, born. First licence 1977. Won 9 races under NH rules as jockey.

1946 Irish trainer and prolific amateur rider (260 winners since 1963 and over 200 point-to-points) JOHN FOWLER born. Trainer of Royal Dipper, Bankers Benefit, and Maid of Money. First licence 1974. Once listed his 'recreations' in *Directory of the Turf* as 'mostly unprintable'.

1951 Irish trainer NOEL MEADE, handler of Sweet Mint and Fane Ranger, born. First licence 1972.

1965 Having had a permit for 13 years, DONALD 'GINGER' MCCAIN finally sent out his first winner, San Lorenzo (R. Langley, 3-1), at Liverpool. He went on to train Red Rum to win three Grand Nationals.

1968 Owner of winners One Wing and Brilliant Gail JOHN COSTELLO died aged 67 following car crash in Co. Tipperary. Also owner of Darragh Stud, Ennis, Co. Clare.

1983 Nine years after retiring as a trainer SAM ARMSTRONG died aged 78. Rider of 50 winners over jumps, Armstrong trained Classic winners Sayajirao (1947 St Leger) and My Babu (1948 2,000 Guineas).

1989 27-year-old NH jockey MICHAEL HAMMOND announced his retirement. Three days earlier he rode the last of his 231 winners, Colombiere, at Catterick. Second in Championship to Scudamore in 1987-88 with 63 winners.

1990 Ayr trainer JOHN WILSON saddled his first treble in 12 years of trying when Impecuniosity (20-1), Persuasive (11-8) and Young Miner (33-1) landed a 1,695-1 treble - and at his home course.

1990 BRUCE RAYMOND rode his first winner on Southwell's flat all-weather track when Gothic Ford obliged. He rode his only jump winner - Grey Charger - 25 years earlier at the same course over hurdles.

1992 The day after announcing that he was launching his Testimonial Year - the first of its kind for a jockey - 36-year-old STEVE SMITH ECCLES broke an ankle in a fall at Lingfield.

1993 Seven-year-old RAPPORTEUR pulled off a 25-1 shock win on the all-weather track at Lingfield. Punters shouldn't have been surprised though - it was the Charles Elsey-trained runner's 14th win at the track.

3 JANUARY

1912 King George and Queen Mary visited the Calcutta races.

1913 American financier James R. Keene died aged 74. Owned Foxhall, which completed a double in the Cesarewitch and Cambridgeshire for William Day's stables at Woodyates, Wiltshire, in 1881.

1924 Former jockey turned trainer REG HOLLINSHEAD, renowned for the quality of apprentices he has produced, born. Trained Remainder Man, runner-up in the 2,000 Guineas and 3rd in the Derby (1978).

1937 AHMED FOUSTOK born. The owner and breeder of prolific two-year-old winner Provideo, which won 16 races as a two-year-old in 1984. Colours: emerald green and red check; emerald green sleeves.

1940 Epsom trainer JOHN SUTCLIFFE JR born. He was responsible for Jimmy Reppin and Right Tack, which won the 1969 2,000 Guineas.

1962 Jockey SIMON WHITWORTH born. Rode first winner, Byroc Boy, at Warwick on May 3 1982.

1967 Jockey GERALD MOSSE born. He partnered 'wonder horse' Arazi as a two-year-old and the 1990 15-1 Arc winner Saumarez.

1967 Jockey ROBERT BELLAMY born. First winner was Molojec for Jenny Pitman on National Day 1987. Also partnered Memberson.

1984 The two events were probably in no way connected, but the Prince of Wales fell off his horse while out with the Cottesmore Hunt in Leicestershire; and Buckingham Palace announced that women would not be allowed into the Royal Enclosure at Royal Ascot if their hats were too small.

1988 Appearing on TV quiz programme *Sporting Triangles*, jockey Gee Armytage revealed her all-round sporting knowledge when she asked Manchester United and England skipper Bryan Robson which sport he was involved in.

1990 Jockey-optician Andy Orkney took the eye when, the day after opening a practice in Leyburn, he rode his first-ever double on The Maltkin and Kersil at Sedgefield.

1992 US jockey ANGEL CORDERO JR injured in a fall at Aqueduct, suffering a broken elbow, three broken ribs and a damaged spleen. He never raced again and announced his retirement in May 1992. Rode 7,076 winners.

1993 10lb-claiming apprentice ED CARVALHO partnered his 42nd mount and rode his first winner, Majestic Moran, at Tampa Bay Downs, USA, at the ripe old age of 43.

1993 Former Dorking-based trainer ROBIN GOW went through the card at Seeb racetrack in Oman, saddling all 6 winners at Oman's most prestigious meeting, which includes thoroughbred, Arab and harness races.

4 JANUARY

1927 Scottish owner-trainer ROBIN DUN (Bright Beach and Cardonagh) born.

1936 Jockey TOMMY JENNINGS, partner of Sempervivum, born. Also rode Mugatpura.

1944 Jockey JACINTO VASQUES, rider of Ruffian and Genuine Risk, born.

1954 Flamboyant, overweight American trainer ROGER STEIN born. The handler of Forty Niner Days caused something of a stir when he brought that animal over to race at Ascot and appeared in the parade ring in a blue tracksuit and, horror of horrors, without a tie.

1967 Former trainer COLIN LAIDLER died, aged 37, after a lengthy illness. His Stenquill won the Emblem Chase at Manchester in 1962.

1990 THE SHANAHAN BAY became the first horse to win 4 times on all-weather surfaces when the Eric Eldin-trained five-year-old won over 6 furlongs at Lingfield.

1991 Henry Cecil's former wife, JULIE CECIL, sent out her first runner as a trainer. Ferox finished last on the all-weather track at Southwell in the Chatsworth Handicap.

1992 STEVE CAUTHEN wed 25-year-old law student Amy Rothfuss in Cincinnati. He was 32.

1992 Jockey FRANKIE DETTORI had an eventful introduction to racing in Hong Kong. Riding at Sha Tin, Dettori apparently hindered the 5–4 favourite Innovation, ridden by local jockey Jackie Tse, who took such exception that he lashed out at Dettori with his whip as they crossed the line almost together in 4th (Dettori's Duet Danseurs) and 5th places. Tse was severely warned by the stewards, who cautioned Dettori for chewing gum. 'They told me it was not a fast food store,' said Frankie.

1993 Tragedy struck for Sir Andrew Lloyd Webber's wife Madeleine when the horse he bought for her, Champion Hurdle hopeful AL MUTAHM, purchased for £80,000, was destroyed after severing a tendon during the Ramsbury Hurdle at Newbury.

5 JANUARY

1842 The first recorded race meeting at Auckland, New Zealand, took place at the Epsom racecourse.

1938 Jump jockey turned starter GERRY SCOTT born.

1945 Jump jockey turned groundsman DAVID CARTWRIGHT born. Best horses Bighorn and Lyford Cay.

1945 Wellingborough owner TIM CORBY born.

1961 CANTAB won at Stratford to become the first Ryan Price winner to be ridden by Josh Gifford.

1963 In a pretty awful winter, TOMMY MCGINLEY rode 3 winners at Ayr, the first UK meeting since December 21 and the last before March 8.

1968 Les Kennard-trained EASTERN DELIGHT, ridden by claimer Ken Begley, won the first race staged in the British Isles since November 25 when he scored in the two-mile 5-furlong hurdle race at Sandown.

1983 WELCOME SIGHT, from the Mick Easterby yard, fell into the River Rye near Malton and was rescued from drowning by Andrew Stringer, who was nominated for a bravery award as a result.

1987 TOT was the first winner of the first NH meeting at Edinburgh.

1988 RAVINELLA was named Europe's joint champion two-year-old along with Warning. She was the first filly to top the rankings since the ratings were introduced in 1978.

1989 ALLERLAD was a shock 100–1 winner at Ayr. Owner-trainer David MacDonald didn't have a penny on, but *Raceform* journalist Alan Amies took £20 each way at 200–1 and collected £4,800.

1992 After a horse collapsed and had to be destroyed before the start of a race in Bombay, Indian police launched an investigation into the involvement of big-time criminals in horse-doping. Bottles of drugs and syringes were discovered at the track, India's top course. Police allegedly arrested the chief security officer of the Royal Western India Turf Club, which runs the track.

1993 Former trainer JACK MORRIS, one of only two people to survive when a plane carrying broodmares from Deauville crashed at Heathrow in 1968, died of cancer in Newmarket Hospital, aged 68.

1993 New fence-style hurdles were introduced on the all-weather at Lingfield and twenty-year-old Josh Caddell rode Faynaz to win the first race over the new obstacles. Gay Kelleway saddled Aberfoyle, her first winner as a trainer, at the same meeting.

6 JANUARY

1907 Former 'king of the selling plates', trainer BOB WARD, born.

1933 Former boss of racing in Singapore, TIM THOMPSON, born.

1938 Jockey DUNCAN KEITH born. The Scot won the 1965 2,000 Guineas on 100-8 shot Niskar and was runner-up in Mill Reef's Derby on Linden Tree. First winner Zator at Folkestone in 1954. Twice disqualified from Ascot Gold Cup when riding Rock Roi in 1971 and 1972, first year for failing dope test, second for interfering with second-placed Erimo Hawk. Gave up riding because of weight problems in 1973.

1943 Kildare trainer VIVIAN KENNEDY born. Was a flat jockey for 26 years and also rode winners over hurdles. Began training in 1983. Best horses trained Flute Player, Living Rough.

1945 After a gap of almost three years, jump racing resumed after the war with a meeting at Cheltenham. Ron Smyth won the Berkeley Hurdle on Forestation for his trainer uncle, Vic Smyth of Epsom.

1951 American trainer SHUG MCGAUGHEY (real name Claude) born in Lexington, Kentucky. He was responsible for Personal Ensign and Easy Goer, which won the 1989 Belmont.

1951 All 6 clear favourites won at Windsor.

1966 Former US Champion Jockey CHRIS ANTLEY born in Fort Lauderdale, Florida.

1987 DE RIGUEUR was disqualified from Ascot's Balmoral Handicap, which had taken place in September 1986, after a Mars Bar was blamed for a positive dope test, costing connections over £10,000.

1991 Racing took place in Beirut for the first time in five years after being stopped during the civil war. The 4-race meeting was attended by 25,000.

1992 Classic-winning jockey TONY MURRAY found dead at his Wiltshire home, aged 41. Won the Oaks on Ginevra in 1972 and the St Leger on Bruni in 1975 and had over 1,100 wins to his credit.

1993 The new look hurdles for all-weather tracks claimed their first victim when Terminus broke his neck in the selling hurdle at Southwell.

1993 Leading Sydney trainer GRAEME ROGERSON'S Total Effect was beaten favourite at Randwick. Later, after being found guilty of failing to report to the stewards a condition which may have affected the running of the horse, he was disqualified for six months and fined AUS$10,000 on two charges relating to the incident. He was granted the right of appeal and allowed to continue to train pending the appeal.

7 JANUARY

1833 JOHN OSBORNE, who became the most popular northern rider of the Victorian era, born in Derbyshire. Nicknamed 'The Bank of England jockey' as a tribute to his honesty and 'The Old Pusher' for his perseverance with seemingly lost causes. Won 12 Classics including 1869 Derby on Pretender. Took up training at Middleham and rode out until the age of 88, a year before he died.

1916 Jump trainer JACK CANN born. First licence 1966. Best horses included Tillingbourne, Royal Beacon, Harlech Lad and Devon Air.

1920 Jump and flat jockey AUBREY BRABAZON born. Rode Vincent O'Brien's treble Cheltenham Gold Cup-winner Cottage Rake (1948-49-50) and dual champion hurdler Hatton's Grace (1949-50). Also won Irish 2,000 Guineas and Oaks. Later trained.

1949 ALBERT 'SNOWY' WHALLEY, who rode his first winner in India aged 23, and won the 1,000 Guineas on Roseway in 1919, died in Newmarket aged 63.

1955 Flat jockey MICK MILLER born. First winner Silky Moss at Carlisle in 1973. 20 winners in 1976 and 1979.

1958 Flat jockey ALAN PROUD born. Rode Ballet Champ to win Ascot's Brown Jack Stakes in 1985. First winner Gold Cheb at Thirsk, 1976.

1968 EL MIGHTY, the no-hoper which had started as one of the leading fancies for the 1967 Derby when a story was published that a punter had 'dreamed' he would win, won a hurdles race at Cagnes Sur Mer. In the Derby, trained by Dave Hanley and ridden by Paul Cook, his odds tumbled from 200-1 to 22-1 but he finished well down the field, behind Royal Palace.

1991 Morley Street's full brother GRANVILLE AGAIN made his British debut over hurdles, winning by 12 lengths at Wolverhampton.

1993 An enormous gamble took place on BIG BEN DUN, trained by Co. Clare Farmer John O'Neill, which ran in the Carrick Hill Handicap Chase at Punchestown. The horse was backed down from 100-1 to 3-1 favourite and won by 10 lengths. It was believed to have taken over IR£150,000 out of the betting ring. Ridden by Sean Donovan, the horse had finished 16 of 19 last time out in a hurdles race.

1993 GEORGE AUBREY BEAUCLERK ELLWOOD was born. Never heard of him? Well, bear the name in mind – he may just end up as Champion Jump Jockey in a few years' time. If he does, his godfather, a Mr Good, will be delighted – he staked £10 at odds of 5,000-1 with William Hill on the infant becoming Champion Jump Jockey before his 30th birthday as a christening present for George.

8 JANUARY

1807   SAM CHIFNEY SR, rider of 5 Classic winners and self-styled best jockey and trainer 'there ever was', died aged 53. In his autobiography, modestly entitled *Genius Genuine*, he wrote: 'In 1773 I could ride horses in a better manner in a race than any person ever known in my time. In 1775 I could train horses for running better than any person I ever yet saw.' Received 200 guineas per year to ride for the Prince of Wales even after his controversial riding of one horse, Escape, saw the Prince give up his racing interests in order to support his jockey. Chifney died in the Fleet Prison for debtors, where he had been sent for failing to pay £350 to a saddler named Latchford.

1917   Former chairman of the Racecourse Association, Air Commodore BROOKIE BROOKS, born.

1928   Flat and NH jockey turned flat trainer MATTHEW MCCOURT born. Rode from 1943 to 1966 and died at the age of 65. First training licence 1968, based at Letcombe Regis. Best horses trained included Van Laser, Annsome Boy, Belfort and Amorous.

1934   Jump jockey turned starter BILL REES born. Son of 1922 Grand National-winning (on Music Hall) jockey Bilby Rees. Bill won 1960 Cheltenham Gold Cup on Pas Seul, rode 51 winners for the Queen Mother. Retired in 1972 after bad leg injuries.

1937   Somerset-born trainer SALLY ANN BAILIE entered the world. After racing over jumps in England she trained in the States, turning out winners like Win and K.C.'s Best Turn. She was the first woman to win a $100,000 and $200,000 stakes race. She also became the first woman to saddle a runner in the Japan Cup.

1959   Queen Mother's first double. DOUBLE STAR and SPARKLING KNIGHT both won at Hurst Park for the Peter Cazalet–Arthur Freeman combination.

1992   Jockey BRENDAN POWELL and his mount Blue Danube became the first-ever fallers in a British all-weather steeplechase when they took a tumble in Southwell's Huntsman's Handicap Chase.

1993   An official crowd of 4,000 attended Southwell's Racing for the Mines meeting, the first race meeting to be used as a political platform. Political figures and racing personalities made speeches at the meeting, whose races were named after pits threatened with closure by the government.

9 JANUARY

1820 Legendary flat trainer MATHEW DAWSON born. Sent out 28 Classic winners, starting with the 1853 Oaks (Catherine Hayes) up to the 1895 St Leger (St Visto). Trained in Newmarket. Died in 1898 after catching a chill while talking to the Prince of Wales.

1930 Flat trainer GEOFFREY WRAGG, son of Harry, born. Trained Teenoso to win 1983 Derby.

1936 Flat trainer WALLY CARTER born. First licence 1988, previously head lad to Brian Swift for twenty years.

1948 Flat jockey ERNIE JOHNSON born. Rode Blakeney to win 1969 Derby. First winner 1965, rode winners in India, Germany, Hong Kong and Kenya.

1953 Marten Julian, famous for his *Dark Horses* annual, born. Has a degree in Theology.

1956 Jump jockey STEPHEN JOHNSON born. Rode 10 winners in 1985.

1968 Amateur rider ALEXANDRA EMBIRICOS born.

1968 The 1943 Derby winner, STRAIGHT DEAL, which was owned by Dorothy Paget and trained by Walter Nightingall, died aged 28.

1969 ARCTIC CORAL at Warwick was David Nicholson's first winner as a trainer. He also rode the 11-10 favourite.

1976 LEONOTIS returned the staggering odds of 400-1 when winning at Randwick in Sydney.

1986 A racecourse worker at St Moritz, where racing takes place on ice and snow on a lake, only just escaped in time from his snowcat tractor, which sank under the ice.

1987 Schweppes announced they were to end their sponsorship of the oft-abandoned Gold Trophy.

1990 Jockey DEAN GALLAGHER became the first ever to lose his claim on two separate occasions. He did so once before a revision of the rules about conditional jockeys and claims allowed him to start the season with a 3lb allowance. His win on Last House at Newton Abbot removed it again.

1990 After ten years as a jockey, NICK ADAMS rode his first treble: Hot Company, Elegant Rose and Count Me Out at Lingfield.

1992 The publication of the International Classifications for 1991 saw Arazi on the best-ever rating for a two-year-old of 130.

1993 Ireland's first and only on-course betting shop, at Leopardstown, operated by the Paddy Power Organisation, closed down after three years, apparently as a result of objections by racecourse bookies.

1993 Just 250 paying customers attended a meeting at Lingfield in atrocious weather. The average attendance is just under 1,000 and doubts were expressed about the strength of the market.

10 JANUARY

1511 An order of the Corporation of Chester decreed that a prize of a silver ball, value 3s 4d (17p), should be run for by horses on the Rood Eye (later Roodee) course at Chester. Some historians dispute this date, and prefer a silver bell, worth 111 shillings and run for on Shrove Tuesday 1540 as the first evidence for racing at Chester (see also 9 February).

1940 Warminster trainer DAVID JERMY born. First licence 1974.

1941 Owner ERIK THORBEK born. Best horses included Danish Knight and Stirabout. Colours: red and white stars and armlet.

1942 Colchester trainer JIM SCALLAN born. Jump jockey from 1965, trainer's licence 1978-79.

1954 Amateur rider LAURENCE KIRKBY born. Steward at Market Rasen.

1959 Flat trainer CHRISTIAN WALL born. Best horse trained Rotherfield Greys with which he won William Hill Stewards' Cup at Goodwood in 1988, landing a 'touch' for Ealing publican/owner Tony Gleeson, who claimed winnings of up to £500,000.

1960 Rotherfield Greys jockey NIGEL DAY born. Rode first winner at Doncaster in 1978.

1961 Flat jockey PHILIP ROBINSON born. In the late 1980s he was the first British jockey to become Hong Kong Champion. Also rode winners of the English (Pebbles, 1984) and Irish (Katies, 1984) 1,000 Guineas.

1963 Flat jockey TONY MCGLONE born. First winner at Wolverhampton in 1980. In 1987 won Kuwait Derby on Saare.

1967 Former jockey ARTHUR WAUDBY died, aged 70. Rode 4 successive winners at Wetherby in October 1928.

1969 RONALD BLINDELL, the owner of Stalbridge Colonist, who defeated Arkle in the 1966 Hennessy Gold Cup, died aged 63.

1975 ALDANITI, owned and trained at the time by Josh Gifford, won on his debut at 33-1 in the Silver Doctor Novices Hurdle Division Two at Ascot. The race was for five-year-olds and was run over two miles. Bob Champion rode him, as he was to do when they won the 1981 Grand National.

1988 Trainer Vincent O'Brien and his stable jockey Cash Asmussen went their separate ways.

11 JANUARY

1857 Flat jockey FREDERICK JAMES ARCHER born in Cheltenham, the son of a jump jockey. He lived only until 1886, when he shot himself in a fit of delirium. By then had been Champion Jockey 13 times, ridden 2,748 winners from 8,084 mounts (including 21 Classic winners) and left estate worth £60,000.

1919 Derby winner CAPTAIN CUTTLE foaled. Twelve days earlier and he would have been officially a yearling when just one day old.

1937 Jockey WALLY SWINBURN born. First flat jockey to achieve over 100 winners in a year in Irish racing history, with 101 in 1977. Father of Walter Swinburn Jr.

1937 Trainer BRIAN SWIFT born. Rode some 200 winners between 1951 and 1961. First trainer's licence 1967. Had flat and jump winners, including the Triumph Hurdle and Stewards' Cup.

1938 Permit trainer GEORGE BARLOW born.

1938 Jockey IVOR MARKHAM, now Raceform race-reader, born.

1943 Flat trainer HENRY (RICHARD AMHERST) CECIL born, the elder of twins in Aberdeen. First licence 1969, having been assistant to Sir Cecil Boyd-Rochfort. Slip Anchor and Reference Point both won the Derby for him. Leading Trainer for the first time in 1976.

1957 Manchester United and England skipper BRYAN ROBSON, owner of Taylormade Boy, born.

1964 French trainer NICHOLAS CLEMENT born. First licence 1989. Trained Saumarez to win the 1990 Arc de Triomphe.

1968 Jump jockey LIAM O'HARA born.

1982 Owners of the Kildangan Stud in Ireland had to pay compensation to the owners of two mares after it was proved that resident stallion Tap On Wood did not cover the mares Quay Line and Pampalina, as stated on certificates issued by the stud. Instead it emerged that they had been covered by a 12-hands high Connemara pony, a teaser at the stud.

1987 Trainer SYD WOODMAN (67) and owner SIR DAVID ROBINSON (82) died. The latter once owned Kempton Racecourse and his Our Babu was the 1955 2,000 Guineas winner.

1988 NELSON BUNKER HUNT's breeding stock sold for almost $47 million in Keeneland.

1990 CHARMIAN HILL, 70, owner of Dawn Run, died.

1991 ERIC EVANS, Dean of St Paul's, officially opened a new betting shop at Old Bailey by placing a £100 charity bet on a loser.

1991 Trainer LEN LUNGO sent out first winner, Cumbrian Ceilidh, at Edinburgh.

12 JANUARY

1934   Jump and flat trainer JOHN ('MICK') BOLTON of Wiltshire born.

1960   Flat jockey ALAN MERCER born. First winner Croft Close at Redcar, 1977; 30 winners in 1979.

1972   Irish jump jockey TOM RUDD born.

1983   Champion Jockey of 1941 HARRY WRAGG retired from training having ridden 13 Classic winners and trained 5 more, including Psidium in the Derby.

1983   Outstanding trainer FRANCOIS MATHET died aged 74. He sent out the winners of 4 Arcs, 6 Prix du Jockey Club, 2 Derbys (Phil Drake, Relko), the 1,000 Guineas with Bella Paola and 4 Coronation Cups.

1990   Riding GOSPEL ROCK at Wetherby, GRAHAM BRADLEY was thrown when the horse bolted, smashed down a concrete post, crashed through a fence and a hedge, raced down the main road and ended up in the car park of The Swan pub – his local!

1990   Trainer BROOKE SANDERS and jockey DALE MCKEOWN teamed up to land their first-ever trebles with Don Keydrop, Solitary Reaper and Oublier L'Ennui at Lingfield.

1991   THE ILLIAD landed a mega-gamble for connections in Leopardstown's Ladbroke Hurdle. Backed from 33-1 in sponsor's ante-post book and started 7-1 third favourite. Reportedly won connections a seven-figure sum, including £400,000 for owner Noel Furlong.

1991   DESERT ORCHID finished 4th of 5 in the Victor Chandler Chase at Ascot. It was the 7th time that trainer David Elsworth's head lad Rodney Boult had been present to see Dessie run, and the 7th time he'd seen him beaten. He never did beat that jinx.

1991   Sixteen-year-old part-time art student EMMA O'GORMAN landed a 267-1 treble on the all-weather at Lingfield, the first of her career.

1993   JAMES FANSHAWE trained his first jump double when Perfay and Fired Earth both won over hurdles at Leicester.

1993   STARMINE won the Dove Claiming Chase at Leicester, returning starting-price odds of 66-1 but not attracting a single bet on the Tote. Just one bet would have produced a 1,530-1 dividend.

1993   YVONNE STAPLETON, formerly secretary of the Lady Jockeys' Association, became the first woman appointed to the investigating team of the Jockey Club's security department.

13 JANUARY

1862   Aged just 22, jockey LUKE SNOWDEN died at Lambourn. He had already ridden 3 Classic winners, the last, Brown Duchess, in the 1861 Oaks.

1920   JOHN HISLOP, owner of Brigadier Gerard and a respected rider and equine writer, born.

1937   HOWARD KASKEL, New York owner of Irish Derby winner (1987) Sir Harry Lewis, born. Colours: white, green hoop; two green hoops on sleeves; green cap.

1941   Jockey BILL SHOEMARK born.

1965   A record 229 runners contested 8 races at Worcester.

1966   Jump jockey NIGEL HAWKE born. He rode Seagram to win the 1991 Grand National.

1967   'The racing fraternity,' observed Mr Justice Melford Stevenson during a court case, 'consists very largely of a bunch of crooks out to relieve you of your money.'

1988   Friday the thirteenth proved lucky for jockey PETER NIVEN, who rode 4 winners for 4 different trainers at Edinburgh to land a 381-1 accumulator.

1988   PARK SLAVE was laid at an astonishing 3,000-1 for the Whixley Novice Hurdle at Wetherby, probably the longest odds ever recorded on a British racecourse. The horse finished 7th.

1990   Lambourn trainer MARK SMYLY, 46, sent out his last runner, ANSWERS PLEASE, at Newcastle. The horse fell. His best horse, Yanuka, was 3rd at 33-1 in the 1979 1,000 Guineas.

1990   REDUNDANT PAL, trained by Paddy Mullins, won Ireland's richest hurdle race, The Ladbroke, at Leopardstown, at 20-1. Having been beaten at 1-5 in a 2-horse race a fortnight earlier, Mullins was called in by the stewards and asked for an explanation. It was later announced that the stewards had accepted Mullins' 'explanation that he had no explanation'.

1992   US jockey MICHAEL EARL SMITH rode 6 winners from 7 mounts at Aqueduct, the first jockey to achieve such a feat at a New York Racing Association track since Jorge Velasquez did it at Belmont Park on July 9 1981. Seventeen days later Smith did it again.

1993   Political riots caused racing in Bombay to be cancelled.

1993   Eyebrows were raised as Irish Derby winner ST JOVITE, trained by Jim Bolger, was rated 135 - 10lb above Derby winner Dr Devious in the 1992 three-year-old classifications.

14 JANUARY

1938 Trainer LE ROY JOLLEY born.

1948 Born today, jockey JOHN WILLIAMS clocked up two Grand National victories - in Norway. His first winner came at Kempton in 1967 and he is proud of his feat of riding Green Ruby, the Ayr Gold Cup and Stewards' Cup winner, in 1986.

1967 Flat jockey ALAN (KEITH) MUNRO born. Ended apprenticeship in March 1990, rode Generous to win Derby in 1991, as well as Irish Derby and King George VI and Queen Elizabeth Diamond Stakes.

1987 It was announced that JOHN SMITH was to succeed John Sanderson as clerk of the course at York.

1991 All-weather racing at Southwell was called off because of the weather. Frost caused abandonment of the meeting.

1991 The Jockey Club reintroduced a yearling entry stage for the Derby and floated the idea that it could be run on a Saturday from 1993. Mixed reactions ensued; it is still run on Wednesday.

1991 Former jockey and trainer BILLY PARVIN, who rode in 16 consecutive Grand Nationals without winning one, died aged 86. He was 2nd on Blue Prince in 1935 and only Michael Scudamore, with 17 straight appearances, bettered his record for consistency.

1992 All conquering MARTIN PIPE continued to rewrite the record-books as he rattled up his 6th consecutive century of winners when Ambassador (Peter Scudamore) did the business at Folkestone.

1992 Gay Kelleway, renowned lady jockey and provider of telephone tips for *Sunday Sport* readers, enjoyed her first winner as an owner when Aberfoyle came home under Aaron Bates at Lingfield.

1993 Jockey Club figures revealed that there were an average of 11,446 horses in training during 1992 with 9,293 at the end of December - 11 per cent fewer than the year before. The last time a lower average was recorded was in 1981, when there were an average of 10,648. In 1992 there were an average of 10.3 runners per flat race and 10.75 for hurdles races.

1993 A champagne reception for jockey JOHN WILLIAMS, who celebrated his 45th birthday by riding a double on Kryptos and Absolutely Fact and was rewarded with a bottle of bubbly by the Lingfield executive.

1993 SABIN DU LOIR, aged fourteen, won his final race, the John Bull Chase at Wincanton, ridden by Peter Scudamore, bringing to an end a career which began with a first victory in a novice hurdle at Southwell on February 25 1983. The horse won £250,000 prize-money and totalled 21 victories in 41 races. He beat Desert Orchid on 4 of the 5 occasions they met. Owned by Brian Kilpatrick.

15 JANUARY

1925 The new venue for racing in the US, Hialeah, opened its doors to 17,000 racegoers for its first meeting.

1935 Con-man jump trainer GEORGE RENILSON born. Con-man? Well, he was owner-trainer of 1978 Scottish National winner King Con . . .

1936 Modest trainer WALTER BENTLEY born (he must be modest, his entry in the *Directory of the Turf* is only two lines long!). Best horse trained Primula Boy.

1940 Jump trainer PAM SYKES of Shropshire born. Took out licence in October 1978. Best horses included Spartan Major, Itsgottabealright.

1940 US trainer BERNARD FLINT born in New Orleans.

1944 Flat trainer ROBERT ARMSTRONG born. Lists his favourite activities as tennis and travel, and he has certainly sent out winners here, there and everywhere since gaining his licence in 1973. Moorestyle, Never So Bold and Shady Heights are probably his best known inmates.

1945 It was announced in the *Sporting Life* that Newmarket stable hands' wages were to rise by 10s per week to £3 10s.

1947 Flat trainer RICHARD CASEY born.

1963 Jump jockey JIM DOYLE born.

1968 LORD BICESTER killed at the age of 70 in a car crash. Owner of NH Handicap Chase winner Winning Coin and the successful Thames Trader and Mariners Log.

1978 Jockey PAUL WEBBER got off the mark for his career, winning on Weeny Bopper at Chepstow.

1992 ANGEL PENNA SR, the Argentinian-born, French-based trainer responsible for the superb Allez France (1974 Arc winner), died. He was 68.

16 JANUARY

1924   Flat trainer JOHN HANSON, owner-trainer of Winter Melody, born.

1957   Jump jockey TONY O'HAGAN, rider of Elsell, born.

1983   Trainer FRANK CUNDELL, who sent out Crudwell to win an amazing 50 races on the flat, over hurdles and fences, died aged 73. Crudwell numbered amongst his victories the 1956 Welsh Grand National, Dick Francis up, and was also placed in another 32 of his 108 races. In addition Cundell, also a vet and successful amateur rider, trained Mackeson Gold Cup winner Super Flash.

1987   William Hill withdrew their sponsorship of the Dewhurst Stakes.

1989   ALEX GREAVES, who hadn't ridden a winner before December, took her total of flat winners at Southwell to 9 from 14 rides and became the leading jockey there when she rode a double on Bronze Cross and Give In. Said her trainer David Barron, 'If this had happened on grass it would have been unbelievable, but because it is Fibresand people think it's a fluke. I don't.'

1991   With the Gulf War looming as the final deadline for their country to pull out of Kuwait passed, the Iraqi authorities nevertheless seemed to have their own ideas about the priorities of life: they allowed racing to take place in Baghdad.

1991   Another cold shoulder for racegoers as Southwell's all-weather meeting fell victim to the frost – for the second time in three days.

1991   'The classifications don't mean a hoot' was the dismissive reaction of WILLIE CARSON upon learning that the international classification had rated flying filly Salsabil 1lb inferior to In The Groove.

1992   When was a runner a non-runner for the first time? Answer, when it was DEEP FLASH, who entered the record-books as the first horse to be declared a non-runner for betting purposes under the newly introduced rule. The 150-1 shot (had anyone actually *backed* it?) refused to race at Taunton in the Unity Farm Hurdle, having come under orders.

1993   Sprinter SCHILLACI set a new Australian record for 1,000 metres when he clocked 55 seconds in the AUS$60,000 Rubiton Stakes at Sandown, beating the previous mark of 55.06 set at Victoria in March 1991 by Worthy Regent.

1993   It was revealed that the state-run New Zealand Totalisator Agency Board had managed to continue accepting bets for a greyhound race three minutes after it had been run. During that time 36 punters placed bets on the Trifecta (first three in correct order), which paid NZ$7,488 (approx £2,500). There were several more win-and-place bets, but a staggering 153 punters placed *losing* bets!

17 JANUARY

1916 Racing columnist SIR DAVID LLEWELLYN, better known as the *Sporting Life*'s Jack Logan, born.

1939 North Yorkshire trainer SARAH HALL (known as Sally) born. Twice winner of the Newmarket Town Plate as an amateur rider, she became a trainer in 1969 and has landed some decent wins in races like Newcastle's XYZ Handicap, Haydock's Victor Ludorum Hurdle and Ascot's Cornwallis and Diadem Stakes. Hallgate and Cool Decision were among her best horses.

1945 BBC rugby correspondent IAN ROBERTSON born. A keen owner, he retained the oval ball connection when naming his horses, and it paid off: Rugby Special and Twickenham both turned out to be winners for him, the latter 11 times – obviously a pair of 'triers'!

1949 Jump jockey PAUL CAMPBELL born.

1962 Irish jump jockey TONY MULLINS born. Associated with Dawn Run, riding her to many victories, but controversially missing out on the 'big ones', the Champion Hurdle and Gold Cup, when Jonjo O'Neill was on board.

1964 Jump jockey DIANE CLAY born.

1965 Lambourn jump jockey ANDREW ADAMS born.

1970 IL TEMPO, aged seven, set a world record time of 3.16.75 for two miles carrying 130lb at Trentham, New Zealand.

1984 The graded stakes panel of the Thoroughbred Owners and Breeders Association announced the unprecedented decision to assign Grade 1 status to all seven Breeders' Cup Championship races when the inaugural meeting was run in November.

1987 GRAHAM BURROWS, stable lad for the Dickinson-trained Badsworth Boy, killed in a car crash.

1988 JOHN REID appointed stable jockey to Vincent O'Brien.

1991 Trainer TED WALSH sent out first winner, Roc de Prince, at Gowran Park in the Thyestes Chase.

1993 Northern owner CLIFFORD ATKINSON died aged 78. He bred all his own runners and had horses in training for 30 years, among them Lady Mere, who was bought by Robert Sangster in 1976 and subsequently won the Princess Elizabeth Stakes.

18 JANUARY

1915 Successful owner CARLO D'ALESSIO born. Best horses included Bolkonski and Wollow, who won successive 2,000 Guineas for him in 1975 and 1976; also dual Ascot Gold Cup winner Le Moss.

1947 Flat jockey DAVID MAITLAND born. Won Royal Hunt Cup on Ardoon, 1975.

1948 Jump jockey ALAN TAYLOR born.

1950 Trainer ROGER CHARLTON born. Saddled Quest For Fame to win the 1990 Derby having received his first licence only in February of that year. Previously assistant to Jeremy Tree.

1950 Owner JAMES WIGAN born. Owned and bred Final Straw, winner of Champagne, Greenham and July Stakes. Colours: Cherry; cornflower blue sash and cap.

1952 France's popular *tierce* bet, requiring punters to select 1st, 2nd and 3rd in a selected weekly race, was launched.

1964 Jump jockey (THOMAS) RICHARD DUNWOODY born. Despite riding Charter Party to Cheltenham Gold Cup triumph and winning several top races on Desert Orchid, he still reckons career highlight to be his 1986 Grand National victory on West Tip. Became champion, 1992-3.

1965 Jump jockey PAUL DENNIS born.

1988 French jockey YVES SAINT-MARTIN, Derby winner on Relko in 1963, closed his career with 2 rides in San Francisco. Born in 1941.

1991 NASHWAN, 1989 Horse of the Year, became a father. The first foal sired by Hamdan Al Maktoum's champion, a chestnut colt out of Ashayer, was born at Shadwell Stud, Norfolk, at 10.00pm.

1991 ALEX 'QUEEN OF THE SANDS' GREAVES won on all 4 of her mounts at Southwell, becoming the first lady jockey to ride a 4-timer in Britain. All 4, trained by David Barron, represented a 212-1 accumulator.

.1992 Judge JONATHAN DIMSDALE announced 6-4 favourite Major Ivor as the winner of the Levy Board Novice Hurdle at Catterick - only to change his mind a few minutes later and place Blackdown, an 8-1 shot, first after seeing a print of the finish.

1993 32-year-old STEVE CAUTHEN said 'I could retire' after negotiations for his 1993 contract with his retainer, Sheikh Mohammed of Dubai, collapsed. Still to resume riding at press time.

1993 There was an incredible coincidence following the East Markham Claiming Stakes at Southwell when the winner, NIKKI NOO NOO, attracted two identical bids. Put in to be claimed for £3,000 her trainer John Hill and a rival bidder both offered £4,011. Under the rules of racing lots were drawn to decide who would own the horse and Hill was the winner.

19 JANUARY

1921 Former *Sporting Life* editor OSSIE FLETCHER born.

1924 Her Majesty's racing manager LORD CARNARVON born.

1932 British Racing School director BARNEY GRIFFITHS born.

1940 Amateur jockey and Jockey Club member CHRIS COLLINS born. Owner of prolific jump winner Credit Call. Colours: white; navy blue collar and cuffs; quartered cap.

1950 Racing commentator TONY O'HEHIR born.

1951 Jump jockey and trainer MARTIN BLACKSHAW born. Rode some 300 winners in UK before moving to France, where he headed the list in 1978. Turned to training in 1980 and was later tragically killed in a car crash.

1957 The Queen Mother's DEVON LOCH, famous for his inexplicable collapse on the run-in of the 1956 Grand National with the race at his mercy, ran his last race, the Mildmay Memorial Chase at Sandown, and finished fourth having broken down. Not the luckiest of horses, all things considered.

1990 Flat jockey PAUL COOK, injured when Madraco fell on the flat at Doncaster in the previous September, announced his retirement. He rode Touching Wood to win the 1982 St Leger, and Glad Rags in the 1966 1,000 Guineas.

1990 Jockey SYLVESTER CARMOUCHE was banned until April after stewards ruled that he had 'hidden' his mount, 23-1 shot Landing Officer, in thick fog for an entire circuit of a one-mile race at Delta Downs, Louisiana, before rejoining the race and storming home by an impressive 24 lengths. Perhaps the main giveaway was the fact that he was seen passing the grandstand only once.

1993 WATER WOO became the mother of the first foal by Derby winner Generous, born at Bill Gredley's Stetchworth Park Stud in Newmarket.

1993 Home Secretary Kenneth Clarke announced that Britain's 9,400 betting shops would be permitted to open until 10.00pm from April 1 to August 31.

1993 Soccer stars Ian Rush, Bryan Robson and Jan Molby scored when the syndicate of which they were members had a 9-2 winner, BOOGIE BOPPER, trained by Martin Pipe, at Folkestone, in the Novice Hurdle.

20 JANUARY

1921   Trainer MAJOR WILLIAM RICHARD (DICK) HERN born. Trained since 1957 and had some of the finest animals of all in his yard: Brigadier Gerard, Henbit, Troy and Nashwan, for example. Winner of every English Classic.

1922   LORD HANSON, who sponsored the Derby via Ever Ready, born.

1931   Mr J. Whitney's fine chaser EASTER HERO won the Wigston Chase at Leicester for the 2nd successive season.

1931   GOLDEN MILLER landed his first victory, winning the Gopsall Maiden Hurdle, worth £83, at Leicester. Went on to win 5 Cheltenham Gold Cups and a Grand National. Put down in 1957.

1941   Twice Champion Amateur Jockey SIR WILLIAM PIGOTT-BROWN born.

1951   36 and 40 went to post for the two divisions of the Rudgate Novice Hurdle at Wetherby, where 158 runners contested the 6 races.

1962   ARKLE won for the first time, in his 3rd race, at 20–1 in the Bective Novice Hurdle at Navan.

1966   Jump jockey GEOFF HARKER born.

1968   Irish jockey CHARLIE SWAN born. An unusual man, obviously, as he rates one of the highlights of his career as finishing 5th on Last of the Brownies in the Grand National, even though he has been his country's Champion Jockey.

1987   Jockey Club launched campaign for Sunday racing.

1988   Jockey GRAHAM BRADLEY fined £500 after dropping his hands and losing on Trout Angler at Ludlow.

1990   NEIL GRAHAM, who took charge of Dick Hern's West Ilsley stables during the trainer's 1988 illness, sent out his first winner from his new Newmarket base when his first runner, Silken Lines, scored at Southwell.

1992   MERRICK FRANCIS, son of former jockey turned thriller writer Dick, sent out his last winner as a trainer with his last runner, Alkinor Rex, at Lingfield.

1993   JOHN FOWLER scored the first treble of his training career as Deep Inagh, Jennycomequick and Will This Do all won at Fairyhouse.

21 JANUARY

1917 The owner of Bollin Emily, Bollin Patrick and Royal Bollin is not, strangely enough, Mr Bollin, but SIR NEIL WESTBROOK, born on this day. Colours: red; white sleeves; red and yellow quartered cap.

1927 Owner of 1979 2,000 Guineas winner Tap On Wood, TONY SHEAD, born. Colours: green and black stripes; green sleeves.

1930 Former Newmarket trainer JOHN POWNEY born.

1932 Jump trainer of Tom's Little Al, BILLY WILLIAMS, born.

1937 French trainer FRANCOIS BOUTIN born. Has handled champions like Nureyev and Miesque but hit world headlines with the arrival of 'wonder horse' Arazi.

1938 Eighteen-year-old BRUCE HOBBS landed a double at Windsor on French Mandate and Flying Minutes, both trained by his father Reg at Lambourn.

1940 LORD TAVISTOCK born. Owner of Japan Cup winner Jupiter Island and Precocious. Colours: purple and white stripes; black velvet cap with gold tassel.

1943 Jump jockey turned commentator RICHARD PITMAN born. Former husband of the formidable Jenny, father of jockey Mark. Self-effacingly described career as '470 winners and 5,000 losers'.

1950 LORD MILDMAY of Flete's Cromwell won the Prince's Chase at Sandown. Some four months later Lord Mildmay, the Champion Amateur who had also ridden Cromwell, went missing after going for an early morning swim and was never seen again. The Prince's Chase was renamed the Mildmay Memorial Chase in 1952, and was duly won by Cromwell.

1959 Flat jockey WALTER WHARTON born. Once described his recreations as 'eating and cigars' – not, one trusts, together.

1968 Former jockey HENRY MORGAN BLETSOE died aged 84. He rode Rubio to victory in the 1908 Grand National at odds of 66–1.

1983 DESERT ORCHID made his jumping debut. He fell in a novice hurdle at Kempton and many thought he had reached the end of the road first time out over timber as he lay winded for twelve minutes. But he got up . . . and the rest, as they say, is history.

1991 MARTIN PIPE completed a nap hand – his 5th consecutive century of winners came up with Trefelyn Cone at Leicester.

1992 JACQUELINE GETTY PHILLIPS, 55, died in New York. Owner of Vincent O'Brien-trained 1976 Irish St Leger winner Meneval. Colours: yellow with white spots.

1992 The disqualification of 12 horses ridden by jump jockey ADRIAN MAGUIRE when he was incorrectly claiming 3lbs was confirmed by the Jockey Club.

22 JANUARY

1819　In a four-mile steeplechase for gentlemen riders at Lismore, Ireland, there were 4 runners, each of which fell at least once. The eventual winner came down 4 times.

1924　Former senior steward of the Jockey Club LORD MANTON born. Owner of Flaming Dome and Pure Bog. Colours: blue; orange sleeves; brown cap.

1945　High Wycombe trainer TIM HARRIS born.

1948　Yorkshire jump trainer THOMAS TATE born.

1963　Jockey twins MICHAEL and RICHARD HILLS were born, sons of trainer Barry. Michael rode his first winner on August 13 1979, but brother Richard had to wait until October 26 to break his duck.

1972　GEOFF PROWSE rode seven winners from as many mounts at Elwick, Tasmania, Australia.

1991　Coalite is announced as the new sponsor of the St Leger.

1991　Eat your heart out, Lester Piggott: still active West Virginian jockey WILLIE CLARK celebrated his 69th birthday. Believed to be the oldest jockey still regularly riding. He had clocked up 1,141 winners from 10,613 mounts, starting in 1947.

1991　Jockey TOMMY LOWREY, who rode Airborne to win the 1946 Derby, died aged 79.

1993　British rider GEORGINA FROST rode a 31-1 treble at Aqueduct, USA, scoring on Jeune Saypa (4-5), Sweet She Ain't (8-5) and One Dumpling (59-10). It took her tally to 12 wins from 65 mounts.

1993　KENT DESORMEAUX won on his first ride at Santa Anita, his first mount after sustaining 14 skull fractures just a month earlier at Hollywood Park.

1993　One-eyed, BELPER won races, Masked Ball managed with only one testicle, Prime Mover, winner of the Oyster Claiming Stakes at Southwell, did it with just one hip, carrying a hole where his left hip had been.

1993　AMRULLAH, without a win in 74 races and fêted as the least successful horse in training, was led into the winners' enclosure at Kempton to mark his retirement.

23 JANUARY

1795 The most famous of Turf administrators, ADMIRAL HENRY JOHN ROUS, was born. First elected a steward of the Jockey Club in 1838. In 1850 he published *The Laws and Practice of Horse Racing*. Recognised as one of the greatest three 'dictators' of the English Turf along with Sir Charles Bunbury and Lord George Bentinck.

1907 Jockey W. KIRK continued an extraordinary winning streak when he rode 4 consecutive winners at Wairoa County in New Zealand to add to the 7 successive winners he had guided home the day before.

1918 79-year-old JACOB PINCUS died at Mount Vernon, USA. As a Newmarket trainer in 1881 he sent out Iroquois, ridden by Fred Archer, to become the first American-bred Derby winner.

1919 Owner–jockey DICK SMALLEY born.

1940 Former Everton footballer Brian Labone born. And what did he call his racehorse? Yes, that's right, GOODISON.

1945 Trainer turned starter IAN DUDGEON born.

1980 Timmatemma gave trainer MARK TOMPKINS his first win, obliging at Market Rasen.

1982 Trainer COLIN HAYES saddled 10 winners in a day in Australia, 7 at Victoria Park, Adelaide, and 3 more at Caulfield - certainly a case of a g'day!

1989 Former jockey turned trainer in France MARTIN BLACKSHAW killed in car crash near Chantilly, aged 38.

1992 BARRY WINDOW, Peter Scudamore up, won at Newton Abbot, an amazing 1,470 days after his previous race on January 14 1988. The horse's trainer? Surprise, surprise - Martin Pipe.

1992 Jockey JASON TITLEY, aged twenty, rode his first double when Grand Habit and Bishops Hall (both Harry de Bromshead-trained) won at Gowran Park.

1993 ANN HILL, trained by Reg Hollinshead, won at Lingfield. Owner Tony Hill said he had named the horse after his wife because 'their back ends are similar'.

1993 The Jimmy George Final Fling Hurdle at Warwick was the first race ever named in honour of a stag night. Friends of Newmarket-based JIMMY GEORGE, advertising manager of *Pacemaker* and thoroughbred breeder, clubbed together to sponsor the race as the first leg of a marathon stag weekend. George wed Jane Jarvis in Sussex the next week. The race was won by Persian Sword, the 5-2 favourite ridden by Richard Dunwoody.

24 JANUARY

1915 GAINSBOROUGH foaled. He became the first horse owned by a woman (Lady James Douglas) to win the Derby, in 1918.

1916 WARNER JONES, joint breeder of Lomond and Rousillon, born.

1928 Former Jockey Club controller of rules PETER TWITE born.

1935 Owner LADY JULIET DE CHAIR born. Colours: Emerald green, black spots; black cap. Best horse Night at Sea (1990 Trafalgar House Sprint winner).

1940 Clerk of the scales PETER SAYER born.

1948 Televised racing began with three jump races broadcast from Sandown by the BBC.

1953 A then record price for a selling hurdler of 1,450 guineas was paid by Brigadier J. M. Evans for Miss Dorothy Paget's four-year-old colt Fourth Act at Kempton.

1954 Trainer JOHN MCCONNOCHIE, formerly assistant to Fred and Mercy Rimell, born.

1956 BAHRAM, undefeated Triple Crown winner of 1935, died in Argentina.

1974 US jockey CHRIS MCCARRON finished last on the first mount of his career - before going on to ride a record 546 winners during the season.

1977 Jump jockey HYWEL DAVIES rode his first winner Mr Know All at Fontwell.

1988 SLIP ANCHOR's first foal born, a colt out of Doumayna.

1988 Basic pay for stable lads breaks through the £100 barrier for the first time.

1990 Having officially retired at Down Royal on October 10 1971 when finishing 4th on his final mount, Lyntim, trainer JIM DREAPER returned to the saddle on Sir Bumble at Fairyhouse.

1991 After ten weeks out with a broken left leg, Champion Jockey Peter Scudamore returned to the saddle at Newton Abbot with a winner, Outside Edge.

1991 Eleven-year-old mare HOPEFUL WATERS achieved an unusual double when she gave birth to a colt foal by Monsanto on the same day that Lingfield winner Comedy River became the first of her progeny to win a race.

1992 QUEST FOR FAME won the allowance Purse at Santa Anita, California, to become the first Derby winner (1990) of the century and the first for 97 years (since Isinglass in 1895) to win as a five-year-old.

25 JANUARY

1919 Thirsk permit-holder LADY ANN BOWLBY born.

1941 Cidade Jardim racecourse, Sao Paulo, Brazil, opened.

1946 Former jump jockey turned bloodstock agent JOHN WOODMAN born.

1953 Former jump trainer MATTHEW DELAHOOKE born.

1970 Jockey DAVID BENTLEY born.

1982 ANTHONY WEBBER rode his 200th winner, Roddy Armytage-trained Applalto, at Leicester.

1983 Embarrassed trainer NELSON GUEST had to cough up £125 for a taxi to drive from Newmarket to Chepstow after it was discovered that his horse Noblissimo had arrived without the necessary passport to enable him to compete in the three-mile hurdle. The taxi made it in time for John Francome to partner the horse to a 7-length victory.

1983 JOHN CRAIG, who owned the Bold Hotel in Stockport and was also the owner of useful horses Megan's Boy, Katmandu and Ebornee-zersdouble, died at the age of 52.

1990 As gales swept Britain, trainer TIM ETHERINGTON had a lucky escape when a 50-foot pine tree crashed through the roof of his house, demolishing the room in which he'd been sitting. At almost the same time, jockey SEAMUS O'NEILL also got lucky, when, on his way home from the abandoned meeting at Taunton, a tree crashed on to his car. He escaped uninjured.

1992 Irish jump jockey TOMMY CULLEN died aged 86. Rode Copper Court to win the 1932 Grand National.

1993 For the first time on-course physiotherapists were introduced at a race meeting. A Jockey Club experiment saw Mary Bromiley and Grant Downe on hand at Leicester to administer to injured jockeys. They saw fifteen jockeys but had no serious problems to deal with.

1993 As Du Trefle won at Leicester to give MARTIN PIPE his seventh consecutive century of winners in a season. His final scores in the previous four seasons were 208, 224, 230 and 224.

26 JANUARY

1892 MANIFESTO fell at Manchester in his first steeplechase, but he went on to become an Aintree institution, running 8 times in the Grand National, winning in 1897 by 201, in 1899 under 12st 7lbs; finishing 3rd in 1900, 1902 and 1903; 4th in 1895 and 6th, aged sixteen, in 1904. He fell in 1896.

1924 Jockey JOHNNY GREENAWAY born. Rider of Dalnamein and Cold Storage.

1938 Two champion hurdlers won races at Newbury, each carrying 12st 7lbs. Winner VICTOR NORMAN took the Sefton Chase and 1937 winner FREE FARE scored in the Weyhill Handicap Hurdle.

1951 Former jump jockey SANDY MAY born.

1961 Ice-hockey star WAYNE GRETZKY, joint owner of Arc winner Saumarez and Golden Pheasant, born.

1968 WILLIE SHOEMAKER broke his right thigh at Santa Anita. He was out for over a year, returning with 3 winners on his first day back.

1968 Former British horses filled the first 3 places in a 5½-furlong sprint at Hialeah, where POLYFOTO (formerly Eddie Reavey) beat ON YOUR MARK (ex-Sam Armstrong) and REET LASS (once Snowy Gray).

1970 A riot broke out at Calcutta racecourse after a hot favourite was beaten by an outsider. There was enormous damage but no fatalities, and racing took place there again within a fortnight.

1983 STUART MURLESS retired aged 65 after training for eighteen years at Loughbrown Lodge, Curragh. Nocturnal Spree won the 1,000 Guineas for him.

1986 ROYAL GAIT raced for the first time, finishing 4th in a 9-furlong race in Seville, Spain. He went on to 'win' the Ascot Gold Cup in 1988, only to be disqualified, then survived a stewards' inquiry to win the 1991 Champion Hurdle. He dropped dead in December 1992 after a hurdles race at Leopardstown, aged nine.

1992 Some £21 million was bet off-course in France on the Prix D'Amerique trotting race, the sport's premier event, run at Vincennes - 10 per cent more than was bet on the Arc de Triomphe off-course in France. The odds-on favourite, Ultra Ducal, was beaten in the last stride by Verdict Gede.

1993 PETER SCUDAMORE took a tumble at the 3rd last in the Aspiring Champions Novice Chase on odds-on favourite (8-15) Capability Brown, but reacted quickly enough to remount and go on to win the 9-runner race.

27 JANUARY

1871   The Royal College of Surgeons was presented with the skeleton of the great racehorse ECLIPSE by Professor John Gamgee of the New Veterinary College of Edinburgh who, in turn, acquired it for £105.

1907   Organised racing began at the St Moritz frozen-lake course with one race for unmanned horses towing a skier and one trotting race.

1928   Inaugural race meeting at Barrackpore, India. The best course in India for facilities, but just 71 days of racing were staged there before the land was sold off for other purposes in November 1954.

1947   Table tennis champion turned assistant trainer (to Martin Pipe) CHESTER BARNES born.

1949   Grand National-winning jump jockey GRAHAM THORNER born. Rode 650 winners in fifteen years. Received trainer's licence in 1981.

1965   BBC Radio racing correspondent CORNELIUS ('I've got a couple of selections for you') LYSAGHT born. Made his name appearing on *Danny Baker's Morning Edition* on BBC Radio 5.

1967   A wholesale pile-up took place in the first division of a novice hurdle at Windsor when CHEQUE BOOK (Paul Kelleway) and MACKEREL SKY (Tommy Jennings) came to grief at the first. The two horses set off the wrong way round the track, meeting the remainder of the field head-on and bringing down three more runners.

1967   SIRIUS III, trained by Peter Cazalet and ridden by David Mould, won the juvenile hurdle event at Windsor, believed to be the first victory in the UK by a Russian-bred horse.

1990   Husband and wife PATRICK and ANTHEA FARRELL both rode in Doncaster's William Hill Golden Spurs Handicap Chase. He finished second on Fleming; she pulled up on J. J. Henry.

1992   Trainer JANE BARCLAY, sister of former jockey Sandy, sent out her first winner when REGAN won over hurdles at Sandown.

1993   Even though he no longer owned the horse, trainer DAVID BARRON withdrew 1991 Lincoln winner Amenable from this year's race. The horse had been claimed for 10,500 guineas by owner Andrew Millar and transferred to Roger Spicer after a race at Southwell, but under Jockey Club Rules the horse's entries remained in the control of Barron who, miffed at losing the horse, withdrew it from the big race.

1993   LADY MURLESS, born Gwen Carlow, wife of trainer Sir Noel, died aged 77. She also trained and her first winner was chaser Golden Crown in 1934. Married Murless in 1940.

1993   Eight-year-old SULUK won over jumps at Southwell for the 15th time, setting a new record for wins at a single track and eclipsing Certain Justice's record of 14 at Fontwell, set in the fifties.

28 JANUARY

1904   Owner MRS MILES VALENTINE born. Cancottage won Maryland Hunt Cup 3 times for her. Won US Grand National twice (with Deux Coup and Down First). Colours: pink, cerise hearts; pink cap.

1919   Trainer PADDY MULLINS born. First licence 1954. Completed Champion Hurdle–Gold Cup double with Dawn Run in 1984 and 1986 – the first time it had been achieved.

1934   Jump trainer RAY PEACOCK born. Best horses include Dad's Lad and Rushmoor.

1941   Owner PETER HOPKINS (Lumen, Vicario De Bray) born. Colours: orange, white chevrons; white cap.

1943   Twice Irish Champion Jockey (1965 and 1970) GEORGE MCGRATH born.

1961   Great jumper MILL HOUSE made his debut and was 4th in a maiden hurdle at Naas.

1962   Flat jockey TONY CLARK born. Rode Ile De Chypre to win Juddmonte International.

1964   Jockey MARTIN BOSLEY Bit Bent: not a libellous headline – that was the name of the rider's first winner, at Fakenham in 1980.

1982   JEFF KING sent out first winner as trainer, having been successful jockey, when 50-1 shot Stephouette, ridden by Ted Waite, won novice hurdle at Huntingdon on an objection.

1988   SUSAN PIGGOTT, wife of Lester, granted trainer's licence.

1989   The Queen's 1977 St Leger winner DUNFERMLINE died of a twisted gut, aged fifteen.

1992   Two-year-old ARAZI awarded top weight of 9st 4lbs in US Experimental Free Handicap – that's 1lb higher than the legendary Secretariat and the second highest rating ever. Court Fleet had 9st 6lbs in 1942 and went on to win Triple Crown. Arazi, who won Breeders' Cup Juvenile, was trained by François Boutin, and rated on a par with Bimelech (1939), Alsab (1941), Native Dancer (1952) and Bold Lad (1964).

1993   The winner of the Albert Handicap at Lingfield was the 3-1 favourite . . . Albert.

29 JANUARY

1879 Equine artist GILBERT 'G.H.' HOLIDAY born in Maida Vale. Well known for his technique of painting horses from unusual angles. Would sit on a saddle in his studio whilst painting. In 1932 paralysed whilst hurdling and died on January 26 1937.

1911 Owner WILFRED SHERMAN, who enjoyed princely success with PRINCELY STAR, winner of 8 races, and PRINCELY SON, winner of 10, born.

1937 Not a dry eye in the house when injury victim Aldanti, ridden by cancer victim Bob Champion, won the 1981 Grand National. The horse's owner, born on this day, was NICK EMBIRICOS. Colours: white; royal blue sash, armlets and cap.

1946 He has a famous name but trainer RICHARD FRANCIS is not a writer of racing thrillers. Born on this day, he began training in 1984.

1957 Trainer PAUL HOWLING born. Rode one winner over hurdles, began training in 1987. Best horse Ski Captain.

1965 Jump jockey DALE MCKEOWN born.

1971 1990 Champion Lady Rider CLARE BALDING born.

1980 Jump jockey BEN DE HAAN rode his first winner, Arctic Princess, at Chepstow.

1982 The Irish Turf Club passed a new rule under which horses which were considered not to have run on their merits could be suspended for up to three months.

1983 GET OUT OF ME WAY (Paul Barton) gave Graham Thorner his biggest training success by winning the William Hill Yorkshire Chase at Doncaster.

1990 SULUK set a record when winning for the 6th time within a month at the same track. He won for the first time at Southwell on January 2 and landed his 6th success for trainer Reg Hollinshead on this day.

1992 It was announced that Carlisle racecourse had elected a female director for the first time in its 86-year history. The role went to ANN BLISS, formerly company secretary of the racecourse.

1993 For the first time in its 150-year history central heating was fitted into Doncaster's weighing-room.

1993 The Queen Mother, Vincent O'Brien, Fulke Walwyn, Fred and Mercy Rimell, Golden Miller, Arkle, Sir Ken, Dick Francis, Dawn Run, Jonjo O'Neill and Fred Winter were inducted into the first Racing Hall of Fame at Cheltenham's Prestbury Park.

1993 The death was announced of SIR JOHN CAREW, 90, oldest member of the Jockey Club, who owned Prince Brownie, winner of the 1950 Valentine Chase at Liverpool, trained by Peter Cazalet.

1891 Bookmakers operated legally for the last time on-course in New Zealand, at Takapuna, where 29 paid the £12 10s (£12.50) licence fee. The last race was won by favourite Sir Artigel, ridden by young jockey Albert Whittaker, who died shortly after in a race fall at Paeroa.

1917 1897 Triple Crown winner GALTEE MORE died in Germany.

1939 NICHOLAS AURIOL DIGBY GASELEE born. Rode over 90 winners as amateur. Trainer since 1976. His Party Politics won 1992 Grand National.

1948 Royal trainer WILLIAM HASTINGS-BASS born. (Later Lord Huntingdon); full name Lord William Edward Robin Hood.)

1949 Jockey DES BRISCOE born.

1951 Dublin trainer ANNE COLLEN born.

1951 Irish trainer JIM DREAPER born. Finished second on Black Secret in 1971 Grand National. Trained Ten Up to win 1975 Cheltenham Gold Cup, and also Carvill's Hill.

1956 Triple Champion Hurdler SIR KEN won under the welter burden of 12st 8lbs in the Elvaston Chase at Nottingham.

1966 Newmarket jockey MICHAEL TEBBUTT born.

1972 Only a few months after retiring, trainer HARVEY LEADER, born in 1893, died. He rode on the flat from the age of 12 and his one Classic winner was 1920 St Leger winner Caligula.

1976 MURIEL NAUGHTON was the first woman to ride over jumps in Britain when finishing 6th on Ballycasey over fences at Ayr.

1982 STUART SHILSTON rode his first winner for the Queen Mother, Sindebele (trained by Fulke Walwyn), at Cheltenham.

1982 CIMA (J. Old up) was trainer Capt. James (Jim) Wilson's 150th winner, scoring in a novice hurdle at Cheltenham.

1987 JONJO O'NEILL sent out his first winner as a trainer when SHELBOURNE won at Ayr.

1990 ALEX GREAVES became the first woman jockey to ride a flat race treble at a single meeting when Irish Passage, Orchard Court and Bronze Cross took her total to 14 wins from 22 mounts at Southwell's all-weather track.

1991 Trainer STAN MOORE sent out his first winner, Dramatic Event, at Windsor.

1993 LEANNE ISHERWOOD became the first Australian woman to ride the winner of the £67,797 Wellington Cup in New Zealand when she scored on outsider Dancing Lord.

31 JANUARY

1883 FRED ARCHER married Helen Rose Dawson, the daughter of his trainer Mathew Dawson's brother, John. She died just a year later shortly after giving birth to a daughter.

1918 Tiverton trainer JOHN BAKER born. Best horses Star Player, Philosophos.

1928 Jump trainer HARRY BELL born. Best horse Sebastian.

1932 Jockey JEAN MASSARD born. Best horses ridden Rose Royale, Le Fabuleux.

1933 Trainer HERBERT JONES born. Best horse Jimsun.

1941 87-year-old LADY JAMES DOUGLAS, the first woman to own a Derby winner (Gainsborough - named after a railway station and not a painter), died. She also bred two other classic winners: Bayuda (1919 Oaks) and Rose of England (1930 Oaks).

1954 Amateur jockey DIANA GRISSELL born.

1957 Jockey DICK FRANCIS announced his retirement, saying he wanted to stop before going rapidly down the scale. Earlier in the month he had been kicked in the stomach and broken a wrist, but the latter accident failed to prevent his career as a writer of racing thrillers taking off in a big way.

1988 First foal of DANCING BRAVE born, a colt out of Lady Moon.

1990 MIDFIELDER was trainer Philip Hobbs' 100th winner, at Windsor.

1991 JULIE KRONE, riding 30-1 shot Quilma in a race at Gulfstream Park, suddenly found an unexpected obstacle in her way when she had to jump a fox sunning himself on the back straight. The leap and swerve did no favours to horses behind, and Julie ran on to be 2nd behind 46-1 winner Hero's Love with 31-1 shot Lady Blessington 3rd. The unexpected 1-2-3 produced a Florida record 'trifecta' payout of 96,751.8-1.

1992 LETS GO SABO, 20-1, won the opening race at Southwell - the first winner for *Coronation Street*'s Ken Barlow, alias actor Bill Roach, but not for his co-owner, actor Bill Waddington (better known as *Street* character Percy Sugden), who has also owned Lucy Lastic.

1992 ALEX GREAVES became first jockey to ride 50 winners on Southwell's Fibresand track when partnering Euroblake to victory.

1992 PETER SCUDAMORE completed his 6th successive 100 winners (and 7th in total) when Run For Free won at Lingfield.

1 FEBRUARY

EACH YEAR Date on which the grass canters at Warren Hill, Newmarket, are traditionally opened to trainers' strings.

1914 Trainer KEN OLIVER born. He made a habit of winning the Scottish Grand National, achieving this five times up to 1992. He wasn't quite so lucky with the Aintree equivalent, finishing second on four occasions. Known as the 'Benign Bishop'.

1927 OLD TAY BRIDGE, runner-up in both the 1925 and 1926 Grand Nationals, dropped dead while at exercise preparing for another attempt. The gelding was thirteen years old.

1941 Owner of Eclipse winner Kalaglow and Young Generation, 3rd in the 2,000 Guineas, ANTHONY WARD born. Colours: emerald green; orange braces; hoops on sleeve; orange cap.

1961 Flat jockey MARK RIMMER born, won 1979 Cesarewitch (Sir Michael), 1988 Lincoln (Cuvee Charlie).

1967 DAVID NICHOLSON rode 2,952-1 4-timer at Haydock (Vilone, Coronado, Black Justice and Bassnet).

1983 Star juvenile hurdler THE GREY BOMBER, unbeaten in five starts, was electrocuted while out on the roads near Denys Smith's stable, where gales had brought down electric cables. Contact between horseshoes and road surface created sparks which triggered off the current. Rider Tommy Nevin was saved by his rubber-soled boots.

1986 CRAIG PHILLIPS of Hacienda Heights, California, won $1,906,491.90 with a 'pick nine' bet at Santa Anita, California.

1991 Trainer TONY FORBES sent out his first winner, Mountain Crash, at Bangor.

1992 94-year-old FRED W. HOOPER became the 14th recipient of the Eclipse Award of Merit, presented in Las Vegas. A veteran owner and breeder, Hopper won the 1945 Kentucky Derby with Hoop Jr, the first horse he ever bought at public auction.

1992 AMRULLAH ran his 72nd race – and suffered his 72nd defeat. This time out he was pulled up in a novice chase at Sandown at odds of 200-1.

1993 KOVALEVSKIA completed a quick-fire treble, winning over two miles on the flat at Southwell, having won over hurdles at Lingfield on grass on January 25 and on the all-weather on January 27.

1993 The Jockey Club brought forward the deadline for overnight declaration of runners from 10.30am to 10.15.

1993 A minor bomb blast rocked Taipa racecourse in Macau. A caller to a Chinese newspaper claimed it was 'the work of disgruntled Taiwanese investors who have lost a fortune since the track opened'.

2 FEBRUARY

1929 Jockey DENNIS DILLON born.

1941 Champion Jump Jockey 3 times (1964–65, 1965–66, joint in 1968–69) TERRY BIDDLECOMBE born.

1948 US trainer NICK ZITO born. Best horse Strike the Gold, 1991 Kentucky Derby winner.

1951 Rider of Safely Kept and Unbridled CRAIG PERRET born.

1959 Jump jockey KIERAN TEELAN born.

1966 Former co-Champion Conditional Jockey RICHARD FAHEY born.

1967 Jump jockey ROBBIE SUPPLE born. Career highlight winning Janneau Armagnac Handicap Hurdle on Jubail at Liverpool.

1968 Trainer FRANK CUNDELL enjoyed a treble at Kempton with French Kilt and Grey Venture ridden by Stan Mellor and Rope Ladder ridden by John Cook.

1983 The Tote announced a minimum £1 bet in all enclosures at racecourses. The minimum had previously been 50p since December 1975.

1986 1971 Derby winner MILL REEF died aged eighteen.

1991 Jump jockey RICHARD ROWE rode his 554th and final winner when Super Sense won at Sandown.

1991 Desert Orchid won the Agfa Diamond Chase at Sandown.

1992 Amateur jockey MAURICE 'MOSSIE' O'NEILL, 38, died in hospital after suffering severe head injuries at Carrigtwohill point-to-point meeting, Ireland.

1992 The Queen's 1974 1,000 Guineas and French Oaks winner HIGHCLERE died in America, aged 21.

1992 LAFFIT PINCAY rode 5 winners at Santa Anita to overtake Bill Shoemaker as the South Californian track's all-time leading rider with 2,250 victories.

1993 Jump jockey DALE MCKEOWN announced his retirement, aged 28. 'I can't make a living out of the game any more,' he said. He had 138 wins to his credit.

1993 Skeletal remains discovered 90 miles south of Lexington, Kentucky, were believed to be those of missing jockey JAMES A. KRATZ, who had disappeared aged 24 in July 1973 after allegedly telling his wife that someone had offered him $2,000 to pull a horse. Kratz had been declared legally dead in September 1980. Wounds to the skeletal skull suggested blows to the head were the cause of death.

3 FEBRUARY

1852 An eventful first day of the Flat race at Lincoln, where the card consisted of a mile weight-for-age event, a hurdle race, and a hunters' flat race. It was the latter which featured the fun and games as the winner was disqualified for being a thoroughbred and the runner-up for having won more than the stipulated amount of prize-money, leaving the race to be awarded to Loddington, which finished 'a bad 3rd of 4'.

1914 Owner ETTI PLESCH born. Owner–breeder of Derby winners Psidium (1961) and Henbit (1980).

1924 The first Grand Prix of St Moritz took place as a flat race at the Swiss frozen-lake course.

1938 ANTHONY MILDMAY won on Davy Jones at Gatwick, where the course is now part of the airport. That combination had led over the 2nd last fence of the Grand National two years earlier only for Mr Mildmay's (later Lord Mildmay of Flete) reins to break and Davy Jones to run out at the last.

1942 Owner JOHN MORETON born. Best horses included Churchwarden and Twin Oaks. Colours: mauve; pink stars; mauve sleeves and cap.

1948 Jockey CLIVE CANDY born.

1950 MICHAEL DICKINSON, English trainer in the US, born. Sent out first 5 in the 1983 Cheltenham Gold Cup: Bregawn, Captain John, Wayward Lad, Silver Buck and Ashley House.

1952 Jockey JOHN CORR born.

1960 BRYAN BURROUGH, owner of 1983 Grand National winner Corbiere, born. Colours: light blue; orange chevrons.

1968 Chaos struck at Taunton when part of the starting gate failed to rise properly for a handicap hurdle race. The recall man failed to see the signal from the starter and the race went on, Indamelia 'winning'. The race was later ruled void.

1990 Jockey WILLIE SHOEMAKER rode his final mount, PATCHY GROUND-FOG, to 4th place at Santa Anita in the Legend's Last Ride Handicap (staged or what?). He had totalled 8,833 winners from 40,350 mounts.

1991 LESTER PIGGOTT rode in India for the first time in 22 years. Scorpio won for him over 6 furlongs in Bombay.

1991 Racing began at Taipa, Macau.

1993 RICHARD DUNWOODY completed his 4th and fastest season's century when Grey Hussar won at Windsor.

1993 Trainer JACK BANKS saddled his first double when Local Style and Mizyan won at Southwell.

4 FEBRUARY

1862   ACE OF HEARTS and THE RUG (wonder if it started at double carpet?) dead-heated at Carmarthen in a four-mile chase, so they staged a run-off – and they dead-heated again.

1937   GEORGE OWEN rode Go Canny and Russian Sentry to win two steeplechases at Haydock. He went on to train 1949 Grand National 66–1 winner Russian Hero.

1937   Welsh trainer DAI BURCHELL born.

1941   Trainer SUSAN DAVENPORT born.

1949   Jockey GEORGES DOLEUZE born. Rode Dunette and Margouillat.

1950   Jump jockey JIM WILSON, rider of Willie Wumpkins and Little Owl, which he rode to victory in the 1981 Gold Cup, born.

1955   Jockey STEVE KNIGHT, rider of 1987 Grand National winner Maori Venture, born.

1957   Jump jockey CHRIS PIMLOTT born. He later became a jockey's agent.

1977   RICHARD ROWE's first mount Royal Rudolf (trained by Josh Gifford) was 3rd over hurdles at Sandown.

5 FEBRUARY

1904   Goodwood racecourse owner DUKE OF RICHMOND born.

1917   Owner-breeder of Derby winner Reference Point LOUIS FREEDMAN born. Colours: yellow; black spots; yellow sleeves and cap.

1921   Trainer DONALD UNDERWOOD, owner of True Song, born.

1926   SCEPTRE, only winner of 4 Classics and 4th in the 1902 Derby, died at Exning stud, Newmarket.

1942   *Daily Mail* racing writer COLIN MACKENZIE born.

1945   BIG RACKET, carrying 114lbs, clocked a record 43.26mph in a 2-furlong race in Mexico City.

1945   Trainer MICK MASSON, handler of Midsummer Star, born.

1950   Scottish trainer LEN LUNGO born. Was Martin Pipe's first jockey.

1957   Beckhampton jockey STEVE RAYMONT born.

1960   Former amateur rider SHARRON MURGATROYD born. Later paralysed in a fall at Bangor.

1960   1987 and 1989 Cambridgeshire winning jockey (Balthus and Rambo's Hall) DEAN MCKEOWN born. Obviously favours fillies – he has three daughters!

1967   LORD PENRHYN, who, as Major Frank Douglas-Pennant, owned the 1908 Grand National winner Rubio, died aged 101.

1987   Schweppes announce their sponsorship of a new handicap at Goodwood, the Golden Mile.

1993   A. P. INDY, winner of the Belmont Stakes, was named Horse of the Year for 1992 at the Eclipse Awards Dinner. The horse won 8 of his 11 starts and earned $2,979,815.

1993   Set to return to the saddle after his fall at the Breeders' Cup in October, LESTER PIGGOTT's comeback in Dubai was postponed as a downpour and the death of a member of the Dubai ruling family caused the postponement of the meeting.

1993   Nine-year-old JINXY JACK became the first recorded example of a horse winning a hurdles race for 4 consecutive seasons when scoring in the Morebattle Hurdle at Kelso. The 1–8 favourite was trained by Gordon Richards and ridden by Neale Doughty.

6 FEBRUARY

1889   Jockey JEM SNOWDEN died in poverty at Bentley, near Doncaster, aged just 45. He won the 1864 Derby on Blair Athol but was partial to the odd tipple and once lost his retainer with the Duke of Westminster after turning up for a Chester meeting the small matter of a week late. Only a subscription organised by Middleham trainers raised the money to pay for his funeral and for a memorial to him.

1900   Former Epsom trainer SNOWY PARKER born.

1939   Stainforth trainer RON THOMPSON born. Best horse Inishpour.

1952   Hampshire trainer LINDSAY BOWER born.

1961   Jockey STUART MORRIS, once Champion Apprentice in Hong Kong, born. His hobby is tropical fish.

1963   Jockey STEVE DAWSON born. Rode 1984 Cesarewitch winner Tom Sharp.

1992   Golden Oldies time at Santa Anita racecourse, where 80-year-old trainer NOBLE THREEWIT saddled the first 2 winners, both owned by 85-year-old former trainer W. R. Johnson.

1992   The *Racing Calendar*, first printed in white from 1773 to 1969, when it changed over to yellow, reverted to white.

1992   Irish Champion MICHAEL KINANE rode a treble on his first appearance at Sha Tin, Hong Kong: Sound Print, Magic Moment, Bust One.

1992   Car park tipsters Alexander Buck (one year) and his son Clifford (three years) were warned off all racecourses and Jockey Club licensed properties - a clear case of passing the Bucks.

1992   Aussie jockey JIM CASSIDY, beaten on a series of short-priced favourites at Warwick Farm, Sydney, issued a threat against punters who had been giving him a hard time. 'Do something about them or I will do it myself!' he stormed to the stewards. 'It's happening all the time and I shouldn't have to put up with it.' Stewards passed the matter on to course security.

1993   ROSEMARY HENDERSON, aged 50, rode Fiddler's Pride, which she also trained, to win the John Hughes Grand National Trial at Chepstow.

1993   JULIE CECIL sent out her first runner over jumps and Aremef duly won the Charlcote Novice Handicap at Stratford.

1993   Former jump jockey MICK HAMMOND sent out his 100th winner since setting up as a trainer when Hamanaka won at Wetherby.

7 FEBRUARY

1591 GEORGE, EARL OF HUNTLY, recorded in his memoirs that horse racing was taking place in Scotland at Leith.

1796 *The Sporting Magazine* reported matches and sweepstake races taking place in Hyde Park.

1829 Foundation stone for Aintree Grandstand laid by Lord Molyneux, who placed a full bottle of sovereigns inside the footings.

1927 Twice Champion Point-to-point rider BERTIE HILL born.

1931 Senior Jockey Club judge MICHAEL HANCOCK born.

1944 Somerset trainer ANN HARDEN born.

1947 Jump jockey JOHN ENRIGHT (Rigton Prince, Supermaster) born.

1950 One of the leading trainers at Churchill Downs, USA, BURK KESSINGER, born in Lexington, Kentucky. Former stockbroker, began training in 1986.

1951 Panamanian jockey in US, RICARDO LOPEZ, born.

1952 Flat jockey TONY IVES born. Successful in Hong Kong and Macau in recent years.

1965 Curragh trainer KEVIN O'SULLIVAN born.

1965 Jockey MICKEY FLYNN (Insure) born.

1976 DIANA THORNE became the first lady to ride a winner under NH rules, at Stratford, riding Ben Ruler.

1988 Trainer JACK WATTS died aged 76. His Indiana won (100-7) the 1964 St Leger. At one time private trainer to Lord Derby.

1989 PETER SCUDAMORE completed the fastest ever 150 winners in a season, beating in the process Jonjo O'Neill's record of 149 winners in a season in 1977-78.

1989 EDDIE DEMPSEY, 77, who rode 100-1 shot Caughoo to win the 1947 Grand National, died in Dublin. His winning National was run in a mist, and Dempsey was accused of only going round once!

8 FEBRUARY

1886 Tattersalls' rules on betting introduced.

1913 Owner–Jockey Club member SIR MARTIN GILLIAT born. Colours: light blue; black cross belts; gold cap.

1918 LORD RAYNE, owner of Celtic Song, born. Colours: gold; scarlet sleeves; royal blue cap.

1938 JOHN HISLOP, who went on to breed Brigadier Gerard, won at Warwick (on Overseas), as did Sir Harry Llewellyn (Talybont), who went on to become an Olympic show-jumper.

1938 Jump jockey turned starter JOHN LEECH born.

1945 TAFFY THOMAS (real name Myrddin Lloyd Thomas) born. Rode first winner at Hurst Park in 1961. Frequent visitor to India, Malaysia and Singapore to ride winter winners.

1947 Trainer KEVIN MCCAULEY born.

1960 Trainer ALEX SCOTT born. Previously assistant to Dick Hern.

1978 SWEET MILLIE won the Widnes Selling Hurdle at Haydock to give Jonjo O'Neill the then fastest century of winners in a season by a jump jockey.

1983 Derby winner SHERGAR kidnapped. A ransom of £2 million was demanded but the horse was never seen again.

1983 The Jockey Club amended its rule 153, under which horses whose jockeys are found guilty of careless riding are automatically relegated to last place. In future it was to be possible for them to be replaced behind the horse(s) with which they interfered.

1985 Newmarket Sausage won at Sedgefield to give trainer GEORGE MOORE his first winner.

1988 1991 Derby winner GENEROUS foaled.

1989 CHRIS ANTLEY rode a winner at Aqueduct, USA, then proceeded to do exactly the same thing on 64 successive racing days at the track, including a 5-timer on March 27, before finally failing to ride a winner on May 1.

1990 An anonymous bidder paid £10,900 at auction for five green leather armchairs used by the Queen, Prince Philip and other Royals to watch racing at Newbury. Auctioneers had reckoned on around £1,000.

1992 WALTER SWINBURN rode his first all-weather winner, Dorset Duke, at Lingfield.

1993 Jockey TONY CHARLTON almost managed to object to himself after winning at Fontwell. Believing that his mount Metal Oiseau had been beaten in a photo-finish by Gallant Effort he lodged an objection to 'the winner', only to discover that the photograph revealed he had won.

9 FEBRUARY

1540   Possibly the earliest recorded reference to a race meeting, which took place at The Roodee, Chester (see 10 January).

1809   Trainer TOM DAWSON born at Gullane, Haddingtonshire. Sent out Pretender to win 1869 Derby from his Tupgill, Middleham, stable. First trainer to completely give up practice of 'sweating' horses by giving them strong gallops while they were wearing heavy rugs and hoods.

1938   Trainer RON BOSS born. Rode 18 winners as a jockey from 1956 to 1959, and as a trainer has won Irish Oaks (Olwyn, 1977) and Queen Mary Stakes.

1951   Jump jockey PETER HAYNES born.

1962   Jump jockey PETER HOBBS born.

1974   Erezev was jockey CHRIS MCCARRON'S first winner at Bowie, Maryland.

1987   Jockey WALTER SWINBURN appealed against a two-year driving ban. It was reduced to six months.

1988   It was announced that CASH ASMUSSEN was to become stable jockey to trainer André Fabre.

1991   All racing – jump, flat and all-weather – called off in Britain and Ireland, because of snow and frost.

10 FEBRUARY

1849 Great US trainer WILLIAM RANSOM JOHNSON died aged 67. In 1807-8 he started horses in 63 races and won 61 of them, acquiring the nickname 'Napoleon of the Turf' and becoming *the* authority on racing.

1899 First jump meeting staged at Haydock Park.

1908 Owner–Jockey ARTHUR HARRIS of Tipperary born. He rode his last winner ten days before his 50th birthday, and at the age of 81 listed his favourite recreation as playing cricket. His best horse was Avondale, winner of 6 flat, 3 hurdle and 3 chase events.

1939 Former Champion Amateur Jockey GEORGE SLOAN born.

1945 192 runners contested 11 races at Windsor, attracting a record crowd for a jump meeting at the course.

1948 Owner–Jockey Club member ANTHONY MILDMAY-WHITE born. His Merry Maker won 13 jump races for him. Colours: light blue and white hoops; light blue sleeves; hooped cap.

1949 Epsom flat and jump trainer ROGER CURTIS born.

1950 Former Jockey Club handicapper MARTYN STEWART born.

1983 Former trainer RICKY VALLANCE died aged 74. Won the 1958 Imperial Cup with Flaming East and the 1973 Hennessy with Red Candle.

1983 WILLIE CARSON visited Buckingham Palace to receive his OBE.

1990 Jockey TIM REED rode a 2,120-1 double on Wrekin Melody (100-1) and Alistair's Girl (20-1) at Catterick.

1992 The Aga Khan sold his disqualified 1989 Oaks winner Aliysa, along with ten other mares, to Sheikh Mohammed.

1993 PETER SCUDAMORE reached 100 winners for the 8th consecutive season at Ascot on Capability Brown, the horse he had fallen from and then remounted to win last time out.

1993 LESTER PIGGOTT made his racing comeback following his fall from Mr Brooks in the Breeders' Cup Sprint at the end of October 1992. He raced at Nad El Sheba racecourse in Dubai. The first of his four mounts was Walk in the Park in the Al Arweeh Stakes (unplaced). He finished 2nd on 2 of his other three mounts.

11 FEBRUARY

1943 JOY SWAINSON, owner of 1977 Schweppes Gold Trophy winner True Lad, born. Colours: emerald green and black stripes on white; black cap.

1949 LORD LONDONDERRY, Jockey Club member since 1915, died in Ireland aged 70. Owned 50-1 1921 St Leger winner Polemarch.

1966 Flat jockey DANA MELLOR, daughter of Stan Mellor, born. Her real first name is Alison.

1981 Off the course through injury since November 1979, ALDANITI won his comeback race, the Whitbread Trial Handicap Chase at Ascot. Next stop Grand National. The rest is history . . .

1984 EDWARD HODSON of Wolverhampton thought he'd cracked it at long last when his 5p yankee bet came up, landing incredible world-record odds of 3,956,748-1. Sadly for Ted he'd placed the bet with a bookie who had a £3,000 payout limit. Is there a moral to that story?

1988 The distance of the $1 million Breeders' Cup Distaff was shortened from one and a quarter miles to 9 furlongs.

1991 MORLEY STREET was voted Champion American Chaser in the Eclipse Awards. Yet the horse was soon to be returned to hurdling in England after failing in three attempts at chasing, and went on to win the 1991 Champion Hurdle.

1991 PETER SCUDAMORE rode his first all-weather winners on Southwell's Fibresand track when Vigano and Tom Clapton obliged.

1993 LESTER PIGGOTT rode a double in Dubai on Bonita and Aghaadir, his first winners since Thamestar at Doncaster on October 24, seven days before breaking his collarbone and two ribs in his fall from Mr Brooks in the Breeders' Cup Sprint. Commented Lester after his first winner, 'Not bad, was it?' The racing was at Jebal Ali racecourse.

12 FEBRUARY

1556   The oldest recorded reference to what is believed to be England's oldest horse race, the Kiplingcotes Derby, was made on this day when a herdsman named Thomas Carter of Helperthorpe said on oath that he 'chauncinge to be at a horse runninge at Kiplingcotes Ashe about Shrovetide last'. The race, held over the Yorkshire Wolds each year on the third Tuesday in March, is believed to have been first run in 1519 and is open to any horse. It is also unique in that the second horse can often win more than the winner in prize-money as first prize is funded by interest on an original prize fund while second prize is the entry fees of the horses entered.

1856   The first race of the season saw FISHERMAN beaten a length at Lincoln, but it was a rare case of 'the one that got away': the horse had another 33 races that year, winning an incredible 23 of them.

1929   Actress LILY LANGTRY died, aged 75, in Monte Carlo. She first raced under the pseudonym of Mr Jersey and was an enthusiastic owner. Following her second marriage, she allowed her horses to race under her real name of Lady de Bathe. Won the Cesarewitch twice, with Merman in 1897 and Yentoi in 1908.

1935   Kidderminster trainer BILL MORRIS born.

1935   Turf Club chief executive CAHIR O'SULLIVAN born.

1937   MALCOLM KIMMINS, Jockey Club member and owner of Zellaman and Glen Berg, born. Colours: dark blue; red stripe; red cap.

1939   Owner of Jan Ekels, Recitation and Sackford, ANTHONY BODIE born. Colours: yellow; navy-blue braces; striped cap.

1948   Politician and racehorse owner NICHOLAS SOAMES born.

1953   Jockey ADRIAN PHILLIPS, partner of Grando King, born.

1969   Jockey BOBBY JONES, who rode Royal Lancer (33–1) to win the 1922 St Leger and was twice 2nd in the Derby, in 1930 and 1931, died aged 64.

1983   65-year-old trainer JACK CALVERT retired after a 33-year career during which he sent out 530 winners, including Move Off, Crosby Don and Dieppe, who won 17 races for him.

1989   81-year-old former trainer WILLIAM HENRY GATEHOUSE HIDE, father of jockey Edward and trainer Tony, died. Trained nearly 500 winners before retiring in 1968.

1993   DAVID NICHOLSON passed his previous best total for a season of 67 when he sent out a treble at Newbury.

1993   Trainer MICHAEL MARSH, who sent out his own Larbawn to win the 1968 and 1969 Whitbread Gold Cups, died aged 77. His horse Topsham Bay, trained by David Barons, won the 1992 Whitbread.

13 FEBRUARY

1914   Owner LORD CADOGAN born. Owner of Green Drill, Narvik. Colours: Eton blue.

1924   Irish trainer JOHN 'BUNNY' COX born. Best horses Highway View, Fort Fox. As a jockey he partnered Quare Times and Quita Que.

1935   Northern Dancer's owner CHARLES TAYLOR born.

1938   Actor, hell-raiser, racehorse owner and ardent punter OLIVER REED born. He owned a horse called Gawnmysun, whose name was selected after several rather more risqué names had been rejected.

1958   Rider of Rathgorman and Canton KEVIN WHYTE born.

1959   LESTER PIGGOTT rode his last hurdles winner, Jive, at Sandown. It was 6-4 favourite and gave Lester his 20th success over hurdles.

1962   Hertfordshire trainer JACKIE PERRIN born.

1964   Former Malton trainer STEVE MULDOON born. Best horse Denham Green.

1968   Nineteen-year-old jump jockey ROGER ROWELL rode his first winner, Vaux-le-Vicomte (5-1), at Plumpton.

1970   Jump jockey RIDLEY LAMB rode his first winner, White Speck, at Catterick.

1988   Saros finished 4th in the San Antonio Handicap at Santa Anita, taking jockey JORGE VELASQUEZ's career winnings past $100 million.

1993   Former Northern jump jockey PHILLIP JAMES died aged 55.

1993   KING CREDO, bred by actor James Bolam, who still owned part of the horse in partnership with actress wife Susan Jameson, won the Tote Gold Trophy at Newbury. Trained by Steve Woodman, ridden by Adrian Maguire.

1993   Trainer KEVIN MORGAN had his first treble, with Irish Ditty (4-1), Nessfield (9-4) and Favoured Victor (7-1), all ridden by Adie Smith.

14 FEBRUARY

1899 Jockey TOMMY BURNS born. Best horses ridden West Indies, Raeburn.

1942 Newmarket trainer JULIE CECIL, former wife of Henry, born.

1950 PAT TAAFFE rode his first winner as a professional, Oberstown's Sister, over hurdles at Thurles, for father Tom.

1951 Tim Molony rode ARCTIC GOLD to win the Great Yorkshire Chase at Doncaster. The horse went on to start 8-1 favourite for the 1951 Grand National, despite being just six years old, but fell while leading at the Canal Turn.

1951 KEVIN KEEGAN, owner, former England soccer skipper and Newcastle manager, born.

1954 Amateur rider HARRY ORDE-POWLETT born.

1954 Former Newmarket trainer RAYMOND HUTCHINSON born.

1965 Colourful racecourse tipster RAS PRINCE MONOLULU, whose catch-phrase was 'I gotta horse', died aged about 80. He was believed to have come from Abyssinia and his real name was Peter Carl McKay.

1966 Trainer CAPTAIN CHARLES ELSEY CBE died aged 84. Trained six Classic winners including Musidora (1,000 Guineas, Oaks 1949) and Cantelo (1959 St Leger).

1967 Amateur jockey ALISON YARDLEY born.

1968 Jockey SEAMUS O'GORMAN born.

1971 Amateur rider TERESA SPEARING, daughter of trainer John, born.

1976 VAL GREAVES became the first lady rider to compete against professionals and to ride over hurdles when she was unplaced on Silver Gal at Catterick.

1989 It was revealed that DAVID PRESTON of Elmbridge had written to the local Town Clerk requesting that Desert Orchid be made a freeman of Elmbridge for his exploits at the borough's Sandown track. Said Town Clerk David Jenkins: 'Perhaps he could be granted common grazing rights.' The request was eventually turned down as 'only a human being can be made a freeman'.

1989 PETER SCUDAMORE rode Avionne to victory at Newton Abbot. It would have been his 1,000th winner had an earlier 'winner' not been subsequently disqualified.

1991 RED RUM and his stablemates were on the move as trainer Ginger McCain, who sent the nation's favourite out to win three Grand Nationals, uprooted from Southport to Cholmondeley.

1993 Trainer SIMON DOW saddled his first winner in France, Salbus, which won the Prix de la Baie des Anges at Cagnes.

15 FEBRUARY

1907   Great American jockey JOHN LONGDEN born in Wakefield, Yorkshire. Rode 6,032 winners in the USA.

1908   Owner of Maigret SIDNEY GILLIAT born.

1912   Jockey BOBBY PETRE, partner of Lovely Cottage, born.

1917   Superbly named racecourse commentator CLOUDESLEY MARSHAM born.

1922   Trainer WILLIAM ELSEY, father of trainer Captain Charles Elsey, died. In 1905 he sent out 63 horses to win 124 races worth £17,297.

1928   Part owner of Cheltenham Gold Cup winner Alverton, killed in the Grand National, SOLNA JONES, born. Also bred No Bombs, famous for failing dope test after eating Mars Bar. Colours: green and pink stripes; pink cap.

1950   Former Champion Lady Rider DIANA WILLIAMS born.

1957   Irish trainer KEVIN PRENDERGAST married Lesley Daly. They went on to have seven daughters: Andrea, Penelope, Louise, Norma, Anne, Amanda, Natasha. Not surprisingly, he listed one of his business interests as 'breeding'.

1964   RYAN PRICE saddled Rosyth (10-1, Josh Gifford up) to win the Schweppes Gold Trophy at Newbury. The horse was considered by the stewards to have made abnormal improvement since his previous race on January 11 and Price was later disqualified from training 'until the end of the season'. Gifford's licence was withdrawn until March 31.

1983   76-year-old owner JOHN MAILES ended a twenty-year drought when Music City won at Newton Abbot.

1983   Former jockey and trainer TED LEADER died aged 80. He rode Sprig to win the Grand National in 1927 and won the Gold Cup on Ballinode (1925) and Golden Miller (1932). Was Champion Jockey in 1925-26.

1989   PETER SCUDAMORE rode the 1,000th winner of his career, Baluchi, at Worcester, to become the third jockey after Stan Mellor (1,035) and John Francome (1,138) to achieve that landmark.

1991   Jockey turned trainer PAUL TULK sent out his first winner, Tasmim (9-1), at Southwell.

1992   HENRY CECIL married Natalie Payne; and jockey CASH ASMUSSEN wed Cheryl Lyn Mallow in Laredo.

1992   Tragedy for point-to-point rider Jill Dawson at the Badsworth meet when Sweet Diana and Herman Blake died beneath her in successive races. Both were odds-on favourites. To add insult to injury, the *Racing Post* reported that the unfortunate Herman Blake was also posthumously disqualified.

16 FEBRUARY

1924 Champion Aussie trainer COLIN HAYES born in Adelaide. He rode 52 winners as an amateur and once sent out 10 winners in a single day. Dual Melbourne Cup winner. His At Talaq won the Cup, having finished 4th behind Secceto in the 1984 Epsom Derby. His first winner was Surefoot in 1947.

1930 South Glamorgan trainer BRYN PALLING born.

1953 Former Champion Apprentice ROBERT EDMONSON born.

1955 Upper Lambourn trainer CHARLES NELSON (Double Schwartz, Minstrella) born.

1956 Newmarket jockey PAUL D'ARCY born.

1969 Newmarket jockey MICHAEL DENARO born.

1993 Super Impose, the biggest stakes winner in Australian racing history, was retired. The horse raced 74 times, winning 20 races and AUS$5,659,290. In his first race at Benalla he won a £200 prize and his last win, in the W. S. Cox Plate, yielded AUS$1.75 million. He was trained by Lee Freedman.

17 FEBRUARY

1898 US owner FRANCES GENTER, whose Unbridled won the 1990 Kentucky Derby, born. She got involved in the sport after receiving literature from a tipster. Her husband Harold invented the pop-up toaster. Colours: light blue; two gold hoops; gold cap.

1944 Jockey PHILIP HEWITT, rider of Pride of Ivanhoe, born.

1947 Owner of Cairn Rouge, CRAIG SINGER, born.

1949 Former Whatcombe jockey DAVID ATKINSON born. Highlight of his career: 'Partnering Party Man to 5 wins in one season'. First winner at Newbury 1965.

1959 Trainer of Eliogarty, BARRY KELLY, born.

1968 TOM DREAPER trained the winner of the Leopardstown Chase for the seventh consecutive year when Peter McLoughlin rode Fort Leney to victory.

1968 Carrying 11st 13lbs, Persian War, trained by Colin Davies and ridden by Jimmy Uttley, won the Schweppes Gold Trophy at Newbury, beating 32 opponents, with Major Rose 2nd.

1981 Sixteen-year-old RICHARD DENNIS rode his first winner, Snowdrop Wonder, at Newton Abbot.

1987 Previous year's Arc winner DANCING BRAVE came off second-best when hit by a car in Newmarket. Fortunately he sustained only minor injuries. Some bright spark later described his condition as 'stable'!

1990 PHIL TUCK, aged 33, rode Midland Glenn to victory at Newcastle then announced his retirement. Rode 10 consecutive winners between August 23 and September 3 1986. Rode 423 winners in all. Once the most superstitious of jockeys, he is now a confirmed sceptic.

1993 Bidding for a record 17th win in 18 outings at Southwell, 1-14 chance SULUK was defeated, thus making him the biggest odds-on loser since 1-14 shot Arum Lily lost at Haydock in December 1988 and upsetting the man who laid out £3,200 to 'buy' £200.

18 FEBRUARY

1857   The first Champion Jockey, NAT FLATMAN, rode Apathy to win the first race of the season at Lincoln (did anyone care?). Apathy was owned and trained by former itinerant tea pedlar Tom Parr.

1880   Trainer of 5 Classic winners THOMAS DAWSON died after leaving his sickbed to watch a trial on the training gallops.

1908   Trainer TED GODDARD born. (Robsons Choice, Tubalcain.)

1948   *Sporting Life* writer GEOFF LESTER born. Once tipped Arazi to win a race, naming him as the third certainty in life after death and taxes. The horse lost.

1950   Jockey TONY MURRAY born at Wantage Hospital, Berkshire – the same place as Lester Piggott.

1950   Amusement and gaming machine manufacturer ALAN PARKER, owner of good jumper Yahoo, born. Colours: yellow; white epaulets; yellow sleeves; black armbands; white cap.

1951   Jump jockey MAURICE BARNES born. Rode Rubstic to win 1979 Grand National at odds of 25-1.

1953   Jockey JOHN BURKE born. Rode both Cheltenham Gold Cup (Royal Frolic) and Grand National (Rag Trade) winners in 1976.

1967   Controversy raged after the Ryan Price-trained HILL HOUSE, ridden by Josh Gifford, won the Schweppes Gold Trophy at Newbury. A dope test showed a high concentration of cortisone and a 171-day enquiry finally concluded that the horse manu-factured some of his own cortisone. Hill House ran 23 more races but never won again, often refusing even to start.

1976   The Queen Mother's 300th winner over jumps as Sunyboy (Fulke Walwyn–Bill Smith) won the Fernbank Hurdle at Ascot.

1991   Trainer FULKE WALWYN died aged 80. Rode Reynoldstown (10-1) to win 1936 Grand National. Trained 4 Cheltenham Gold Cup winners, 6 Hennessy Gold Cup winners, 7 Whitbread Gold Cup winners.

1991   Jump jockey RICHARD ROWE, who still regarded the highlight of his career as riding his first winner, Retaliation, at Stratford in 1978, despite winning the Whitbread Gold Cup, announced his retirement. Best horses included Kybo, Royal Judgement.

1993   Nineteen-year-old PHILIP HIDE, nephew of former jockey Eddie, rode his first double as Duke of Aprolon and Fighting Words, both trained by Josh Gifford, won at Sandown.

1993   Robert Massey rode his first winner, and 150-1 chance. Stylus, trained by David Nicholson, produced the longest odds victory since 250-1 Equinoctial at Kelso two seasons previously. Stylus strolled the Somerby Novice Hurdle at Leicester by 15 lengths.

19 FEBRUARY

1910   ALBERT WHITTAKER rode 7 winners from 7 mounts at Huntley, New Zealand.

1916   One of America's finest jockeys, EDDIE ARCARO, born. Won 4,779 races during 31-year career, including the Kentucky Derby 5 times.

1930   Newmarket trainer WILLIAM HOLDEN born. Best horse Royal Yacht.

1932   Florida-based owner of 1992 Irish Derby winner St Jovite VIRGINIA KRAFT PAYSON born. Colours: white; royal blue frame and sleeves; white armlets.

1933   Owner JOHN MEDLER born. Best horse Merchant's Dream. Colours: red with white band and armlets.

1957   Jockey STUART WEBSTER born.

1966   Determined to bring his campaign for the banning of jockeys using whips to a greater audience, WALTER HOYSTEAD held up the runners for the Fulham Hurdle – at gunpoint. The bizarre hostage-taking at Flemington, Melbourne, delayed the start of the race for sixteen minutes, during which time police bargained with Hoystead before finally persuading him to give up his weapon and be led away. He was later fined AUS$80.

1968   Cousins WILLIE and ARTHUR STEPHENSON sent out 3 winners each. Arthur scored at Doncaster with Mid Day, Pravona and Battledore while Willie was on target at Doncaster with Spring Spirit and at Newbury with Vulmot and San Miguel.

1988   Jump jockeys PETER SCUDAMORE and BRUCE DOWLING were given a 21-day ban each for reckless riding after becoming involved in a mid-race fracas.

1993   Jockey TIM REED wore spurs as he won at Edinburgh on Palanquin.

1993   Top stallion DOMINION died of a coronary, aged 21. He produced 13 European pattern race winners including Primo Dominie.

1993   TOUGH COOKE, trained by Dick Allan, won at Edinburgh having been off the course for 1,032 days through injury.

1993   SIR ROBIN MCALPINE, owner of 1984 Oaks winner Circus Plume, died aged 86. He was born 'Robert' in 1906 but changed his name by deed poll. A Jockey Club member, he also owned champion French filly First Bloom.

20 FEBRUARY

1883 Racing began at Bombay, where all the Indian Classics are run.

1924 NAT SHERWOOD, owner of Venture to Cognac and Billy Larkin, born. Father of Oliver and Simon. Colours: orange and green halved; quartered cap.

1926 Owner of Dahlia, Empery and Youth NELSON BUNKER HUNT born.

1931 Former Newmarket trainer DAVID RINGER born.

1935 Yorkshire trainer ERNIE WEYMES born.

1945 Seattle Slew's owner KAREN TAYLOR born.

1950 Jockey GERARD RIVASES (Dankaro, Mariacci and Vitiges) born.

1950 Owner of 5-times winner Mayday Melody ROWENA NURSE born. Colours: red; black disc; checked cap.

1967 Trainer REG DAY celebrated his 84th birthday. Began his career in 1900. Trained 1925 St Leger winner Solario and Sweet Solera (1961, 1,000 Guineas and Oaks) to win Classics. Rode at the last steeplechase meeting at Newmarket in 1907.

1968 BROUGH SCOTT broke his arm when Nautical Hitch fell at Doncaster.

1993 WILLIE SHOEMAKER reportedly negotiated an out-of-court $1 million settlement with Ford, who built the car he was driving on the night of the car crash which paralysed him.

1993 Lady jockey MAXINE JUSTER wed Kent cricketer Graham Cowdrey.

1993 A record Hong Kong *tierce* (1-2-3) dividend of HK$390,697 for HK$10 was declared when 140-1 chance Lucky Express beat First Touch, 12-1, and Active King, 100-1, at Sha Tin. The previous highest had been HK$381,755, set in November 1990.

1993 Having made his comeback from injury only ten days earlier, LESTER PIGGOTT was back in hospital after sustaining a gash over his left eye when the well-named Beat Them Up reared up cantering to the start. He had earlier ridden his first Hong Kong winner since 1986 on 7-1 shot So Easy.

1993 MARTIN PIPE scored his 1,500th winner over jumps in Britain when Milford Quay (Peter Scudamore up) won at Chepstow.

1993 Lingfield's going was described as faster, rather than standard, for the first time in the four-year history of the all-weather surface. And 67-year-old trainer Charlie Moore saddled his first flat double after 35 years with Invocation and Carlowitz.

1993 Not surprisingly, SPRING HILL SPIRIT, one of the favourites for a maiden race at South Durham point-to-point, failed to take a hand in the finish. For the 7-2 shot displayed on the number board wasn't even at the course, having never been declared for the race. Backers received their cash back.

21 FEBRUARY

1596   The 5th EARL OF RUTLAND, a keen racehorse owner in the reign of Queen Elizabeth I, recorded the fact that his runner won the 'forest race of Galteresse'.

1860   HARRY GRIMSHAW rode a treble at Nottingham on the opening day of the season. He went on to win the 1865 Derby on Gladiateur but died the next year at the age of 25 when a trap he was driving at night overturned.

1905   Eccentric owner DOROTHY PAGET born. Hated most men. Usually seen in public wearing a heavy overcoat. Huge punter. Owned 5-times Cheltenham Gold Cup winner Golden Miller. Won 1943 Derby with Straight Deal. Provided Sir Gordon Richards with first winner as a trainer when The Saint won at Windsor in 1955.

1923   Trainer SEAMUS MCGRATH, owner of Levmoss, born.

1960   Jockey NICKY HOWE born. Best horses included Fine Sun.

1960   Jockey PETER KAVANAGH, rider of Redundant Pal, born.

1967   The Isle of Man parliament, the Tynwald, voted to allow cash betting after Lieutenant Governor Sir Peter Stallard gave the casting vote in favour while commenting that he did so only 'with grave misgivings'.

1967   1970 Triple Crown winner NIJINSKY (Northern Dancer–Flaming Page) born.

1968   Jump jockey MICK BROWN born.

1987   Record-breaking jump trainer MICHAEL DICKINSON flew out to launch a new training career in Maryland, USA, declaring that he had 'no plans to train again in England'.

1989   After HELLO ROCKY had jumped atrociously and had eventually fallen in a novice hurdle at Huntingdon, the stewards were told by jockey BARRIE WRIGHT that the horse was deaf and that this was a contributing factor. What?

1990   PETER SCUDAMORE rode his 1,200th winner, Run For Free, at Warwick.

1992   The Jockey Club disclosed that its security officers were investigating suggestions that a number of all-weather races may not have been run entirely honestly.

1993   Trainer GARY JONES, returning to action following a heart attack, seemed to have offered coincidence backers the bet of the season by saddling Cardiac at Santa Anita on his first day back. The horse finished 2nd, although his Marble Maiden was a winner.

1993   CHARLES O'BRIEN, younger son of Vincent, saddled his first runner as a trainer, Yukon Gold, which finished 4th in the 11-runner Baltinglass Hurdle at Punchestown.

22 FEBRUARY

1924 International owner HENRYK DE KWIATKOWSKI born. Best horses include 1982 Eclipse Award Horse of the Year, Conquistador Cielo, Danzig and Polonia. Colours: white; red cross belts; red and white hooped sleeves.

1947 Official founding of the Royal Calcutta Turf Club, although racing had been going on there since 1769.

1948 Australian jockey RON QUINTON, eight times Sydney champion, born.

1948 Former jump jockey LOUIS JONES born.

1952 Trainer JAMES BETHELL born.

1955 Jump jockey turned trainer RIDLEY LAMB born. Rode 85 winners in the 1980–81 jump season. Rode The Thinker to win the 1987 Cheltenham Gold Cup.

1960 LESTER PIGGOTT married Susan Armstrong, daughter of Newmarket trainer F. L. (Frederick) Armstrong. They have two daughters, Maureen and Tracy.

1965 Jockey KIERAN FALLON born.

1966 SICA BOY, who won the Arc in 1954, died at the Whitsbury Manor stud.

1989 Former NH jockey ALBERT POWER died at the age of 68. Rode Overshadow to win the 1953 Irish Grand National.

1990 ALEX GREAVES rode a treble at Southwell, taking her total to 19 wins from 33 mounts.

1990 DEAR MIFF, unplaced at Wincanton, was the first runner sent out by former England soccer international turned trainer Mick Channon.

1991 Trainer DICK HERN's new Kingwood stables at Lambourn officially opened. He had been formerly based at West Ilsley, Newbury.

1992 With two to jump, PLAT REAY was leading the field in the Bidford Handicap Chase at Stratford, ridden by Carl Llewellyn. As the horse jumped the fence there was a flash from a camera and the horse fell. After something like that had developed it seems likely that the jockey snapped . . .

1993 One-time 'wonder horse' ARAZI covered his first mare, Sheikh Mohammed's Optimistic Lass, at Newmarket's Dalham Hall stud.

23 FEBRUARY

1904 Trainer MARCUS MARSH born. His father, Richard, trained at Newmarket for King Edward VII. Marcus trained 1934 and 1952 Derby winners Windsor Lad and Tulyar having been dismissed by his uncle, Fred Darling, after placing his own bets, instead of doing so through Uncle Fred!

1927 Berkshire trainer JOCELYN REAVEY born. Began training following the death of husband Eddie in 1981. Listed her recreation as 'spoof', a gambling game played with coins.

1933 *Sporting Life* starting price reporter and compiler of the Ringlets column JOHN STUBBS born.

1935 The oldest continually run 100,000-dollar stakes in the US, the Santa Anita Handicap, took place for the first time at the California track.

1939 Golden Miller ran his final race, unplaced in the Newbury Handicap Chase.

1942 Winchester trainer BARRY STEVENS born.

1946 Amateur jockey PHILIP SCOULLER born.

1965 Jump jockey WILLIE HUMPHREYS born.

1968 Jockey PETER HUTTON born. He won German St Leger on Goodbye Fancy in 1988.

1968 MILL REEF was born in America. Went on to win the Derby, Eclipse, King George, Arc and the Coronation Cup.

1972 Three-times Grand National winner (Red Rum twice, Red Alligator) BRIAN FLETCHER was unconscious for ten days following a fall at Teesside. He was advised never to ride again.

1992 The Queen made the presentation of the Queen's Cup at Randwick, Australia, when Aquidity, trained by Tommy Smith, was the winner. She also opened the new grandstand at the course.

1993 The Jockey Club confirmed that Martin Pipe's hurdler HER HONOUR failed a post-race dope test after finishing 6th of 8 when 6–4 favourite in the Walton Hurdle at Kempton on January 22.

1993 MANSFIELD HOUSE, trained by Folkestone handler Peter Upson, raced on an unexpected surface when his horsebox crashed on the A604 dual carriageway road near Huntingdon. Mansfield House escaped and raced off down the road, but was eventually caught before he could damage himself.

24 FEBRUARY

1938 JOHN PAUL CAMPO, trainer of 1981 Kentucky Derby and Preakness Stakes winner Pleasant Colony, born.

1944 Lewes trainer ROGER HOAD born. (Bash Street Kid.)

1946 Jockey TERRY STURROCK (Sky Diver) born.

1947 The 13 French challengers entered for the Lincolnshire were lumped together with a 5-1 quote at the first call-over of prices at the Victoria Club. 100-1 outsider Jockey Treble won the race.

1950 Jockey GUY GUIGNARD born. (Baiser Vole.)

1951 Former Middleham trainer DAVID MOORHEAD born.

1953 Thirteen-year-old gelding PALANO won at Southwell - the 2nd victory of his career. The 1st had been 30 races and almost six years before in April 1947 at Ludlow. Things got better, though, and his 3rd win was recorded on March 19 1953.

1954 English trainer in America CHRIS SPECKERT born.

1967 At Lingfield RAWA RUSKA (20-1) and LADY'S MAN (100-7) gave trainer John Bolton his first winners in his own right, although he had previously held a licence for Auriol Sinclair when ladies were not permitted to be official trainers.

1968 Marcus Brutus won at Lingfield to give owner CHARLES ST GEORGE his first winner over jumps, sixteen years after his first flat winner.

1979 Trainer J. C. WILLIAMS sent out a world record 8 winners at Waterford Park, West Virginia. He had 14 runners on the card, competing in all 12 races, and he also sent out 2 runners-up.

1982 Hollywood Park in Inglewood, California, was selected as the site for the inaugural Breeders' Cup Championship on November 10 1984.

1990 Jump jockey MALCOLM BASTARD called it a day after riding Royal Charge to victory at Doncaster. In fifteen years he had ridden 'about 100' winners. And, yes, he had a father.

1992 A foal out of grey seven-year-old HALVOYA by Indian Ridge was born two months early at Campbell stud near Bury St Edmunds. She made veterinary history by being the earliest premature thoroughbred recorded in Britain to survive.

1992 Jockey BRENDAN POWELL broke his leg in a fall at Doncaster.

1993 DAVID NICHOLSON became only the 4th jump trainer (after Martin Pipe, Jenny Pitman, Gordon Richards) to break the £500,000 prize-money barrier in a season when Barton Bank won the Whitlenge Novice Chase at Warwick.

1993 Police launched an investigation after the wheels fell off horseboxes belonging to trainers Philip Mitchell and Mick Naughton in separate incidents.

25 FEBRUARY

1937 US-based owner of 1,000 Guineas and Oaks winner Midway Lady HARRY RANIER born. Colours: grey; maroon sash and armlets; quartered cap.

1938 BRYAN MARSHALL rode his first winner over jumps, Carlore, for Noel Murless in a selling hurdle at Manchester.

1942 Former amateur jockey JO BERRY born. Wife of trainer Jack.

1953 Trainer ROBERT WILLIAMS born. Twice won York's John Smith Magnet Cup.

1954 Trainer MICHAEL BLANSHARD born. His recreation is archaeology and he has dug up winners like Ardrox Lad and Lemhill.

1956 Former Champion Amateur Jockey NICKY RICHARDS born.

1958 Jockey JIM DAVIES born.

1958 PATRICIA COOKSEY born at Newton Falls, USA. The first female jockey to ride in the Preakness Stakes, the second to ride in the Kentucky Derby and the first to ride a stakes race winner at Churchill Downs. All-time leading woman rider at Churchill Downs. Had 1,126 mounts in 1991, winning on 144 of them, clocking up $1,791,053 prize-money.

1962 US trainer in Ireland PETER HILL born.

1981 Brooks Law won at Warwick to give jockey LESLIE BLOOMFIELD his first winner.

1984 Jockey HYWEL DAVIES, riding Solid Rock, fell at the last at Doncaster. On his way to hospital he 'died' and was revived three times. He raced once more at Doncaster, riding Le Frac City - and fell again. He never raced there again.

1988 Triple Champion Hurdler SEE YOU THEN retired after pulling up lame at Wincanton. On the same card 1984 Cheltenham Gold Cup winner BURROUGH HILL LAD returned to action after a lay-off of over two years. He finished last of three.

1988 Jockey RICHARD GUEST really came down to earth with a bump, recording his 8th fall in just five days at Wincanton.

1993 Jockey CHARLIE SWAN rode the first 4-timer of his career at odds of almost 400-1 when Minella Man, So Pink, Tug of Peace and Who's Fooling Who won for different trainers at Tipperary.

1993 The Jockey Club revealed that Geoff Lewis-trained Flash of Straw - backed from 25-1 in the morning to 4-1 SP favourite for the HMS Cromer Handicap at Yarmouth on August 20 1992 - had been doped. The horse finished 6th of 12.

1993 BILLY NEWNES rode his first winner since returning from a detached retina injury sustained when a filly head-butted him at Hoppegarten, Germany, the previous August. The name of his 16-1 Lingfield winner was Observation Post.

26 FEBRUARY

1789 The great unbeaten ECLIPSE died of kidney failure at the age of 24 at 7pm. (There is some discrepancy in records as to whether this happened on February 26 or 27.)

1839 Jem Mason and LOTTERY beat 16 rivals in 14 minutes 53 seconds to win the Grand Liverpool Steeplechase, the race which was to become known as the Grand National. This was also the race in which rider CAPTAIN BECHER fell, tumbling into the brook which was subsequently named after him. DICTATOR became the first horse to die in a Grand National, falling at the second brook.

1909 Trainer PADDY SLEATOR born. He was responsible for Another Flash and Scottish Memories, winners of the 1960 Champion Hurdle and 1961 Mackeson Gold Cup respectively. In the early 1960s he caused a storm by sending a string of fit horses from his Co. Wicklow stables to Arthur Thomas's Warwickshire yard from which, ridden by Bobby Beasley, they farmed good autumn and early winter races. Outraged English trainers made representations to the authorities and the enterprise was halted.

1916 Twice Champion Apprentice FRED RICKABY born.

1918 A stand at Happy Valley, Hong Kong, collapsed and caught fire and 600 people were burned or crushed to death.

1933 SIR JAMES GOLDSMITH, owner of Garnishee and Zongalero, born.

1937 The King George VI Chase, inaugurated as a tribute to the newly installed monarch, was run for the first time at Kempton and won by J. V. Rank's SOUTHERN HERO, ridden by Jack Fawcus. Trained by Gwyn Evans at the Druids Lodge stables in Salisbury.

1955 Unfortunately named jump jockey MALCOLM BASTARD born.

1957 Jump jockey TONY CARROLL born.

1968 The death was reported of owner of The Tetrarch, DERMOT MCCALMONT, aged 80. Flying two-year-old The Tetrarch, known as the 'Spotted Wonder', is still believed by many to have been the fastest racehorse of them all.

1985 Jump racing's only jockey–optician, ANDY ORKNEY, made a spectacle of himself rode his first winner, Golden Ty, at Nottingham.

1991 Trainer LADY ELIZA NUGENT opened her account with Battle Drum at Nottingham.

1991 One of Ireland's greatest jockeys, TOMMY BURNS, who later became a trainer, died aged 92. Rode 21 Irish Classic winners, the first, the Irish St Leger, at age seventeen on Captive Princess.

1992 DAVID BARRON became the first trainer to send out 50 winners on Southwell's all-weather track when Papa Westray won the Buckingham Handicap.

27 FEBRUARY

1901   Argentinian trainer in America HORATIO LURO born. (Princequillo, Northern Dancer.)

1915   Trainer CYRIL MITCHELL born. Handled Peter O'Sullevan's good horses Be Friendly and Attivo.

1919   Owner JACK JOSEPH born. His Tassilo was 1968 Massey Ferguson Gold Cup winner. Colours: royal blue with red spots; black cap with white spots.

1932   Jockey GRENVILLE UNDERWOOD born.

1934   Triple Grand National winning trainer TIM FORSTER (Well To Do, Ben Nevis, Last Suspect) born. Probably one of the most pessimistic men in racing. He allegedly keeps a motto in his study: 'The situation is hopeless and getting worse'. Prior to Last Suspect's Grand National triumph he advised connections to 'meet back at the weighing-room after we've caught him'.

1935   Jockey ALAN LILLINGSTON born.

1937   Trainer LORD HEAD born. Border Incident and Uncle Bing were amongst his charges.

1938   Owner SIMON TINDALL born. Best horses include No-U-Turn, Krug, Charlie Muddle. Colours: royal blue; yellow sleeves; white cap.

1952   Federico Tesio's broodmare Romanella, in foal to his Derby Italiano winner Tenerani, gave birth to dual Arc winner RIBOT, named after an obscure nineteenth-century French painter. The foal was born at the National Stud, West Grinstead.

1955   Jump jockey BARRIE WRIGHT born.

1970   Former US Champion Jockey KENT DESORMEAUX born.

1973   Brantridge Farmer won at Fontwell to make AURIOL SINCLAIR the first lady trainer to send out 100 winners.

1978   Love From Verona and Nick Henderson won at Fontwell to give BARRY HILLS his first winner over jumps as a trainer.

1992   77-year-old former Epsom-based jockey and trainer Albert Patrick 'Manch' Taylor died.

1993   82-year-old trainer NOBLE THREEWIT sent out Devoted Brad to win the San Rafael Stakes at Santa Anita, USA.

1993   56-year-old GEORGE TURNER, believed to be the oldest active jump rider in the country, rode Rathmichael to win at Bolventor point-to-point in Cornwall, the first winner he'd ridden there in 25 years of trying.

28 FEBRUARY

1844 DISCOUNT won the Liverpool and National Chase (The Grand National's earlier title). The horse acquired his name when new owner Mr Quartermaine beat former owner Mr Payne down to a bargain price.

1913 Former Epsom trainer PHILIP NUNNELEY born.

1920 Owner PRISCILLA HASTINGS born. Her Taxidermist stuffed the opposition in both the Whitbread and Hennessy Gold Cups in 1958. Also owned Murrayfield, King's Troop. Colours: primrose; black hoop; armlets and cap.

1933 Northern trainer PAT ROHAN born. He went off to train in Bahrain.

1935 Trainer ARTHUR PITT born.

1938 Rugby enthusiast and trainer DONALD FAIRGRIEVE born.

1938 Five-times Cheltenham Gold Cup winner GOLDEN MILLER won it for the final time, amazingly enough in an optional selling chase at Birmingham.

1943 Champion jump jockey RON BARRY born. Rode The Dikler to victory in the 1973 Gold Cup, and won the US Colonial Cup twice on Grand Canyon, in 1976 and 1978. Became an inspector of courses.

1944 Owner of Obratztsovy, Whitstead and Lake City, HARRY DEME-TRIOU born. Colours: dark blue and light blue hoops; maroon cap.

1946 Labour party politician, racegoer and tipster ROBIN COOK born.

1950 Jockey TAFFY DAVIES born. Best horse ridden Barona.

1956 Scottish trainer JOHN WILSON born.

1958 Trainer NIGEL TINKLER born in Harrogate. By the age of sixteen he'd ridden a winner on the flat, over hurdles and over fences in Scotland.

1958 It was L for victory as Winston Churchill's LE PRETENDANT won the Ashford Novice Hurdle at Kempton by 20 lengths, ridden by jockey Johnny Gilbert for trainer Walter Nightingall.

1976 KEVIN MOONEY rode his first winner, Amarind (trained by Fulke Walwyn), over fences at Kempton.

1980 Eighteen-year-old SONNY SOMERS won over sticks at Lingfield to register his 2nd success of the season at an age seldom equalled and never exceeded.

1987 PRINCESS ANNE made her National Hunt debut, finishing last of 4 at Kempton.

29 FEBRUARY

1836   WILLIAM LYNN staged the first steeplechase at Aintree, won by The Duke, ridden by the soon-to-be-immortalised Captain Becher.

1916   Jockey BRYAN MARSHALL born. The rider of consecutive Grand National winners in 1953 and 1954, Early Mist (20-1) and Royal Tan (8-1), he died in 1991.

1932   Daventry trainer ANNE COCKBURN born.

1940   US trainer of Seattle Slew, BILLY TURNER, born.

1948   Vet STEPHEN BORSBERRY born. Owner of prolific Beverley course specialist Rapid Lad, where he has won 12 times. The horse also won twice over hurdles. Colours: emerald green; black stripes on body; black and emerald green hooped cap.

1984   JOHN FRANCOME rode his 1,000th winner over the sticks in Britain on Observe at Worcester. One of the backers of that winner was William Hill punter ALBERT FULLER of Mottingham, London, who was celebrating his 100th birthday by visiting his local betting shop where Hill's gave him a free £100 bet.

1991   HELLENIC PRINCE threw jockey John McLaughlin during the 3-runner Tarragon Handicap Hurdle at Lingfield and set off for the unsaddling area, where the jockey finally caught him, remounted and went back to try to finish 3rd. But by then the hurdles had been removed and the judge had left his box, so the 3rd-place money of £231 went begging. Perhaps they should have waited for the field to come round for the next race.

1992   Hereford staged what might well have been the worst jump race ever. The February Novice Selling Hurdle attracted 13 runners, none of whom had ever finished in the first three of a race. Nine of the runners duly failed to get round the two-mile 3-furlong track - 6 were pulled up, 2 fell, 1 unseated rider - including the 5-2 favourite Orithyia. The last of the 4 to finish, Northern Glint, was tailed off. The 3rd horse, a 50-1 shot, finished at 'one pace', the runner-up, a 20-1 chance, found 'no extra on the flat' and the winner, Arr Eff Bee, which had form figures of PPPB, went off at 50-1 with virtually no betting support. It was ridden by Ian Lawrence, trained by Peter Smith and, to rub salt into the wounds, 'there was no bid for the winner' following the race. Oh yes, the time for the race: 5 minutes 12.4 seconds - 29.8 seconds slower than average.

1 MARCH

1839 R. Ackermann published a set of four prints depicting the 'first steeple chace on record', allegedly run overnight in 1803 by the 3rd Dragoons, who were stationed at Ipswich and raced from the barracks to Nacton Church. There is just the slightest element of doubt about the authenticity of this event.

1843 For the first time, the fledgling Grand National, known as the Liverpool and National Chase, became a handicap, framed by William Topham. VANGUARD won with 11st 10lbs. Peter Simple carried top weight of 13st 1lb. Winning jockey Tom Olliver became the first to win the race in successive years.

1906 The forerunner of the famous St Moritz frozen-lake course meeting took place at 3.00pm when 12 riderless horses and a mule raced.

1939 Jockey TOMMY KELSEY, who partnered Rapid River, born.

1944 COTTAGE RAKE, who would win 3 Cheltenham Gold Cups (1948–1949–1950), made his racecourse debut, unplaced on the flat at Thurles.

1945 Owner and rock singer ROGER DALTREY born.

1947 US owner PETER BRANT born. Owner of Waya, Triptych, Merce Cunningham. Colours: dark green; light green yoke and armlets.

1969 TUESDEE TESTA, 27, became the first female jockey to win a race at a major US thoroughbred track when she rode Buz On to victory at Santa Anita, California.

1986 CRAIG B. SINGER's Sondrio (Ire) won the inaugural Breeders' Cup Special Stakes, the $130,000-added Gulfstream Park Breeders' Cup.

1989 Beau Ranger gave Martin Pipe his 150th winner of the NH season. He was the first trainer to achieve this feat.

1991 PAT DAY became only the 6th rider in history to reach the $100 million mark in prize-money when he finished 2nd on Wild Sierra at Oaklawn Park. Those who got there before him were Bill Shoemaker, Laffit Pincay, Angel Cordero, Chris McCarron, Jorge Velasquez.

1992 Jockey DAVY (D. L.) JONES, who rode Red Rower to win the 1945 Cheltenham Gold Cup, died in Cheltenham aged 84. Won the Kenya Derby aged 62 and was still riding there until the stewards stopped him when he was 65.

1992 Family fortunes were buoyant for the COSTELLO clan when they dominated the point-to-point meetings at Quin and Lismore, Dermot and Tom Jr riding a treble apiece, John sending out 3 winners and father Tom another 2.

1993 Trainer BILL TURNER had his first jumps double when Cleeveland Lady and Shaston both won at Plumpton.

2 MARCH

1781 A Minute of the Doncaster Corporation recorded that Mr John Carr should be paid 100 guineas 'for his trouble in architechting and directing' the work of constructing Doncaster racecourse's grandstand, which had set them back £2,637.

1838 Renowned trainer JOHN PORTER born at Rugeley, Staffordshire. Took over at Kingsclere stables in 1868 and sent out 7 Derby winners including Ormonde (1886). Retired in 1905, having trained the winners of 1,063 races worth £720,021 over 43 seasons. Founded Newbury racecourse 1906. Died 1922.

1938 The second King George VI Chase was won by front-running AIRGEAD SIOS for trainer Vic Tabor, beating just 3 opponents.

1948 NATIONAL SPIRIT completed a Champion Hurdle double for trainer Vic Smyth, who had changed the horse's name from Avago.

1948 Former jump jockey ROY DAVIES born.

1954 The opening race on the Cheltenham Festival card was the Birdlip Selling Hurdle, won by Mull Sack and up-and-coming teenage jockey LESTER PIGGOTT.

1959 Former Clwyd trainer CATHIE LLOYD-JONES born. Claims to have been the youngest trainer to be granted a public licence – she was 21 when she received it. Owned, trained and rode a winner at Cheltenham in 1982.

1959 Born on this day, jump jockey LORNA VINCENT's first-ever rides over hurdles and fences were both winners. The highlight of her career? 'Beating John Francome in a photo-finish the day before my 21st birthday.'

1968 Trainer GEORGE OWEN, who had been without a runner since the foot-and-mouth epidemic hit his Tarporley stable on November 17, bounced back with a winner as Brian's Best won at Warwick, ridden by Roy Edwards. Two days later, the horse came out again at Warwick – and won for the second time.

1985 HIERONYMOUS was jockey Peter Scudamore's first ride for, and his first winner for trainer Martin Pipe. He scored at Haydock Park.

1986 The Santa Anita Handicap became the world's first such event with a guaranteed value of $1 million.

3 MARCH

1847 For the first time, the Grand National Handicap Chase was run at Liverpool. Won by nine-year-old Matthew. Since 1839 the race had been known variously as the Liverpool Chase, Grand Liverpool Chase, Liverpool and National Chase.

1918 Legendary television commentator PETER O'SULLEVAN born. Best horses include sprinter Be Friendly and Triumph Hurdle winner Attivo. His autobiography *Calling The Horses* was a bestseller, but he once told me he didn't think his local library had enough copies of it in stock. Awarded CBE. Described his 'most fortuitous racing experience' as 'contracting pneumonia on eve of intended association with equally unskilled partner in wartime novices chase at Plumpton – an excursion which neither horse nor rider could reasonably have been expected to survive'.

1923 Australian-born but Irish-based jockey GARNIE BOUGOURE born. Best horses ridden Noblesse, Ragusa, Pourparler.

1934 Trainer PETER CALVER born. Vet who once trained Grand National winner Highland Wedding.

1944 Jockey HARRY WHITE born. Best horses ridden include Think Big, Greenland Park.

1948 Newmarket trainer SIR MARK PRESCOTT born. He handled Spindrifter, who won 13 races as a two-year-old, 10 of them consecutively, a record for the century at the time.

1949 *Racing Post* editor MICHAEL HARRIS born.

1952 Newmarket trainer LORD JOHN FITZGERALD born. As an amateur he rode in 104 races, winning 2 of them!

1963 Trainer and tennis fan CHARLIE BROOKS born. Formerly assistant to Fred Winter.

1967 Jump jockey ALAN MCCABE born.

1983 Owner of 1969 Northumberland Plate winner Even Say, 72-year-old SID TERRY, died.

1985 Jockey BILL SHOEMAKER became the first rider to reach $1 million in career earnings as Lord at War won the Santa Anita Handicap.

1991 LESTER PIGGOTT rode Delage to win the Indian Turf Invitation Cup in Madras at odds of 10–1.

1992 PETER SCUDAMORE became the first jump jockey to ride 1,500 winners when Slavi won the Ranvet Novice Hurdle at Warwick.

1993 SULUK extended his record-breaking run at Southwell to 17 wins from 19 jump outings in the Palacegate Racing Selling Hurdle, a race sponsored by his owners. He was 4–6 favourite for trainer Reg Hollinshead and jockey Stephen Wynne.

4 MARCH

1846 One of the oddest named horses to compete anywhere, let alone Liverpool, HORNIHIHARRI HO, fell in the Liverpool and National Chase. The horse was owned by Mr H. L. Carter, and the bookies who freely offered 33-1, referred to it as Hurry Harry.

1868 Grand National favourite CHIMNEY SWEEP broke a leg without even jumping a fence - he hit a course-marking rock.

1902 Jockey Club member SIR JOHN CAREW POLE born.

1939 Hong Kong trainer GEOFF LANE born.

1946 Racing writer and *Daily Telegraph* tipster TONY STAFFORD born. In March 1993 a disgruntled reader wrote to the newspaper about Tony's recent tipping column. 'His *coup de grâce* came when he featured 7 of the 8 runners. Needless to say, the unmentioned nag, Rosgill, won at 9-1.' I bet no one ever complimented you on the winners, Tony.

1948 Kelso clerk of course JONNIE FENWICKE-CLENNELL born.

1954 Arundel trainer LYDIA CLAY born. First licence 1986. Best horses include Dancing Brig and Royal Partner. Has listed her recreations as 'good food, good wine, good company' - good for her!

1968 Jockey RON VIBERT rode his 100th winner as a pro when Prince Gin won at Warwick.

1978 RED RUM made his last racecourse appearance. Running for the 110th time, he finished unplaced in the Greenall Whitley Brewers Handicap Chase at Haydock. Rummy won 3 flat races, 3 over hurdles and 21 chases, totalling £115,234 in prize-money.

1980 PRINCE CHARLES raced in public for the first time, at Plumpton, finishing 2nd on Long Wharf behind Classified, ridden by TV commentator Derek Thompson.

1985 Jockey JONATHAN LOWER rode first winner, Silver Ace, at Windsor.

1989 Trainer MARTIN PIPE sent out 2 runners at Hereford, 2 at Newbury and 2 at Haydock - they all won.

1989 A colt called ARAZI was born. For a while it would seem that a better name for him might have been Champion the Wonder Horse.

1993 The Jockey Club announced a £5,000 reward for information leading to the conviction of 'any person who commits a serious offence in relation to racing' following recent doping cases.

5 MARCH

1840   The final day of the inaugural three-day meeting at Flemington, Australia. The meeting was named after local butcher Bob Fleming.

1840   WEATHERCOCK fell at Becher's during the Grand Liverpool Steeplechase at Aintree. His jockey, Barker, was injured and taken, suffering from concussion, to a nearby farmhouse - where he was still lying three days later, connections of the horse having made no effort to ascertain his state of health. 12-1 Jerry won.

1845   CURE ALL walked from Grimsby to Aintree to win the Grand National - and then had to walk back again.

1855   The first meeting took place at Riccarton, Christchurch, New Zealand.

1937   Former jockey DAVID EAST born.

1940   Owner of Precocious (Gimcrack and Molecomb Stakes winner) LADY TAVISTOCK born. Her Jupiter Island won Japan Cup, setting a record time of 2.25 minutes for the one and a half-mile trip. Colours: saffron and white diamonds; saffron and white striped sleeves; saffron cap.

1948   Staffordshire trainer SALLY OLIVER born. Best horse Aonoch.

1952   French trainer ELIE LELLOUCHE born in Tunisia.

1957   Jump jockey GEORGE KNIGHT born.

1962   Trainer HON. IAN MATTHEWS born. Best horses Tivian, Ra Nova.

1965   Owner and breeder of Heavenly Note LORD RONALDSHAY born. Colours: white; red spots; red sleeves; red cap. A well red man?

1966   Jump jockey DECLAN MURPHY born. Best horses ridden include Keep Hope Alive, Kingsmill. Won Irish Champion Hurdle in 1989.

1968   A horse announced as being lame and unable to run won a hunter chase at Doncaster after being heavily backed. VERONICA BELL, supported from 7-1 to 9-2, scored after what trainer Gordon Richards described as 'a misunderstanding'.

1983   No SPs were returned when Michael Dickinson-trained BREGAWN won at Hereford and his SILVER BUCK at Market Rasen.

1993   Pontefract racecourse was reunited with an oil painting by DAVID DALBY of the 1824 Badsworth Gold Cup, which had hung at their club stand entrance until the early 1960s, when it had gone missing. It had turned up for auction at Sotheby's for an estimated £20-£30,000.

1993   Kelso staged its richest ever race, the 16-runner Hennessy Cognac Special Novice Hurdle, won by MAJED ridden by Peter Niven for Mary Reveley at 15-8 favourite.

1993   ROGER SPICER completed his first double as a trainer when Sir Telimar and Modest Hope won on the flat at Southwell.

6 MARCH

1838   The first race meeting took place at Melbourne, Australia. There were two races, bullock trucks served as the grandstand, a clothes prop was the winning post and bets were struck and settled in rum.

1858   LITTLE CHARLEY won the Grand National, ridden by William Archer, whose fourteen-month-old son, Fred, would become one of the finest jockeys of all time.

1907   GLADYS 'POSY' LEWIS born. Probably the first woman jump trainer. Owned and trained 1959 and 1961 Welsh Grand National winner Limonali.

1944   Former Darlington trainer IAN VICKERS born.

1955   Former jockey TOM O'RYAN born.

1958   Jockey BENJY COOGAN born.

1963   Jockey GARY STEVENS born in Caldwell, Idaho. Champion in North America. Won 1988 Kentucky Derby on Winning Colors.

1967   First winner for trainer TIM BROOKSHAW, Dufton Park (Johnny Lehane), at Wolverhampton in a selling chase.

1968   20-1 shot South Rock gave TONY DICKINSON his first winner as a trainer and seventeen-year-old jockey MICHAEL DICKINSON his first victory at the 4th attempt in a selling chase at Chepstow.

1990   At Warwick, Shaston gave jockey HYWEL DAVIES his 600th winner, while SIR JEST became trainer Arthur Stephenson's 250th winner at Sedgefield.

1992   Twelve-year-old AMRULLAH was beaten for the 73rd time in 73 races in a novice chase at Sandown. Said trainer John Bridger, 'If he were mine I'd retire him, but the owner likes to see him run.'

1993   78-year-old SCOBIE BREASLEY sent out Chou-Chou Royale at 39-1 to win the Cockspur Gold Cup in Barbados, his 3rd consecutive winner of the race, the premier prize there. Sandy Hawley rode as Breasley announced his intended retirement to his native Australia.

1993   RAPPORTEUR, ridden by Billy Newnes, won his 15th race in an event named after him at Lingfield, a post-war record for any flat course, for trainer Charles Elsey.

1993   Trainer JEREMY TREE died. In a career of almost 40 years the 67-year-old sent out 4 classic winners: Only for Life and Known Fact in the 2,000 Guineas; Juliette Marny and Scintillate in the Oaks. His Rainbow Quest won the 1985 Arc. Succeeded Noel Murless at Beckhampton in 1953.

1993   CHARLIE WHITTINGHAM sent out his 9th winner of the prestigious Santa Anita Handicap when his grey Sir Beaufort won at 11-8.

1993   Former jump jockey MICHAEL WILLIAMS sent out his first flat race winner when Knock to Enter won at Lingfield.

7 MARCH

1661 First recorded meeting at Epsom Downs. King Charles II was in attendance – in an open-top bus, perhaps?

1691 The diary of the Chester Recorder noted: 'We rode to Farne race where I run against Sir Edmund Ashton, Mrs Morte, Mr Mackworth and Captain Warburton. Mrs Morte won the race.'

1916 Canadian owner DONALD G. WILLMOT born. His With Approval won the Canadian Triple Crown in 1989 and Izvestia did likewise in 1990.

1919 Owner of Sammy Davis, Acclimatise and Archbishop JOCELYN HAMBRO born. Colours: emerald green; white hooped sleeves; white cap.

1931 DEREK WEEDEN born. Thirteen years a jump jockey, then a trainer.

1934 A race which would not be allowed today, the National Hunt Juvenile Chase for four-year-olds, at Cheltenham, was won by Fred Rimell, on Captain's Choice, trained by his father at Kinnersley.

1948 Northern jockey JIMMY (BREWIS) WALTON born.

1950 Worcester trainer MICHAEL OLIVER born. Trained West Tip to win 1986 Grand National.

1953 Trainer DAVID ARBUTHNOT, whose riding career produced one winner, born. Best horses include Rinja.

1959 Champion South African jockey FELIX COETZEE born.

1960 Lightweight jockey MARTIN FRY born.

1964 The great Arkle won the first of 3 consecutive Cheltenham Gold Cups, starting at 7–4 and defeating Mill House, the reigning champion and 8–13 favourite.

1967 ANDY TURNELL rode his first winner over fences, Sweeney Todd (trained by Brian Trafford), at Plumpton. On the same card hurdler INDIAN SCENE won at 33–1 and was returned at 198–1 on the Tote.

1982 Jockey JOHN THORNE died in Oxford's Radcliffe Infirmary, aged 55, following the fall of Bend a Knee in a point-to-point at Mollington. He rode his own Spartan Missile to be runner-up in the 1981 Grand National.

1990 Jockey REG CRANK, 35, retired, signing off on Sally's Dove at Bangor, the 250th winner of his twenty-year career.

1993 FRANKIE DETTORI won the Young Jockeys World Championship, in Japan, for the 2nd year running when he won 3 of the 4 races.

1993 Macau Jockey Club trainer LEUNG WING LEUNG was assaulted by thugs in Taipa, the 3rd attack on racing people in as many months, following incidents involving Champion Jockey Geoff Allendorf and Irish rider John Egan.

8 MARCH

1622 The first recorded race at Newmarket, a match between horses owned by Lord Salisbury and the Marquess of Buckingham for £100.

1890 Wetherby trainer PERCY VASEY born. His father, J. Vasey, trained at Woodborough, Nottinghamshire, in the early 1880s. Rode 27 winners as an amateur in Malaysia. Also played cricket for Malaya from 1919 to 1927. Trained in England from 1937. Died aged 92.

1900 FLYING FOX, 2,000 Guineas, Derby and St Leger winner in the previous year, was sold for a record 37,500 guineas when the Duke of Westminster's stable went under the hammer.

1924 Jockey DAVE DICK born. He was the man who went on to win the 1956 Grand National on ESB when Devon Loch collapsed under Dick Francis. Dave Dick thus became the first jockey to complete the Spring Double, having won the 1941 Lincolnshire Handicap on Gloaming.

1934 US trainer VINCENT TIMPHONY born.

1937 US trainer DICK DUTROW born.

1939 Jockey JEAN CRUGUET born. Rode San San, Hurry Harriet, Seattle Slew.

1950 Vincent O'Brien-trained COTTAGE RAKE won the Cheltenham Gold Cup for the 3rd successive season, ridden by regular pilot Aubrey Brabazon.

1952 Jockey GARY MOORE born. Rider of Gold River, Bering, Ravinella.

1958 Trainer and breeder of oriental chickens ANABEL KING born. Best horses include Queensway Boy, Viridian.

1964 ALAN MERRIGAN, who rode The Thinker and Durham Edition, born.

1970 Jockey JAMIE O'HANLON born.

1983 MICHAEL DICKINSON reached a fastest training century when Sir Wimpy won at Warwick.

1987 ZANY TACTICS, aged six and carrying 126lbs, set a world record time of 1.06.8 for 6 furlongs at Turf Paradise, USA.

1993 TEMPERING won for the 14th time on Southwell's all-weather flat track, ridden by Steve Wood for trainer David Chapman.

1993 After 48 hours of virtually continuous chiropractor treatment for a slipped disc, Australian jockey MICK 'THE ENFORCER' DITTMAN won the AUS$650,000 Group 1 Australian Cup at Flemington on Veandercross to become the first jockey since Pat Hyland in 1970 to complete the Newmarket Handicap–Australian Cup double. (He'd won the Newmarket race two days earlier.)

9 MARCH

1870 The Colonel's Grand National victory was a record 5th in the race for jockey GEORGE STEVENS, who died the following year when he was thrown by his own hack at home in Cheltenham.

1920 Florida trainer WARREN A. (JIMMY) CROLL JR born. First winner 1940. Best horses include Housebuster and 1987 Belmont Stakes winner Bet Twice.

1945 Jockey HENRI SAMANI born. Rider of Kalamoun, Blushing Groom.

1961 Newmarket jockey PETER BLOOMFIELD born.

1982 After working disappointingly, SEA PIGEON was retired by trainer Peter Easterby. The versatile dual Champion Hurdler, which also ran in the Derby, had earned £275,687.22 prize-money.

1988 Successful sire and 1972 2,000 Guineas winner HIGH TOP was put down, aged nineteen.

1989 ANTHONY TORY, aged 27, was an appropriate winner of the opening race at Wincanton on Sirrah Jay. The Stewart Tory Chase was named after his grandfather.

1991 Welsh racing history was made when TIM JONES and PIP NASH became the first brother and sister pair to ride winning doubles on the same day at the same point-to-point meeting at Llanfrynach. This had only ever been achieved anywhere when David Turner and Josie Bothway each landed 2 winners at Ampton in 1977.

1991 Jockey JILL DAWSON won the Ladies' Open point-to-point race at Brocklesby Park for the 8th successive year, on Sweet Diana. Her first 3 wins were on Witchin, the next 3 on Sweet Diana then Roscoe Boy.

1992 Unique New York gave HYWEL DAVIES his 700th winner at Plumpton.

1993 The Jockey Club introduced their Raceguard Line, inviting anyone with information about doped horses or other serious racing offences to ring 071-935 7151. The number is still in operation, 24 hours a day.

10 MARCH

1870 Jockey Arthur Yates told his friend, the popular gentleman rider GEORGE EDE, 'Don't ride the brute, he'll kill you,' before Ede went out to partner Chippenham in the Sefton Chase at Aintree. Ede died after he and the horse fell at the fence before the water jump.

1896 HARRY STRAUSS, the man who invented the totalisator, was born in Baltimore. Bet he would have enjoyed a game of Monopoly!

1919 WILD ASTOR became the only horse to win 3 races at the age of eighteen when he scored at Warwick.

1951 Legendary Limerick punter, bookie and owner JOHN PATRICK MCMANUS born. Owner of Jack of Trumps and Deep Gale. Colours: emerald green; gold hoop; white cap.

1953 Jockey ARTHUR WRAGG, brother of Harry and Sam, died aged 41. In his best season, 1933, he rode 46 winners. In 1934 at Newcastle the brothers finished first, second and third in a race.

1959 MAGIC WIND breezed in at odds of 300–1 when winning at Doomben in Brisbane, Australia.

1986 Televisions were allowed in betting shops for the first time since the shops became legal in 1961.

1989 DR DEVIOUS, who was to win the 1992 Derby, was foaled.

1992 ROYAL GAIT, disqualified as winner of the 1988 Ascot Gold Cup, won the Champion Hurdle. The James Fanshawe-trained, Graham McCourt-ridden runner had to survive a twenty-minute Stewards' Inquiry. He was the first novice to win for 36 years.

1993 SULUK did it again at Southwell. The 8–11 favourite won his 18th race on the all-weather course, over hurdles.

1993 DIANE CLAY rode a 111–1 treble at Southwell for her father, Bill, who also had an 8–1 winner at Bangor.

1993 Trainer NIGEL TWISTON-DAVIES reached his first half-century when Dandy Minstrel won at Folkestone.

1993 EDDIE DELAHOUSSAYE, 41, became the 14th jockey in North America to ride 5,000 winners when Ackler won at Santa Anita.

11 MARCH

1922 Jockey RUSS MADDOCK born. Best mounts, Althrey Don, Park Top.

1924 Former amateur rider CYNTHIA SHEERMAN born.

1932 Bristol trainer RICHARD HOLDER born. Best horses include Star of a Gunner and Ikdam, winners of Lincoln (1987) and Triumph Hurdle (1989) respectively.

1933 Trainer–owner ALISTAIR CHARLTON born. Best horse Ida's Delight.

1947 Hang gliding jockey GORDON HOLMES born. Also a fully trained equine dentist. Best horse ridden Burlington II.

1949 Jockey DERMOT HOGAN born.

1954 PETER O'SULLEVAN enjoyed his first success in fifteen years as an owner when Pretty Fair won at Windsor.

1957 Northern jockey MICK WOOD born.

1960 Talon gave jump jockey GRAHAM BRADLEY his first success, at Sedgefield.

1961 The Victorian Totalisator Agency Board set up the Commonwealth's first legalised off-course betting system, in Melbourne.

1965 Arkle won the Cheltenham Gold Cup but the 3rd-placed horse, STONEY CROSSING, was a former Australian Olympic show-jumper which had never raced in the UK before.

1988 Successful sire BUSTED died following a heart attack, aged 25. England's Horse of the Year in 1967, he sired 1974 St Leger winner Bustino.

1989 SCOBIE BREASLEY, 75, former Champion Jockey (1961 to 1963), sent out Sandford Prince to win the Cockspur Gold Cup, the premier race in Barbados, where he set up as a trainer.

1989 PAT EDDERY rode his first Australian winner, Concordance, at Rosehill, Sydney.

1992 Keep Talking (ridden by Marcus Armytage) gave 97-year-old JIM JOEL his 12th Festival triumph, in the four-mile National Hunt Chase, 34 years after his first success at the Cheltenham Festival (Caesar's Helm in the Mildmay of Flete Chase). On the same day 66-year-old trainer JOHN WEBBER, who first sent runners to the Festival in 1958, finally managed a winner when Elfast won the Mildmay of Flete.

1992 Sportscast, which broadcast horse and dog racing to pubs and clubs, went off air after parent company British Aerospace pulled the financial plug.

1993 Tenesaint was the 3rd successive winner of Towcester's John Wrathall Memorial Hunters Chase to be trained by CAROLINE SAUNDERS, for whom Wrathall rode until his death in a road accident in France four years earlier. Teaplanter won the other two.

12 MARCH

1727   TREGONWELL FRAMPTON died. He was the first great dictator of the turf, and keeper of the running horses to William III, Queen Anne, George I and II. He was 86.

1924   Five-year-old chestnut RED SPLASH won the first Cheltenham Gold Cup. Ridden by Dick Rees, trained near Bicester by Fred Withington, the son of a parson, and owned by Captain E. Wyndham.

1930   Arkle's jockey, PAT TAAFFE, born; died 7 July 1992.

1936   GOLDEN MILLER won the Cheltenham Gold Cup for the 5th successive time, returning odds of 21–20 favourite.

1946   BOBBY O'RYAN rode Distel to win the Champion Hurdle. The jockey was enjoying a purple patch – it was his 7th win in a row.

1964   Riding The Pouncer at Stratford, jockey TERRY BIDDLECOMBE dropped his whip. He offered fellow jockeys £10 for a loan of theirs, and when no acceptance was forthcoming grabbed one out of the hand of another rider and rode his horse home to win by a head.

1966   JOHN LONGDEN rode his 6,032nd and last winner on George Royal at Santa Anita, setting a world record finally broken by Willie Shoemaker in 1970.

1991   A legend was born as DESTRIERO land a massive gamble for owner Noel Furlong in Cheltenham's Supreme Novices Hurdle. Estimates of the scale of the gamble range from £1 to £3 million.

1991   Omerta gave jockey ADRIAN MAGUIRE his first winner in Britain when the Martin Pipe-trained runner scored at Cheltenham.

1992   Jockey JAMIE OSBORNE ended the Cheltenham Festival with 5 winners – Flown, Young Pokey, Nomadic Way, Remittance Man and Dusty Miller – a record equalling that set by Fred Winter in 1959, when he won on Flame Gun, Fare Time, Top Twenty, Clair Soleil and Gallery Goddess.

1992   RUSHING WILD won the Foxhunters Chase to become the first horse in 25 years to win at the Festival on his debut under Rules. Master Tammy had done it in 1967 in the National Hunt Chase.

1992   COOL GROUND won the Cheltenham Gold Cup but controversy surrounded the defeat of Martin Pipe-trained Carvills Hill and the tactics adopted by trainer Jenny Pitman – her Golden Freeze stayed close to the market leader, whose jumping seemed to suffer. She was later cleared of any offence.

1992   Havant cleaner RICHARD MUSSELL collected £567,066.25 from Ladbrokes from a 5-winner Cheltenham accumulator.

1993   HARRY HASTINGS, last seen out winning the Waterford Crystal Supreme Novices Hurdle, returned to action 2,922 days later in the Ayrshire Hunters Challenge Cup – and fell 5 out.

13 MARCH

1905   Owner ISIDORE KERMAN born. Allegedly named his best horse Kybo after the initials of advice his mother had once given him: Keep Your Bowels Open! Colours: white; red cross and blue cap.

1920   HEINZ JENTZSCH born. German champion trainer 28 times.

1928   DICK REES (*né* Frederick Bilbo) rode five-year-old Patron Saint to win the Gold Cup, beating his elder brother Bilby on Vive.

1933   REYNOLDSTOWN won for the first time in the Wolverhampton Dunstall Hurdle. Went on to win 2 Grand Nationals

1946   Trainer CHARLES BOOTH, who lists his recreations as 'wine, women and song', born. Best horses include Ruddy Drake, Barrie Baby.

1948   The highest ever number of runners for a flat race in England, 58, contested the Lincolnshire Handicap, Commissar winning at 33–1. The race was run at Lincoln.

1952   Former Lambourn trainer JOHN NELSON born.

1956   Ledbury permit trainer TIM HOULBROOKE born.

1968   Bangor and Uttoxeter, the last courses where racing was still forbidden following the foot-and-mouth outbreak the previous October, were finally cleared.

1969   Jockey TONY CULHANE born. Best horses ridden include Time To Go Home, Umbelata.

1983   Jump jockeys NEIL CLAY (86 winners) and COLIN ASTBURY (90) announced their retirements.

1986   PETER SCUDAMORE broke his Cheltenham Festival duck on Solar Cloud in the Triumph Hurdle. Also a first for trainer David Nicholson.

1986   Paddy Mullins-trained DAWN RUN completed the first-ever Champion Hurdle–Gold Cup double, taking the second leg ridden by Jonjo O'Neill. There were riotous scenes after the race as Jonjo was carried shoulder-high into the winners' enclosure.

1989   After 38 unsuccessful racecourse appearances fourteen-year-old jumper PANEGYRIST finally got his head in front at Ayr. Commented jockey Joe O'Gorman: 'He'll be useful if they give him a bit of time.'

1990   PAST GLORIES finished third behind Kribensis in the Champion Hurdle, returning 150–1 to become the longest-priced placed horse in the history of the race.

1993   Olympian, 6–4 favourite, is the shortest-priced winner so far of Sandown's Imperial Cup.

14 MARCH

1933 Owner of 1992 Oaks and St Leger winner User Friendly BILL GREDLEY born. Colours: yellow; black stripes on sleeves; white cap.

1944 LORD HALIFAX, owner of 1978 Derby winner Shirley Heights, born. Colours: light blue; chocolate sleeves; hooped cap.

1945 Trainer TAFFY SALAMAN born.

1953 Taunton trainer BRIAN FORSEY born.

1954 Jockey PAUL RICHARDS born. Best horse ridden Mayotte.

1960 Jump jockey TONY GORMAN born.

1963 Jump jockey DERRICK MORRIS born.

1964 Jump jockey MICHAEL BOWLBY born. Best horse ridden Brown Windsor.

1976 WILLIE SHOEMAKER rode his 7,000th winner, Royal Derby, at Santa Anita.

1986 CARL LLEWELLYN rode his first winner, Starjestic, at Wolverhampton.

1989 Buckingham Palace announced that The Queen had appointed WILLIAM HASTINGS-BASS to take over at her West Ilsley stables when Major Dick Hern's lease expired at the end of the year.

1991 Jenny Pitman-trained GARRISON SAVANNAH won the Cheltenham Gold Cup, ridden by her son Mark, 24. Mark ended the day in hospital after cracking his pelvis riding Run to Form in the final race, one and a half hours after his Gold Cup triumph.

1992 American SYDNEY CRAIG, owner of a chain of health clubs, received a 60th birthday present from his wife Jenny: a horse called Dr Devious, which, less than three months later, went on to win the Derby.

1992 It really wasn't jockey TONY IVES' day. Riding in Macau, he was weighing in after partnering Mountview to victory when he caught his foot on the bottom of the scales and tripped, hitting a table and knocking himself unconscious. When he came round he declared himself fit enough to ride Good Luck Swoopy, which played up in the stalls, trapping Ives' leg, injuring him and forcing him to forfeit the rest of his rides for the day.

1993 Racing at Mahalakshmi, Bombay, was postponed following violence in the city, causing the loss of the most important three-year-olds' race in the Indian calendar, the Poonawalla Breeders' Million. British jockeys John Lowe, Chris Rutter, Michael Wigham and Kieran Fallon flew back to England after bombs had killed hundreds in the week leading up to the meeting.

15 MARCH

1651 A match for 1,000 crowns was run in France at the Bois de Boulogne between PRINCE D'HARCOURT'S mount and that of the DUC DE JOYEUSE. The horses were fed on bread made with beans and aniseed and for two days before the race each given between 200 and 300 fresh eggs, according to contemporary accounts. Pity anyone down-wind of the runners as the Duc's horse was blown to victory.

1855 First meeting run at Thirsk. Local schoolmaster GEORGE NICHOLSON was appointed clerk of the course, a position he held for twenty years until he finally landed the bet of a lifetime in the Autumn Double – and promptly dropped dead with excitement.

1935 Roads to the course were blocked and trains jam-packed as crowds streamed to see the Cheltenham Gold Cup duel between winner GOLDEN MILLER, ridden by Gerry Wilson, and the runner-up by 3/4 length Thomond II, ridden by Billy Speck.

1936 Huntingdon and Windsor clerk of the course HUGO BEVAN born.

1939 FREDDIE MAXWELL'S first winner as a trainer was Irish Salmon at Down Royal. He went on to send out 425 British flat winners.

1945 SOLARIO, the 1925 St Leger winner which also won the Ascot Gold Cup, died at Newmarket. In July 1932 Solario was sold at Newmarket for 47,000 Guineas, then a record price for a horse sold at auction in England.

1948 Jockey GRAHAM SEXTON, rider of a winner at every Flat racecourse in Britain, born. He started with Calisto at Wolverhampton in 1966.

1953 Trainer JEAN DE ROUALLE born. Best horse Caerlina.

1962 CASH ASMUSSEN (real name Brian) born. Rode Suave Dancer to win the 1991 Arc de Triomphe.

1973 First meeting took place at Evry in France.

1980 RICHARD DE PASS rode 7 winners from 7 mounts at Florida Downs, USA.

1983 MERCY RIMELL became the first woman to train the winner of the Champion Hurdle when Richard Linley brought home Gaye Brief at 7-1.

1990 100-1 shot NORTON'S COIN staggered the crowd and broke the track record in winning the Cheltenham Gold Cup for dairy farmer Sirrell Griffiths, for whom he represented a third of his entire stable.

1992 JULIE KRONE became the first female to win a riding title at a major Florida track when she completed the 59-day Gulfstream Park season with 72 wins, taking her career total to 2,344.

1993 Former trainer E. BARRY RYAN (73) died in New York.

1993 JOHN BAKER, who trained Star Player to win the 1991 Chester Cup, died aged 75.

16 MARCH

1903   Owner FRANK HILL born. Best horses Be Cautious, Be Patient. Colours: petunia; gold sleeves; green cap.

1940   PRINCE REGENT, probably the best chaser of the 1940s (Cheltenham Gold Cup winner 1946), raced in public for the first time, unplaced on the flat at Baldoyle.

1942   Trainer BILL WATTS born. Best horses included Waterloo and Teleprompter, winner of the 1975 Arlington Million.

1949   TV racing commentator GRAHAM GOODE born. Appropriate initials!

1955   Worcester broke all records for entries: 472 horses were entered for an 8-race card. 121 of them finally went to post.

1961   Trainer GARETH CHARLES-JONES born.

1966   JACKIE BRUTTON became the first woman trainer officially to train a winner in Great Britain over the sticks when Snowdra Queen won at Cheltenham in the United Hunts Challenge Cup.

1971   Jockey JASON TITLEY born.

1989   York rider KEN HOLMES won the Kiplingcotes Derby, reputedly the oldest race in Britain, first run in 1519, for the 3rd time. He rode Paddy From Wales to win the four and a half-mile event over the Yorkshire Wolds.

1989   Not a dry eye in the house as DESERT ORCHID became the first grey to win the Cheltenham Gold Cup. Ridden by Simon Sherwood, 5-2 favourite.

1989   Bookie VICTOR CHANDLER took an on-course bet at Cheltenham of £90,000 for 4-9 shot RUSCH DE FARGES. The horse lost.

1993   ATTADALE was backed from 1-10 to 1-16 in a novice hurdle at Sedgefield after one punter risked £3,000 on the horse at 1-10 and a further £8,000 at 1-16. Fortunately for him, the Len Lungo-trained runner duly obliged, giving the bold gambler a profit of £800 for his £11,000 stake.

1993   MONTELADO became the first horse to win consecutive races at the Cheltenham Festival. Having won the National Hunt Flat Race which closed the previous year's meeting he won the first race of this year's, the Trafalgar House Supreme Novice Hurdle, for jockey Charlie Swan and trainer P. J. Flynn.

1993   MARTIN PIPE trained his first championship winner when Granville Again, partnered by Peter Scudamore, won the Champion Hurdle at 13-2.

1993   FISSURE SEAL won Cheltenham's American Express Gold Card Handicap Hurdle at 14-1. The horse was owned by four dentists who named him after a seal used to stop decay in children's teeth.

17 MARCH

1859 The Union Steeple Chase and the Welter Race – both £3 to enter – were run at Market Rasen, as evidenced by the earliest surviving racecard for the course, which also declared: 'Should the weather prevent the races coming off on the day fixed, the stewards will have the power to postpone them from day to day, or week to week, until they come off, and all entries to remain the same.'

1928 Trainer DEREK KENT born. Best horse Grand Canyon, dual Colonial Cup winner in 1976 and 1978.

1941 Trainer PAUL FELGATE born. Best horses include Gemini Fire, Shuttlecock Corner.

1950 Point-to-point trainer JOHN PORTER born.

1956 Jump jockey SIMON MCNEILL born. Recreation windsurfing. Best horse ridden Katabatic.

1958 Jockey BRENT THOMSON born.

1967 A *Daily Telegraph* survey into feeling about a Tote monopoly revealed that just 5 per cent of those polled wanted bookmakers abolished.

1969 Irish jockey ULTAN SMYTH born.

1983 Trainer MICHAEL DICKINSON sent out the first 5 in the Cheltenham Gold Cup: winner Bregawn, followed by Captain John, Wayward Lad, Silver Buck and Ashley House.

1988 FORGIVE 'N' FORGET, the winner in 1985, was destroyed after breaking a leg during the Cheltenham Gold Cup. Trainer David Barons is convinced to this day that disappointing favourite Playschool was 'got at'. Charter Party won the race for trainer David Nicholson and jockey Richard Dunwoody.

1989 Former trainer HUGH SIDEBOTTOM died aged 83, having trained from 1936 to 1957.

1991 ENRICO CAMICI, 78, the greatest Italian jockey, died of a heart attack. Rode Ribot throughout his unbeaten 16-race career and rode 4,081 winners.

1993 PAUL CARBERRY rode a winner with his first Cheltenham Festival ride – just as his father, Tommy, had done on Tripacer in 1962 – when Rhythm Section won the Guinness Festival Bumper.

1993 OLYMPIAN, which had won the Imperial Cup at Sandown on the Saturday, collected a £50,000 bonus courtesy of bookmakers Sunderland, sponsors of that race, when the Martin Pipe-trained runner won the Coral Cup Handicap Hurdle at Cheltenham. The bonus was for winning the Imperial plus any Cheltenham Festival race.

18 MARCH

1875 TOMMY PICKERNELL rode his third Grand National winner, Pathfinder – but not without a problem or two before the race. Having imbibed a spot of Dutch courage, he had to ask a fellow jockey in which direction he and his mount should be facing.

1912 Trainer LUCIEN LAURIN born. Took over as trainer of Secretariat when he was nearly 60 years old and on the verge of retiring, having trained the winners of 1,137 races and amassed prize-winning earnings of $6,434,303. Took Secretariat to the 1973 Triple Crown.

1921 DICK REES, 6-times Champion and the first jump jockey to ride over 100 winners in a season, won the Grand National for the first and only time on Shaun Spadah, the only one of the 35 starters to complete the course without falling. Despite a broken collar bone, HARRY BROWN remounted his National horse The Bore to finish 2nd. Yet bravery had little to do with it – he had substantial each-way bets riding on the 9–1 favourite!

1949 ALEX 'HURRICANE' HIGGINS born. One of his early jobs was as a stable lad.

1952 Champion jockey PAT EDDERY born, one of thirteen children in Dublin. First Derby winner Grundy, first Arc winner Detroit. His father Jimmy was Champion jockey in Ireland.

1957 Author and owner LADY SOPHIA MORRISON born. Colours: straw; brown hoop on cap.

1978 Giant jockey CHRIS KINANE (6ft 2¹/2ins) rode his first winner, Hard Outlook, at Lingfield.

1981 WILLIE WUMPKINS, thirteen years old, won the Coral Golden Hurdle at Cheltenham for the 3rd consecutive year, at odds of 13–2. Ridden by Jim Wilson, who had partnered the horse to win at 10–1 the previous year and at 25–1 the year before. The trainer who achieved what Fulke Walwyn described as 'one of the greatest training feats I have seen in my life' was Jane Pilkington of Stow-on-the-Wold, the mother-in-law of the jockey.

1991 ALEX GREAVES became the first female jockey in its nineteen-year history to win a coveted William Hill Golden Spurs Award, receiving the award for Apprentice of the Year.

1992 Industrial action by stable lads in support of a claim for better rates of overtime pay caused the opening meeting of the season at San Siro, Milan, to be abandoned.

1993 SHAWIYA became the first filly to win the Daily Express Triumph Hurdle. Ridden by Charlie Swan, trained by Michael O'Brien, she returned 12–1.

19 MARCH

1860 The first meeting at Baldoyle, Ireland, took place.

1880 Brothers TOMMY, HARRY and JOHN BEASLEY finished 1st (Empress), 5th (Woodbrook) and 8th (Victoria) in the Grand National.

1907 George Stern rode OB to victory in the Lincoln. OB, trained by Richard Carter in France, became the first horse to win it twice. The feat was matched in 1957 and 1958 by Our Babu.

1935 Irish trainer PADDY PRENDERGAST born. Learned his trade as assistant trainer to the late 'Sunny Jim' Fitzsimmons in New York and Florida.

1937 Former window-cleaner turned trainer and 'king' of selling races and betting touches KEN PAYNE born.

1938 Market Rasen trainer MICHAEL CHAPMAN born. Best horse Quistador.

1939 Gloucester trainer DAVID 'THE DUKE' NICHOLSON born. His best season as a jockey was 1966–67, when he rode 63 winners. Partnered Mill House to win 1967 Whitbread Gold Cup. Took out licence to train in 1968 while continuing to ride. His Charter Party won Cheltenham Gold Cup in 1988.

1941 Jockey Club member and owner of What A Buck LORD VESTEY born. Colours: royal blue; white striped sleeves.

1944 Trainer PETER MAKIN born. Best horses Powder Blue and sprinter Elbio.

1945 Lambourn trainer HARRY COTTRILL announced his retirement. His Adam's Apple won the 1927 2,000 Guineas and Lovely Rosa the 1936 Oaks.

1949 WILLIE SHOEMAKER made his first public riding appearance, finishing 5th on Waxahachie at Golden Gate Fields.

1958 SIMON SHERWOOD born. As a jockey rode 8 Cheltenham Festival winners, 2 Whitbread Gold Cups and 2 King George VI Chases.

1965 Lightweight jockey JIMMY CARTER born.

1968 L'ESCARGOT, who went on to win the Grand National and Gold Cup, was the 13–2 winner of Cheltenham's Gloucestershire Hurdle, ridden by Tommy Carberry.

1968 Chancellor Roy Jenkins doubled betting tax to 5 per cent.

1987 THE THINKER won the Cheltenham Gold Cup for trainer Arthur Stephenson, who was so blasé about the race that he watched it on TV at Hexham racecourse.

1993 PAUL SMITH ECCLES, younger brother of Steve, rode his first winner at the age of 21 when Elegant Friend won at Fakenham.

1993 RED RUM and DESERT ORCHID competed in a 1-furlong walking race at Cheltenham's Comic Relief Charity Fund Raising Day at which £130,000 was raised. Rummy just beat Dessie.

20 MARCH

1888 The Duke of Portland's DONOVAN won the Brocklesby Stakes at Lincoln. He ended the two-year-old season with 11 wins from 13 outings and went on to win both the Derby and St Leger.

1891 Four previous Grand National winners – Ilex, Gamecock, Roquefort and Voluptuary – were among the 21 who went to post for the Grand National, won by 4-1 favourite COME AWAY.

1915 Respected American trainer BURLY COCKS born.

1924 Owner of Irish Oaks winners Regal Exception and Caterina ROBIN SCULLY born. Colours: grey, lemon sleeves; orange cap.

1928 JOHN BENSTEAD born. Trained dual Cambridgeshire winner Baronet.

1929 Jockey TOMMY LOWREY (later to win the 1946 Derby on 50-1 shot Airborne) rode his first winner, Rose Cottage, at Lincoln.

1941 Twice Champion Apprentice BOBBY ELLIOTT born.

1945 Jockey MAURICE PHILIPPERON born. Rode Homeric and Admetus.

1948 SHEILA'S COTTAGE, trained by Neville Crump, won the Grand National. Two days later, during a photo session, the horse showed its appreciation of the ride given by jockey Arthur Thompson by biting off the top of one of his fingers.

1967 Stockton racecourse was renamed Teesside Park.

1968 Jimmy Uttley partnered PERSIAN WAR (4-1) to the first of his 3 successive Champion Hurdle victories. On the same day Barry Brogan rode a double on 20-1 shot Hustler in the Cotswold Chase and 8-1 chance Spaniard in the George Duller Handicap Hurdle.

1975 ROYAL CADET became the first horse in the country to be ridden by a professional female jockey when partnered by Jane McDonald to finish 11th in an apprentices' race at Doncaster.

1980 Concert Hall gave GEOFF LEWIS his first winner as a trainer at Doncaster.

1989 Equine artist MICHAEL LYNE died in his 77th year. Best known for a series of paintings of chases at Aintree between 1965 and 1975.

1992 Trainer DEREK SHAW sent out his first flat winner, Coleridge (50-1), in the Cystic Fibrosis Research Cup at Doncaster.

1993 NORWICH, doped at Doncaster in 1990, won on his US debut in the San Francisco Mile Handicap at Golden Gate, California.

1993 Uttoxeter became the first British racecourse to offer racegoers the attraction of Bungee Jumping. Lord Oaksey raised £1,000 for the Injured Jockeys Fund by diving head-first from the 200ft crane at the course. On the day, Uttoxeter attracted a record crowd of 10,343, who saw Mister Ed (25-1) win the Midlands Grand National to give trainer Roger Curtis his biggest success.

21 MARCH

1860 JOHN (BARHAM) DAY, who rode 16 Classic winners and trained another 7, died in his 67th year. Despite his success he failed to ride or train a Derby winner.

1871 THE LAMB was literally a dream Grand National winner for owner Lord Poulet, who had 'seen' Tommy Pickernell riding the horse to victory in his slumbers. Upon waking he booked that jockey for the mount, and the combination duly obliged at 11-2.

1899 Jockey TOD SLOAN rode 5 winners from 5 mounts at Ingleside, California.

1902 SHANNON LASS's Grand National win earned the south coast village of Telscombe a new church. Local squire Ambrose Gorham restored the church in the village with his £2,000 winnings.

1929 LORD JOHN (GEOFFREY TRISTRAM) OAKSEY born. Rode as an amateur from 1955 to 1975 but became best known for his fronting of Channel 4's racing coverage.

1942 The Cheltenham Gold Cup was won by MEDOC II ridden by Frenchie Nicholson. The race was run in thick fog but radio listeners weren't told that by commentator Raymond Glendinning, who was mindful of the fact that his broadcast was almost certainly being monitored by foreign sources with a vested interest in knowing the weather conditions over England.

1944 Jockey TIM NORMAN born. Rode Anglo to a shock 50-1 Grand National victory in 1966.

1944 Trainer CHARLES VERNON MILLER born. Best horse trained Bighorn.

1962 Jockey NICKY CONNORTON born. Once rode 9 winners in 4 racing days in Malaysia. Best horse ridden Fascadale.

1964 Possibly the most open betting race ever run as the Grand National starting price showed 100-7 the field with Time, Pappageno's Cottage, Laffy and Flying Wild all co-favourites at that rate. The 33-runner event was won by 18-1 shot Team Spirit.

1970 A record one and a half-mile time of 2 minutes 23 seconds, equivalent to a speed of 37.76mph, was clocked by FIDDLE ISLE, carrying 124lbs at Santa Anita Park, California. The time was equalled in 1980 by the great John Henry, at the same track.

1992 LESTER PIGGOTT's bid to win the Lincoln for the first time was foiled by his son-in-law, William Haggas, trainer of winner High Low. Lester finished 2nd on Mudaffar, trained by brother-in-law Robert Armstrong. It had been 42 years since Lester had first ridden in the race, riding Prince Danilo.

1993 'Hall of Fame' rider ERIC GUERIN (69) died. Rode Native Dancer to win the Preakness and Belmont Stakes in 1953.

22 MARCH

1903 JOHN BIGG, owner of 1959 Grand National winner Oxo, born. Colours: green, pink and white striped sleeves; pink cap.

1913 PETER NELSON, trainer of 1974 50-1 Derby winner Snow Knight, born. He was also responsible for Knockroe, who set a record time for one and a half miles when winning the Weetabix Wildlife Handicap at the 1973 Derby meeting at Epsom.

1916 Owner LAVINIA, DUCHESS OF NORFOLK, born. Her Moon Madness won the 1986 St Leger. Colours: sky blue; sky blue and scarlet quartered cap.

1921 CHARLIE ELLIOTT, later to ride 14 Classic winners, pulled off a double on the first 2 rides he had in public, Rakings and Golden Myth at Nottingham.

1922 STEVE DONOGHUE rode Granely to win the 1922 Lincoln for financier Jimmy White, who enjoyed a small flutter. A former bricklayer from Rochdale, White had been confined to his office and unable to watch the race so had dabbled a mere £1,000 at 20-1, 'just in case'. Five years on the fearless gambler crashed on the stock exchange and committed suicide.

1922 Owner-trainer of Forty Light TONY BETHELL born. His Starlight Lad won 11 races. Colours: salmon pink; white hoop on cap.

1929 A record 66 went to post for the Grand National, won by a 100-1 shot for the second successive year, Gregalach. Largest-ever field for a jump race.

1931 Former Newmarket trainer JOHN WAUGH born.

1939 THE HON DAVID SIEFF born. Owner of Double Shuffle, 1969 top two-year-old filly Mange Tout and 12-times winner Backgammon. Colours: green and gold halved; sleeves reversed; striped cap.

1948 Trainer BILL O'GORMAN born. Best horses include Provideo, Brondesbury, Superlative. Father of jockey Emma.

1960 Amateur rider CHRIS BEALBY born. Best horses ridden include Green Bramble, Sun Lion.

1984 PROVIDEO won his first race as a two-year-old, at Doncaster. Went on to set a twentieth-century record of 16 wins in a season, trained by Bill O'Gorman.

1993 ADRIAN MAGUIRE completed his first century of winners in a season when Trendy Auctioneer won at Plumpton.

1603 Racing recorded at Leicester.

1840 Colburn's *Kalendar of Amusements* for 1840 described the Leamington Grand Steeple Chase to be held this day in glowing terms: 'In point of interest and attraction this race is second to none in the kingdom; it is a joyous and animating scene, and worthy of being paid a visit, not only by the lovers of sport but by those of the *beau monde* who delight in seeing and being seen, for the attendance is always numerous and fashionable.'

1877 Jockey FRED HOBSON, who had the curious style of holding on to his saddle every time he jumped a fence, won the Grand National in his only appearance in the race, riding 15–1 Austerlitz.

1919 Owner-trainer of Credit Call, URSULA 'URKIE' NEWTON, born.

1934 GOLDEN MILLER won the Grand National for the only time.

1945 10-times Champion Jockey STEVE DONOGHUE died in his 61st year. He rode the winners of 14 Classics, including 6 Derbys, and partnered Brown Jack to 6 consecutive victories in Royal Ascot's Queen Alexandra Stakes from 1929 to 1934.

1948 Newmarket jockey RAY MCGHIN born.

1955 Upper Lambourn trainer OLIVER SHERWOOD born. Champion Amateur Rider 1979–80. Trainer of The West Awake, Arctic Call.

1968 JOSH GIFFORD at Lingfield and JIMMY MORRISEY at Ludlow both rode trebles.

1979 DAVID ELSWORTH saddled his first winner as a trainer, Fortune Cookie, at Devon.

1986 ROYAL GAIT, later to be disqualified from the Ascot Gold Cup and to win the Champion Hurdle, won for the first time, in his 3rd race, at Madrid over 9 furlongs in heavy ground.

1989 PRINCE CHARLES lost his first 'winner' as an owner-breeder. Devil's Elbow, which had finished 1st in a hurdles race at Worcester in December 1988, was disqualified following a Jockey Club inquiry. A test revealed prohibited substances and trainer Nick Gaselee was fined £2,000, although he was cleared of administering the substances intentionally.

1991 ALEX GREAVES became the first woman to ride the winner of the Lincoln Handicap when she won on 22–1 shot Amenable.

1991 LESTER PIGGOTT's first all-weather winner in Britain was La Masaas at Lingfield.

1992 Owner JIM JOEL, real name Harry Joel Joel, died at the age of 97. He never married. First Classic winner was Picture Play in the 1944 1,000 Guineas. At the age of 92 he saw his Maori Venture win the Grand National. Colours: black; scarlet cap.

24 MARCH

1876 For the 3rd time in four years CAPTAIN JAMES MACHELL trained the Grand National winner as 25-1 chance Regal went in.

1882 Only 3 of 12 runners finished in the Grand National. 10-shot SEAMAN, ridden by Lord Manners, beat Cyrus and Zoedone.

1885 The Brocklesby Stakes at Lincoln was won by a small chestnut flecked with white, named The Bard. For the rest of the season it was a question of to win or nothing else for The Bard, who devised a plot his namesake would have baulked at as he ran 16 times as a two-year-old and was never beaten. Trained by Martin Gurry at Park Lodge, Newmarket.

1911 The one-eyed GLENSIDE (20-1) was the only horse to complete the Grand National course without falling. The other 3 to finish were all remounted.

1922 Only 3 of 32 starters got round in the Grand National, won by the 100-9 chance Music Hall, and for the first time the RSPCA protested about the severity of the course.

1927 Owner of 1986 Royal Hunt Cup winner Patriarch PETER WINFIELD born. Colours: royal blue and red quarters; white sleeves; black cap.

1935 Vicomte's owner, TREVOR BARKER, born. Also owned 11-times jump winner Follower. Colours: green with white hoop and armlets; green cap with white star.

1937 VISCOUNT CHELSEA (CHARLES G. J. CADOGAN) born. Owner of Roman Holiday and Money Market. Colours: dark brown; Eton blue epaulets and cap.

1947 Surrey trainer TONY INGHAM born. His career as a jockey ended when he fractured his skull at Folkestone. Took out trainer's licence in February 1977. Best horses included Song of Songs and Levaramoss.

1951 Press Association racing writer RODNEY MASTERS born.

1956 The Queen Mother's horse DEVON LOCH, ridden by Dick Francis, inexplicably jumped and fell while on the Grand National run-in. At the time, it looked certain to be the winner. E.S.B. came through then to win at 100-7.

1968 Jump jockey DAVID BURCHELL born.

1982 COLIN BROWN (The Go-Boy) and PHIL TUCK (Highland Linnet) both rode their 100th winners at Southwell.

1988 ARTHUR FREEMAN, who rode Mr What to win the 1958 Grand National, died at the age of 62.

1988 Jockeys announced a ban on media interviews because of worries over 'trial by television' amid controversy over jockeys' use of the whip.

25 MARCH

1799 Over £250,000 was bet on the outcome of a race at Newmarket between northern champion HAMBLETONIAN, the 1795 St Leger winner, and DIAMOND, one of the best horses based in the south of the country. Hot favourite Hambletonian, ridden by Frank Buckle, won by half a neck from Diamond, ridden by Irish professional Dennis Fitzpatrick.

1887 A huge gamble went wrong when SPAHI, who had never raced in a hurdle or chase, was made 9-2 favourite for the Grand National. He fell as Gamecock won, but then proceeded to come out and win 24 hours later, carrying 12st 12lbs in the Champion Chase.

1892 CAPTAIN RODDY OWEN won the Grand National on 20-1 chance Father O'Flynn. The army officer later died in Africa, where he had a Kenyan waterfall, Owen Falls, named in his honour.

1904 MOIFAA won the Grand National at 25-1. Legend has it that the horse was shipwrecked off the coast of Ireland on the way over from his native New Zealand. Sixteen-year-old Manifesto ran in the race for the 8th and last time, coming in 8th. Previous record: 1st (1897, 1899), 3rd (1900, 1902, 1903), 4th (1895).

1927 The BBC broadcast the Grand National for the first time. Meyrick Good and George Allison were the commentators as Sprig, the 8-1 favourite, won.

1933 Jockey LIONEL BROWN born. Best horses ridden include Copsale, Farm Walk.

1933 Former Loughborough permit holder LORD CRAWSHAW born.

1934 PETER HARRIS born. Owner of Bachelor's Hall, winner of the Hennessy and Mackeson Gold Cups and King George VI Chase. Colours: emerald green; red sash; yellow sleeves and cap.

1938 Seventeen-year-old BRUCE HOBBS became the youngest Grand National winning jockey as he partnered Battleship to a 40-1 victory.

1946 Newmarket trainer BEN HANBURY born. He had 50 winners as a jockey. His Midway Lady won the 1986 Oaks and 1,000 Guineas.

1956 Trainer KEVIN BISHOP, owner of Tiepolino, who won 12 chases including Liverpool's Topham Trophy, born.

1958 Wantage trainer MICHAEL ROBINSON born.

1961 Two Russian horses, GRIFEL and RELJEF, raced in the Grand National. Unseated rider and pulled up respectively.

1968 Former champion jockey DOUG SMITH sent out his first winner as a trainer with his first runner, Owen Anthony, at Doncaster.

1991 Jockeys ALAN MUNRO and ALLAN MACKAY fined for starting from the wrong stalls in a race at Folkestone.

26 MARCH

1886   Owner A. J. Douglas backed his 25–1 Grand National winner OLD JOE to win a sizeable sum – and promptly gave trainer George Mulcaster (£1,000) and jockey Tommy Skelton (£1,380) the race prize-money.

1906   Northern jockey BILLY NEVETT, who won 3 wartime Derbys at Newmarket (1 on Dante), born. He was 6 times runner-up in the Championship to Gordon Richards. Died May 1992. Rode 2,068 winners from 12,356 British mounts in 33 seasons.

1924   Trainer WALTER WHARTON born. Best horses included Night Off, Vaguely Noble. Trained the latter to win the Observer Gold Cup after which the horse was sold for a then world record public auction price of 136,000 guineas to American plastic surgeon Dr R. Franklyn. Trained by E. Pollet, Vaguely Noble won the Arc.

1926   WILLIAM WATKINSON rode Jack Horner to win the Grand National. Three weeks later Watkinson was killed in a fall at Bogside.

1938   JOHNNY ROE, 9 times Champion Irish Jockey between 1963 and 1974, born. Became a trainer and went to Macau.

1940   Panamanian jockey turned trainer BRAULIO BAEZA born. Still remembered for partnering Roberto to inflict the only defeat of his career on Brigadier Gerard, in the 1972 Benson & Hedges Gold Cup. Retired as jockey in 1976 with 3,140 victories to his credit.

1954   Former jump jockey DEREK OLDHAM born.

1955   For the 3rd successive year Vincent O'Brien saddled the Grand National winner as Quare Times (100–9) completed a sequence begun by Early Mist (20–1) and continued by Royal Tan (8–1).

1955   New York trainer GEORGE RUSSELL ARNOLD II born. First winner La Yo Quiero at Delaware Park, July 25 1975.

1960   The Grand National was televised for the first time and won by Merryman II, trained by Neville Crump and ridden by Gerry Scott, who became a starter, at 13–2 favourite.

1960   Newmarket trainer JAMES EUSTACE born.

1966   Drake's Drum, bought by Beatle PAUL MCCARTNEY for his father, won the 6-furlong Hutton Plate, the race before the Grand National, and was led in by the star, who was attending Aintree races for the first time. He later saw Tim Norman ride 50–1 shot Anglo (formerly known as Flag of Convenience) to victory in the National.

1968   Knotty Pine, ridden by Frank Durr, gave MICHAEL JARVIS his first winner as a trainer, at Doncaster.

1993   Jockey GARY STEVENS won 3 of the 4 races the inaugural International Jockeys Challenge in Dubai, to give his US team, including Kent Desormeaux, victory. No betting was permitted.

27 MARCH

1873   DISTURBANCE won the Grand National. His trainer, Captain James Machell, had an unusual party piece of jumping on to his mantelpiece from a standing start. No time was recorded for this National – the timekeeper's watch stopped.

1903   AMBUSH II, owned by King Edward VII, became the first horse to represent a reigning monarch in the Grand National, but fell as Drumcree won.

1908   RUBIO (66–1), the first US-bred Grand National winner, previously pulled a regular hotel bus to and from Towcester station.

1918   Jockey ALEC RUSSELL born. In July 1957 he rode all 6 winners at Hamilton. Retired in October 1973 and died in February 1990.

1934   Rider of Noholme and Blue Mountain DICK BROADWAY born.

1935   LORD SUFFOLK born. Breeder of Oaks winner Ginevra and owner of Irish Minstrel. Colours: violet; green sleeves and white cap.

1955   Upper Lambourn trainer KIM BRASSEY born. Best horses include Indian Rajah, Sharp Romance, Darweesh, Destroyer, Amigo Sucio.

1955   Former US Champion Jockey CHRIS MCCARRON born. Rode a record 546 winners in 1974.

1968   FRANKINCENSE, ridden by Greville Starkey, set a twentieth-century weight-carrying record for trainer John Oxley when winning the Lincoln under 9st 5lbs at odds of 100–8.

1984   BILL SMITH rode his 500th winner, Special Cargo (trained by Fulke Walwyn), for the Queen Mother in the Alanbrooke Memorial Handicap Chase at Sandown.

1989   Just 16 runners lined up for a 6-race jump card at Chepstow, where Peter Scudamore rode one of the least rewarding trebles ever at odds of 1–7, 1–7 and a walkover.

1989   Gossip columnist NIGEL DEMPSTER won a £10,000 wager when his horse My Purple Prose won for the 3rd time in the season, at Chepstow, at evens.

1993   Red Indians were brought in to perform a rain dance at Newbury, which had been suffering drought conditions. There were no immediate indications that their gyrations were effective.

1993   LYNDA RAMSDEN became the first woman to train the William Hill Lincoln winner when her High Premium, ridden by Kieran Fallon, won at 16–1. For good measure she also sent out 3rd-placed Will of Steel.

1993   Liskeard man SIMON EDWARDS, 28, rode Ballysheil (3–1) to win at Kilworthy point-to-point – and also won a bride. Girlfriend Jackie Oliver had refused his marriage proposal until he broke his duck. After the race he proposed again – and she accepted.

28 MARCH

1884   The winner of Chester's Dee Stakes, a failure in the Derby, VOLUPTUARY had never before run in a steeplechase, but today won the Grand National. The horse's unorthodox career continued as he went on to become a theatre star, appearing at the Drury Lane theatre in a production of *The Prodigal Daughter*, in which he was called upon to leap a water jump every night.

1919   The Grand National was won by POETHLYN as it resumed after a four-year gap during the war. For the first time in the history of the race a runner, All White, was pulled up to enable his jockey, T. Williams, to throw up. A pre-race seafood snack had come back to haunt the jockey, who eventually restarted and ran on to be 5th.

1924   Jockey BILL O'NEILL, riding outsider Libretto in the Grand National, fell, but undaunted he hitched a lift on a passing loose horse, the favourite Conjuror II, caught his own mount, remounted – and promptly fell again. Master Robert (25-1) won the race.

1931   EASTER HERO, dual Cheltenham Gold Cup winner of 1929-30, ran for the last time, dead-heating in the Champion Chase at Liverpool over two miles 7 furlongs the day after being brought down in his third unsuccessful attempt to win the Grand National.

1942   Many might be surprised to learn that, as well as Richard Burridge, Desert Orchid had another part-owner, SIMON BULLIMORE, born today. He acquired a quarter of the horse for £100 plus his share of the upkeep.

1954   Curragh trainer and former jockey DECLAN GILLESPIE born.

1958   Owner and commentator PETER O'SULLEVAN landed his first flat winner when Just Friendly scored at Lincoln.

1966   Jockey LUKE HARVEY born. Best horses ridden include Katabatic, Cool Ground.

1984   Trainer MICHAEL DICKINSON sent out his final British winner over jumps, Mister Donut at Fakenham.

1988   SUSAN PIGGOTT, wife of Lester, trained her first winner with a full licence, Raahin at Folkestone.

1989   Owner RICHARD BURRIDGE announced that he was setting up a fan club for popular Gold Cup-winning Desert Orchid.

1990   GOD'S SOLUTION attempted to win the same race for the 6th consecutive year at Catterick. Formerly the See it Live in Yorkshire Handicap and the Race Around Yorkshire Handicap, the name of the 6-furlong race was changed to the God's Solution Handicap in honour of the grey which, partnered by Alex Greaves, finished 3rd.

1991   Readers checked that the date wasn't April 1 when the *Sun* informed them that SHERGAR had been discovered in the Channel Islands.

An eighteenth-century handbill showing the results of
a meeting at Chester, 2 May 1791 (*Hulton Deutsch*)

Even before the television age, certain jockeys became stars

Above: A study of three celebrated horsemen, Chifney, Wheatty and Robinson, published in the *Sporting Review*, 1842 (*Hulton Deutsch*)

Opposite, top: A more formal portrait of Chifney (1786–1854) by C. Turner (*Hulton Deutsch*)

Opposite, bottom: The jockey Butler (*Hulton Deutsch*)

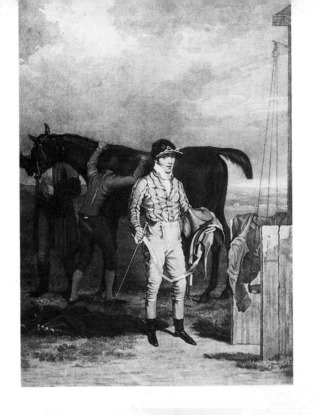

One of the all-time greats, Fred Archer, who tragically shot himself after the death of his wife (*Hulton Deutsch*)

Hornpipe *leaping over* Pepperpot *his Rider and the Farmers Son at* Lincoln Races
Friday the 8th Sept.r 1797

Above: This image of the 1791 Derby shows the difficulty artists had in portraying motion before photography allowed them to study natural movement more closely (*Hulton Deutsch*)

Below: Edward VII leads in Persimmon after winning the 1896 Derby (*Hulton Deutsch*)

Bay Middleton, winner of the 1836 Derby (*Hulton Deutsch*)

Horse-racing today is big, big business. The top-priced horse at the 1989 Keeneland Selected Yearling Sale was this colt by Northern Dancer out of Mrs Penny, which fetched $2.8 million

1881   Amateur CHARLIE CUNNINGHAM rode in 7 races at Rugby's jump meeting, winning 6 of them and finishing 2nd in the other.

1901   2lbs of butter won the Grand National for the Arthur Nightingall ridden GRUDON. The race was run in a snowstorm, and in an inspired move owner-trainer-breeder Bernard Bletsoe packed the horse's hooves with the butter, which helped him keep his footing when all about were losing theirs.

1917   MAN O'WAR, perhaps America's most famous racehorse ever, was foaled. He won 20 of his 21 races starting at odds-on in every one of them, and was universally known as Big Red.

1925   Thirsk permit trainer LAURENCE GRIFFITHS born.

1935   For the first time the National was won by two Furlongs - Frank Furlong, jockey, and Noel Furlong, owner-trainer. The horse was REYNOLDSTOWN (22-1).

1940   Irish jockey PADDY KIELY born. Best horses ridden included General Symons, Ivor's King.

1947   The Grand National took place on a Saturday for the first time at the request of prime minister Clement Attlee 'in the interests of British industry'. The 100-1 win of CAUGHOO did little for the interests of British punters.

1949   Jump jockey STEVE JOBAR (real name Robert) born. Won Triumph Hurdle in 1980 on Heighlin. Also partnered Pacify.

1949   Cullompton trainer RICHARD TUCKER born. Best horses include Friar Tuck, Prince Ebony.

1958   MR WHAT won the Grand National, but never won again in 33 attempts.

1958   Grass Court (Geoff Littlewood up) was BILLY NEVETT's first winner as a trainer.

1991   Arkle's jockey turned trainer, PAT TAAFFE, underwent successful heart transplant surgery.

1992   GIANFRANCO DETTORI won the Premio Pisa in Italy on Worldwide. Second was That'll Be the Day, ridden by his son Frankie.

1992   TONY IVES rode LET US FAMOUS to win the first Macau Derby at Taipa, returning odds of 4-6.

1993   Jockeys RICHARD DUNWOODY and ROGER MARLEY were arrested for disorderly behaviour hours after attending the Jockeys Association Awards ceremony in London. Dunwoody later apologised: 'I deeply regret the incident, and the adverse publicity it might have brought to the ceremony and to my profession. I was upset at Roger Marley's arrest and this unfortunately led to my own.'

30 MARCH

1883 The smallest-ever field of 10 turned out for the Grand National. Won by Zoedone (100-7) whose jockey, Count Charles Kinsky, was also a diplomat at the Austro-Hungarian Embassy.

1898 Racing took place at Folkestone, Kent's only surviving racecourse, for the first time. It got underway with a 2-day jump card.

1906 For the first time 4th-place prize-money was paid in the Grand National, and 100-6 chance Crautacaun was the first beneficiary. Ascetic's Silver was the 20-1 winner.

1928 Only 2 horses - 100-1 outsider Tipperary Tim, the winner, and runner-up Billy Barton (33-1) - of 42 starters finished the Grand National.

1931 One of the two famous EASTERBY brothers born, MICHAEL WILLIAM. Perhaps slightly overshadowed by his older brother, Miles Henry, universally known as Peter. Mick trained Mrs McArdy to win the 1977 1,000 Guineas, ridden by Eddie Hide.

1945 Owner of Via Delta and The Ripleyite ERIC CLAPTON born. Both horses won races for him before he apparently decided that it was too expensive a hobby to keep up. Colours: emerald green and yellow stripes; hooped cap.

1951 Newmarket trainer JOHN GOSDEN born. Began training in England in 1988, having previously been a leading handler in the USA and earlier, in 1974, assistant to Sir Noel Murless.

1962 MC HAMMER (real name Stanley Burrell) born. Highly successful owner in the USA who enjoys the odd flutter - 'I only bet within my means', he once told journalists.

1963 Film star GREGORY PECK attended the Grand National to watch his horse Owen's Sedge compete. It finished 7th behind 66-1 chance Ayala, which was trained by Lester Piggott's father, Keith.

1968 PAT EDDERY had his first British ride when Dido's Dowry came sixth at Liverpool.

1970 SECRETARIAT, the great US Triple Crown winner, foaled. Became known as Super Red.

1974 RED RUM won the Grand National for the 2nd consecutive time, at 11-1, ridden by Brian Fletcher, trained by Ginger McCain.

1990 Former England soccer international turned trainer MICK CHANNON sent out his first winner, Golden Scissors, at Beverley. Fifteen minutes later he sent out his 2nd when Wessex Boy won at Wincanton.

1991 RICHARD DUNWOODY completed his first century of winners on Mulloch Brae at Towcester.

31 MARCH

1905 Jockey FRANK MASON had been paid £300 not to ride in any races for two weeks so as not to risk injury and jeopardise his chances on 6-1 Grand National 2nd favourite Kirkland. The move paid off when the horse won.

1921 GORDON RICHARDS rode his first winner, Gay Lord, at Leicester. Last horse home in the race was named Toilet.

1923 Jockey GEORGE SLACK born. Best horses ridden included Tudor Line, Bandalore.

1927 Carlisle trainer STAN PAYNE born. Best horses handled include Stan's Folly and Pleasant Polly.

1933 Former Cock of the North JOHNNY SEAGRAVE born. Rode 76 winners in 1969 and partnered Music Boy to win the Gimcrack Stakes in 1975, when he also won the Ayr Gold Cup on Roman Warrior.

1970 Native Bazaar gave jockey DICK MARSHALL his first winner, at Warwick.

1973 RED RUM won the Grand National for the first time, ridden by Brian Fletcher, beating fellow 9-1 joint favourite Crisp in a close finish. Crisp, ridden by Richard Pitman, produced one of the finest exhibitions of jumping and front running ever seen in the race.

1978 JIM BOLGER sent out his first English winner, Beparoejojo, at Liverpool.

1979 Cheltenham Gold Cup winner ALVERTON, ridden by Jonjo O'Neill, broke his neck and was killed while attempting to jump Becher's in the Grand National, which was won by the first Scottish winner, Rubstic, 25-1 (trained by John Leadbetter in Roxburghshire).

1990 East and West Germany met for the first time at a race meeting since the erection of the Berlin Wall in 1961, at Hoppegarten in East Berlin. Brent Walker sponsored one of the races and trainer HEINZ JENTZSCH sent out three winners from as many runners. British jockey Peter Bloomfield won on Kassu.

1991 Eddie Delahoussaye on BEQUEST equalled the world record time of 1 minute 57.4 seconds, set by Double Discount in 1977 on the same course, when winning the Santa Barbara Handicap over 10 furlongs at Santa Anita. Two Filipinos cleaned up when they won the 'pick nine' bet at Santa Anita, collecting $1,015,215.80.

1993 Trainer MARTIN PIPE broke the £1 million win-and-place prize-money barrier for the second time (the first was in 1990-91) when Pragada and Sweet Glow were 2nd and 4th at Ascot.

1993 GAY KELLEWAY sent out her first winner on the flat when Tyrone Flyer won at Catterick.

1 APRIL

1974 There is some dispute about the date – some say today, some say late March and some April 15 – but there is no doubt that the horse born (probably) on this day, ECLIPSE, was one of the finest of all. The name was appropriate as he was foaled during an eclipse of the sun. Eclipse remained undefeated in 18 races.

1926 Owner JIM JOEL celebrated the first of 355 jumping wins when Hamlet won over hurdles at Bournemouth.

1929 Amateur FRANK WISE wore an artificial leg when riding Alike to win the Irish Grand National at Fairyhouse. He also lost the tops of three fingers on his right hand during the war. We have been unable to confirm that the trainer's instructions to his jockey were 'Hop to it'.

1941 GAIE JOHNSON HOUGHTON, former Champion Lady Rider, born.

1941 Cheltenham permit-holder NORTON BROOKES born.

1944 Trainer NIGEL ANGUS born. Best horses include Swinging Junior, Roman Warrior.

1950 Trainer MERRICK FRANCIS, son of jockey turned author Dick, born.

1957 Newmarket jockey NEIL CROWTHER born.

1972 CLIVE BRITTAIN saddled his first winner as a trainer, Vedvyas, at Doncaster.

1974 LINDA GOODWILL won the first 'mixed' race, the Lads And Lassies Handicap at Nottingham, riding Pee Mai.

1978 LUCIUS won the Grand National in which Red Rum had hoped to land an unprecedented 4th win. A bruised heel caused Rummy to be withdrawn 24 hours before the race.

1989 MRS CAROLINE CARR of Hampshire was licensed as a clerk of the scales, the only woman to hold the title at that time.

1991 At nineteen, DEBORAH RYAN became the youngest female to make a book at a racecourse when she represented her father, Pat, at Wetherby.

1991 Trainer PETER CHAPPLE-HYAM sent out his first winner, Noble Flutter (Paul Eddery up), at Warwick. Not much more than a year later he had a Derby winner and a 2,000 Guineas winner to his credit.

1991 The *Racing Post* entertained readers with an April Fool report that Desert Orchid was to go show-jumping ridden by Harvey Smith.

1991 JACQUI OLIVER became the first female jockey to record a treble over the jumps when Bolshoi Boy, Noble Ben and Shu Fly all won at Uttoxeter.

1993 Amendments in legislation finally permitted betting shops to remain open from 6.30pm to 10pm between April 1 and August 31.

2 APRIL

1821 Durdham Down at Bristol staged the first officially recorded hurdle race, run in three heats of one mile each with five hurdles in each heat.

1838 The 'Emperor of Trainers' ROBERT ROBSON died aged 73 with 34 classics to his credit, including 12 Oaks and 7 Derbys, although the St Leger eluded him. He phased out the accepted tradition of 'sweating' horses by giving them gallops while they were wearing heavy rugs and a hood.

1919 Former jump jockey TOMMY WYSE born.

1925 GERALD FOLJAMBE rode two jump winners at Malton, Leicestershire, despite having had a leg amputated below the knee (not, though, on this day).

1936 TONY COLLINS, trainer of betting coup horse Gay Future, born.

1937 Trainer BARRINGTON (BARRY) HILLS born. Rode 9 winners as an apprentice and has nearly as many sons – 5 in all, including jockey twins Michael and Richard. Won the Arc in 1973 with Rheingold.

1938 Jockey Club member and owner of Preraphaelite GURNEY SHEPPARD born. Colours: light blue; red striped sleeves; hooped cap.

1945 Thirteen-year-old HEIRDOM won the Irish Grand National.

1946 Owner of Broadsword LORD NORTHAMPTON born. Colours: olive green; orange sleeves and cap.

1949 WILLIE SHOEMAKER rode his first winner, Shafter V, at Golden Gates.

1953 Gloucester trainer ROBIN DICKIN born. Had over 100 wins.

1954 VINCENT O'BRIEN had his licence suspended for three months following an inquiry into inconsistencies in the running of his star chasers, Royal Tan, Lucky Dome, Knock Hard and Early Mist. O'Brien issued a statement declaring: 'I am completely in the dark as to what, if any, offence I am alleged to have been guilty of.'

1960 Trainer of Repeat the Dose TIM ETHERINGTON born.

1963 Trainer PETER CHAPPLE-HYAM born. Sent out Rodrigo De Triano to win 1992 2,000 Guineas and Dr Devious to win 1992 Derby.

1977 CHARLOTTE BREW became the first woman to ride in the Grand National. She and Barony Fort made it to the 4th from home before the horse refused. Red Rum won the race for the 3rd time at 9–1 and was ridden by Tommy Stack.

1987 WAYWARD LAD, whose record of £217,923 prize-money from 28 wins in 55 outings had been bettered only by Dawn Run, retired on a winning note in the Whitbread Label Gold Cup at Liverpool, scoring at 7–1.

3 APRIL

1840 Set to carry 13st 3lbs in the Cheltenham Cup Chase, the great jumper Lottery nevertheless won the four-mile race. It was the highest weight he ever carried to victory.

1908 Owner of 1968 Cheltenham Gold Cup winner Fort Leney and 21-times winner Prince Tino SIR JOHN THOMSON born.

1925 Northumberland jump trainer ANDY SCOTT born.

1930 Jump jockey PETER PICKFORD born.

1937 Trainer LIAM BROWNE of Kildare, Ireland, born. Snooker-playing handler with over 600 winners to his credit since 1971. As a jockey rode winners of the Lincoln, Tetrarch and Pretty Polly Stakes.

1942 Buckfastleigh trainer NEIL KERNICK born. Professional jump jockey from 1960 to 1981.

1951 Jump jockey PETER WARNER born.

1958 Jockey CHARLIE MANN born. Best horses ridden include Classified.

1978 MICHAEL ROBERTS rode his first winner in Britain – Pakeha for Gavin Hunter at Ayr.

1982 GERALDINE REES became the first lady to complete the course in the Grand National, finishing 8th and last on Cheers. Meanwhile 48-year-old DICK SAUNDERS became the oldest winning jockey, riding Grittar to victory.

1986 Two days before he was due to ride the well-fancied Classified in the Grand National, jockey STEVE SMITH ECCLES claimed he was hijacked in his own car. He was sleeping off a couple of jars in the back of his Mercedes and woke up to find it moving. Surprised, he sat up, saw someone driving and said, 'What the hell do you think you're doing?' The driver stopped and ran off. Smith Eccles went on to finish 3rd in the big race.

1993 ALISON DARE from Gloucestershire won on Russki at Chaddesley Corbett point-to-point to become the most successful woman rider in the sport's history with 174 winners.

1993 MORLEY STREET, ridden by Graham Bradley, won the Grade 1 Martell Aintree Hurdle for the 4th successive season.

1993 JUDY HIGBY tried to place a bet with bookie Richard Halling at his Tring betting shop on the morning of this day that the Grand National would not take place. The bookie, not wanting to take her money, declined the request. That afternoon one of the most bizarre events in British sporting history saw the Grand National collapse into fiasco. After one false start a second was signalled but only 9 horses stood their ground. The rest set off and completed varying amounts of the course, with Jenny Pitman-trained Esha Ness, ridden by John White, crossing the line 1st at 50–1 only for the race to be declared void.

4 APRIL

1913 Only 2 of the 22 starters got round without falling in the Grand National - 100-9 chance COVERTCOAT beat 25-1 shot Irish Mail by a distance.

1922 Former senior Jockey Club starter MICHAEL SAYERS born.

1926 French trainer PHILIPPE LALLIE born.

1929 Trainer JOHN WINTER born. Son of 1911 Oaks winner Cherimoya's jockey, Frederick Neville Winter, and brother of top jump jockey and trainer Fred Thomas Winter. John took over Newmarket's Highfield stable on the death of his father in 1965. Won Royal Ascot's Wokingham Stakes in 1967 with Spaniard's Mount.

1943 Longchamp racecourse in Occupied France was bombed by the British just before racing began - but the meeting went ahead.

1943 Trainer of Jer PETER BEVAN born.

1951 Irish trainer MOUSE (MICHAEL) MORRIS born. Claims hang-gliding as a favourite recreation but when his feet are on the ground has trained good horses like Buck House.

1953 Former jump jockey ANSON GONSALVES born.

1953 Amateur rider CHARLIE SAMPLE born. Won Horse & Hound Grand Military Gold Cup.

1957 French jockey JEAN-LUC KESSAS born.

1959 Trainer TONY FOWLER born.

1964 Jump jockey BRUCE DOWLING born. Best horses ridden Delius, Miss Nero.

1981 Not a dry eye in the place as one-time invalid ALDANITI and former cancer victim BOB CHAMPION combined to win the Grand National.

1991 The Queen Mother visited Aintree racecourse for the first time since the infamous Devon Loch collapse of 1956, to open their new £3 million Queen Mother Stand.

1991 1987 Cheltenham Gold Cup winner THE THINKER was put down after breaking a leg during an early morning gallop.

1991 American jockey MARK SALVAGGIO, 31, rode 3 winners at 3 different tracks for trainer Tim Ritchey. Broken Silence (9-10) won the 1.00pm at Philadelphia Park; Barbara's Cutlass (13-10) was successful in the 2.50 at Delaware Park and Don't Throw Stones (46-10) completed the treble, winning the 9.10 at Penn National.

1992 With five days remaining before the General Election, topical tip PARTY POLITICS won the Grand National at the generous odds of 14-1. A week earlier Mr Major won at 16-1 at Ascot and on April 3 Hung Parliament was placed at Kempton. On April 6 9-4 joint favourite Political Issue went in at Kelso as coincidence backers had a field day - or week.

5 APRIL

1912 Owner ALEX PICKEN born. Best horses included Current Gold, winner of the National Hunt Handicap Chase at Cheltenham. Colours: maroon; gold sash and cap with maroon spots.

1915 Oriental Park racecourse, Havana, Cuba, was the scene of the World Heavyweight Championship clash between Jack Johnson and Jess Willard. Underdog Willard triumphed in the 26-round event despite later claims by Johnson that he threw the fight.

1916 Actor and owner GREGORY PECK born. Best horses include Owen's Sedge and Different Class, with both of which he tried to win the Grand National. The former was 7th in 1963, and the latter was brought down in 1967 but finished 3rd in 1968.

1924 The legendary BROWN JACK was born. When he died, aged 25, his heart was found to weigh 19lbs (the average is 11 to 12lbs), which may help to explain how he won a Champion Hurdle and, most memorably, the Queen Alexandra Stakes at Royal Ascot on a record 6 consecutive occasions from 1929 to 1934.

1929 1932 Derby winner APRIL THE FIFTH was foaled.

1932 Australasian champion and 'wonder horse' PHAR LAP died in what are still believed by many to be suspicious circumstances.

1935 THEFT (ridden by Gordon Richards) set a trend by winning the Greenham Stakes at Newbury only to finish runner-up in the 2,000 Guineas. The same thing happened to Masham (1959), Romulus (1962), Silly Season (1965), Tower Walk (1969), Mill Reef (1971), Kris (1979) and Bairn (1985).

1940 What was to be the last Grand National for six years was won by BOGSKAR, at 25-1, ridden by Mervyn Jones and trained by Lord Stalbridge.

1940 Jockey BRIAN ROUSE born. Rode John Dunlop-trained Quick as Lightning to win the 1,000 Guineas in 1980 at 12-1. One of his daughters became a Page Three Girl.

1946 The first Grand National since 1940 was won by LOVELY COTTAGE, ridden by Captain Robert Petre of the Scots Guards, trained by Tommy Rayson and starting at 25-1.

1978 CRIQUETTE HEAD sent out her first winner as a trainer when Animation obliged at Rouen.

1986 The Grand National produced the intriguing possibility that TV commentator Des Lynam might have to interview himself after the race. He had leased 200-1 outsider Another Duke, who fell as 15-2 chance West Tip won the race.

1990 GINGER MCCAIN saddled an Aintree winner for the first time since Red Rum, 13 years earlier, when Sure Metal won at 100-1.

6 APRIL

1854 VIRAGO, trained by John Day for moneylender Henry Padwick, landed a double in the one-mile 2-furlong City and Suburban and the two-mile 2-furlong Great Metropolitan at Epsom. A tough filly, she went on to win 2 more races at York in April before taking the 1,000 Guineas on May 4.

1925 Former senior Irish handicapper MICHAEL BYRNE born.

1933 Solihull jump trainer KEN BRIDGWATER born. Best horse trained Winnie the Witch.

1938 Magician PAUL DANIELS, a keen racegoer and owner, born. One trick proved beyond even his conjuring powers when he sponsored the Paul Daniels Magic Handicap at Redcar and attempted to win it with his own That's Magic, which could only manage 15th place in the 18-strong field.

1945 PAT DONOGHUE, son of recently deceased jockey Steve, was granted a temporary licence to train.

1962 The Queen Mother's LAFFY won the Ulster Harp National at Downpatrick, trained by Peter Cazalet and ridden by Willie Robinson.

1967 BRENDA JOHNSON became the first woman officially to train a winner at Liverpool when Minto Burn, ridden by Brian Surtees, won the Foxhunters Chase. She bred the horse, too.

1968 Trainer BILL WATTS sent out his first jump winner, Prospect Pleases, at Leicester, almost immediately followed by his first flat winner, Rasping, at Catterick.

1983 FULKE WALWYN sent out his 2,000th winner when Noble Heir won at Ascot.

1992 Topical tip POLITICAL ISSUE, 9–4 joint favourite, won at Kelso just three days before the General Election.

1992 History was made in the Kelso betting ring when two bets of £2 and another of £10 were struck about COUNTESS CROSSETT to win the Sprouston Claiming Hurdle at 5,000–1 – believed to be the longest price ever laid on a British racecourse. Bryan Hazell of Hexham accepted the tenner and watched nervously as the horse, returned at 500–1, finished 9th of 17.

7 APRIL

1920 WILLIAM ARTHUR STEPHENSON, predominantly a jump trainer, born. His favourite course was Wetherby rather than one of the glamorous tracks. Took out his first licence as a trainer in 1959 and handled horses like Rapid River and Blazing Walker.

1949 LUCA 'bookmakers are like leeches' MATEO CUMANI born. Rode 85 winners in Italy, France and the UK. Trained Kahyasi to win the Derby and Commanche Run to win the St Leger.

1967 RED RUM (trained by Tim Molony) saw a racecourse for the first time and dead-heated in a selling plate for two-year-olds at, significantly enough, Liverpool, ridden by Paul Cook.

1969 RED RUM won a jump race for the first time – the two-mile Bilton Hurdle at Wetherby, ridden by Paddy Broderick.

1977 Steve Cauthen rode 6 winners in a day at Aqueduct for the 2nd time. He set a record by achieving it for the 3rd time in November.

1979 Steve Cauthen rode his first winner in England - Marquee Universal at Salisbury.

1979 DAVID ELSWORTH sent out his first winner on the flat, Raffia Set, at Salisbury.

1982 Former jockey and trainer RUFUS BEASLEY died aged 75. Had three Cambridgeshire win, Sterope (twice) and Jupiter, and rode the 20-1 1936 St Leger winner, Boswell.

1990 MR FRISK, ridden by Marcus Armytage (16-1), set a new record time of 8 minutes 47.8 seconds for the Grand National. On the same day, MR FRISKY won the Santa Anita Derby.

1991 Twenty-year-old jockey RODNEY DICKENS died 33 minutes after arriving at hospital having been thrown from his horse in a race at Sportsman's Park, Cicero, Illinois.

1992 ARAZI, the 'wonder horse', won the Prix Omnium II at Saint-Cloud on his three-year-old debut. Steve Cauthen had the ride.

1993 Amateur JOHNNY GREENALL became the first jump jockey to lose his claim for the 3rd time when Overheard won at Ludlow. He first lost it when he rode his 30th winner only for the Jockey Club to change the rule to 40, which he duly achieved . . . but the Club intervened once again to make it 55.

1993 Sweet Duke won the Alpine Meadow Handicap Hurdle to give PETER SCUDAMORE a winner with his final ride before his retirement. The Nigel Twiston-Davies-trained runner scored at 5-2 favourite as Scudamore took his final total of wins to 1,677 (or 1,678, depending on which record-book you believe).

8 APRIL

1844 Lottery, winner of the first Grand National, ran and won his last race, at Windsor. He ended his days pulling a cart in Neasden.

1897 The first running of the Lady Dudley Challenge Cup, the major event in the point-to-point calendar, took place at Crowle, Worcestershire, over three miles. Twelve ran and both the winner, 6-1 chance Triton (ridden by E. E. Green), and runner-up, Scholarship (8-1, ridden by Mr Munby), were owned by R. Cave Brown.

1922 Jockey CHARLIE SMIRKE, age 15, rode his first winner, an unnamed Vitala filly in the Highfield Selling Plate at Derby.

1947 The experiment by the Totalisator of running one pool for win and place with 4s as the minimum unit, and the pool equally divided between win and place, came to an end. It had been in operation since March 1931.

1967 Writing in the *Daily Express*, Charles Benson said, 'He can safely be ignored, even in a race noted for shocks.' But FOINAVON, ridden by John Buckingham, took advantage of an almighty pile-up at the 23rd fence to produce a 100-1 surprise in the Grand National - it was a mega-shock, too, for a friend of mine who had decided to pocket the bet someone had given him to put on Foinavon on the grounds that it could not possibly win.

1968 A course record 97 runners contested the card at Edinburgh.

1985 GEORGE DUFFIELD rode his 1,000th winner in Britain - Color Blind at Warwick.

1985 GAMBLER'S CUP gave John Francome his 1,138th and last winner over the sticks, at Huntingdon.

1985 STEVE CAUTHEN rode his first Henry Cecil-trained winner, Abha, at Nottingham.

1985 DESERT ORCHID raced in blinkers for the only time, and was pulled up in the Welsh Champion Hurdle.

1991 BILL SHOEMAKER (59) was partially paralysed following a car crash in California.

1991 As the leaders came towards the finish of the Oswell Westminster Handicap at Newcastle, the jockeys were shocked to see a group of deer grazing on the track. They scattered just in time and Buzzard's Crest, ridden by George Duffield, went on to win. West with the Wind's jockey Kevin Darley commented, 'Fortunately, the deer spotted us, but it could have been very nasty indeed.' Those jockeys must have been staggered . . .

9 APRIL

1910 Punters' friend PHIL BULL, the instigator of the Timeform ratings service, was born in Hemsworth, Yorkshire. He died aged 79.

1917 Irish trainer (MICHAEL) VINCENT O'BRIEN born. His astonishing tally of winners includes 3 Grand National triumphs, 4 Cheltenham Gold Cup victories and 6 Epsom Derby winners. Has won every British classic, plus 9 Irish St Legers, 6 Irish Derbys, 5 Irish 2,000 Guineas, 4 Irish Oaks, 3 Irish 1,000 Guineas and 3 Arc de Triomphes. Rode his first winner as an amateur in 1940. The trainer of legendary horses such as Hatton's Grace, Royal Tan, Sir Ivor, Nijinsky, Alleged, The Minstrel and many more.

1920 Trainer GEORGE VERGETTE born. Best horses include Purple Silk and King of Diamonds.

1939 Trainer of Hallgate and Not So Silly ALAN BAILEY born.

1943 Worcester trainer (FRANCIS) JOHN YARDLEY born. Best horses include Diamond Head, Low Profile.

1945 Northern jockey LAWRENCE BROWN died.

1964 Epsom jockey ROY CARTER born.

1966 TONY MURRAY's first ride was Cleodora at Warwick.

1969 Amateur rider PIP NASH born.

1983 JENNY PITMAN became the first woman trainer to saddle a Grand National winner as Corbiere, bearing the name of a Jersey lighthouse, obliged.

1984 CHRIS LORETH rode 8 winners from 10 mounts at Exhibition Park, Vancouver, Canada.

1985 JOHN FRANCOME's last mount was The Reject at Chepstow, which fell. Has ridden since in celebrity and charity events.

1990 Irish jockey DAVID PARNELL was killed in a car crash, aged 24. Rode his first winner, Razzo Forte, at Tralee in 1980. Retained by Kevin Prendergast and rode 32 winners in 1987. Won Ulster Oaks and Ulster St Leger.

1991 Hong Kong trainer PETER TSE YAN-SID was fined £44,000, believed to be a racing record, following the doping of three horses in his stable in February.

10 APRIL

1915 Owner of Calve, Relfo and Bold Rex LORD GRANARD born.

1923 Former Turf Club senior steward DENIS MCCARTHY born.

1932 Actor and owner OMAR SHARIF born.

1937 STAN MELLOR MBE, who rode 1,035 winners under NH rules, born. Became a trainer at Pollardstown stables in Wiltshire from 1972. Best horses trained include Pollardstown and Lean Ar Aghaidh. Champion Jockey 3 times.

1947 Jockey BRIAN FLETCHER, who twice won the Grand National on Red Rum, born. He also won it on Red Alligator, and was only the second jockey of the century to score a hat-trick of wins in the race. Retired on medical advice in 1976 as a result of repeated head injuries.

1948 Malton jump trainer JOHN PARKES (Call Collect) born.

1948 Owner of Junk Bond and Tidemark LORD DE LA WARR born.

1949 Trainer CHRIS POPHAM born. Best horses include Roll-a-Joint and Panto Prince.

1949 Amateur jockey PETER CRAGGS born. Won William Hill Scottish National on King Con in 1978.

1965 Two racecourses staged their last meetings: Bogside and Rothbury.

1965 Trainer GORDON RICHARDS of Greystoke, Cumbria, sent out his first winner, Playlord, at Bogside.

1983 PETER ROGER, Headmaster of St Michael's Junior School, Kirkby, Merseyside, set a record of 40 minutes for completing the Grand National course – without a horse! He raised £6,000 for school funds in the process.

1989 Labour MP Tony Banks tabled a motion in the House of Commons calling for the Grand National to be banned unless the course passed the safety standards of animal welfare groups.

1992 If ever a horse was 'weighted' to win it must have been Tommy Cuthbert-trained Mils Mij, running at Ayr in the Ayrshire Agricultural Society Handicap Hurdle. Amateur William Hurst lost a staggering 4st to ride the horse which, appreciating his rider's effort, duly stormed to victory. It was the first time Hurst, at the age of 36, had ridden a winner.

1993 At the age of 65, STUART OLIVER rode Valoroso to win at Sandon point-to-point, North Staffordshire. On the same card BARRY LEAVY made one of the most optimistic objections of all time when, after falling from Local Customer before the final fence, he objected to winner Mount Argus. Not surprisingly, the stewards declined the opportunity of awarding the race to a riderless horse.

11 APRIL

1770 ECLIPSE beat Bucephalus in a match at Newmarket. Co-owner William Wildman won a bet of 600–400 guineas on Eclipse.

1872 Metairie racecourse in New Orleans, which had become the leading American track during the previous 35 years, staged its last day's racing. It was ruined by competition from local fairgrounds.

1887 LORD LYON was destroyed at the age of 24. In 1866 he had won the Triple Crown – the 2,000 Guineas, Derby and St Leger.

1904 KEITH PIGGOTT, Lester's father, who trained Ayala to win the 1963 Grand National, born. Son of the jump jockey Ernie Piggott, Keith rode his first winner at Newbury on his fifteenth birthday before gaining weight and turning to the jumps, riding 350 winners over the sticks.

1945 Owner DAPHNE THRELFALL born. Best horse Huntingdale. Colours: flame and gold.

1946 Trainer of Monksfield and Stranfield DES MCDONOGH, born. He paid just 740 guineas for Champion Hurdler Monksfield.

1948 Breeder of Generous DAVID NAGLE born.

1957 JOHN BUCKINGHAM made his racecourse debut, finishing unplaced on Royal Oak at Stratford. He later achieved fame when he rode Foinavon to a sensational 100–1 Grand National victory.

1966 GRAHAM SEXTON rode his first winner, Calisto, at Wolverhampton.

1970 LOTTIE LEHMAN at Sedgefield was Mary Reveley's first winner as a permit-holder.

1989 Five-times Champion jockey DOUG SMITH was found dead at his Newmarket home, aged 71. Rode 2 2,000 Guineas winners, Our Babu (1955) and Pall Mall (1958), and 2 1,000 Guineas winners, Hypericum (1946) and Petite Etoile (1959). Trained Sleeping Partner to win the 1969 Oaks. Smith was Champion from 1954 to 1959, except in 1957, when Scobie Breasley broke the sequence.

1992 Trainer JIM BOLGER saddled 5 of the 7 winners at The Curragh. One of the beaten horses was his 8–11 favourite St Jovite, who went on to be runner-up at Epsom and winner of the Irish Derby. This was his first flat 5-timer although on August 12 1991 he sent out 5 winners on a mixed card at Gowran Park.

1993 The first 3 home in a point-to-point at Dromoland, Ireland, were disqualified. Winner Carrow Villa Boy's rider Paul McMahon weighed in 6lbs light and was thrown out; Another Goose, the runner-up, had taken the wrong course and 3rd-placed Platinum Lady lost out when rider Joe Hogan admitted to missing out a fence. That left 4th-placed Ballycasey Girl VI to take the honours by default.

12 APRIL

1876 The final flat race meeting took place at the Cottenham Pastures course in Cambridge. The aptly named Cottenham won the first race on the card and the last went to Mandeville, owned by Newmarket trainer Tom Jennings, whose father had been landlord of The Swan at nearby Bottisham.

1923 SIR CECIL BOYD-ROCHFORT, Royal trainer from 1943 to 1968, saddled his first winners, Plumb Square and Young Pole, in successive races at Pontefract. He trained 13 Classic winners during his career. Stepfather of Henry Cecil.

1928 Former Jockey Club medical consultant DR MICHAEL ALLEN born.

1934 Former Champion Jockey in Kenya FRANK MORBY born.

1937 Former Cock of the North EDDIE HIDE born. He was 6th in the all-time list of British jockeys when he retired with over 2,500 winners to his credit, including 1973 Derby winner Morston.

1946 Jockey PAUL COOK born. Once rode 3 winners at 3 separate meetings during the course of one day. In 1966, he won 1,000 Guineas, English and Irish St Legers on Glad Rags.

1947 Cheltenham Festival was postponed until this date because of inclement weather, and for the last time the Champion Hurdle and Gold Cup were both run on the same day, a Saturday on this occasion. National Spirit won the Champion, Fortina the Gold Cup.

1958 Amateur rider SHARON OLIVER born. Best horse ridden Aonoch.

1992 English-born female apprentice LEANNE CROOK was fatally injured when she fell from Spotted Wonder during the Welter Handicap at Doomben, Brisbane, Australia. The horse, making a challenge, hit the metal running rail and came down, and Leanne rolled along the ground before hitting her head against an upright. She was dead on arrival at hospital.

1992 LORENZO MAZZONI returned to the saddle in Turin, Italy, almost a year after a fall which had left him in a coma for twelve days. He won on his comeback mount, Mopaz Binari.

1993 CHARLIE SWAN rode his first Irish National winner when Ebony Jane landed the big race at odds of 6-1. Cheltenham Gold Cup runner-up Rushing Wild was put down after fracturing his pelvis during the race.

1993 Australian trainer JOHN WHEELER landed an unusual double. He sent out Veandercross to win the AUS$200,000 Queen Elizabeth Stakes, a Group 1 race at Randwick, Sydney; then an hour later and 500 miles away in South Australia at Oakbank, his Touch Judge took the AUS$100,000 Great Eastern Steeplechase.

13 APRIL

1913 American trainer CHARLIE WHITTINGHAM born in San Diego, California. Sent out his first winner in 1934 and went on to be champion trainer in prize-money terms in 1970–73, 1975, 1981 and 1982. His Sunday Silence won the 1989 Kentucky Derby, Preakness Stakes and Breeders' Cup Classic.

1915 Trainer of Privy Councillor (1962 2,000 Guineas) and Rose Dubarry TOM WAUGH born.

1923 Lord Derby's TRANQUIL won the 7-furlong Berkshire Handicap at Newbury on her way to beating Derby winner Papyrus in the St Leger, for which she started at 100–9.

1928 American owner-breeder RICHARD KIRSTEIN born. Best horses include Polish Patriot and Cacoethes. Cacoethes, 3rd in the 1989 Derby, was originally named Our Friend Elvis. Colours: pink and purple quarters; pink sleeves; purple armlets; quartered cap.

1946 Ross-on-Wye trainer JOHN (ANDREW CHILD) EDWARDS born. Best horses trained include Pearlyman, Yahoo and Little Polveir.

1952 Twice Champion Jump Jockey turned trainer JONJO O'NEILL born. The high-point of his riding career came when he completed the double he'd begun with a 1984 Champion Hurdle win on Dawn Run by winning the 1986 Gold Cup on the same horse. Set a then record of 149 winners when landing the Championship for first time in 1977–78. Best horse trained Vicario di Bray.

1964 French jockey FREDDIE HEAD rode his first winner, at Fontainebleau.

1968 Then a jockey, JACK BERRY returned to action for the first time since breaking his leg – only to fall from Oban Bay at Carlisle in his first race back and fracture a wrist.

1968 PAUL DAVEY, private trainer to David Robinson, sent out 5 winners: London Boy and River Peace at Doncaster and Floretti, Carlburg and Little Green Man at Teesside Park.

1973 Double Sensation won at Thirsk to give BEN HANBURY his first success as a trainer.

1982 BOB CHAMPION announced his retirement as a jockey after Josh Gifford-trained Lumen won a hurdle race at Wetherby. Champion's first win was on Altercation at Plumpton in 1968. It was followed by 420 more.

1988 JOSH GIFFORD recorded his 1,000th winner as a trainer, Ballyhane.

1993 Coventry City FC manager BOBBY GOULD had his first winner as a part-owner when Homemaker won at Warwick.

1993 Jockey BILLY NEWNES completed his set when victory on Queen of the Quorn at Newcastle meant he had ridden a winner at every Flat course in Britain.

14 APRIL

1812   The earliest date on which a Classic was run. The unpronounceable CWRW, ridden by Sam Chifney Jr at 7–1, won the 2,000 Guineas.

1885   A good day for FRED ARCHER, who rode a treble on Greenore, The Bard and Mate at Northampton, where the racecourse closed in 1904.

1924   Jockey TOMMY 'T.P.' BURNS born. He was the rider of Ballymoss which, in 1958, became the first horse trained in Ireland to win the Arc de Triomphe.

1939   Jockey Club chief executive CHRISTOPHER HAINES born.

1944   Nottingham trainer CHARLES (CHUCK) SPARES born. Best horse trained Ibn Majed.

1950   Trainer TED WALSH born. Best horse Roc de Prince. Rode Daring Run and Hilly Way as a jockey.

1952   Former amateur jockey LINDA SHEEDY born.

1962   Dublin trainer EDWARD LYNAM born. Best horse trained Tantum Ergo.

1968   Jockey ALEX 'QUEEN OF THE SAND' GREAVES born. Made her name on the all-weather track at Southwell. First woman to ride the Lincoln winner.

1969   Former jockey and trainer TOMMY DENT died aged 65. Rode his first winner in 1920 at Pontefract, and began training at Penrith in 1949.

1989   2–5 favourite Spoilt Son, ridden by M. Birch, won at Thirsk to give trainer ALEX (ARCHIBALD) SCOTT his first winner.

1989   Pass the Peace was trainer MICHAEL BELL's first winner, at Newbury.

1990   Trainer ROGER CHARLTON sent out his first winner, Deploy (Pat Eddery), at Haydock, from his Beckhampton House stables. By June 6 he had sent out Sanglamore to win the French Derby and Quest for Fame to win the English.

15 APRIL

1882 The Jockey Club Argentino was founded.

1902 Owner LURLINE BROTHERTON born. Her Freebooter won the 1950 Grand National and for a short period Red Rum raced in her blue, silver and scarlet colours, although this was before he won the National. Plates from every one of her winners - 255 over jumps, 112 on the Flat - are displayed on the walls of her home near Malton.

1940 Eccentric racing pundit JOHN MCCRIRICK born. Old Harrovian, failed bookmaker, *Sporting Life* 'hack', 1979 Campaigning Journalist of the Year. The racing industry is divided as to whether he is a good or bad thing. I side with the former camp.

1950 ASTRAKHAN (Willie Smyth-Tommy Burns) was the first winner on the flat, at Hurst Park, for the then Princess Eiizabeth.

1952 Trainer JEREMY TREE saddled his first winner, Court Life, at Birmingham.

1959 Jockey JOHN WHITE born. Rider of The Tsarevich and Brown Windsor.

1964 Jockey JOHN CARROLL born. Best horse ridden Paris House.

1978 TOM MORGAN rode his first winner, Cocoa, at Phoenix Park.

1980 TONY MCGLONE rode his first winner, Ashgayle, at Wolverhampton. He won the 1983 Barbados Guineas and the 1987 Kuwait Derby, the latter on Saare.

1989 Jockey MARK BIRCH rode his 1,000th winner, Bollin Patrick, at Thirsk on his wife Joyce's birthday. The colt's dam, Bollin Charlotte, had given him his first victory in July 1968. Just to round off the day he later had to jump off one of the horses which completed a treble for him when it refused to pull up.

1990 Jockey TIM HAMEY, one of the few to have completed the National (Fabra, 1931) and Gold Cup (Koko, 1926) double, died aged 84.

1991 MARTIN PIPE became the first trainer in history to win £1 million in a jump season when Colour Scheme won at Southwell.

1992 NIJINSKY died in the USA at the age of 25 and was buried between Secretariat and Riva Ridge at the Chalborne Farm Horse Cemetery. By Northern Dancer, bred in Canada, Nijinsky won the 1970 2,000 Guineas, Derby and Irish Derby plus the King George VI and Queen Elizabeth Stakes, followed by the St Leger. He was second behind Sassafras in the Arc.

16 APRIL

1875 FRED ARCHER rode Peeping Tom, owned by the unfortunately named Captain Bastard, to win one of the earliest of sponsored races, the Newmarket International Free Handicap. The town of Newmarket put up the £300 prize-money and the Jockey Club gave £100 to the runner-up.

1887 Royal trainer CAPTAIN SIR CECIL BOYD-ROCHFORT born at Middleton near Mullingar in Co. Westmeath. He would be Champion Trainer on 5 occasions.

1913 Arguably the fastest two-year-old ever to race, THE TETRARCH, trained by Atty Persse, won on his debut at Newmarket.

1916 Former Swaffham trainer REX CARTER born.

1919 Owner of Mesopotamia and Knockroe VICTOR MCCALMONT born. Colours: light blue and scarlet (quartered); white cap.

1941 Irish trainer MICHAEL KAUNTZE born. Rode as amateur from 1957 to 1968, with, he says, 'conspicuous lack of success'. Best horses trained Etoile de Paris, Kooyonga.

1944 North Yorkshire trainer of Allten Glazed and Umbelata MICK NAUGHTON born.

1948 Owner-trainer of Gambling Prince GILL JONES born.

1949 Jockey SANDY HAWLEY, who rode Nobiliary and Youth, born.

1955 Jockey IAN JOHNSON born.

1955 Owner of hurdles winner Parlour Moor CHARLOTTE MORRISON born. Colours: white; crimson hoops; black cap.

1960 Jockey PAUL BRADWELL born. Best horses include Standaan.

1964 Jockey STEVE HORSFALL born. Best horses ridden include O. I. Oyston, Kerens Star.

1968 Five months after a car crash which nearly killed him and his family, WILLIE CARSON returned to the saddle on Bikini in the Elveden Maiden Stakes at Newmarket, but finished unplaced.

1983 French ace YVES SAINT-MARTIN rode a double at Thirsk on Deportment and Our Dynasty.

1983 Trainer NEVILLE CRUMP celebrated his 5th Scottish National victory when Canton (Kevin Whyte) won the Ayr marathon.

1986 JONJO O'NEILL and STEVE SMITH ECCLES were riding in a hurdle race at Cheltenham. Smith Eccles was telling a joke when Jonjo fell. 'He got a pretty severe kicking, but he couldn't wait to get back into the weighing-room to hear the end of the joke,' said Smith Eccles.

1993 Taunton's evening meeting, sponsored by William Hill, was the first for which Britain's betting shops were officially permitted to stay open after 6.30pm.

17 APRIL

1907 Jockey DAVY JONES born. He rode Red Rover to victory in the 1945 Cheltenham Gold Cup carrying 3st of dead weight. Reported to have ridden winners on the Flat, over hurdles and over fences on the same afternoon at Liverpool.

1915 ADAM CALDER, the owner-trainer of top hunter-chaser Flying Ace, born.

1934 Bagshot trainer BRIAN GUBBY born. Best horses include Gabitat, Green Dollar, Red Dollar.

1935 DALE BAIRD, who in 1990 became the world's most prolific winning trainer, was born in Martinsville, Illinois. He saddled his 6,000th winner in August 1992. He also at that stage boasted 4,600 winners as an owner, 349 of them in the 1981 season (the world record for a single season was held by Jack Van Berg with 496 in 1976).

1939 Jockey Club member and owner of Greenwood Lad CHRISTOPHER SPORBORG born. Colours: navy blue; cerise sleeves; striped cap.

1939 FULKE WALWYN rode his last winner, Mansur, at Uttoxeter.

1950 Owner of Trempolino and Saumarez BRUCE MCNALL born.

1950 'Travel and excitement' are the self-confessed recreations of owner PETER SMITH, born today. His Stargazer won at 100-1 at Plumpton in November 1987. Colours: chocolate and pink.

1952 Trainer of New Halen and Petty Bridge PAUL JAMES born.

1962 Trainer of Just So PAUL NICHOLLS born. As a jockey rode Playschool.

1963 Former Irish Champion Jump Jockey TOM MORGAN born.

1970 RICHARD HANNON sent out his first winner, Ampney Prince, ridden by Frankie Durr at Newbury.

1982 KEN OLIVER won the Scottish National for the 6th time when David Dutton rode Cockle Strand to victory in the Ayr feature.

1990 Trainer ROBBIE CONNOLLY died, aged 31, of motor neurone disease.

1992 Flamboyant owner 'Teasie Weasie' Raymond died aged 80. The high-society hairdresser owned 1963 Grand National winner Ayala and the 1976 victor Rag Trade. His colours were ice blue and wine and he caused a sensation by wearing coloured morning suits to Royal Ascot.

1993 FRANKIE DETTORI rode a 15,969-1 4-timer at Newbury on Tissisisat (20-1) for the Queen, Linpac West (25-1), Inchinor (7-2) and Winged Victory (11-2). This was his first 4-timer at one meeting.

18 APRIL

1915   ANNE, DUCHESS OF WESTMINSTER, owner of Arkle, born. Her famous colours of yellow, black belt and gold tassel were also carried by Cheltenham Gold Cup winner Ten Up and Grand National winner Last Suspect. Triple Gold Cup winner Arkle is still revered as probably the greatest jumper ever.

1916   Trainer RON MASON born. Best horses included Sovereign Path, Track Spare. Before becoming a trainer in 1959 he had been a successful speedway rider at Manchester's Belle Vue. Liked a tilt at the ring and was often spectacularly successful.

1918   Former senior Jockey Club handicapper DAVID SWANNELL born.

1921   Owner-trainer of Memberson PETER DUFOSEE born.

1939   INFRA RED, 4th dam of Mill Reef, won the Princess Elizabeth stakes, ridden by Willie Stephenson at Epsom for trainer Captain Cecil Boyd-Rochfort.

1945   Newark trainer MELVYN LEACH born. Best horse Lallax.

1947   Self-confessed alcoholic and compulsive gambler, but brilliant jockey, BARRY BROGAN born. The Irishman was never Champion Jockey but he rode The Dikler to win the 1971 King George VI Chase and Even Keel to win the Benson & Hedges Gold Cup.

1947   GEORGE BOYD saddled his first winner, Backbite, at Bogside. He went on to become Scotland's most successful trainer in the next twenty years, sending out Rockavon to win the 1961 2,000 Guineas at 66-1. Retired in 1969.

1951   Rails bookmaker VICTOR CHANDLER, rated as one of the bravest layers around, born.

1964   Racecourse commentator SIMON HOLT born.

1977   The *Sporting Life* carried the following paragraph, open to various interpretations: 'John Higgins fractured a bone in his left leg in a fall from Mrs Higgins at Edinburgh on Monday, and will be out of action for a month.'

1989   PETER SHILTON's unraced two-year-old, Between the Sticks, scored on his racecourse debut at Newmarket at attractive odds of 33-1. But the former England goalkeeper, who is fond of the occasional flutter, arrived at the course too late to back the animal.

1991   JULIE CECIL sent out her first winner as a trainer when Lester Piggott rode Golan Heights to victory at Newmarket.

1991   HOPSCOTCH, ridden by Peter Scudamore, won the Park Financial Hurdle at Cheltenham – a record 6th win in a season at the track.

19 APRIL

1770 The great ECLIPSE beat Diana, Pensioner and Chigger for the 100 guineas King's Plate at Newmarket. Dennis O'Kelly bought out William Wildman's half-share in the horse for 1,100 guineas.

1877 FRED ARCHER won on all 6 of his mounts at Newmarket.

1928 Jockey DOUG PAGE born. Rider of Albergo.

1939 FULKE WALWYN fractured his skull in a fall from Grosvenor Bridge at Ludlow. He was subsequently obliged to retire from riding.

1945 *The Racing Calendar* announced that the Jockey Club was to appoint a Public Relations Officer. No sniggering at the back!

1952 Great American champion NATIVE DANCER, winner of 21 of his 22 races, born. His only defeat was by Dark Star in the 1953 Kentucky Derby.

1956 Trainer PAUL DALTON born. He is obviously something of a pessimist - his Burton-on-Trent stables are called Noah's Ark. Perhaps his winners go in two by two.

1957 ARKLE foaled at the Ballymacoll stud, Co. Meath. His dam was Bright Cherry, a useful type over two to two and a half miles, but his sire, Archive, although classically bred, proved virtually useless on a racecourse and stood at a mere 48 guineas.

1964 French jockey FREDDIE HEAD got off the mark with his first winner, Zamboanga, at Fontainebleau.

1976 Jack De Lilo was PETER SCUDAMORE'S first ride over jumps, finishing 4th at Chepstow.

1978 Five-year-old UBEDIZZY, trained by Steve Nesbitt, finished 2nd at 20-1 behind Boldboy in the 6-furlong Abernant Stakes at Newmarket but behaved so badly in the unsaddling enclosure afterwards, trying to savage his lad, and anyone else who went anywhere near him, that the horse was banned from ever running in Great Britain again. His jockey, Andy Crook, was also born on this day in 1955.

1978 JONJO O'NEILL beat Ron Barry's record of 125 wins in a season, set in 1972-73, when Majetta Crescent won at Perth. Peter Scudamore subsequently smashed Jonjo's record of 149. It was a fair old afternoon for Jonjo, who rode 5 winners from 5 rides.

1984 Lady jockey VICKI HARRIS rode her first winner, Tit For Tat, at Southwell.

1987 Britons ANTHONY SPEELMAN and NICHOLAS COWAN picked up $1,627,084 (after federal income tax of 406,768 was withheld) on a $64 9-horse accumulator bet at Santa Anita, California.

1993 A bay colt out of Its in the Air was born at Gainsborough Stud, Newbury - the last foal by NIJINKSY, who died in 1992.

20 APRIL

1880 TRISTAN won a star-studded two-year-old race, the 5-furlong Westminster stakes at Epsom. Tristan went on to win the Ascot Gold Cup in 1883; the 3rd horse, Voluptuary, won the Grand National in 1884 and the unplaced Hackness went on to win the 1882 Cambridgeshire, at odds of 100–12.

1915 Owner CARLO VITTADINI, whose Grundy won the 1975 Derby, born. Also owned Italian Derby winners Ardale, Ortis and Orange Bay. Colours: dark blue; yellow hoop armlets; and spotted cap.

1920 Fernley was the first 'winner' for MRS FLORENCE NAGLE – but was disqualified. In 1966, Mrs Nagle contested a court case forcing the Jockey Club to license women trainers.

1924 Newmarket trainer GEORGE (GERRY) BLUM born. Trained Venus of Stretham to win 11 races; also responsible for Stay Low.

1935 Hertfordshire trainer KEN IVORY born. Best horses include Go Bananas and Dawn's Delight.

1946 Trainer of Skywalker MICHAEL WHITTINGHAM born.

1946 PAT TAAFFE rode his first winner, Ballin Corona, on the Flat at Phoenix Park for trainer Micky Gleeson.

1949 Legendary US jockey WILLIE SHOEMAKER rode his first winner. On the same day 40 years later, in 1989, he once again rode a winner at the same track – Golden Gate Fields in California.

1961 Irish trainer DANNY MURPHY born.

1966 Racecourse commentator IAN BARTLETT born.

1992 WINGCOMMANDER EATS, 6–1, beat Mayfair Moss, 14–1, in a 10-runner selling race at Newton Abbot for which there were only 45 possible dual forecast combinations. The Tote dividend for the dual forecast was £1,002.80.

1992 The Martin Pipe-trained 1–2 favourite RIVERSIDE BOY disappeared before the start of the Real British Coal Novice Chase at Uttoxeter. Puzzled connections eventually discovered that the horse had broken loose from the lad looking after him in the pre-saddling area, found a nearby exit gate open and strolled off along the road. The race went ahead without him and he was eventually discovered some time later, three miles away from the course.

21 APRIL

1887 Jockey CHARLIE CUNNINGHAM rode 5 winners at Kelso. Small beer for him – on March 29 1881 he had ridden 7 at Rugby.

1918 LORD DERBY born. Owner of Arlington Million winner Teleprompter and Ascot, Goodwood and Doncaster Cups winner Alycidon. Colours: black; white cap.

1926 Owner of Aureole, Dunfermline and Highclere HER MAJESTY THE QUEEN born. Colours: purple; gold braid; scarlet sleeves; black velvet cap; gold fringe.

1929 US trainer ALLEN JERKENS born. Handled the very useful Beau Purple, which won a string of important races in 1962 over a variety of distances.

1930 FULKE WALWYN rode his first winner, Alpine Hut (Morgan Lindsay) at Cardiff. It was also his first ride under NH rules.

1934 The Queen's stud manager MICHAEL OSWALD born.

1943 BARRY IRWIN born. Californian owner of Prized, the first horse to win million-dollar races on both turf (Breeders' Cup) and dirt (Molson Million) in the same season (1989). Colours: green; black ball with green shamrock; black sleeves and cap.

1979 Irish jockey NIALL BYRNE, aged seventeen, rode his first winner, High Simbir, at Naas.

1979 NO BOMBS won the Sean Memorial Hurdle at Worcester only to be disqualified for failing a dope test due to consuming a Mars Bar!

1989 Quick-thinking horsebox driver IVAN HUGHES saved the lives of three people trapped on the roof of a blazing building in Newmarket by driving his empty horsebox up to the building so that they could jump on to it and escape safely.

1990 JENNY PITMAN was fined £200 by stewards at Ayr after striking unfortunate jockey JAMIE OSBORNE in the face! Pitman's horse Run to Form had collided with the rails, and Jenny blamed Jamie, who was riding Dwadme. The stewards, however, apportioned no blame for the incident.

1993 A professional punter from the north-east known to invest heavily only on big odds-on 'certainties' suffered a £40,000 setback at Catterick where he staked one wager of £15,000 at 1–10 on Jizyah, 2nd of 2, and another of £18,000 at 1–6 on Carbon Steel, 3rd of 3. He also placed other, smaller, bets on the pair. He retired licking his wounds.

22 APRIL

1754 MR CORKER's bay mare was ridden 300 miles in three days on a course at Newmarket, to win a wager of £100.

1783 The first recorded meeting at Catterick racecourse took place.

1875 Sandown Park, the first fully enclosed course, opened its gates to the public.

1915 Former chief executive of the Jockey Club SIDNEY KENT born.

1916 A record-breaking purchase as a 5,500-guinea yearling, LA FLECHE, proved to be a bargain when she won the 1892 1,000 Guineas, Oaks and St Leger. She died on this day at Sledmere stud, Yorkshire.

1922 Part-owner of Theatrical and Arazi ALLEN PAULSON born.

1925 Would you buy a used horse from this man? GEORGE 'ARFUR DALEY' COLE, an owner with trainer Patrick Haslam, born.

1929 DANA BRUDENELL-BRUCE born. Part-owner of Cheltenham Gold Cup winner Alverton and Circus Ring; also Irish St Leger success Opale. Colours: black, yellow sleeves; scarlet cap.

1934 Owner of Gustav Dore LORD PORTMAN born. Colours: old gold; royal blue fleur-de-lys and cap.

1935 Former Newbury permit-holder DAVID NUGENT born.

1947 The photo-finish was introduced in Britain at Epsom.

1952 Former jockey BOB WEAVER born.

1957 JACK BERRY rode his first winner, Sarsta Girl (Charlie Hall), at Wetherby, over hurdles at 10-1.

1966 Jump jockey GUY UPTON born. Best horses ridden Membersun and Golden Celtic.

1967 Trainer GEORGE 'BUSTER' FENNINGWORTH, who won 52 races in the 1962 season from his Hurgill Lodge and Belle Isle, Richmond stables, was killed in a car crash en route to Ayr races.

1968 BOB LAWSON, aged 17, rode his first winner, Portland II, at Alexandra Park.

1989 MARTIN PIPE became the most successful trainer over one season when High Bid at Uttoxeter became his 181st winner of the campaign, passing the record formerly held by Henry Cecil, who set it in 1987.

1990 Retired Curragh trainer MICK CONNOLLY, 77, died – just 6 days after his son Robbie had died of motor neurone disease.

23 APRIL

1624 JOSEPH STRUTT, whose 1801 volume *Sports and Pastimes of the People of England* chronicled many sports, including horse racing, reported on this day that for the first time the prize for the St George's Bell, run at Chester on Shrove Tuesday since 1540, would be kept permanently by the winner. The prize was a silver bell worth some £10.

1846 Jockey THOMAS CANNON was born at Eton. He went on to ride 13 (including 1882 Derby winner Shotover) and train 2 Classic winners. He was the father of Mornington Cannon and the great grandfather of Lester Piggott. At one stage in his career he accepted a £9,000 lump-sum retainer to ride for three seasons for Mr George Baird, for whom he partnered Busybody to win the 1884 1000 Guineas and Oaks.

1875 Tom Cannon rode Lord Dupplin's KALEIDOSCOPE to win the main event of the day at Sandown.

1949 Owner-trainer PETER BROOKSHAW born.

1951 Leading American trainer PETE VESTAL born in New York.

1982 Leading thoroughbred owner and breeder JOHN R. GAINES announced plans for the multi-race, multi-million-dollar Breeders' Cup Series at the annual Kentucky Derby Festival 'They're Off' awards luncheon in Louisville, Kentucky.

1984 SILVER BUCK, winner of the 1982 Cheltenham Gold Cup, ran his last race. He won the HS Commercial Spares Handicap Chase over three miles 100 yards at Wetherby, starting at 11-8 favourite. He won 34 of his 48 races, collecting prize-money of £177,179.

1990 Gladtogetit won at Sligo to give ADRIAN MAGUIRE his first success under rules.

24 APRIL

1855 There were dubious dealings at Newmarket as James Merry's Lord of the Isles, trained by William Day, beat Henry Padwick's St Hubert by a neck in the 2,000 Guineas, the latter trained by Day's father, John Barham Day. When the Day family later explained to the two owners that St Hubert had 'allowed' Lord of the Isles to win in expectation of the compliment being returned in the Derby, the two owners rapidly disabused their trainers of such thoughts and made alternative training arrangements. In the event, Wild Dayrell won the Derby that year.

1924 Owner of Weareagrandmother – the name was inspired by a famous remark by Margaret Thatcher – former gentleman rider, punter, sometime MP, columnist for the *Sporting Life*, star of dog food commercials SIR CLEMENT FREUD born. Lists his recreations as *boules* and backgammon. Colours: black; orange hooped sleeves; black cap with orange spots.

1932 Trainer of Mon's Beau GILES BEESON born.

1945 GORDON RICHARDS won a race at Newmarket riding bareback after the saddle slipped on the Aga Khan's Leventina with 2 furlongs of the race remaining. Richards still returned, 'with all his gear intact'.

1958 English trainer in America IAN JORY born. Handled Best Pal.

1961 NICK GASELEE rode his first winner, One Eyed Gunner, at Folkestone.

1967 Guy's Master was, appropriately enough, the first Flat winner for trainer GUY HARWOOD, winning at Alexandra Park.

1969 PAT EDDERY rode his first winner, Alvaro, at Epsom. Pat was seventeen at the time. 'My overwhelming feeling on passing the post was one of relief,' said Eddery, who rode the horse for trainer Major Michael Pope and had made his racecourse debut 390 days earlier on Dido's Dowry at Aintree.

1985 Private Views won at Worcester to give jockey ANDREW ADAMS his first winner.

1986 Trainer ALEX STEWART married Katherine Domvile, but could have been forgiven if he seemed rather reluctant to take the plunge. Some while earlier, Stewart had been one of four racing friends who had struck a bet between themselves that whichever of them was first to become engaged would buy the others dinner in the restaurant of their choice. Also in the wager were fellow trainer Jamie Toller, assistant trainer Chris Thomson Jones and Teddie Beckett of the British Bloodstock Agency. They ended up dining at Le Pavillon on the Champs Elysées in Paris, enjoying an expensive meal complete with the best champagne – and a £1,500 bill for Stewart.

25 APRIL

1878 The first running of Newmarket's Craven Stakes was won by Thurio, owned by Prince Soltykoff, which beat Sefton by 1/2 length. The runner-up went on to gain some small consolation by winning the Derby.

1905 STEVE DONOGHUE rode his first winner, Hanoi, at Hyères in France.

1917 Owner-breeder of Calibina (Wokingham Stakes, Stewards' Cup) and Shapina ALEC BADGER born. Colours: tangerine; royal blue hooped sleeves; striped cap.

1920 Luton trainer PHILIP ALLINGHAM born.

1923 Owner of The Brianstan and Le Johnstan STANLEY POWELL born. Colours: white; black star; green sleeves; white cap.

1925 Trainer of My Swallow and Deep Diver PAUL DAVEY born. Private trainer to David Robinson from 1967 to 1974.

1941 Jockey GIANFRANCO DETTORI, father of Frankie, born. Best horses ridden include Bolkonski and Wollow.

1945 Dual purpose trainer MIKE O'NEILL born. Best horses trained include Joveworth on the flat and Precious Boy over jumps.

1951 Goodwood clerk of the course ROD FABRICIUS born. Also acting clerk of the course at Aintree on the fateful 'void race' day in 1993.

1968 Jockey DALE GIBSON, rider of Very Adjacent and Starlet, born.

1978 JOHN FRANCOME was banned until June 3 and fined £750 for his part in the 'John Banks' affair.

1989 ANOTHER CLEM beat 9 other runners to win the 5.45 race at Punchestown – but no one backed the winner, because bookmakers' clerks, Tote staff and the official timekeeper all refused to work. They objected to an 8-race card ending so late. 'Their move was scandalous, and an insult to the public,' declared the *Sporting Life*.

1991 Trainer LAZ BARRERA, who trained Affirmed to win the US Triple Crown in 1978, died of pneumonia, aged 66.

1992 TOPSHAM BAY, owned by Michael Marsh, won the Whitbread Gold Cup. Mr Marsh also owned and trained Larbawn to win the race in 1968 and 1969.

26 APRIL

1721 The famous FLYING CHILDERS beat Speedwell in a four-mile match at level weights at Newmarket. This was the first outing for probably the first truly great racehorse. Owned by the Duke of Devonshire, Flying Childers proved his ability by giving one of the best racehorses of the time, Fox, a stone and beating him by 360 yards.

1851 DEFAULTER, SQUIRE OF MALTON, REINDEER and PULCHERRINA ran a quadruple dead-heat in the Omnibus Stakes at The Hoo. It seems that even in those days the name Omnibus was synonymous with four of them coming along at the same time!

1918 Trainer of Flosuebarb and Ginger Boy JOHN HOOTON born.

1924 Trainer of Lady Senator and Rory's Rocket PETER ASHWORTH born. Professional jockey from 1936 to 1955.

1936 Former amateur rider SIR EDWARD CAZALET born.

1939 Thirteen-year-old BRIENZ, who had been 3rd in the Derby ten years previously behind Trigo, won the Ely Handicap Chase at Cardiff, ridden by Tommy Carey.

1943 GORDON RICHARDS rode Scotch Mist to victory at Windsor. It was his 2,750th winner, two ahead of Fred Archer's record total.

1943 Jockey RON ATKINS, rider of Moyne Royal and Mon Plaisir, born. Also a trainer.

1950 Jockey KEVAN LEASON born. Best horse ridden Goldhills Pride. Caused no little surprise when he announced in 1990 that henceforth he would be known as Karen and would continue his life as a woman.

1953 Irish jockey MICHAEL FURLONG born. Best horse ridden Bannow Rambler.

1961 JOSE ADEON SANTOS born in Chile. He was top American money-earning jockey in 1986, 1987, 1988 and 1989 with earnings of $11,329,297, $12,407,355, $14,877,298 and $13,847,003 in the respective years.

1992 SUDDEN BLESSING won the Golden Horse Cup at Wang Chuen, Canton, China, partnered by jockey Za Na from Mongolia. This was the first winner at the first meeting in China since the Communists took over in 1949. A crowd of 4,000 turned up and also saw the same horse win the Guangzhev Derby on the same card. However, few benefited as there was no betting allowed. Shortly afterwards the authorities decided to ban racing once again.

27 APRIL

1852 STOCKWELL, owned by Lord Exeter, won the 2,000 Guineas partnered by J. Norman.

1857 Emperor Napoleon II opened Longchamp. Along with some 10,000 other interested parties, he observed the first day's racing at the new course. The first race was won by Eclaireur.

1927 Owner of Cheltenham Gold Cup winner Burrough Hill Lad STAN RILEY born. Colours: kingfisher blue; black and orange hooped sleeves; orange cap.

1937 SUPERIOR GUARD lived up to his name by winning both the 2nd and 3rd races on the card at Avondale, New Zealand.

1939 GRASSHOPPER, ridden by Keith Piggott, won the last race to be run at Ely, Cardiff.

1944 Senior steward of the Jockey Club LORD HARTINGTON born. Colours: straw; straw and brown checked cap.

1944 Owner of Gazeley stud near Newmarket and breeder of Venetian Palace and Positive PATRICK MCCALMONT born.

1952 Jockey Club member GEORGE WEIR, owner of Arctic Explorer and Crimson Silk, born. Colours: light blue; chocolate sash; checked cap.

1966 JOHN DUNLOP's first winner as a trainer was Tamino at Newmarket in the Palace House Stakes. Ron Hutchinson rode.

1969 British trainer SAM HILL, who died in Bath in February 1993, aged 76, trained all 6 winners at Ootacamund, Tamil Nadu, India. All 6 races were handicaps and his winners were St Roma (April Plate), Smokey (Mudumalai Plate), Precious (Ootacamund Cup), Fair Elaine (Palani Plate), Queen o'Scots (Guindy Plate) and Fair Scholar (Kundah Plate).

1971 ARTHUR STEPHENSON sent out 5 winners at Kelso - all ridden by different jockeys.

1989 PETER SCUDAMORE rode a 4-timer at Towcester - and the 3rd of his winners, Gay Moore, made him the first jump jockey ever to ride 200 winners in a season.

1992 PROSEQUENDO was Mark Dixon's first flat winner as a trainer, scoring at Wolverhampton.

1992 Trainer JENNY PITMAN and jockey MICHAEL BOWLBY were cleared of breaking any rules over the controversial running of Golden Freeze in the Cheltenham Gold Cup when the horse took on front-running hot favourite Carvills Hill. A Jockey Club hearing concluded that the horse ran on his merits and that the tactics employed were legitimate.

28 APRIL

1925 Dual code Newmarket trainer HARRY THOMSON JONES born. Touching Wood, Tingle Creek and Devon Ditty are among the stable stars he has handled. In 1971 on the day his Athens Wood won the St Leger he also sent out Ramequin to win a novice hurdle at Fakenham. There's versatility for you.

1929 Popular newspaper racing correspondent of the *Daily Telegraph* P. E. (PETER) SCOTT, who wrote as Hotspur, born.

1932 Scarborough trainer ROY ROBINSON born. Swift Albany and Impus were among the best inmates of his jumping yard.

1943 Trainer of Willie Wumpkins and Meladon ADRIAN MAXWELL born.

1953 New York trainer DELMAR WILLIAM CARROLL II born. Best horses include Pleasure Cay, Stay the Course, Bed o'Roses.

1958 Banbury jump trainer MARK WILKINSON born. Rattlin' Jack and Smart Star are among the best of his horses.

1961 Upper Lambourn trainer JOHN AKEHURST born. Son of Epsom trainer Reg, John won as an amateur rider and lists as one of his major achievements scoring a hole-in-one at Frilford Heath Golf Club at the 11th on August 24 1991. He's trained a couple of decent horses, like Master Lease and Rhodes, along the way.

1972 The unbeaten dual Arc winner, Ribot, died of a twisted intestine at the Darby Dan stud in Kentucky, aged twenty.

1973 Jockey DOUG BARROTT was killed by a fall from French Colonist in The Whitbread Gold Cup.

1984 The Queen Mother's SPECIAL CARGO won the Whitbread Gold Cup in what many consider to be the greatest steeplechase ever. Second in the Sandown race was Lettoch, a short head down, and 3rd, a further short head behind, was Diamond Edge, on which Royal jockey Bill Smith was riding his last race, having opted for that mount in preference to Special Cargo.

1990 MR FRISK, Marcus Armytage up, became the first horse to complete the Grand National-Whitbread Gold Cup double in the same season for owner Mrs H. Duffy and trainer Kim Bailey.

29 APRIL

1794 The *Kentish Gazette* carried an advertisement for a 'very singular game of cricket to be performed on horseback', to be played at Linsted Park on Tuesday May 6. Whether they were jockeys having a go at cricket or cricketers having a go at riding is not recorded.

1890 1867 Derby winner HERMIT died, aged 26.

1901 Odds-on favourite (7–10) Alard Scheck finished last of 5 as J. Winkfield partnered bay colt HIS EMINENCE (3–1) to victory by 1½ lengths in the 27th Kentucky Derby for owner-trainer F. B. Van Meter.

1904 1–4 chance PRETTY POLLY, ridden by Willie Lane for trainer Peter Gilpin and owner Major Eustace Loder, won the 1,000 Guineas by 3 lengths. She went on to win 22 of her 24 starts. She was an even hotter winning favourite in the Oaks, returning 8–100, and was 2–5 winner of the St Leger.

1921 Both the 2,000 Guineas (won by Craig An Eran) and the 1,000 Guineas (won by Bettina) were run on the same day at Newmarket.

1940 Former Royal jump jockey DAVID MOULD born. Rode Border Mask to win the 1970 Hennessy and Tingle Creek to win the 1973 Benson & Hedges Handicap Chase. Married show-jumper Marion Coakes.

1944 England soccer international turned trainer FRANCIS LEE born.

1947 Former trainer RICHARD MITCHELL born.

1961 Jockey JOHN QUINN born. Best horses State Jester and Past Glories.

1967 There were emotional scenes at Sandown as the hugely popular Mill House, so often second-best to the immortal Arkle, won the Whitbread Gold Cup for Fulke Walwyn and David Nicholson, holding off a late challenge by Kapeno. Mill House's regular rider Willie Robinson missed the race because of a broken leg but was introduced to the Queen Mum, crutches and all.

1971 Jockey ADRIAN MAGUIRE born. Best horses Omerta, Cool Ground.

1987 MARK QUALEY and JOHNA MCCUTCHEON were married by Judge Robert L. Andrew – in the winners' enclosure at Gulfstream Park, Florida, after the running of the Herecomesthebride Stakes.

1991 At Hexham there were 7 co-favourites for the 10-runner Law Society Legal Handicap Hurdle. FINGERS CROSSED, one of the 6–1 market leaders, was the winner. It is believed to be only the second time so many horses have headed the market together.

1991 Aussie trainer BILL MITCHELL was banned for twelve months after 2nd-placed Livistone Lane tested positive to three prohibited substances in Randwick's Doncaster Handicap on March 30. In May the ban was lifted and an all-time high fine of AUS$40,000 was imposed instead.

30 APRIL

1851   Nine racegoers died when the train taking them to their homes in Manchester from Chester races crashed.

1874   Thousands flocked to Williamstown racecourse to see the 'brothers' race' run. It was a sweepstake of 100 sovereigns, contested by three brothers – Lords Charles, William and Marcus Beresford. The race was run over three miles, each horse carrying 12st, and Lord William, riding Woodlark, was the winner by a short head.

1894   Coalminer NATHAN RICHARDS married dressmaker ELIZABETH DEAN. Neither had the remotest connection with horse racing but their son, Gordon, became Champion Jockey on 26 occasions.

1917   Trainer of Deep Run and Nocturnal Spree STUART MURLESS born.

1929   BBC Radio racing commentator PETER BROMLEY born.

1947   Trainer of Persian Heights and Ile de Nisky GEOFF HUFFER born. It is strongly rumoured in the business that in a previous incarnation Huffer was a member of the pop group Mungo Jerry.

1955   Jump jockey RICHARD HOARE born. One of the few jockeys whose entire name could be construed as an insult.

1956   Jockey DAVID NICHOLLS born. Rider of Soba and Chaplin's Club.

1965   The first-ever Ascot jump meeting took place. The Inaugural Hurdle was won by the favourite Sir Giles, trained by Fulke Walwyn, ridden by Willie Robinson. The Kennel Gate Chase was won by Another Scot, ridden by Tim Norman. The two-day meeting included Flat races.

1965   MARY KEIM became the only woman to train the winner of the Kentucky Oaks (and still is) when her Amerivan, which she also owned, was partnered by Ron Turcotte.

1969   After just 100 yards of the 2,000 Guineas, 15–8 favourite RIBOFILIO, trained by Fulke Johnson Houghton, was already struggling. After 3 furlongs the horse was tailed off, and Lester Piggott had pulled it up after 4. Right Tack (15–2), ridden by Geoff Lewis, went on to win. Dope tests on Ribofilio proved negative.

1982   Jump jockey RONNIE BEGGAN rode his first winner, B. & K. Emperor, at Aintree.

1983   THE QUEEN opened the National Horse Racing Museum in Newmarket.

1992   RAG TIME BELLE won at Redcar to bring home the bacon for Gloucester pig-breeder-owner Roger Hughes, pig-keeper-trainer Malcolm Eckley and breeder Victor Wadge, a bacon farmer.

1992   Weighing-out procedures were modified so that breast plates, breast girths, martingales and neck straps would no longer count towards a Flat jockey's weight although they would still be included for jump jockeys.

1 MAY

1915   Trainer of Mac Joy and Blue Rondo KEN BAILEY born.

1943   A crowd of 65,000 saw 2–5 favourite COUNT FLEET win the Kentucky Derby by 3 lengths for jockey J. Longden and trainer G. D. Cameron. Ten ran. Count Fleet also won the Preakness and Belmont Stakes.

1954   For the first time net prize-money for the Kentucky Derby topped $100,000 and the connections of DETERMINE (the first grey to win the race) collected $2,050 more than that for their horse's 1 1/2-length win over 16 opponents. The horse was ridden by R. York, trained by Willie Molter and paid 4.3–1.

1960   Flat jockey STEVE CAUTHEN, the 'Kentucky Kid', born in Covington, Kentucky. British Champion for the first time in 1984, having won the American equivalent in 1977. The only jockey to have completed that double since Danny Maher in 1908.

1961   Betting shops became legal in Britain.

1965   BILL SHOEMAKER rode Lucky Debonair to win the 91st Kentucky Derby against 10 rivals at odds of 4.3–1 for trainer Frank Catrone.

1971   The great BRIGADIER GERARD won his first race as a three-year-old, the 2,000 Guineas, ridden by Joe Mercer, returning odds of 11–2 and beating Mill Reef in the process.

1975   Pickets were out on duty at the 1,000 Guineas meeting at Newmarket where striking stable lads provoked ugly scenes during which Willie Carson was dragged from his horse.

1976   HONEST PLEASURE became the first horse to carry over $1 million win-and-place betting money in the Kentucky Derby. In all, $1,651,253 was riding on the odds-on shot, which finished 2nd, ridden by Angel Cordero Jr. Bold Forbes (3–1) was the winner.

1982   Eddie Delahoussaye rode 21–1 chance GATO DEL SOL to win the Kentucky Derby. Nineteen ran. The prize-money was $428,850. The grey, trained by Edwin Gregson, won only 7 of his 39 starts but still chalked up prize-money of $1,340,207 during his career.

1985   Six-year-old DESERT ORCHID finished unplaced in his only flat race run over two miles at Ascot. He started at 33–1.

1990   PAT EDDERY rode the second 5-timer of his career, booting home a 354–1 quintet at Bath.

1990   Ascot held its first evening jump meeting for 25 years.

1990   Trainer COLIN TINKLER sponsored a race at Redcar, calling it the 'Very Much Alive Marie Tinkler Stakes' in honour of his former wife. Tinkler won it with his own Ghadbbaan, ridden by daughter-in-law, Kim.

2 MAY

1517   The DUKE OF SUFFOLK took on a sportsman called Nicolle Dex in a horse race in France, 'from the Elm at Auvergney to within St Clements Gate for 80 crowns'. Despite, or perhaps because of, giving his horse no hay for three days and restricting his own diet to white wine, the Duke finished second.

1870   The first horse to win the Triple Crown (in 1853) – 2,000 Guineas, Derby and St Leger – WEST AUSTRALIAN, died.

1893   Irish jockey JIM PARKINSON had his first winner, his own horse Noiseless, at Birr. He was later warned off for over twelve months for foul riding but overcame that to be Champion Trainer 23 times.

1911   Jockey-trainer KEN GETHIN born. Died in 1989. Won 1952 1,000 Guineas on Zabara. Trained at Epsom after retiring as a jockey.

1959   WILLIE SHOEMAKER survived an objection from the runner-up to ride his 2nd Kentucky Derby winner, TOMY LEE, which got home by a nose from Sword Dancer and 15 others. Trained by Frank Childs, the horse paid 3.7–1. The race was run in a post-war record temperature of 94°F.

1962   Jump jockey BILLY MORRIS, who rode The Ceiriog to win the Swedish Champion Hurdle, born. Self-nominated highlight of career: 'Decided not to get married in 1981'.

1964   NORTHERN DANCER, ridden by Bill Hartack, trained by H. A. Luro, was the neck winner of the 12-runner 90th Kentucky Derby at odds of 3.4–1. In the process he set a new track record of 2 minutes.

1970   DUST COMMANDER was a surprise winner of the 96th Kentucky Derby, beating 16 opponents and returning odds of just over 15–1 for jockey M. Manganello and trainer Don Combs. Diane Crump, 15th on Fathom, was the first female to ride in the race.

1974   WYE racecourse staged its last meeting.

1991   Melton Mowbray trainer NORMA MACAULEY landed the first double of her nine-year career at Redcar.

1992   LESTER PIGGOTT rode his 30th Classic winner in England on Rodrigo De Triano in the 2,000 Guineas. His first was 38 years earlier – the longest-ever span between first and 'last' Classic wins.

1992   Hong Kong punters marked the first full night meeting held at Happy Valley on a Saturday by breaking through the $1 billion mark on Totalisator turnover (£73 million).

1992   The biggest ever sum of win money placed on a Kentucky Derby candidate was heaped on to 'wonder horse' Arazi. $1,460,470 was shovelled on to the French-trained 9–10 favourite which finished only 8th – the worst placed odds-on favourite in the history of the race.

3 MAY

1769   The great racehorse ECLIPSE appeared in public for the first time in a race at Epsom. Prior to the race professional gambler Dennis O'Kelly, later to own the horse, made a bet which became one of the most famous of racing quotes: 'Eclipse first, the rest nowhere.' He was right – Eclipse won by a furlong with the other horses finishing too far behind to be officially placed.

1842   The great northern mare ALICE HAWTHORN won the Chester Cup. She won 52 of her 71 races.

1939   Jockey JIMMY UTTLEY born. Rode 50 flat winners before becoming too heavy and switching codes although, unusually, he rode only over hurdles – won Champion Hurdle on Persian War 1968, 1969, 1970.

1940   BILLY NEVETT rode his 1,000th winner on Thixendale at Thirsk. He went on to win three wartime Derbys, Owen Tudor (1941), Ocean Swell (1944) and Dante (1945).

1948   Trainer BROOKE SANDERS born. She had 40 wins as a jockey.

1952   BEN JONES trained a record 6th Kentucky Derby winner as HILL GAIL stormed to a 2-length victory at odds of 11-10 with Eddie Arcaro, who was winning his 5th Kentucky Derby.

1971   MARION H. VAN BERG died, having been the owner of a record 4,775 winners in North America since 1937, including 393 in 1969 alone.

1979   ONE IN A MILLION became the first horse running in the name of a company to win an English Classic when Joe Mercer rode the Henry Cecil-trained even-money favourite to victory in the 1,000 Guineas in the colours of textile firm Helena Springfield Ltd.

1990   WILLIE CARSON completed his set of English Classic wins by riding Salsabil to a 6-4 victory in the 1,000 Guineas.

1990   PAT DAY became the most successful rider at Churchill Downs when he rode his 926th winner there, surpassing Don Brumfield's total.

1991   LITE LIGHT won the 117th Kentucky Oaks. Her time of 1.48⁴/₅ seconds for the 9-furlong event annihilated the previous best of 1.50 set by Fran's Valentine in 1985 and netted her owners, the Lewis Burrell Sr family (which includes rapper MC Hammer), record winnings of $207,285.

1992   Two-year-old BURST became the first filly to complete the Australian two-year-old Triple Crown when she added the Champagne Stakes at Randwick, Sydney, to the Golden Slipper Stakes and A. J. C. Sires Produce. Trainer Clarrie Connors and jockey Shane Dye had also combined to complete the treble the previous year.

4 MAY

1780   The Derby was run for the first time, over one mile. The winner was Sir Charles Bunbury's Diomed, ridden by Sam Arnull, which went some way towards consoling Bunbury for losing to Lord Derby in the toss to decide whose name the new race should carry.

1898   Lieber Karl, 1-3 favourite, was beaten by a nose in the 24th Kentucky Derby, going down to 3-1 chance PLAUDIT.

1905   Belmont Park, New York, opened and the main race, the Metropolitan Handicap, produced a dead-heat between Syonsby and Race King. The attendance was 40,000.

1935   OMAHA was the 4-1 winner of the 18-runner 61st Kentucky Derby for jockey W. Saunders and trainer J. Fitzsimmons. The next year Omaha finished 2nd in the Ascot Gold Cup.

1940   Eight went to post for the 66th Kentucky Derby and 35.2-1 chance GALLAHADION was the shock 1 1/2-length winner.

1945   The death of former jockey CHARLES WOOD was announced. Born in 1856, he won the Triple Crown on Galtee More in 1897.

1946   Trainer NEVILLE CALLAGHAN born.

1953   WALTER SWINBURN SR rode his first winner, Metalon, at Warwick.

1957   Trainer DR JON SCARGILL PhD born. Claims to have no recreations – 'work all day and night'.

1968   DANCER'S IMAGE, ridden by R. Ussery, trained by L. C. Cavalaris and returning odds of 3.6-1, finished 1 1/2 lengths ahead of Forward Pass in the 14-runner 94th Kentucky Derby. But the joy of owner Peter Fuller was stifled when 'because of the finding of prohibited medication of Dancer's Image', Forward Pass was awarded the race and the prize-money of $122,600 went to owner Calumet Farm. Forward Pass was the 2.2-1 favourite. This was the first time the winner had ever been disqualified.

1974   CANNONADE won the 100th Kentucky Derby, worth $274,000 to owner J. M. Olin. Returning 6-4, the Angel Cordero Jr-ridden winner beat a record 22 rivals by 2 1/4 lengths. Trained by W. C. Stephens. A record crowd of 163,628 crammed in.

1983   Game Trust at Cheltenham provided RICHARD DUNWOODY with his first winner.

1985   Angel Cordero Jr rode SPEND A BUCK to a 5 3/4-length triumph in the 111th Kentucky Derby. The horse returned odds of 4.1-1 against 12 opponents and was trained by Cam Gambolati.

1988   Husband and wife ROBERT and THERESA Elwell raced against each other in the Audi Grand Prix Chase at Cheltenham. Theresa was 2nd on Mister Skip while Robert fell at the 14th on White Paper.

5 MAY

1839 Freudenau racecourse, Austria, opened for business. During the Second World War it was badly damaged by bombing, which left 250 craters on the track.

1904 The first jockey ever knighted, GORDON RICHARDS, born at Oakengates, Shropshire. His father, Nathan, was a coalminer and Gordon was one of 12 children. He went on to ride 4,870 winners, claimed 26 Championships and had 14 Classic victories to his credit.

1931 Trainer BERNARD SECLY born. Among his best horses was Katko.

1950 GORDON RICHARDS celebrated his 46th birthday by winning on Abernant at Sandown, becoming in the process the first English jockey to ride 4,000 winners.

1955 Trainer ROBIN GOW born.

1959 Jockey ANTHONY POWELL born, partner of Maid of Money.

1962 DECIDEDLY set a new track record of 2 minutes $2/5$ second in winning the 88th Kentucky Derby against 14 rivals, partnered by Bill Hartack and trained by H. A. Luro, and returning 8.7-1.

1973 SECRETARIAT, one of the all-time greats, was the $2^1/2$-length winner of the 99th Kentucky Derby, ridden by Ron Turcotte in a track record-breaking time of 1 minute $59^2/5$ seconds for trainer Lucien Laurin. Thirteen ran. The horse returned odds of 6-4 and went on to land the Triple Crown, eventually winning 16 of 21 races for prize-money of $1,316,808.

1979 SPECTACULAR BID landed odds of 3-5 when winning the 105th Kentucky Derby under R. J. Franklin, trained by Bud Delp, beating 9 opponents. The horse went on to win 26 of his 30 career starts, totalling prize-money of $2,781,457.

1982 Jockey WILLIE CARSON wed Elaine Williams and went on to win the Cheshire Oaks on Swiftfoot to celebrate the occasion, despite being fined £8 for forgetting to take his medical record-book to the track.

1984 Hawkley, at Kempton, provided ADAM SHOULTS with his first winner.

1986 Jump jockey ANTHONY TORY rode his first winner, Kilton Jim, at Fontwell.

1987 SIS (Satellite Information Services) began its daily broadcasts to betting shops, opening up with a service to shops in Bristol and Colchester.

1990 TIROL set a fastest electronic time for the 2,000 Guineas of 1 minute 35.84 seconds.

1990 UNBRIDLED was the $3^1/2$-length winner of the 116th Kentucky Derby for jockey C. Perret and trainer Carl A. Nafzger. At 92 Mrs Frances Genter became the oldest winning owner, winning prize-money of $581,000.

6 MAY

1920   Jockey Club member JOHN HENDERSON born. Certainly an A grade owner – his Acquit won 4 races, Accord 6, Acquaint 5, Acre Hill 3 – and he bred Accord. Colours: white; Eton blue hoops on sleeve and cap.

1926   Lingfield steward MICHAEL WARD-THOMAS born. Owner of Amari King and Lady Martha. Colours: white; red sleeves; checked cap.

1932   Owner of Ascot Gold Cup winner Precipice Wood ROBERT MCAL-PINE born. Colours: McAlpine tartan; yellow sleeves; green and yellow quartered cap. Also owner of Coed Cochion, Cormorant Wood.

1938   Trainer GEOFFREY COATSWORTH born.

1942   Former jockey turned trainer VINCENT ROSSITER born. Rode first winner 1970. Best horse partnered Glenstal.

1944   Trainer B. A. JONES won the Kentucky Derby for the 3rd time in 7 runnings when 7.1-1 chance Pensive beat 15 rivals by 4½ lengths, ridden by C. McCreary.

1955   Outpoint's jockey PADDY O'BRIEN born.

1956   Trainer of Fidway and Pukka Major TIM THOMSON JONES born. Champion Amateur Jump and Flat Jockey; 231 wins all told.

1959   Jump jockey turned sculptor WILLIE NEWTON born. Rode first winner in 1978. Served time as apprentice in England, Ireland and France. Best horse ridden Chrysaor.

1962   Jump jockey ROBERT CHAPMAN, rider of Desert Hero, born.

1971   JOHN MATTHIAS's first winner, Garden Games, at Beverley.

1972   MERIEL TUFNELL won the Goya Stakes, the first ladies' race, on 50-1 shot Scorched Earth at Kempton and became the first woman to ride a winner under Jockey Club rules.

1974   JACK BERRY sent out his first winner on the flat, 20-1 outsider Fiona's Pet, at Wolverhampton, ridden by his wife, Jo.

1978   STEVE CAUTHEN rode Affirmed to win the Kentucky Derby, later becoming the first jockey to complete the Kentucky-Epsom Derby double when he won on Slip Anchor in 1985. Affirmed went on to land the Triple Crown.

1984   Morwray Boy at Doncaster was CHRIS RUTTER's first winner.

1991   Racing closed ranks when a controversial *Cook Report* TV programme criticised Martin Pipe's training methods. Suddenly, those who had previously given him only grudging praise rallied round him.

1992   DAVID ELSWORTH became the first trainer to be given the go-ahead to operate from two yards, Whitcombe Manor and Whitsbury.

1992   Great stallion BLUSHING GROOM, sire of Arazi and Nashwan, was put down at the age of eighteen.

7 MAY

1887   BENDIGO, ridden by John Watts and carrying 9st 7lbs, won the first running of Kempton's Grand Jubilee Handicap for trainer Charlie Jousiffe and owner Buck Barclay, starting 4–1 favourite. The horse had also won the first-ever Eclipse Stakes at Sandown in 1886.

1914   SCOBIE BREASLEY born. The Aussie jockey who made it big in England later became a trainer in Barbados. Real name Arthur Edward. He won the Derby twice, in 1964 on Santa Claus and in 1966 on Charlottown. Nicknamed after the Australian trainer Jim Scobie.

1914   Lester Piggott's grandfather FRED RICKABY won the opening race on the card at Harpenden's final meeting.

1940   Trainer JOHN SPEARING born. Best horses trained include Run and Skip, Cree Bay, Rapid Lad.

1955   WILLIE SHOEMAKER won the first of 4 Kentucky Derbies on Swaps (2.8–1), trained by M. A. Tenney. Ten ran.

1958   Champion Lady Rider in 1987–88 CAROLYN EDDERY born. Wife of jockey Pat.

1977   Hot favourite and subsequent Triple Crown winner SEATTLE SLEW, the 1–2 shot, duly won the Kentucky Derby by 1¾ lengths for jockey J. Cruguet and trainer William H. Turner. Fifteen ran.

1982   CHAPLIN'S CLUB finished 2nd in his first-ever race, at Lingfield, ridden by P. Colquhoun. He went on to set and then equal a twentieth-century record of 9 handicap wins in a season.

1988   Roan filly WINNING COLORS lived up to her name, prevailing by a neck for jockey G. L. Stevens in the 114th Kentucky Derby, for which seventeen went to post. Trained by D. Wayne Lukas. Jockey Bill Shoemaker, riding in his 26th Derby, had now landed 4 wins.

1990   MARTIN PIPE sent out 4 winners, including his 200th of the term for the 2nd consecutive season.

1990   Jockey TERRY SMITH failed to ride ROSSA PRINCE to victory – despite the fact that the race was a walkover as his horse was the only one entered. The horse bolted before the race at a point-to-point meeting at Tweseldon and couldn't be recaptured in time to complete the course. To compound matters, Smith was fined £25 for declaring the wrong colours.

1991   TOULON became the first French winner at Chester since 1952. The André Fabre-trained runner won the Chester Vase at odds of 9–4.

1992   49-year-old Puerto Rican-born ANGEL CORDERO announced his retirement having suffered a broken elbow, broken ribs and a damaged spleen in a 4-horse pile-up at Aqueduct. He scored 7,076 winners during his career, bettered only by Laffit Pincay (7,758) and Bill Shoemaker (8,833).

8 MAY

1788 The first Royal winner of the Derby was the Prince of Wales' odds-on shot SIR THOMAS, ridden by the Lester Piggott of his day, William South, who was in his 54th year.

1915 REGRET became the first filly to win the Kentucky Derby, ridden by J. Notter and trained by James Rowe Sr, at odds of 2.65-1. Sixteen went to post. For the first time the winner collected a five-figure sum in winnings - $11,450.

1920 Record prize-money of $30,375 went to PAUL JONES, the 6.2-1 winner of the 17-runner 46th Kentucky Derby, ridden by T. Rice, trained by William Garth.

1922 Trainer for Jimmy Tarbuck and Frankie Vaughan DOUG MARKS born. Fan of Nottingham Forest FC. Rode Godiva to win both the 1,000 Guineas and the Oaks in 1940 for trainer W. Jarvis.

1924 US trainer LAZ BARRERA born. Responsible for 1978 US Triple Crown winner Affirmed.

1935 Ascot and Cheltenham steward SIR JOHN COTTERELL born.

1937 WAR ADMIRAL was the 8-5 favourite, 1 3/4-length winner of the 63rd Kentucky Derby, ridden by C. Kurtsinger and trained by George Conway. Twenty ran. Mary Hirsch, whose No Sir ran 13th, was the first woman trainer to have a runner.

1941 GORDON RICHARDS broke his left leg after being kicked by a filly at the start of a race at Salisbury. He was out of action for the rest of the season, which allowed 39-year-old Harry Wragg to take over as Champion Jockey.

1945 VE Day coincided with the 1,000 Guineas at Newmarket. Despite the party atmosphere, noted a contemporary report of the day's proceedings, 'the stewards did not exchange hats, nor did the bookmakers pay out any bonuses'. Lord Derby's Sun Stream, ridden by Harry Wragg, won the 1,000 Guineas, his 7th victory in the classic. He bred all 7 winners.

1947 Trainer turned starter NICK VIGORS born.

1955 Jockey LINDSAY CHARNOCK born. Rider of Gentilhombre.

1969 For the first time since its first publication in 1773 the *Racing Calendar* was printed in yellow, only reverting to white on February 6 1992.

1982 STEVE SMITH ECCLES rode his 300th winner, Orange Tag (Nicky Henderson), at Market Rasen.

1985 US jockey RANDY ROMERO rode 6 winners from 8 mounts at Churchill Downs.

1990 BLACK SAPPHIRE opened trainer James Fanshawe's winning account when scoring at Salisbury.

9 MAY

1800   CHAMPION, a son of Pot-8-os, ridden by William Clift, won the Derby and later added the St Leger to that achievement.

1892   One of the famous jockey BEASLEY brothers, WILLIE, 2nd in the 1888 Grand National on Frigate, died from injuries sustained in the Kildare Hunt Plate at Punchestown. Of the other brothers, Tommy died in 1905 and Harry in 1939.

1893   For the first time, admission was charged for entrance to the Chester races. Over 45,000 paid 1s (5p) each day during the three-day meeting.

1912   Welsh jockey EVAN WILLIAMS born. He rode Golden Miller to win the 1936 Cheltenham Gold Cup.

1914   The 40th Kentucky Derby was won by 17-20 favourite OLD ROSEBUD (ridden by J. McCabe, trained by F. D. Weir) in a new track record of 2 minutes 3²/5 seconds. Seven ran.

1934   Trainer HUGH O'NEILL born. Trained Milton Burn.

1934   Former Irish Champion Jockey BUSTER PARNELL born.

1936   Actor-owner ALBERT FINNEY born. Once reportedly bought all the tickets for a performance of a show he was in so that he could take the day off to see his horse run. It was a non-runner!

1940   Trainer 'RICHARD' FULKE JOHNSON HOUGHTON born. Trained Ribocco and Ribero to win the 1967 and 1968 St Legers. Other top horses trained include Ile De Bourbon, Habitat, Ribofilio, Hot Grove.

1945   LORD ASTOR's Court Martial was his third 2,000 Guineas winner.

1955   SIR GORDON RICHARDS, Champion Jockey 26 times, sent out his first winner as a trainer, THE SAINT, owned by Miss Dorothy Paget, at Windsor.

1975   Champion Trainer-to-be MARTIN PIPE sent out his first winner when Len Lungo rode HIT PARADE to victory in a selling hurdle at Taunton.

1982   LUCA CUMANI had first Classic winner when Pat Eddery piloted Old Country to victory in the Derby Italiano in Rome.

1987   Trainer SIR NOEL MURLESS died at the age of 77. Knighted in 1977, he had retired the year before, having trained 19 Classic winners, among them Crepello (1957), St Paddy (1960) and Royal Palace (1967) in the Derby. In 1967 he became the first trainer to accumulate winning prize-money of over £250,000 in a single season, saddling the winners of 60 races in all.

1989   The great racehorse PARK TOP was put down at the age of 25.

1992   FLYING SPEED, the 2nd of 6 winners for the yard during the day, won at Warwick to chalk up the 4th consecutive double century of winners for Martin Pipe.

10 MAY

1881 Japan's Emperor Meiji paid his first visit to the Negishi racetrack, which had been constructed for the exiled English to stage meetings.

1904 Owner of Linwell SIR DAVID BROWN born.

1905 Only 3 runners lined up for the 31st running of the Kentucky Derby. 1-3 favourite AGILE cruised home by 3 lengths.

1929 BRYAN MARSHALL rode his first winner, Cheviotdale, for Atty Persse at Kempton.

1943 Jockey BRUCE RAYMOND born. Rider of Petong and Bob Back, 1988 was his best season, producing 77 wins. First winner Arctic Bar at Birmingham in June 1961.

1950 TOMMY WESTON rode his last winner, Lindum Hill, at Doncaster. Born in 1903, he had 11 Classic winners, including Sansovino in the 1924 and Hyperion in the 1933 Derbys. Having joined the Royal Navy during the war, he was torpedoed off Freetown and drifted on a raft in the Atlantic for three days.

1957 NH jockey DAVID DUTTON, rider of Cockle Strand, born.

1963 Jump jockey NEIL FEARN born. Best season 23 winners, 1985-86.

1968 Twice Champion Apprentice GARY 'THE ANGRY ANT' BARDWELL born. Partnered Not So Silly to win the 1987 Ayr Gold Cup.

1977 EDDIE HIDE rode his 2,000th winner, TRIPLE FIRST, at York.

1985 Goodwood held its first evening meeting.

1986 Jockey MICHAEL BLACKMORE was killed in a fall at Market Rasen.

1989 Former Champion Jump Jockey JOHN FRANCOME caused a storm when, on behalf of Channel 4, he rode a horse called Gaasid around Chester racecourse to give viewers a rider's-eye view of the unique, tight course via a special TV camera which was fixed to his helmet. But Gaasid was due to run in the Chester Cup that afternoon. He started at 5-1 2nd favourite and finished 5th. His trainer, Reg Akehurst, had known nothing about the morning gallop and sacked the staff who had arranged it.

1991 Jump jockey KEVIN MOONEY rode his 296th and final winner, By Line, at Taunton. He won the Whitbread Gold Cup on the Queen Mother's Special Cargo in 1983-84.

1992 BILLY NEVETT, who rode three Derby winners died aged 86. He rode for 3 generations of the training Peacock family, Dobson, Matthew and Richard. Rode his last winner on Setting Star at Manchester on the last day of the 1956 season.

1992 US trainer GARY JONES watched his Kostroma win in a photo-finish with Danzante in the Wilshire Handicap. Having watched the replay three times he commented, 'I still think I lost – but I'm gonna take the money anyway!'

11 MAY

1870   FORMOSA finished runner-up to Our Mary Ann, to whom she was conceding 30lbs in the Chester Cup, and DISTURBANCE won the Dee Stand Stakes. Two years earlier Formosa had won the 1,000 Guineas, Oaks and St Leger after running a dead-heat in the 2,000 Guineas, and three years later Disturbance won the Grand National.

1887   Winner MONTROSE (10-1) came home 2 lengths clear of the other 6 runners in the 13th Kentucky Derby.

1923   LORD WHITE, responsible for Ever Ready's sponsorship of the Derby, born. Best horse owned Exclusively Raised. Colours: red and white stripes; white sleeves; yellow cap.

1932   Jockey DENIS WARD, partner of Torch Singer and P.C. 49, born.

1941   SUSAN CRAWFORD born. Reckoned to be the finest living British equine artist. She often hides her trademark of a gremlin in her most important works. Has painted 16 Derby winners and exhibited at Royal Academy of Arts. Once claimed to be the winner of 'a midnight steeplechase on Ayr racecourse'.

1955   BILLY NEVETT rode his 2,000th winner when Vanished Sage won at Ripon. His first winner, Stockwood, came 31 years earlier at Carlisle.

1957   Former Champion Apprentice JIMMY BLEASDALE born.

1962   Jump jockey ADRIAN SHARPE, who has a winner of the Swedish Grand National to his credit, born.

1968   OPTIMISTIC PIRATE (10-1) gave Paul Cole his first winner as a trainer, scoring at Beverley.

1968   JOHN LOWE rode his first winner, Pally's Double, at Kempton.

1979   Jockey BOB CHAMPION fell from Fury Boy in a novice chase. Getting to his feet to catch the horse, it lashed out and kicked him in the testicles. This incident was believed to have led eventually to Champion's discovery that he had cancer.

1982   CASH ASMUSSEN rode his first European mount, Levening Bleu, finishing 7th at Saint-Cloud.

1989   STEVE CAUTHEN was riding Mountain Kingdom in the Ormonde Stakes at Chester when he suddenly felt his nearest rival snapping at his heels - literally. Lazaz took a bite at Cauthen's boot as they raced up the home straight.

1991   For the 2nd successive season American trainer D. WAYNE LUKAS sent out the winners of 3 major races: the Shuvee Handicap at Belmont was won by A Wild Ride (Tis Juliet the previous year), the Pimlico Special by Farma Way (Criminal Type) and the Dogwood Stakes at Churchill Downs by Be Cool (Patches).

12 MAY

1780   HEROD died, aged 22. He was Champion Sire for 8 consecutive years, from 1777 to 1784. In 1781 his progeny won 121 races – a record not beaten until 1866 by the offspring of Stockwell. Herod sired the unbeaten Highflyer and the first Oaks winner, Bridget.

1897   TYPHOON II led all the way in the 23rd Kentucky Derby and jockey F. Garner just got him home a neck clear of his 5 opponents to win at odds of 3–1 on a heavy track. The trainer was J. C. Cahn.

1899   FRED RICKABY rode Beatitude to win the first Flat race at Haydock Park, the Golborne Stakes.

1909   The US Preakness Stakes returned to Pimlico, where it had last been run in 1889, having started there in 1873. EFFENDI was the winner. In the interim the race had been run at Gravesend, Brooklyn.

1917   OMAR KHAYYAM, foaled in England, became the first foreign-bred colt to win the Kentucky Derby. The 12.8–1 chance beat 14 opponents under jockey C. Borel for trainer C. T. Patterson. Record prize-money of $16,600 went to owners Billings & Johnson.

1929   Composer and racehorse owner BURT BACHARACH born.

1937   Owner-breeder BILL SHAND KYDD born. His Matchboard won 11 chases, and Brown Windsor (12–1) won the Whitbread Gold Cup in 1989. He rode almost 50 winners under rules and 78 point-to-points. Colours: yellow and white stripes; royal blue sleeves and cap.

1956   Jockey MICHAEL WILLIAMS born. Best horses ridden include Mighty Marine, Wiggburn.

1960   PRINCE ALY KHAN, who in 1959 became the first owner in England to win more than £100,000 in a single season (£3,087 more), was killed in a car crash in Paris. Four days earlier his Sheshoon had looked sure to win a race at Longchamp when it stumbled and was beaten. He had remarked, 'I'm afraid my luck is beginning to run out.' His final winner was 1959 1,000 Guineas and Oaks victor Petite Etoile at Kempton in the Victor Wild Stakes. He had 65 horses in training with Alec Head, 4 with Noel Murless and 1 in Ireland. His Saint Crespin won the 1959 Arc. He had 6 studs in Ireland, 90 broodmares in France and 40 mares and 3 stallions in Venezuela – the latter in case of nuclear holocaust in Europe!

1976   STEVE CAUTHEN's first mount in public, 136–1 shot King of Swat, finished 10th of 11 in a race at River Downs, USA.

1988   *Today* newspaper tipster FRED SHAWCROSS set a British record by going through the 7-race card at York.

1990   Trainer MARTIN PIPE broke the record for winners in a season, which he set himself the previous year, when HUNTWORTH at Warwick became the 209th of his campaign.

13 MAY

1851   The famous re-match between Lord Eglinton's FLYING DUTCHMAN and Lord Zetland's VOLTIGEUR, both Derby and St Leger winners, took place at York. Flying Dutchman's jockey, Marlow, had started with a small disadvantage in the first confrontation between the two in the 1850 Doncaster Cup – he was rolling drunk! Voltigeur, ridden by Flatman, won by 1/2 length, but in the rematch in 1852 the result was reversed with Dutchman a length to the good.

1864   An unnamed colt by Vedette and Katie Stewart won the Stonehenge Plate from three rivals at Salisbury, but the race had to be rerun when it was discovered that the judge hadn't been in his box. So they did it all a second time and the unnamed colt triumphed again.

1891   With none of the 4 runners wishing to set the pace KINGMAN finally won the slowest Kentucky Derby ever in 2 minutes 52 1/4 seconds, ridden by I. Murphy and trained by Dud Allen.

1911   MERIDIAN equalled the track record and set a new Kentucky Derby record as he won the 37th running of the race by 3/4 length under jockey G. Archibald. Seven ran as the 2.9-1 shot stormed home in 2 minutes 5 seconds for trainer Albert Ewing.

1922   The 48th Kentucky Derby was won by 6–5 favourite MORVICH (ten ran). Ridden by A. Johnson; trained by Fred Burlew. Record prize-money of $46,775.

1939   Newmarket trainer TONY HIDE born. Blessed with the middle name Gatehouse, he rode as a professional from 1954 to 1968.

1952   CHOIR BOY was the Queen's first winner since she came to the throne, scoring at Newmarket. Ridden by Harry Carr; trained by Cecil Boyd-Rochfort.

1959   Jockey ROBERT EARNSHAW born. Rode Silver Buck to win the 1982 Cheltenham Gold Cup. He rode 215 winners in his 11-year career.

1970   MILL REEF made his racecourse debut, winning at Salisbury on his way to a 1971 Derby triumph.

1975   Trainer HENRY PEACOCK, son of Dobson, who sent out 100 winners in 1932 and trained 6 Northumberland Plate winners, died.

1976   LUCA CUMANI trained his first winner, Three Legs, at York.

1977   JOSH GIFFORD's Retaliation won at Salisbury to provide jockey Richard Rowe with his first success.

1982   ARDROSS (Henry Cecil–Lester Piggott) became the first horse in the race's 56-year history to win the Yorkshire Cup 2 years in succession when he landed odds of 2–5.

1992   PETER NIVEN and GRAHAM MCCOURT both chalked up their 100th winners of the season at Perth. Niven became the first Scottish jump jockey to achieve the feat when Henbury Hall won.

14 MAY

1779   DICK GOODISON rode Bridget to win the first running of the Oaks for the 12th Earl of Derby, after whose Epsom country house the race was named.

1807   Derby winner ELECTION triumphed in the race on his debut. But someone knew how good he was – he started 3–1 favourite.

1885   Even money favourite JOE COTTON was winner by a neck of the 11th Kentucky Derby, partnered by E. Henderson, trained by Alex Perry. Ten ran.

1886   BEN ALI was the 1.72–1 winner of the 12th Kentucky Derby, for which bookmakers did not operate, having failed to reach a licence agreement with the track management. Set a new Derby record time of 2 minutes 36^1/$_2$ seconds.

1890   RILEY (originally named Shortfellow – his dad was Longfellow) won the 16th Kentucky Derby by 1^3/$_4$ lengths at odds of 4–1, ridden by I. Murphy and trained by Edward Corrigan. Collected record prize-money of $5,460. Six ran.

1927   Favourite WHISKERY (12–5), ridden by L. McAtee and trained by F. Hopkins, was the winner of the 15-runner 53rd Kentucky Derby.

1929   The colours of LORD ROSEBERY – who, as a youngster, wagered that he would marry the richest woman in England, own a Derby winner and become prime minister – were carried by a winner for the last time (he died a week later) when Annis won the Norfolk Stakes at Newmarket. Born in 1847, Lord Rosebery's Ladas won the 1894 Derby; he married Hannah, daughter of the banker Baron Meyer de Rothschild, and became prime minister in 1894.

1932   Trainer JUMBO WILKINSON born. Real name Benjamin. He rode as a professional from 1950 to 1967 and trained Hardy Lad, Kelso Chant and Be My Guest.

1932   Senior Jockey Club handicapper GEOFFREY GIBBS born.

1946   Champion Jump Jockey (joint with T. Biddlecombe in 1968–69; winner in 1969–70 and 1971–72) BOB (BERTRAM ROBERT) DAVIES born. Obtained BSc (Agric) Hons degree at Wye College in 1967. Won 1978 Grand National on Lucius.

1955   Trainer CAROLINE CLARK born.

1979   Saudi Arabian owner PRINCE KHALID BIN ABDULLAH had his first winner, Charming Native, at Windsor. In 1986 he owned 80 British winners. In 1990 his Quest for Fame won the Derby and in 1993 the Commander-in-Chief gave him his 2nd Blue Riband. Born 1937. Colours: green; pink sash and cap; white sleeves.

1991   Top US jockey PAT DAY rode his 1,000th winner at Churchill Downs, where he is the leading rider.

15 MAY

1834 Racing first held at Chantilly, France.

1839 The Derby was run in a snow flurry and won by BLOOMSBURY, who beat 20 opponents at odds of 25-1.

1876 Jockey B. Swim rode VAGRANT, trained by James Williams, to victory in the 2nd Kentucky Derby, beating 10 opponents. The winner was 9-5 favourite.

1894 CHANT was the 1-2 winner of the 20th Kentucky Derby, strolling home by 6 lengths from 4 opponents. Ridden by F. Goodale; trained by Eugene Leigh.

1916 Owner of Guiburn GEORGE PYKETT born.

1926 Thirteen contested the 52nd Kentucky Derby. The Idle Hour stock farm produced 1st, BUBBLING OVER, ridden by A. Johnson, and 2nd, Bagenbaggage. The winner paid $1.90 to $1 stake. Trainer H. J. Thompson.

1931 Herefordshire trainer GORDON PRICE born. Best horses include Stan's Pride, Pearl Run.

1934 Middleham trainer ENRICO INCISA born.

1940 FRED WINTER had his first mount in public, partnering Tam o'Shanter for his trainer father, Fred Sr, at Newbury. The race was a nursery handicap and Winter's mount was 9th of 21. Two weeks later the partnership scored in an apprentice race.

1942 Irish trainer MICHAEL CUNNINGHAM born. Inmates of his yard included Greasepaint, 3 times placed in the Grand National, Cairn Rouge and Champion Hurdle winner For Auction. Dual purpose stable.

1948 Jockey STEVE BROOKS rode 6 winners from 8 mounts at Churchill Downs, USA. His winners returned 10.4-1, 16.8-1, 4.4-1, 3.2-1, 4.6-1 and 5.2-1. His other 2 mounts were both beaten favourites.

1962 COMMANDER IN CHIEF, trained by Eric Cousins, came 3rd on his debut at Wolverhampton as a three-year-old.

1965 Three Six won at Ayr, giving EDDIE HIDE his 1,000th winner.

1982 JACK KAENEL, just sixteen years old, became the youngest winning rider in the Preakness Stakes when his Aloma's Ruler scored. The previous youngest was eighteen-year-old Steve Cauthen, who won in 1978 on Affirmed.

1990 SERIOUS TROUBLE was never in any as he won at Brighton at a starting price of 1-33 for Sir Mark Prescott and jockey George Duffield.

16 MAY

1793   Jockey WILLIAM CLIFT rode Waxy to win the Derby. A unique character, Clift once answered an inquiry by the Duke of Dorset about a winner he'd just ridden in the following manner: 'Hang me, you see I won, that's enough for you.' When he was 80 he would walk from Newmarket to Bury St Edmunds and back (28 miles) 'just to give my legs a stretch'.

1832   KING WILLIAM IV gave an eve of Derby banquet at St James's Palace for members of the Jockey Club, during the course of which he presented the club with a gold-mounted hoof of the great racehorse Eclipse.

1884   Isaac Murphy rode BUCHANAN, the first maiden winner, to a 1-length victory at odds of 3–1 in the 10th Kentucky Derby.

1925   Black colt FLYING EBONY was the 3.15–1 winner of the 51st Kentucky Derby, ridden by E. Sande and trained by W. B. Duke. Twenty ran. This was the first Derby to be broadcast on network radio, by Louisville station WHAS.

1927   Rider of Galloway Braes and Pointsman BERT MORROW born.

1929   Former Champion Apprentice (1947–48) DENNIS BUCKLE born.

1935   Jockey turned TV commentator JIMMY LINDLEY born. His 3 Classic winners were Only For Life in the 1963 2,000 Guineas, Kashmir II 3 years later in the same race and 1964 St Leger winner Indiana. Son of an Eastbourne restaurateur. In 1957 he finished 3rd in the Champion Hurdle on Retour de Flamme.

1948   Trainer COLIN JACKSON born.

1952   Owner-trainer of Lochtillum JAMIE DOUGLAS-HOME born.

1956   Former jump jockey turned agent ROBERT KINGTON born.

1959   BALI HA'I was the Queen Mother's first winner on the Flat, at Sandown. Ridden by Willie Snaith; trained by Cecil Boyd-Rochfort.

1960   Jockey KEVIN HODGSON born. Partnered Polly's Brother to win the 1983 Ayr Gold Cup and also rode Hallgate.

1965   Former jump jockey JESSICA CHARLES-JONES born.

1967   Jockey RICHARD GRUBB rode 7 winners from 8 mounts at Woodbine, Canada.

1992   LESTER PIGGOTT rode Rodrigo De Triano to win the Irish 2,000 Guineas.

1992   Nineteen-year-old jockey NEIL VARLEY rode his first winner, Splice, in the Coral Handicap at Newmarket, his 15th ride.

1992   EDDIE HIDE came out of retirement to ride 10–1 shot Charming Gift to victory at Newmarket in the Cambridge Evening News Celebrity Riders Handicap over one mile. Greville Starkey on 3–1 favourite China Sky was 2nd and Stan Mellor 3rd on Jurran.

17 MAY

1868 Berlin's Hoppegarten racecourse celebrated its first official day's racing.

1875 An estimated turn-out of 10,000 spectators watched the first running of the Kentucky Derby at the Louisville Jockey Club track, later to become known as Churchill Downs. The race was won by ARISTIDES, which beat 14 rivals, ridden by O. Lewis and trained by Andy Anderson.

1881 HINDOO (ridden by J. McLaughlin, trained by James Rowe Sr) was the winner by 1³/₄ lengths of the 6-runner 7th Kentucky Derby.

1924 BLACK GOLD, the 7–4 favourite, won the 50th Kentucky Derby by ¹/₂ length from 18 rivals. Jockey J. D. Mooney; trainer Hedley Webb; owner Mrs R. M. Hoots. The winner's prize-money was $52,775.

1930 A starting machine was used for the first time to dispatch the 15 runners in the 56th Kentucky Derby. GALLANT FOX won by 2 lengths, ridden by E. Sande, trained by James Fitzsimmons.

1939 Jump jockey ALAN MACTAGGART born.

1945 Racing writer JONATHAN POWELL born. Author of *Champion's Story*, about Bob Champion, which was made into a film.

1954 Jockey MICHAEL ROBERTS, the first to ride 200 winners in a season in South Africa, born in Cape Town. South African Champion 11 times, he landed the British title in 1992, winning a £100 bet at odds of 100–1 (payout £10,000) with William Hill, placed by me for his agent, Graham Rock.

1957 THE QUEEN enjoyed her first treble as Pall Mall, Atlas and Might and Main, all won at Haydock.

1959 Former Champion Jockey in Zimbabwe GLENN FRENCH born.

1962 Jump jockey BRIAN STOREY born. Partnered Mighty Mark to win 1988 William Hill Scottish National.

1963 Worcester trainer KARL BURKE, who rode 48 winners from 900 rides as a professional jockey between 1979 and 1990, born.

1969 HENRY CECIL sent out his first winner, Celestial Cloud (5–1) (Bill O'Gorman), at Ripon.

1991 CADDY and DOMINIC'S CROSS, scheduled to race at Kilbeggan, were both later discovered to have been doped. Trainer Francis Flood withdrew Dominic's Cross, which would have started favourite, while Caddy was tailed off.

1992 CULTURE VULTURE (Richard Quinn–Paul Cole) became the first English-trained winner of the French 1,000 Guineas since Fairy Legend in 1927.

18 MAY

1820 SAILOR won the Derby, and became the only horse ever to do so on his own birthday.

1880 'The dustiest Derby of all' says the Kentucky Derby's official history. 'Some estimates had the dust five inches deep.' However, with only 4 rivals to beat, FONSO churned through the dust, ridden by George Lewis, to win by 7 lengths for trainer Tice Hutsell at odds of 7-1.

1898 Racing began at Southwell on the Rolleston course.

1929 Twenty-one ran in the 55th Kentucky Derby, won by 2-1 chance CLYDE VAN DUSEN. Ridden by L. McAtee; trained by, would you believe, Clyde Van Dusen. This was the last gelding to win the race.

1930 Jockey LIAM WARD born. Rode Sindon to win the Irish Derby in 1958. Irish Champion in 1959 and 1961.

1947 Triple Grand National winning jockey BRIAN FLETCHER born. Partnered Red Alligator in 1968; Red Rum in 1973 and 1974.

1959 WILLIE CARSON made his racecourse debut, finishing 5th on Marija, trained by Gerald Armstrong, at Redcar.

1965 ERNIE JOHNSON, who in 1969 would partner Blakeney to Derby success, rode his first winner, Abel, trained by Ian Balding, at York.

1973 Jockey IAN JENKINSON rode his first winner at Windsor, then followed up with 5 more in the same week from as many rides.

1976 STEVE CAUTHEN rode a hat-trick at River Downs, USA, having made his racecourse debut just 6 days earlier.

1985 LESTER PIGGOTT, on Liquidator, took on JOHN FRANCOME on Shangoseer in a match on the flat at Warwick. Piggott won after Francome predicted: 'Whatever beats me will win.'

1986 EDDIE HIDE, who had over 2,500 winners during his career, rode his last official winner on American Liberty at Sha Tin, Hong Kong.

1988 MTOTO won the £15,000 Festival Stakes at Goodwood, but he and the rest of the 6 runners were disqualified and the race declared void. They had all taken the wrong course due to marker dolls being left in the wrong place. All bets voided, no prize-money paid.

1991 American raider FOURSTARS ALLSTARS, ridden by Mike Smith and trained by Irish-born Leo O'Brien, won the Irish 2,000 Guineas at 9-1 to become the first American-trained winner of an Irish Classic.

1992 PAT EDDERY passed Doug Smith's total of 3,111 winners when Source of Light won at Bath to put him 4th in the all-time British lists behind Sir Gordon Richards (4,870), Lester Piggott (4,406 at the time) and Willie Carson (3,331 at the time). The world record is held by Bill Shoemaker with 8,833.

19 MAY

1838   Promising jockey SAMUEL DAY, second son of top trainer-jockey John Barham Day, was just nineteen when he died after taking a fall while out hunting. He had already won the 1837 St Leger on Mango – the youngest jockey to do so.

1875   VINAIGRETTE was the first winner of the Kentucky Oaks, then run over one and a half miles. The filly collected winnings of $1,175.

1923   Twenty-one lined up for the 49th Kentucky Derby, won by 19.2–1 chance ZEV. Ridden by E. Sande; trained by D. J. Leary. Record prize-money of $53,000 was paid to the winner's connections.

1928   REIGH COUNT beat 21 others to win the 54th Kentucky Derby for jockey C. Lang and trainer B. S. Michell, paying $2.06 to a $1 stake. As a four-year-old Reigh Count came to England to win the Coronation Cup and finish runner-up in the Ascot Gold Cup.

1934   Arkle's first jockey, MARK HELY-HUTCHINSON, born.

1938   Trainer turned starter's assistant MAC TURNER born.

1939   Film director and owner LORD PEMBROKE born. Best horses include Athlete, Major Knight. Colours: turquoise; white sleeves; dark blue cap.

1941   Newmarket trainer MICK RYAN born. He trained Katies to win the Irish 1,000 Guineas and has also sent out the winners of every Dutch Classic. Trained for flamboyant owner and mega-gambler Terry Ramsden, who backed Mr Snugfit to win him a seven-figure sum with a series of enormous each-way bets in the 1986 National. Starting at 13–2 favourite, the horse came 4th.

1947   With 2 winners at Worcester GORDON RICHARDS set up a race-riding world record of 3,261 winners. The previous best had been British-born Champion Jockey of Belgium Sam Heapy's 3,260.

1955   Former jump jockey PADGE GILL, rider of Analog's Daughter and Belsir, born. Real name Padraic. First winner Crest Fallen at Naas, June 3 1982. One of the few jockeys to list the highlight of his career as a fall. The tumble in question was at the 23rd fence of the 1985 Grand National. He had been riding Royal Appointment.

1957   Jump jockey DAVID WILKINSON born.

1982   Ray Cochrane won at Goodwood for the first time when Carlton Opal scored.

1983   Deutschmark gave trainer Geoff Wragg his first Goodwood victory.

1989   Anti Matter won at Stratford to give trainer MARTIN PIPE his 200th winner of the season.

20 MAY

1784 The Derby was run over its current distance of one and a half miles for the first time. Colonel O'Kelly's 3-1 favourite Sergeant, ridden by John Arnull, won the 11-runner race.

1863 MACARONI's Derby victory was of vital importance to Newmarket, where he was trained by Jem Godding at his Palace House stables. The victory shattered the myth that the Heath at Newmarket was too firm for the working of horses in the summer and re-established the area's reputation. Ridden by T. Chaloner at 10-1. The victory also pleased the local vicar at All Saints Church who, for once, was allowed to celebrate with a peal of the bells which trainer Godding hated so much.

1879 LORD MURPHY, who went on to become the race's first winner to compete (without success) in England, triumphed at 11-10 in the Kentucky Derby, ridden by C. Shauer and trained by George Rice.

1887 Jockey MORNINGTON CANNON rode his first winner, Flint, in the City Bowl at Salisbury. He was thirteen. He received a present from trainer Charles Morton - a sovereign with which to buy himself sweets!

1930 RON SMYTH rode his first winner, Maryland Point, at Newmarket.

1935 Jockey BRIAN CONNORTON born.

1937 Owner LORD IVEAGH born. His Parnell won the Irish St Leger. Colours: terracotta; black seams, collar and cuffs; quartered cap.

1940 Trainer of Valley Victory and Fourstars Allstar LEO O'BRIEN born.

1963 Newmarket trainer DAVID COSGROVE born.

1964 A world record for the most races won by an owner in one day was set as Audley Farm, USA, saw 8 of its horses win at 6 different tracks: Aqueduct, Pimlico, Suffolk Downs, Lincoln Downs, Greenwood and Aksar-Ben.

1967 11-4 favourite DANELLA won the Thirsk Hunt Cup - the first success for rookie trainer Peter Makin.

1967 Jump jockey JONOTHAN LOWER born.

1967 Newmarket jockey JIMMY QUINN born. First winner Tarleton at Ayr on March 25 1985. Best horse ridden Amongst the Stars.

1972 BRIGADIER GERARD won his first race as a four-year-old at 1-4 in the Lockinge Stakes at Newbury.

1974 STUART WEBSTER's first winner was Hei Land Jamie at Pontefract.

1989 PAUL COOPER won £250,000 for a £16.50 tricast at Thirsk, as Miss Daisy (20-1), Halvoya (25-1) and Roysia Boy were 1, 2 and 3.

1992 Newton Abbot trainer GERALD PENFOLD stunned when his hunter-chaser Seal Prince, 9-4 favourite, collapsed and died after winning the 4.30 at Worcester - the very same race in which Penfold's best horse, John Sam, had been killed when favourite twelve months earlier.

21 MAY

1788 Both horses in a 2-horse, one-mile match at York carried an incredible 30st. Mr Maynard's mare ran (!) out the winner against Mr Baker's horse.

1801 Sir Charles Bunbury's ELEANOR became the first filly to win the Derby. Shortly before the race Cox, her trainer, died, having told the priest ministering to him: 'Depend upon it, that Eleanor is a hell of a mare.' The only recorded death-bed tip, perhaps? The day after the Derby Eleanor also won the Oaks.

1873 Jockey MORNINGTON CANNON was born. His unusual name might be explained by the fact that on the very same day his jockey father, Thomas, won at Bath on a horse called Mornington. The new-born would later ride 6 Classic winners.

1878 For the first time French *pari mutuel* machines were available for betting on the 4th Kentucky Derby. DAY STAR, ridden by J. Carter and trained by Lee Paul, was the winner over 8 others, at odds of 3–1.

1904 ORMONDE, which won the 1886 Triple Crown of 2,000 Guineas, Derby and St Leger for the 1st Duke of Westminster, was destroyed at stud in California. The horse's skeleton was returned to be exhibited in England.

1944 New York trainer MICHAEL DAGGETT born.

1945 The then Princess Elizabeth made her first visit to a racecourse, attending Ascot's Whit Monday meeting where she saw Sun Up become the first winner of an Ascot race to be trained by a woman. FLORENCE NAGLE was the trainer of the horse, though for 'official' purposes it was listed as being trained by her head lad, R. Brown.

1964 The last meeting took place at Lincoln racecourse.

1967 Jockey BILL ELLIOTT, who had retired the previous year, died of cancer, aged 52. He rode winners on the flat and over hurdles, winning the Ayr Gold Cup, Irish St Leger and the Ascot Stakes.

1967 Jockey DENNIS MCKAY rode his first winner. He went on to become Champion in Trinidad and Jamaica.

1988 CNOC NA CUILLE, the horse that carried the Princess Royal to her first victory over jumps, collapsed and died after finishing 3rd in a race at Warwick.

1990 Then playing for Newcastle, soccer striker MICK QUINN had his first winner as an owner when Land Sun scored at Wolverhampton, trained by former England international Mick Channon.

1993 American KING LEATHERBY, 60, became only the third trainer to reach a career total of 5,000 winners. The others are Jack Van Berg and Dale Baird.

22 MAY

1828   For the first time the Derby (run this year on a Thursday) finished in a dead-heat, but CADLAND, ridden by Jem Robinson, beat The Colonel (Bill Scott) in a run-off. The only other dead-heat took place in 1884, when St Gatien and Harvester shared the spoils, but there was no run-off.

1844   One of the most scandalous races of all time was run. Running Rein finished 1st in the Derby, but was subsequently disqualified when it was discovered that he was Maccabeus, and four years old. The race was awarded to Colonel Peel's Orlando, ridden by Nat Flatman. In the race itself the favourite The Ugly Buck was the victim of deliberate foul riding and the 2nd favourite, Ratan, was not only 'got at' but also pulled by jockey Sam Rogers. Another runner, Leander, was struck into and had to be destroyed, at which time investigations revealed that he, too, was older than three.

1867   HERMIT won the Derby. It snowed before and after the race. Owner Henry Chaplin won £120,000 by backing the 1,000-15 winner, while gambler the Marquis of Hastings lost £102,000 on the race. His success must have been extra sweet for Chaplin: he had been engaged to marry Lady Florence Paget who had run off with Hastings.

1877   BADEN-BADEN won the 3rd Kentucky Derby, ridden by W. Walker and trained by Ed Brown, at odds of 8-1. Leonard, 2nd at 7-5, became the race's first beaten favourite.

1935   Malton trainer JIMMY FITZGERALD born. His Forgive 'n' Forget won the 1985 Cheltenham Gold Cup.

1941   Trainer of Grey Desire DON PLANT born.

1955   Popular commentator and Timeform Director JIM MCGRATH born.

1958   Trainer MIKEY HEATON-ELLIS born.

1961   Jump jockey MARTIN HILL born.

1965   Jockey ANDREW WHITEHALL born.

1979   STEVE CAUTHEN rode his first Goodwood winner, Pit Your Wits, in the Tangmere Handicap.

1986   CASH ASMUSSEN rode his first Goodwood winner, Gulf King, in the Halnaker Stakes.

1989   Trainer LIAM CODD saddled his first runner on the flat, Madraco, at Bath. The horse not only won, but also set a new track record.

1990   Kawtuban gave WILLIE CARSON his 3,000th win in Britain,

1992   Yorkshire student Emily Debenham, aged 21, rode her first winner in America when Victory Leader won at Garden State, New Jersey.

1992   A jury awarded former jockey Benito Narvaez $4.4 million after ruling that officials at Tampa Bay Downs in Florida were responsible for the fall which left him paralysed in 1990.

1853   Perhaps America's greatest racing hero, LEXINGTON, won his first race, the Association Stakes, for three-year-olds at Lexington as Darley – he was renamed by new owner Richard Ten Broeck. After a great racing career the horse became the most successful stallion in US history, leading the sire list for 16 seasons.

1873   The first Preakness Stakes, run at Pimlico, attracted 7 runners for its one and a half-mile trip and was won by SURVIVOR by 10 lengths – still a record margin of victory.

1883   LEONATUS (9–5 favourite), ridden by W. Donohue, came home by 3 lengths in the 7-runner 9th Kentucky Derby. The horse won all 10 of his starts as a three-year-old, earning a total of $21,335.

1928   Trainer of triple Champion Hurdle winner Persian War (1968, 1969 and 1970) COLIN DAVIES born. Formerly a very useful racing driver, he completed the 1964 Grand National riding Claymore (66–1).

1928   Jockey WILLIE SNAITH born at Newcastle-upon-Tyne. He won the Sussex Stakes at Goodwood on Landau for the Queen in 1954. Nicknamed 'The Pocket Hercules'.

1936   Owner ROBERT SANGSTER born. His emerald green colours with royal blue sleeves, white cap and green spots have been associated with some fine horses including Derby winners The Minstrel and Golden Fleece. His Alleged was a dual Arc de Triomphe winner. Son of Vernon Sangster, the pools promoter, he first became a leading owner in 1977 when 15 of his horses won a total of £352,501.

1953   Melton Mowbray trainer KEVIN MORGAN born.

1955   Alexandra Park staged London's first evening meeting.

1966   Jockey TONY MURRAY rode his first winner, Guardian Oak, at Windsor.

1977   STEVE CAUTHEN fell from Bay Streak as the horse broke a foreleg at Belmont Park, New York. Steve broke his right wrist and three fingers.

1989   A bullock on the course delayed the 2.15 race at Beverley.

1990   LAFITTE PINCAY became the first jockey to take his mounts' earnings past $150 million prize-money in his career.

1992   Sharpitor and Sea Goddess won at Haydock and Love Returned scored at Lingfield to give trainer WILLIAM JARVIS his first treble.

1992   Jockey Omar Gonzalez wondered what was happening when his filly RED put on a bizarre display after winning at Palermo, Buenos Aires. She reared and plunged, eventually dropping Gonzalez, after which she jumped and bucked before collapsing in the sand. It took her fifteen minutes to return to normal. Trainer Enrique Solo blamed the incident on a lack of oxygen to the brain causing her to lose control of her limbs. Others were not so sure!

24 MAY

1798   SIR HARRY became the first Derby winner to be sired by a previous winner of the race, Sir Peter Teazle, which triumphed in 1787.

1848   SURPLICE won the Derby. The horse had been sold by Lord George Bentinck, much to his subsequent regret. Parliament took the day off after the same Bentinck proposed a motion that the House should adjourn for the day in order to attend the races. This Derby Day motion subsequently became an annual event, and the House duly adjourned for the next 40 years, when the political climate changed and the motion was defeated, although it continued to be moved into the early 1900s.

1871   BARON MEYER DE ROTHSCHILD, the first Jewish member of the Jockey Club, won the Derby_with Favonius.

1923   Owner DANIEL SCHWARTZ born. Part-owner of 1982 Derby winner Golden Fleece, Solinus, Danzatore and 1985 Irish Sweeps Derby winner Law Society. Colours: black and red.

1929   The Queen's representative at Ascot SIR PIERS BENGOUGH born. Owner of April Rose (winner of 6 chases) and Charles Dickens (3rd in 1974 Grand National). Colours: black; silver sleeves; green cap.

1933   Former Malton trainer TED CARTER born. Took out licence in 1977. Trained Rimondo, Megan's Boy.

1946   Taunton permit trainer JENNY HEMBROW born.

1947   The Earl of Harewood, a member of the Jockey Club since 1920 and senior steward in 1940, died aged 64.

1963   Jump jockey MARTIN BRENNAN born.

1968   Irish jockey JOHN EGAN born.

1968   Jockey GARY HIND, partner of Sesame, born.

1972   Having won the first-ever ladies' race under official rules just 18 days earlier MERIEL TUFNELL and Scorched Earth did it again in the 2nd such race, run at Folkestone over one and a half miles.

1989   Great race mare TRIPTYCH, placed in the Arc, Prix de Diane and Washington DC International, was killed after running into a truck at Claiborne Farm, Kentucky.

1992   German jockey Hans Strompen, aged 34, was killed in a fall in the Preis vom Rhein chase at Baden-Baden. His mount Sherlock Holmes fell and as the jockey hit the ground his helmet was knocked off and his mount rolled on top of him, fracturing his skull. He had ridden over 100 winners and was regularly used by Sherlock Holmes' trainer, Rudi Hinterberger.

1993   Jockey FRANKIE DETTORI, who had recently received a police warning for possession of drugs, was refused a licence to ride in Hong Kong.

1814   England had produced the great Eclipse – now the USA produced on this day a foal by Duroc out of Miller's Damsel, named AMERICAN ECLIPSE, which proved to be just that, retiring undefeated after beating all comers, including Henry in an epic confrontation over 3 heats at the Union course in New York for $20,000. The race produced a betting turnover of 10 times that amount.

1864   WILLIAM I'ANSON's Blair Athol (14–1) won the Derby. He was the last owner to have to contribute towards the cost of policing the course and paying the judge's fee.

1887   George Baird's 100-9 MERRY HAMPTON (I wonder what the name meant?) won the Derby having never previously seen a racecourse. He was the last maiden winner.

1898   JEDDAH was the first 100-1 shot to win the Derby.

1926   Breeder of Mtoto and Raffindale and owner JOHN MOORE born. Colours: pink and lilac quartered.

1941   Former Champion Apprentice BRIAN LEE born.

1945   Sedgefield trainer FRED WATSON born.

1953   Trainer of Grand National winner Mr Frisk KIM BAILEY born. Took out licence in 1978 and trained Kings Fountain and Shifting Gold.

1955   Dual purpose Derbyshire trainer JOHN MACKIE (real first name William) born. Responsible for Vanroy, Old Malton, Sacre d'Or.

1957   Devon-based trainer of Sporting Simon BRIAN MILLMAN born.

1960   Jockey NIGEL (FREDERICK) COLEMAN born. Won 1989 Triumph Hurdle on Ikdam, rode first winner Walmari at Stratford on October 24 1981.

1960   Owner-breeder of Cheeny's Brig BRUCE MACTAGGART born.

1984   PETER NIVEN rode his first winner, Loch Brandy, at Sedgefield.

1985   JULIE BOWKER, who listed her favourite recreation as 'training with St Helens rugby team', rode her first winner, at Doncaster on Misha at 3–1.

1991   JOIE DE SOIR, which had raced down the field at Southwell on November 30 1990, became the first horse to begin his career on the all-weather and go on to win a listed race when scoring in the Crawley Warren Heron Stakes at Kempton, returning 16–1. Trained by Fulke Johnson Houghton; ridden by Paul Eddery.

1992   ELIZABETH MAJOR, the prime minister's daughter, made her riding debut on 10–1 shot Milly Black at Huntingdon in the Mencap Support Stakes. She fell as she passed the post in 6th place in the two-mile flat race. She was later passed fit, and exhaustion and heat were blamed for the incident.

26 MAY

1869   A horse from the north won the Derby at Epsom – a very rare occurrence. PRETENDER (11–8 favourite) was ridden by Johnny Osborne and trained by Tom Dawson at the Tupgill stable, Middleham; he beat 21 rivals by a head.

1886   Ormonde gave FRED ARCHER his 5th and final Derby victory.

1908   Actor and owner ROBERT MORLEY born. He died on June 3 1992.

1916   Professional gambler ALEX BIRD born. He died in 1991.

1916   Owner-trainer of Derby winners Blakeney and Morston ARTHUR BUDGETT born. He also bred the pair who won in 1969 and 1973. Retired at the end of the 1975 season.

1925   Owner of Shutford stud TIM ROOTES born.

1928   Owner of 1967 Observer Gold Cup winner Vaguely Noble, LIONEL BROOK HOLLIDAY born. Colours: white, maroon hoop, armlets and cap.

1932   DOUG SMITH rode his first winner on Denia, owned and trained by his master, Major F. B. Sneyd, at Salisbury.

1933   Owner and gambler HORATIO BOTTOMLEY died. An MP, he brought off a £50,000 coup when Northern Farmer (20–1) won for him the 1899 Stewards Cup. He was once asked during a court case: 'You keep racehorses, I believe?' 'No,' he replied. 'They keep me.'

1937   MAJOR DERRICK CANDY, father of Henry, trained his first winner, his mother's five-year-old Mountain Ash, at Bath.

1943   DOUG SMITH rode his first winner for King George VI on Knight's Daughter at Newmarket.

1948   Jockey MARTIN O'HALLORAN born. He partnered Bachelors Hall and Celtic Ryde.

1956   Jockey JAMES EVANS, rider of Gambling Prince, born.

1988   Sixteen-year-old GREY TARQUIN won a handicap chase at Taunton.

1990   Former Champion Hurdler COMEDY OF ERRORS (1973 and 1975) was put down at the age of 24.

1990   Versatile trainer DAVID ELSWORTH became the first to complete the Irish Grand National (Desert Orchid) and Irish 1,000 Guineas double when In the Groove became his first Classic winner, at the Curragh.

1992   Manchester-born jockey MICHAEL RICHARDSON rode Maureen Star to victory in the Swedish 1,000 Guineas. He also boasts a Czech 1,000 Guineas success.

1992   1975 Derby winner GRUNDY died in Japan, aged twenty.

27 MAY

1835   Jockey BENJAMIN SMITH, winner of 6 St Legers, died aged 65 at Littlethorpe near Ripon. He once won a race on Ironside at York despite a broken leg after being kicked at the start.

1846   PYRRHUS THE FIRST won the first officially timed Derby in 2 minutes 55 seconds; jockey Bill Scott, riding Sir Tatton Sykes, was raging drunk and missed the break. His mount made up most of the lost ground only to go down by a neck.

1857   BLINK BONNY won the Derby at odds of 20-1. Two days later she also won the Oaks.

1906   Trainer of Bandalore and Happy Spring STAN WRIGHT born.

1911   Trainer of Crimson and The Plumber's Mate TED SMYTH born.

1917   Former Champion Jump Jockey JACK DOWDESWELL born.

1932   Writer, racegoer and punter JEFFREY BERNARD, of Low Life column fame, born.

1932   Trainer of Gentilhombre NEIL ADAM born. Lists his recreations as 'listening to the Inkspots and Nana Mouskouri'.

1936   MAHMOUD (100-8, Charlie Smirke up) won the Derby in fastest-ever time of 2 minutes 33⅘ seconds.

1948   Newmarket trainer of Mummy's Pleasure, Hawkley and Godstone PATRICK HASLAM born.

1950   Jockey PHILIP WALDRON born. Aldie gave him his first winner at Bath in 1969. Runner-up in the 1980 Derby on Master Willie.

1950   CHARLES COOPER lost his NH riding allowance at Hereford when piloting Paricutin to victory. All his 15 winning rides - 8 hurdles and 7 chases - were on the same horse.

1980   REDNAEL, ridden by Tommy Carmody, was trainer Tony Dickinson's final winner when scoring at Uttoxeter. His total was 562 in 13 seasons. Among his big winners were Santon Brig (1974 Scottish Champion Hurdle), Gay Spartan (1977 Sun Alliance Chase).

1981   WILLIE SHOEMAKER rode his 8,000th winner, War Allied, at Hollywood Park.

1985   SPEND A DUCK won a world record for one-race winnings of $2.6 million when landing the Jersey Derby in New Jersey, USA.

1990   A new world record was set as 196,517 paid to attend racing at Fuchu, Tokyo, where the Japanese Derby was being run.

1991   MARTIN PIPE broke yet another record as he passed his own best of 224 winners in a season when Myfor won at Devon.

1992   Owner CHARLES ST GEORGE died aged 66. Among his best horses were Arc winner Rheingold, St Leger winner Bruni and Oaks winner Ginevra. Colours: black; white chevron and cap. Born June 21 1925.

28 MAY

1839 The grandstand at Ascot was used for the first time, admission price 5s (25p).

1879 SIR BEVYS (jockey George Fordham; trainer J. Hayhoe of Newmarket) was the 20-1 winner of the 100th Derby. Owned by Baron Lionel Rothschild, who raced as Mr Acton. The poet laureate Alfred Tennyson staked £5 on the winner 'because Sir Bevys was the hero of one of my early poems'.

1884 ST GATIEN (100-8) and HARVESTER (100-7) dead-heated in the Derby. On the agreement of the owners there was no run-off although next day Harvester's owner, Sir John Willoughby, objected to St Gatien on the grounds of incorrect entry. The objection was later withdrawn.

1898 American jockey TOD (a nickname which was originally 'Toad') SLOAN rode 5 winners from 5 rides at Gravesend, USA.

1913 Popular TV racing host, he of the doffed hat, JOHN RICKMAN born.

1918 EDWARD ADDISON OBE, owner of Bold Connection and All Systems Go, born. Colours: light blue and red hoops, white cap, light blue spots.

1935 Former Sussex permit trainer SIR KENNETH KLEINWORT born.

1937 Owner-trainer of Pounentes BILLY MCGHIE born. Pounentes won the 1983 Mackeson Gold Cup at odds of 7-1.

1952 TULYAR (ridden by Charlie Smirke, trained by Marcus Marsh) was the Derby winner at 11-2 favourite, becoming the Aga Khan's 5th and final winner of the race. The second-largest field ever - 33 - turned out for the race.

1970 Jump jockey DAWSON LEES born.

1984 JOHN FRANCOME won on Don't Touch at Fontwell to pass Stan Mellor's record of 1,035 wins.

1990 MARTIN PIPE sent out 9 winners at 6 different meetings.

1993 Trainer OWEN BRENNAN saddled the first treble of his 25-year career - and his son Martin rode all three, at Towcester.

29 MAY

1769   The great ECLIPSE won the Noblemen's and Gentlemen's Plate at Ascot.

1857   Two days after winning the Derby, BLINK BONNY also won the Oaks. Her offspring Blair Athol was a Derby winner.

1860   The first meeting took place at Randwick, Sydney.

1863   Jockey GEORGE BARRETT born. In 1891 he rode Common to win the 2,000 Guineas, Derby and St Leger.

1872   The Derby was run over its present course for the first time and won by CREMORNE (ridden by Maidment, trained by W. Gilbert, 3-1 2nd favourite).

1915   Bloodstock agent JACK DOYLE born.

1925   Wetherby clerk of the course PAT FIRTH born.

1927   Former *Sunday Express* racing writer TOM FORREST born.

1930   Trainer of Dom Edino MAURICE AVISON born.

1939   LOVER'S FATE, ridden by Dave Dick, was perhaps an appropriately named winner of the 16-runner Golden Apple Stakes at Hurst Park, open only to horses with female owners (in this case, Mrs Thurston).

1945   Record-breaking trainer MARTIN PIPE, son of a bookmaker, born.

1948   Former Champion Amateur Jockey RICHARD SMITH born.

1959   Racecourse judge RICHARD HANCOCK born.

1967   VULMIDAS won for the 10th time in 13 starts at Wetherby.

1967   ROY EDWARDS rode 4 winners from 5 mounts at Uttoxeter.

1980   PETER SCUDAMORE married Marilyn Kington, sister of former jump jockey Robert.

1982   The great jumping mare DAWN RUN made her racecourse debut in an amateurs' flat race at Clonmel, finishing unplaced. She was ridden by owner Mrs Charmian Hill.

1990   Prince's Court (Kevin Mooney) was Fulke Walwyn's last winner as a trainer, at Uttoxeter.

1993   South African jockey BASIL MARCUS became the first jockey since 1979 to land a five-timer at Sha Tin, Hong Kong.

1993   New Zealand horse ROUGH HABIT, ridden by Jim Cassidy, became the first animal to win Brisbane's Doomben Cup for three consecutive years.

30 MAY

1877   FRED ARCHER scored the 1st of his 5 Derby victories on Silvio.

1945   Marlborough trainer RICHARD HANNON, Champion Handler of 1992, born. He has triplets – Henry, Richard and Elizabeth – with whom he was famed for playing a unique form of the gambling game Find the Lady when they were babies.

1953   Former Champion Lady Rider FRANCA VITTADINI born.

1953   Former jump jockeys, twins MARK and RICHARD FLOYD born.

1962   LESTER PIGGOTT suspended until July 28 after being adjudged to have made 'no effort to win the race' when riding Ione at Lincoln to finish 2nd behind stable companion Polly Macaw. Trainer R. C. Ward had his licence to train withdrawn.

1965   Jump jockey TONY CHARLTON born.

1967   CAPTAIN JOHN FAWCUS, Champion Amateur Jockey over jumps before the Second World War, died after a motoring accident on the way to Uttoxeter. He was 59. He won the Welsh National 4 times and the Scottish on 3 occasions, and also won the latter as a trainer, with Game Field in 1958.

1981   The whole of trainer JACK BERRY's family rode in public. He raced at Kempton, while his wife Jo and sons Alan and Martin were all in action at Ayr.

1983   Record British money winner PEBBLES, winner of the 1984 1,000 Guineas, made her debut, finishing unplaced at Sandown.

1989   MONICA DICKINSON saddled her last runner as a public trainer, Half Decent, which finished unplaced at Uttoxeter.

1992   For the first time a trotting race was included in a Tote jackpot. The 2,100-metre Prix du Tote, run at Lingfield and won by Turkey, contributed to the £7,869.30 payout for one lucky winning ticket.

1992   RICHARD DUNWOODY broke his own record for prize-money earned by a jump jockey in a single season when Four Trix at Stratford took his total to £923,974 – £1,501 up on the previous season.

1992   MARY REVELEY began the day needing to send out 2 winners to become the first woman to train 100 in a season. Watertight, ridden by Peter Niven at Market Rasen, duly obliged to put her on the 99 mark but her final runner on this last day of the season, Peacework in the End of Term Chase, shattered a hind leg and was put down.

1992   At the close of the jump season MARTIN PIPE was Champion, having trained 224 winners, while PETER SCUDAMORE had ridden 175.

1992   The Laughing Lord won over hurdles at Stratford to give trainer ARTHUR STEPHENSON a career total of 2,951 winners, setting a new record and overtaking Arthur Yates, who trained for 50 years from the late nineteenth century.

31 MAY

1764   GIMCRACK raced for the first time, beating 5 rivals at Epsom for a £50 prize. He won 26 of 36 races and is one of the few horses commemorated by a race, the important two-year-old Gimcrack Stakes at York, founded in 1846. Oddly enough, he only raced twice at York during his career, and was beaten on both occasions.

1785   GEORGE, PRINCE OF WALES, had his first runner at Ascot, Rosaletta, which finished 2nd to Colonel O'Kelly's Soldier in a 2-horse race. Later in the same day, however, she won an event run in 3 two-mile heats – a busy afternoon's work!

1863   The first Grand Prix de Paris was run over one mile 7 furlongs at Longchamp.

1865   GLADIATEUR (5-2 favourite), ridden by H. Grimshaw, became the first French winner of the Derby. The horse went on to win the 2,000 Guineas and St Leger.

1911   Horses and people were reportedly killed when a fierce torrential storm hit the racing town of Epsom.

1913   Founding secretary of the Jockeys' Association PETER SMITH born.

1944   Owner of Master Willie and Time Charter ROBERT BARNETT born. The former won the Benson & Hedges Gold Cup, Coral Eclipse and Coronation Cup and was runner-up in the Derby while the latter won the Oaks, Champion Stakes and King George VI and Queen Elizabeth Diamond Stakes. Colours: cherry; black sash; primrose and white quartered cap.

1945   *Daily Mirror* tipster CHARLES FAWCUS born.

1955   Alabama-born trainer in New York THOMAS KEITH BOHANNAN born.

1961   The Derby was won by PSIDIUM, bred in Ireland by Mrs Arpad Plesch. Ridden by a French jockey; trained in England. Psidium was by a French sire out of an Italian mare. Truly a cosmopolitan winner.

1965   Saratoga's attendance record of 73,435 was established.

1970   ARKLE was put down at the age of thirteen.

1975   LESTER PIGGOTT rode his 3,000th British winner at Kempton.

1980   BOB CHAMPION rode his first winner since defeating cancer and his first-ever on the flat when Ripon scored at Fairhill, USA.

1988   The first betting shop on a British Rail station was opened by the Arthur Prince company at Fenchurch Street station. It was banned from offering odds about trains running late!

1991   ALEX GREAVES became the first woman jockey in Britain to ride out her claim, with a double at Hamilton Park on Love Jazz and Mac Kelty, bringing her total of winners to 75 since she got off the mark in December 1989.

1 JUNE

1881 IROQUOIS became the first American-bred horse to win the Derby. He was owned by tobacco millionaire Pierre Lorillard and trained by Jacob Pinkus at Newmarket's Terrace House stable, which eventually became the headquarters of Tattersalls. Fred Archer rode the horse.

1904 GEORGE THURSBY became the first amateur rider to be placed in the Derby, finishing 2nd on John O'Gaunt. He repeated the achievement on Picton two years later. Nobody has done it since.

1929 Owner of Shoemaker and Formidable PETER GOULANDRIS born. Colours: emerald green and royal blue halved horizontally; blue sleeves; quartered cap.

1931 Trainer of A.20 FERGUS SUTHERLAND born.

1933 Trainer NEVILLE BYCROFT born (Gunner Mac, Contact Kelvin).

1943 Dual purpose jockey from 1958 to 1976 turned trainer KEN WHITE born. Nicknamed 'Stoker'. As a jockey he partnered 1975 Champion Hurdler Comedy of Errors to triumphs in the Irish Sweeps Hurdle and Scottish Champion Hurdle. Also rode Chatham to win the 1970 Mackeson Gold Cup.

1947 Former jump jockey turned stud owner RICHARD EVANS born.

1952 Jump jockey RAY GOLDSTEIN born. Rode his first winner, Turk, in 1977 and has partnered Royal Stag and Flying Ziad.

1953 Jockey GORDON RICHARDS was awarded a knighthood in the Queen's Coronation Honours List.

1955 Knock Hill's jockey GEORGE MERNAGH born.

1957 NICKLEBY, at Stratford, was BRYAN MARSHALL'S last winner as a jockey. He rode 517 jump winners in Britain and was Champion Jockey in 1947–48.

1959 Trainer STEVE KETTLEWELL born.

1967 JOE MERCER rode a treble at Brighton as The Rift, Rebel Call and Matadora were successful.

1969 Newmarket trainer WILLIAM O'GORMAN died aged 56. Like his son now, he specialised in sprinters and won the 1958 Stewards' Cup with Epaulette and the King's Stand Stakes with Drum Beat and Majority Blue.

1982 JOHN FRANCOME rode his 120th winner of the season, Buckmaster (John Edwards), to level his score with the injured Peter Scudamore. Francome then quit for the season in order to share the Championship with Scu. Ten years and several more Championships for Scu later, Francome admitted, 'I now regret that decision.'

1985 DERMOT WELD sent out 5 winners at Phoenix Park where, SHERKHRAINE won to become the first winner sired by Shergar.

2 JUNE

1871 Jockey GEORGE STEVENS, 38, who rode a record 5 Grand National winners, was injured while riding his hack up Cleeve Hill at Cheltenham. His hat blew off and frightened the horse, which ran away with him. It threw him off, he hit his head, and died next day.

1920 Irish racing commentator MICHAEL O'HEHIR born.

1920 MAJOR GILES LODER became the last serving officer (Scots Guards) to own a Derby winner when his Spion Kop did it at 100-6.

1930 Newbury trainer GAY KINDERSLEY born. Handler of Pactolus and Traumatic. Rode successfully as an amateur until breaking his back in 1965, although he defied doctors to ride again. Champion Amateur Jump Jockey in 1959-60.

1940 Trainer JACK CLARK born.

1945 Former jockey CHARLES WOOD died in his 91st year. He partnered St Gatien to a Derby dead-heat with Harvester in 1884, and in 1887 was Champion Jockey.

1954 LESTER PIGGOTT rode his first Classic winner – 33-1 Derby victor Never Say Die, trained by Joe Lawson at Newmarket.

1957 Irish trainer KEVIN CONNOLLY, who moved to Macau, born.

1960 Former jump jockey turned trainer JAYO KINANE born.

1960 INDIGENOUS set the fastest time recorded for 5 furlongs when clocking 53.6 seconds, hand-timed, at Epsom.

1982 PHILIP BLACKER retired after a jumping career of 327 winners, including the Whitbread Gold Cup on the Stan Mellor-trained Royal Mail. Became a successful sculptor.

1982 Jonacris and Havenwood supplied PAUL FELGATE with his first training double, ridden by Mick Miller, at Ripon.

1982 GOLDEN FLEECE (3-1 favourite) won the Derby for jockey Pat Eddery, trainer Vincent O'Brien and owner Robert Sangster. Commented Eddery: 'He's the best I've ever sat on.'

1984 Trainer MICHAEL DICKINSON failed to win with his last British runner over jumps, Compton Lad, at Stratford.

1988 TONY BUCKMASTER (42) shocked the Queen when he 'streaked' at the Epsom Derby in front of the Royal Box.

1993 On the 40th anniversary of the Coronation, The Queen's Enharmonic, ridden by Frankie Dettori, was a 12-1 winner at Epsom.

1993 Odds-on favourite Tenby displaced in the Derby; one punter lost a bet of £112,000.

3 JUNE

1824 JEM ROBISON won the Derby on Cedric to launch an amazing bet he had made. He followed it up by riding the winner of the Oaks and completed his winning treble by getting married on the Saturday.

1840 QUEEN VICTORIA, accompanied by the Prince Consort, made her only visit to the Derby, won by 50-1 chance Little Wonder.

1874 GEORGE FREDERICK won the Derby at 9-1. The result clobbered the bookies as it was the ninth birthday of Prince George Frederick.

1885 HARRY CUSTANCE became the first man to ride the winner of the Derby (Thormanby (1860), Lord Lyon (1866), George Frederick (1874)) and also to start the race.

1908 SIGNORINETTA won the Derby at odds of 100-1. Two days later she proved it was no fluke by also winning the Oaks.

1914 VICTOR SMYTH rode his first winner, Dick Whittington, at Manchester. He went on to ride Brownhylda to win the 1923 Oaks and to train 1952 1,000 Guineas winner Zabara.

1921 Jockey TOMMY CUSACK, who partnered Secret Service, born.

1930 Author and point-to-point rider GEOFFREY SALE born.

1947 One of the turf's most fearless gamblers, CHARLES HANNAN, died aged 88. He once lost £10,000 on a game of darts.

1950 Five-year-old CITATION became the money-spinner of all time when winning his 32nd race from 45 starts at Albany, California, taking his total to £330,225 ($1,085,760). Stymie (£328,030, or $918,485 for 131 races) held the old record.

1952 GOLDEN CHANCE (Fred Rimell) was Barry Hills' first ride, finishing 10th at Birmingham.

1989 Jump jockey PETER SCUDAMORE completed a record-breaking season with 221 wins to his credit. Trainer Martin Pipe had 208.

1990 US jockey CHRIS MCCARRON broke both legs and an arm in a fall at Hollywood Park. He returned to the saddle on August 23.

1990 The 1888 Ascot Gold Cup was stolen in a raid on the Co. Kilkenny home of former Turf Club senior steward Major Victor McCalmont. Police later said they believed it had been melted down. Its estimated value was some £70,000.

1992 DR DEVIOUS, ridden by John Reid and trained by Peter Chapple-Hyam, won the Derby. His last outing had seen him finish 7th in the Kentucky Derby. The 8-1 2nd favourite was only the 2nd horse to try the 'Durby-Derby double' – the first, Bold Arrangement, was 2nd in the US and unplaced in the Epsom equivalent in 1989. RODRIGO DE TRIANO, Lester Piggott's mount, was at 13-2 the longest-priced Derby favourite since 7-1 chance Lavandin won in 1956. Rodrigo was unplaced.

4 JUNE

1794 The smallest field ever to contest the Derby, just 4, produced a 6–1 winner in the shape of DAEDALUS.

1844 The Emperor of Russia, Nicholas I, and the King of Saxony attended Ascot races where they saw ALICE HAWTHORN, winner of 52 races in 72 starts, win the Queen's Vase.

1913 Suffragette EMILY DAVISON brought down the King's horse, Anmer, when she ran on to the course during the Derby. She later died in Epsom Hospital. The race was 'won' by Craganour, which was later disqualified, the race being awarded to 100–1 shot Aboyeur.

1918 Gainsborough (8–13) was the first Derby winner to be owned by a woman, LADY JAMES DOUGLAS, who had already made history when the same horse won the 2,000 Guineas, making her the first woman to win a Classic in her own colours.

1919 GRAND PARADE became only the 2nd black horse to win the Derby, 106 years after the 1st, Smolensko.

1924 TOMMY WESTON, aged 21, rode 9–2 favourite Sansovino to win the 27-runner Derby for trainer George Lambton. He was given £1,000 by owner Lord Derby, and within an hour was celebrating with his wife – on a wooden merry-go-round horse on Epsom Downs.

1933 Levy Board chairman SIR JOHN SPARROW born.

1937 Owner of Oaks runner-up Frontier Goddess CHRISTOPHER SPENCE born. Colours: emerald green; black striped sleeves; black cap.

1938 JIMMY STOUT rode Pasteurised to win America's Belmont Stakes for trainer G. M. Odom, who became only the second man to have both trained and ridden winners of the race (Delhi in 1904).

1947 Trainer RICHARD LEE born. Handler of Miss Nero and Delius. Rode as an amateur, 'but not as successfully as my wife, Carol'.

1948 BOB CHAMPION, MBE, born. Fairytale Grand National winner when partnering former crock Aldaniti to victory after beating cancer. Rode 421 winners under rules in England. Now a trainer.

1949 NIMBUS won the Derby by a head from Amour Drake – and it was the first time the race was decided by a photo-finish camera. The winner was bred by bookmaker William Hill, ridden by Charlie (real name Edward) Elliott, trained by G. Colling and returned 7–1.

1982 DEREK KENT left his Sussex stables to train in Hong Kong. His former stable jump jockey Peter Haynes took over.

1983 ALEC STEWART sent out his first winner as a trainer, OPALE, at Catterick.

1985 WILLIAM JARVIS sent out his first winner as a trainer, DORSET COTTAGE, at Beverley.

5 JUNE

1901 Volodyovski became the first Derby winner to be bred by a woman, LADY MEUX.

1902 American jockey DANNY MAHER rode Lord Wolverton's Osboch to victory in the first running of the Coronation Cup, formerly the Epsom Cup, renamed to commemorate the crowning of King Edward VII. George Challoner trained the winner.

1907 ORBY (100-9), from the Colonel McCabe stables at Glencairn, Co. Dublin, became the first Irish-trained Derby winner.

1907 Owner of Nearly a Hand and Righthand Man MURIEL HAGGAS born. Colours: white; black braces; red cap.

1907 JIMMIE LEE rode 6 winners from 6 mounts at Churchill Downs, USA: Bucket Brigade (5-1), Mattie H. (5-1), Woolstone (3-1), Alencon (7-5), Wing Ting (9-1) and Foreigner (3-1).

1927 Trainer of Red Desire, Brython and Barry's Gamble TOMMY 'SQUEAK' FAIRHURST born. Trains at Middleham, North Yorkshire.

1930 Official handicapper ANTHONY ARKWRIGHT born.

1931 LADY TRACE clocked $55^1/5$ seconds (40.76mph) over 5 furlongs at Epsom – a record for a two-year-old. It was equalled by Scarlet Pimpernel (1953), Cerise (1954) and Kerrabee (1960).

1937 Barnsley trainer STEVE NORTON, handler of Goodbye Shelley, born.

1937 The Belmont Stakes was won by WAR ADMIRAL, ridden by C. Kurtser in a new track record for the one and a half-mile trip of 2 minutes $28^1/5$ seconds.

1938 Former champion jockey in Melbourne ROY HIGGINS born.

1939 Two of the first 3 home in the Park Chase at Napier Park, Hastings, New Zealand, were ridden by jockeys other than those who set out on them! Wykemist finished 1st but the 2nd horse, Kikiroki, had fallen, only to be remounted by spectator, Mr Marquand, while the 3rd, Begorrah, which had fallen and was loose, was caught by a Mr Greene, who rode him in.

1946 South African jockey JOHN GORTON born. Rode his first winner in England in 1966. Sleeping Partner gave him a Classic success when winning the 1969 Oaks. In 1974 he retired to train in South Africa.

1949 Rider of Master H. JOHN WESTON born.

1967 Jockey JOHNNY SEAGRAVE enjoyed himself at Edinburgh, where his 6 rides produced 4 winners, a 2nd and a 3rd.

1971 The 103rd running of the Belmont Stakes was won by PASS CATCHER (ridden W. Blum; trained E. Yowell) returning odds of over 33-1.

1982 TIME CHARTER notched a first Classic victory for trainer Henry Candy and jockey Billy Newnes when she won the Oaks.

6 JUNE

1894 LORD ROSEBERY, the Prime Minister, saw his horse Ladas win the Derby at the shortest odds ever, 2-9.

1905 Trainer of Pandofell and Cawston's Pride FREDDIE MAXWELL born. Pandofell won him the Queen's Prize, Yorkshire Cup, Ascot Gold Cup and Doncaster Cup in 1961. Retired 1977, died June 2 1991.

1919 The great American horse MAN O'WAR ran and won for the first time at Belmont Park. He was beaten just once in 21 starts.

1921 GORDON RICHARDS rode the first double of his career on John Charles and Spiral Spin at Lewes.

1923 STEVE DONOGHUE rode the Derby winner for the 3rd consecutive year. Papyrus (100-15) completed the hat-trick begun by Humorist in 1921 and Captain Cuttle in 1922.

1934 The Maharajah of Rajpipla's WINDSOR LAD (15-2) won the Derby ridden by 27-year-old Charlie Smirke, whose licence had been returned only the previous October after being warned off for five years following an incident in which his mount had failed to start in a race.

1945 CLAUDE 'THE PUNTERS' PAL' DUVAL, racing writer of the *Sun*, born. Once forced to run naked around the outside of the Jockey Club HQ by his editor for having unsuccessfully predicted the outcome of an appeal to the Jockey Club.

1953 Jockey GORDON RICHARDS finally managed to win the Derby - on Pinza - for the only time. It was his 28th and final mount in the race.

1962 Seven horses fell in the Derby as the field came down Tattenham Hill. King Canute II broke a leg. The 6 jockeys on the other fallers all ended up in hospital. The race was won by Larkspur, trained by Vincent O'Brien, ridden by Aussie Neville Sellwood, who was killed the following November when his mount, the ironically named Lucky Seven, fell at Maisons-Laffitte.

1979 TROY, ridden by Willie Carson and trained by Dick Hern, won the 200th Derby.

1987 HENRY CECIL set a record for the fastest half-century of wins in a Flat season when Space Cruiser won at Haydock. However, one of his winners was later disqualified so Gatchina's win at Goodwood on June 9 became the record-breaker.

1991 YVONNE DURANT became the first woman to ride the winner of a Norwegian Classic when Helensville won the Norsk 1,000 Guineas.

1992 USER FRIENDLY gave 45-year-old jockey George Duffield his first Classic winner when she won the Oaks for trainer Clive Brittain, beating the smallest field for 76 years.

7 JUNE

1808 A £50 plate race produced an extraordinary result as Honest Harry, Miss Decoy, Beningborough and Peteria ran a quadruple dead-heat.

1864 Run over one and a half miles, America's first Derby was run at Paterson - while the Civil War was still in progress. The Jersey Derby, as it was known, was won by NORFOLK, owned by Theodore Winters of California and trained by Mr Ansell, which defeated 11 opponents in front of a crowd of 10,000.

1936 The world's most prolific trainer, JACK VAN BERG, born. Sent out his 5,000th winner, Art's Chandelle, at Arlington Park, Chicago, on July 15 1987. Best horse the Nebraskan has trained was Alysheba.

1947 PEARL DIVER (40-1, ridden by G. Bridgland) won as the Derby was run on a Saturday for the first time during peace-time.

1952 French trainer PATRICK BIANCONE born. His best horses were All Along and Sagace, both of which won the Arc de Triomphe.

1957 CARROZZA (100-8), leased from the National Stud, gave the Queen her first Classic win, ridden to victory in the Oaks by Lester Piggott.

1960 Trainer of Minster Son (winner of the 1988 St Leger) and Prince of Dance NEIL GRAHAM born.

1961 Jockey DEREK BROWN born. Gained his first win as a professional on Floyd at Newbury on July 19 1985.

1975 WALLY WHARTON, rode his first winner, Persian King (20-1), at Warwick.

1986 Trainer DERMOT WELD and jockey MICK KINANE won the first 5 races at Phoenix Park - finished 2nd, beaten 1/2 length, in the 6th.

1986 DANZIG CONNECTION gave trainer Woody Stephens his 5th consecutive victory in the Belmont Stakes.

1989 TERIMON, ridden by Michael Roberts and trained by Clive Brittain, finished 2nd in the Derby at the immense odds of 500-1 - the longest-priced horse to be placed in the race. The winner was 11-8 favourite Nashwan, ridden by Willie Carson.

1989 BILL SHOEMAKER rode his only winner at Epsom.

1990 QUEST FOR FAME (7-1) won the Derby to give first-season trainer ROGER CHARLTON an English-French (Sanglamore) Derby double.

1992 FRANKIE DETTORI gained his 2nd Classic victory when he partnered POLYTAIN to win the French Derby. His first was on Temporal in the 1991 German Derby. Polytain also created history by becoming the first horse to graduate from the claiming ranks to land this prize.

1992 Hong Kong punters staked a record £14.3 million on the 9th race at Sha Tin.

8 JUNE

1921 Owner-trainer of Rock Saint GEOFFREY GREGSON born.

1933 Owner of 1991 Grand National winner Seagram SIR ERIC PARKER born. Colours: light blue; white cross-belts; red cap.

1945 Worcestershire trainer ROD JUCKES born. Best horse trained Rachel's Delight.

1945 Lord Derby's SUN STREAM (6–4) added the Oaks to her earlier success in the 1,000 Guineas.

1946 W. A. (ARTHUR) STEPHENSON sent out his first winner as a trainer when he partnered his own horse T.O.D. to victory in the Whitsuntide Open Hunters' Chase at Hexham.

1952 JONATHAN PEASE born. Trainer of Golden Pheasant, Roman Prose and Swink, he has sent out a string of big-race winners in France, where he is based, and has also worked in England, Australia, New Zealand and America.

1953 Owner and rock singer BONNIE TYLER born.

1953 Jockey FRANK BARLOW broke his leg in a fall from Widow Lady at Nottingham and missed the rest of the season.

1956 GREVILLE STARKEY rode his first winner, Russian Gold, at Pontefract for Tom Jones.

1985 CREME FRAICHE (5–2) became the first gelding to win the Belmont Stakes when beating 10 opponents for jockey E. Maple and trainer Woody Stephens.

1989 Eleven-year-old sprinter RAPID LAD won at Beverley for the 11th time.

1991 JET SKI LADY, 50–1, was the 10-length winner of the Oaks, trained by Jim Bolger and ridden by Christy Roche. The horse equalled the longest odds returned for an Oaks winner.

1991 JULIE KRONE became the first woman jockey to ride in the Belmont Stakes, finishing 9th of 11 on Subordinated Debt as 4.1–1 chance Hansel won for jockey J. D. Bailey and trainer Frank Brothers.

1992 JAMIE OSBORNE won the 8-nation World Jump Jockey Championship in Australia. Ireland's Anthony Powell was 2nd.

1992 It was revealed that Cheltenham had been staging races over the wrong distances for nearly twenty years. The Gold Cup and the Champion Hurdle had both been run over half a furlong longer than their official distances. The errors came to light in a full remeasurement of Cheltenham and other courses carried out the previous year. Also affected was the Whitbread Gold Cup, which had been run over three miles 5^{1}/$_{2}$ furlongs instead of the advertised three miles 5 furlongs 18 yards.

9 JUNE

1888   SIR DIXON, owned by brothers Phil and Mike Dwyer, won the Belmont Stakes. It was their 3rd consecutive winner of the American Classic and 5th in the previous 6 runnings. The horse was ridden by J. McLaughlin, who also rode the other 4 victors.

1945   Trainer the HON. GEORGE LAMBTON, born in 1860, sent out his final winner, Golden Cloud, at Newmarket. He trained 13 Classic winners, including Sansovino (1924) and Hyperion (1933) in the Derby. His 1924 autobiography *Men and Horses I Have Known* is an acknowledged classic of racing literature.

1948   RON SMYTH's first winner as a trainer was Turkestan, at Brighton.

1953   Beckhampton trainer FRED DARLING died at the age of 69 with 19 Classic successes to his credit. Among them were 7 Derby winners. He died leaving an estate valued at £99,082.

1955   Jump jockey STEVE SMITH ECCLES born. First winner October 1975. Rode See You Then to a Champion Hurdle treble.

1959   Newmarket trainer ADRIAN LEE born.

1962   At 22, CREGGMORE BOY was the oldest recorded runner in a race as he finished 4th in the Furness Selling Chase at Cartmel.

1964   Jump jockey EAMON MURPHY, whose career highlight was riding a treble including the Imperial Cup for the Queen Mother on Insular at Sandown, born.

1965   Northern jockey ANDREW BACON born.

1967   Trainer BILL ELSEY celebrated his first Classic win as Edward Hide rode Pia to win the Oaks at 100–7.

1973   SECRETARIAT completed the US Triple Crown, winning the Belmont Stakes by 31 lengths in a record time of 2 minutes 24 seconds.

1979   TUDOR CHIEF won at Naas to give jockey Patrick Shanahan his first success.

1979   Jockey MARK DWYER rode his first winner, Colneagh Emperor, at Limerick Junction.

1979   Flamboyant trainer ROD SIMPSON sent out his first winner, Lady Tartown, at Warwick, ridden by David Atkinson.

1983   PEBBLES, who went on to become the record British prize-money winner, won for the first time in the Kingsclere Stakes at Newbury, ridden by Philip Robinson. Trained by Clive Brittain, she won the 1,000 Guineas, Eclipse, Champion Stakes and Breeders' Cup Turf.

1986   WILLIE CARSON rode his 2,500th British winner, Flower Bowl, at Leicester.

1990   Irish-trained GO AND GO (Dermot Weld–Michael Kinane) was the first European-trained winner of the Belmont Stakes in the USA.

10 JUNE

1868   GENERAL DUKE won the second running of the Belmont Stakes and prize-money of $2,800.

1871   Harry Bassett, ridden by W. Miller, won the Belmont Stakes. Believed to be the first race on which an American bookmaker opened an ante-post book. James E. Kelly obliged in the preceding winter.

1902   Jockey HARRY WRAGG born in Sheffield. Nicknamed the 'Head Waiter' because of his famed late challenges in races. He rode 13 Classic winners. During his 27-year career as a jockey he rode 1,762 winners from 11,658 mounts in Great Britain and Ireland. In 1947 he began training at Abington Place, Newmarket. He trained 5 Classic winners including Psidium in the 1961 Derby.

1935   First trainer of 1984 Cheltenham Gold Cup winner Burrough Hill Lad JIMMY HARRIS born. His riding career ended when he sustained a broken back after a fall at Huntingdon in 1971. He went on to train at Melton Mowbray from a wheelchair.

1935   Irishman HARRY BEASLEY rode Mollie (unplaced) in the Corinthian Plate at Baldoyle, Dublin, at the tender age of 83.

1937   Jockey turned trainer EDDIE HARTY born. He rode Highland Wedding to win the 1969 Grand National. Also rode in the Olympic Games in 1960. Best horses trained included Fifty Dollars More.

1939   Pulborough trainer GUY HARWOOD born. Rode 14 winners under NH rules. As a trainer won the 2,000 Guineas with To-Agori-Mou (1981) and the 1986 Arc de Triomphe with Dancing Brave.

1944   Brownie, Bossuet and Wait a Bit finished in a triple dead-heat at Aqueduct, USA, in the Carter Handicap.

1960   Jockey EDDIE HARTY married Patricia on his 23rd birthday.

1966   Hotly fancied for the forthcoming July Handicap in Durban, South Africa, SEA COTTAGE was shot at and hit in the leg by a gunman later sentenced to imprisonment. Incredibly enough the horse recovered in time to run, albeit managing only 4th.

1967   JACK JARVIS, trainer of 9 Classic winners, was knighted.

1989   ALIYSA (11–10) favourite, owned by the Aga Khan, won the Oaks, beating Snow Bride by 3 lengths. She lost the race 528 days later when the Jockey Club disqualified her for having a prohibited substance in her system. Legal arguments over the case raged on for years and the Aga Khan removed all his horses from Britain in protest.

1992   Jockey DAVID NICHOLLS was banned for 2 successive 4-day periods after being hauled before the stewards following 2 consecutive races at Hamilton's appropriately titled 'Saints and Sinners' meeting.

11 JUNE

1907 Owner-breeder of 1971 Derby and Arc winner Mill Reef PAUL MELLON born. Colours: black with gold cross front and back; black cap with gold stripe.

1926 Owner of Harmon JOHN ASPINALL born.

1940 French trainer FRANCOIS DOUMEN, handler of King George VI Chase winners Nupsala and The Fellow, born. Top gentleman rider in France for 10 years with 100 wins to his credit.

1944 Apprentice HUBERT JONES became the first jockey to ride 8 winners on a single programme when he achieved the feat from 13 mounts at Caliente, California.

1946 Trainer of Cheltenham Gold Cup winners Burrough Hill Lad and Garrison Savannah and Grand National hero Corbiere JENNY PITMAN born. She rode winners as a point-to-pointer. Formerly married to Richard Pitman. Born Jenny Harvey.

1955 Jump jockey turned clerk of the course SAM MORSHEAD born. His first ride (1973) was a winner; his first ride over fences was a winner; his first 2 rides for Fred Rimell were winners.

1962 English jockey in Italy DAVID PRICE born. First winner Acushla McRea at Windsor in August 1981.

1968 Irish jockey WARREN O'CONNOR, rider of Kooyonga, born.

1977 SEATTLE SLEW (2-5 favourite), ridden by J. Cruguet for trainer William H. Turner Jr, won the Belmont Stakes and completed the Triple Crown. Innkeeper John Esposito, whose tavern conveniently bordered Belmont Park's stable area, painted his picket fence in the winner's colours – a tradition which he then kept up every year.

1983 The largest field to contest the Belmont Stakes, 15, turned out as 13-5 chance CAVEAT, ridden by Laffit Pincay Jr and trained by Woody Stephens, won the race.

1988 For the first time a woman saddled a placed horse in the Belmont Stakes. Diane Carpenter's KINGPOST finished 2nd to winner Risen Star (21-10), ridden by Eddie Delahoussaye and trained by Louie J. Roussel III.

1989 PHIL BULL, founder of the Timeform ratings service, died aged 79.

1989 Scu beat Shoe when Champion Jump Jockey Peter Scudamore defeated all-time winning-most flat jockey Willie Shoemaker 2-1 in a best-of-3 charity challenge series at Cheltenham. Both jockeys carried 10st 7lbs (Shoe normally rode at 7st 7lbs or less) and there was no betting on the races, held on a Sunday.

1990 Australian jockey GAVAN EADES was suspended for six months for spitting at apprentice jockey Ricky Maund as their horses pulled up after the Swan Hill Cup, which Maund had won on Mr Classic.

12 JUNE

1729   In his ancient tome *An Historical List of Horse Matches Run*, JOHN CHENY records details of a meeting at Oswestry, Shropshire, at which 'a free purse of 30 guineas was run for weight 12st, 3 guineas entrance and won by Lord Molyneux's Bay Gelding Tickle Me Quickly'.

1825   Brazil's first race meeting took place at Praia Vermelha, Botafogo.

1884   Trainer Mat Dawson declared that his great horse ST SIMON had more 'electricity' about him than any other horse he had ever known. So it couldn't have come as a shock to him when the animal romped home by 20 lengths in the Ascot Gold Cup as a three-year-old. St Simon went on to become an outstanding stallion: 9 times Champion Sire. The horse died at the age of 27, after which his skeleton was presented to the Natural History Museum.

1917   Rider of Distel BOB O'RYAN born.

1930   Turf Club member CHRISTOPHER GAISFORD ST LAWRENCE born.

1932   Frome trainer DON TUCKER born.

1936   Trainer of Goldhill's Pride TOMMY CRAIG born.

1938   Trainer of Set Point and Sheriff's Star and wife of former England cricketer Colin Cowdrey LADY HERRIES born.

1940   This year's Derby was scheduled to be run at Newbury, but the meeting never took place and the Derby was run at Newmarket instead. PONT L'EVEQUE won it.

1945   Jockey ALFRED GIBERT born. Best horses ridden include 1971 Derby 3rd, Irish Ball, Tennyson and Green Forest.

1964   Trainer IAN BALDING sent out his first winner, ATHOLL, at Sandown.

1982   BARRY HILLS sent out his 800th winner when Reves Celestes (Robert Street) won at Bath.

1982   Jockey BOB CHAMPION was awarded the MBE, and OSSIE FLETCHER, who served for 23 years as the editor of the *Sporting Life*, received the OBE in the Queen's Birthday Honours.

1982   JOHN CARR rode his first winner, Jolly Burglar, at Leicester.

1992   The 8-race card at Canterbury Downs, USA, was something of a family affair as jockey DAVID ESSMAN rode 2 winners but was outshone by his wife KOKIE WARHOL, who rode 4.

13 JUNE

1769 ECLIPSE won the King's Plate at Winchester.

1913 PRINCE EUGENE won the Belmont Stakes for trainer James Rowe, who recorded his 8th winner of the race.

1927 Trainer of A Kinsman JOHN BROCKBANK born.

1932 Wiltshire trainer ROBERT SHEPHERD born. Best horse trained, Fearless Imp.

1948 Jockey SANDY BARCLAY born. Once retained by Sir Noel Murless, he also rode for the Queen. Champion Apprentice in 1966. Rode Caergwrle to win the 1968 1,000 Guineas and Lupe to win the 1970 Oaks.

1954 Jockey GEORDIE RAMSHAW rode his first winner, Fairy Princess, at Lingfield.

1954 Irish jockey TONY QUINN born. Partnered Twinburn.

1958 Champion jump jockey PETER SCUDAMORE born – on a Friday, although he claims not to be superstitious. Rode first winner in 1979, and retired in 1993.

1961 Epsom trainer SIMON DOW born. In 1976 he was rated the top UK boy athlete over 800 metres with a time of 1 minute 58.5 seconds. Best horses trained include Highland Bounty and Itsagame.

1975 Friday the thirteenth was bad news for jockey EDWARD HIDE, who broke his leg in a bad fall from Bewerley at York. At the time he was three winners ahead of Lester Piggott in the title race. He never won it during his career although he finished 2nd in 1957.

1976 A lucky Friday the thirteenth for US jockey PAT DAY, whose 7 mounts at Churchill Downs produced 5 winners.

1992 Irish trainer JIM BOLGER landed his 1,000th winner when Wangola won the Eadestown EBF race at Naas.

14 JUNE

1843   The first running of the Royal Hunt Cup was won by NAT FLATMAN on Lord Chesterfield's Knight of the Whistle, which returned 5–1 for owner Lord Chesterfield. Gary Owen, Epaulette and Bourra Tomacha triple dead-heated for 2nd.

1892   Jack Watts partnered MILFORD to victory in the Coventry Stakes at Royal Ascot for a certain Mr Jersey, which name concealed the identity of actress Lily Langtry – it was not the done thing for women to own horses then.

1910   The Royal meeting began and was subsequently known as Black Ascot because it came five weeks after the death of King Edward VII and everyone was in mourning.

1916   Trainer GEORGE SPANN born. Best horses trained included Polar Flight and Flame Gun. Rode from 1932 to 1954.

1936   The final race meeting took place at Shanghai's Kiangwan course.

1951   Jockey BRIAN BARKER born.

1955   Lady jockey CHARLOTTE BREW born. The first woman to ride in the Grand National – she reached the 27th fence in 1977 before Barony Fort refused.

1972   Jockey JIMMY FORTUNE born. Best horses ridden include Joveworth.

1972   Jockey DARRYLL HOLLAND, 1990 Champion Apprentice, born.

1991   Chinese jockey TSE WAI-HO was banned for four months and fined £4,685 on betting-related charges in Hong Kong. He had earlier admitted to giving tips in return for 'the services' of a prostitute and local schoolgirl.

1991   GARY CARTER became only the 2nd British jockey (Paul Cook, on July 4 1981, was the 1st) to win at 3 racecourses in 1 day. Luvly Jubly, trained by Jack Berry, won at Southwell in the 1.30, Romany Rye scored for trainer Geoff Wragg in the 4.00 at York while Able Susan, also trained by Wragg, won the 8.15 at Doncaster.

1991   Polish-bred SERAFIN won the Swedish Grand National for the 4th consecutive year. John McLaughlin was the 4th jockey to win the race on the horse.

1991   Peter Chapple-Hyam's Cambrian Hills gave him his first Goodwood training success.

15 JUNE

1915   For the first time the Derby took place at a course other than Epsom. Seventeen went to post at Newmarket for the race, won by 11-10 favourite Polymelus, ridden by Steve Donoghue.

1918   Owner of Song, Coral Diver and Normandy BRYAN JENKS born. His Fearless Fred won 21 chases. Colours: flame; white cross-belts; checked cap.

1918   JOHREN won the 50th running of the Belmont Stakes over one and $^3/_8$ miles. Bred in England by Harry Payne Whitney.

1947   MARCEL BOUSSAC won his 8th French Derby with Sandjar.

1949   Trainer (CHARLES) ROBIN BARWELL born.

1963   Jockey TOM TAAFFE, who has 4 Ladbroke Hurdle victories to his credit, plus both the Irish Champion Hurdle and Irish Grand National, born. Best horses ridden include Fredcoteri and Feroda.

1963   Trainer 'SUNNY JIM' FITZSIMMONS retired, weeks before his 89th birthday. 48,000 racegoers watched at Aqueduct, USA, as he received a tray engraved with the names of his 148 stakes winners.

1967   Jockey GEORGE DUFFIELD rode his first winner, Syllable, for trainer Jack Waugh at Yarmouth.

1967   There was an unusual sight at Uttoxeter's evening meeting, where three sisters made a book. Mrs Olive Harris, Mrs June Muggleston and Mrs Dorothy Harrison, the three daughters of trainer Arthur Birch, already owned 8 betting shops.

1967   There was a dramatic finale to the jump season as JOSH GIFFORD landed a treble at Uttoxeter to take his total to 122, just 1 more than the previous record total of 121 set by Fred Winter in 1952-53. Gifford took 58 more rides (529 in total) to set his record.

1982   Embarrassment for Ascot when one of their 'jobsworth' stewards refused entry to the owners' and trainers' bar to Vincent O'Brien on the grounds that he did not have the correct badge.

1988   Tote turnover at Royal Ascot topped £1 million in a day for the first time.

1990   Champion jump jockey PETER SCUDAMORE was awarded the MBE.

1991   PETER O'SULLEVAN was awarded the CBE.

1991   WAVE HILL won at Bath: Henry Cecil's 2,000th domestic winner.

1992   Trainer WILL PEARCE, 42, was found dead with a shotgun nearby on the gallops at Sutton Bank, adjacent to his yard at Hambleton near Thirsk. He was believed to have had severe financial problems, but just two days previously had landed an alleged £250,000 gamble when his Father Hayes (backed from 14-1 in the morning to a 4-1 starting price) won the Hanover Square Handicap at Sandown.

16 JUNE

1752 The first race meeting in the Haydock area was held at Golborne Heath, a £50 cup sponsored by the Newton Hunt.

1904 THROWAWAY (10-1) won the Ascot Gold Cup. The race is alluded to in James Joyce's famous novel *Ulysses*.

1923 Jockey GEORGE SMALL born. Rode his first winner, Mamie's Choice, at Taunton in 1953, and partnered Go Slow and Baulking Green.

1925 Gordon Richards won at Royal Ascot for the first time.

1934 United Racecourses managing director TIM NELIGAN born.

1937 Trainer of Canasta Lad and Zeta's Son PETER BAILEY born. Also handled Strombolus and Prince Rock. First licence 1965.

1941 Northern Rails bookmaker FRANCIS HABBERSHAW born.

1944 Trainer of Turkoman GARY JONES born.

1945 Founding editor of the *Racing Post* GRAHAM ROCK born. Later became agent for jockey Michael Roberts and landed a now legendary bet of £100 at odds of 100-1 with William Hill when Roberts won the Championship in 1992.

1955 Jockey COLIN MAGNIER born. Won 1982 Champion Hurdle on 40-1 shot For Auction and was runner-up in the 1983 Grand National on Greasepaint.

1967 Apprentice ERNIE JOHNSON rode a double on Zeno (George Todd) and Fraxinus (Bill Wightman) at Sandown.

1976 JORGE TEJEIRA won on 8 of the 12 mounts he had during the day at Keystone, Pennsylvania, and Atlantic City, New Jersey.

1981 STOCKTON racecourse held its final meeting.

1982 RYAN PRICE won the Bessborough Stakes at Royal Ascot with Spin of a Coin (Brian Rouse), then announced that he would retire at the end of the season.

1988 GREVILLE STARKEY fell inexplicably from Ile De Chypre, 4-1 2nd favourite, when ahead in the final furlong of the King George V Handicap at Royal Ascot. In October a jury in a drug-smuggling case heard that Starkey fell after a blast of high-pitched sound was directed at the horse from a high-tech ultrasonic gun. It became known at the Stun Gun incident, although no conclusive proof was ever produced.

1992 A punter who decided to have a bet on impulse collected £130,800 from William Hill when he landed a £100 treble on the last 3 races of the day at Royal Ascot.

1992 The McBeans Nursery in Lewes, Sussex, unveiled a white moth orchid named Dessie in honour of DESERT ORCHID. It was displayed for the first time at the Three Counties Show, Malvern, and cost £12.95 or £19.95 depending on size.

17 JUNE

1882   1881 Kentucky Derby winner Hindoo won his last race to bring his career details to 31 wins, 3 2nds and 2 3rds from 36 races, producing $71,875 prize-money.

1937   Jockey JOHN COOK born. Originally a flat jockey, he turned to jumping after completing his national service stint with the Navy. Rode Specify to win the 1971 Grand National. In 1972 broke his leg so badly that he was forced to retire.

1954   Riding Never Say Die in the King Edward VII Stakes at Royal Ascot, LESTER PIGGOTT was involved in a skirmish with Rashleigh on the final bend. The stewards suspended Piggott for the remainder of the meeting and the Jockey Club then ruled that because of his 'dangerous and erratic riding' and 'complete disregard for the rules of racing and for the safety of other jockeys' his licence was to be withdrawn and he would be able to regain it only if he spent at least six months working for a trainer other than his father.

1962   Jump jockey RONNIE BEGGAN born.

1962   FRED WINTER rode the Fulke Walwyn-trained MANDARIN to a memorable victory in the Grand Steeplechase de Paris at Auteuil. After the 3rd of the 21 fences Mandarin's rubber bit broke and they carried on with 'no brakes and no steering'.

1964   TARNYA (MICHAELA JANE) DAVIS born. The first woman to ride a winner on King George Day at Kempton (1986).

1967   Apprentice ERNIE JOHNSON rode his first hat-trick as Ballyfall, Rex Pactum and Camisado all won at Warwick.

1982   ARDROSS (Henry Cecil–Lester Piggott, 1–5 favourite) won the Ascot Gold Cup for the 2nd consecutive year. On the same day Indian King, ridden by GREVILLE STARKEY, set a track record at Ascot in winning the Cork and Orrery.

1989   Champion jump jockey turned trainer JOSH GIFFORD awarded MBE.

1992   Irish jump jockey TOMMY CARMODY, Champion in 1985 and 1988, announced his retirement aged 35. A shoulder injury sustained at Naas in January had led to the decision.

1992   LAFFIT PINCAY rode his 2,419th winner at the Hollywood Park track to overtake the existing record-holder for the track, Bill Shoemaker.

1992   The Richard Hannon-trained LYRIC FANTASY won the Queen Mary Stakes at Ascot in a record 59 minutes 72 seconds – the first sub-minute juvenile 5 furlongs at the course. Michael Roberts rode the filly, who was named after a painting by Augustus John.

1992   COLOUR SERGEANT won the Royal Hunt Cup to become the Queen's first Royal Ascot winner since 1979. The Lord Huntingdon-trained horse also set a course record of 1 minute 38.07 seconds.

18 JUNE

1867   GEORGE FORDHAM rode 6 winners in 7 races at Stockbridge. He dead-heated in the other race but was beaten in the run-off.

1930   A fierce thunderstorm hit Ascot and lightning struck and killed a Mr Hobein of Southport, who was sheltering beneath a bookmaker's umbrella. The course was flooded and racing abandoned after the 2nd race, the Royal Hunt Cup, won by The MacNab, ridden by Freddie Fox.

1932   Owner GEORGE PERRATT born. Best horses include Mr Melody and Border Squaw. Colours: maroon and black stripes; gold sleeves; maroon and black quartered cap.

1939   One of the top trainers at Churchill Downs, LYNN WHITING, born. He began training in 1968 and won his first Churchill Downs title in 1978.

1941   Trainer FRED DARLING scored his 7th and last Derby winner, Owen Tudor (25-1), and also trained runner-up Morogoro (11-2).

1957   Jockey RAY COCHRANE born. Best known as a Flat jockey but rode 8 hurdles winners. Partnered Kahyasi to win the 1988 Derby. Won the 1,000 Guineas and Oaks on Midway Lady in 1986.

1963   Jockey JOEY BROWN born. Won Crown Plus Two and Daily Mirror Apprentice Championship. First winner 1981. Best horse ridden Mailman. Described his early career as 'Five successful years with I. A. Balding; one and a half disappointing years with R. M. Whittaker and a disappointing year with N. Tinkler'.

1964   For the first time since the Royal Ascot meeting was established the whole Gold Cup day card was abandoned due to torrential rain.

1966   A record Tote jackpot of £63,114 3s was paid for 5s (25p) at Ascot.

1989   Four-year-old colt FROSTY THE SNOWMAN set a world-record time of 1 minute 44.45 seconds for 9 furlongs at Woodbine, ridden by Dave Tenna.

1991   LESTER PIGGOTT won the King Edward VII Stakes at Royal Ascot on Saddler's Hall – his first Royal Ascot winner for 6 years.

1992   DRUM TAPS (Lord Huntingdon) won the Ascot Gold Cup, ridden by Lanfranco Dettori, who was lucky to avoid being bitten on the backside by Walter Swinburn's mount Arcadian Heights. 'I heard Walter scream at me on the home turn and I couldn't see what had happened. I thought perhaps I had pulled out in front of him.' In fact, Swinburn was warning him that his horse was attempting to take a chunk out of Dettori's rear end. Following a stewards' inquiry trainer Geoff Wragg was ordered to equip the horse with a net muzzle in all future races. The horse won again in 1993.

19 JUNE

1867 Filly RUTHLESS won the first Belmont Stakes, the oldest of the US Triple Crown races, run at Belmont Park, USA, over one and $5/8$ mile, ridden by Gilpatrick for owner F. Morris. Trained by A. J. Minor. Four ran. Prize-money was $1,850 dollars.

1877 ADMIRAL JOHN ROUS, the man who established the authority of the Jockey Club in British racing, died at the age of 82.

1910 JERRY M., 2nd in the Grand National earlier in the year, was injured while winning the Grande Steeplechase de Paris. He didn't reappear for almost two years, going on to win the 1912 National.

1917 Owner SIR DAVID WILLS born. His Happy Laughter won the 1953 1,000 Guineas and he bred 1959 Kentucky Derby winner Tomy Lee. Colours: blue; white cross-belts, collar and sleeves; white cap with blue spots.

1922 Owner of 6-race winner State Jester and Old Newton Cup winner Mint ERIC BARBER born. Colours: yellow; brown spots on body; yellow and brown hooped cap.

1924 The first meeting took place at Naas, Ireland.

1931 THE DUKE OF ATHOLL born. Owner of good jumpers Far Bridge (1984 Tingle Creek Chase) and Boraceva (NH Chase, Cheltenham, 1989). Colours: black and old gold stripes; hooped sleeves; quartered cap.

1942 Malton trainer KEITH STONE, who moved to Macau, born.

1943 Trainer turned starter SIMON MORANT born.

1946 Irish trainer OLIVER FINNEGAN born.

1947 French jockey FREDDIE HEAD born. Several times French Champion, he won the Arc on his grandfather's horse Bon Mot in 1966. Also partnered Three Troikas, Zino and Miesque, winning the 1987 1,000 Guineas on the latter.

1951 Owner-trainer of General Harmony SARAH JENNINGS born.

1957 Melton Mowbray trainer JOHN WHARTON, handler of Tom Sharp, Snakesong, Blue Indigo and Mr Quick, born.

1967 VAL FAGGOTTER rode 4 winners at Edinburgh.

1987 GAY KELLEWAY was the first woman to ride a Royal Ascot winner when Sprowston Boy, trained by her father, Paul, won the Queen Alexandra Stakes by 8 lengths at 12-1.

1989 AL-TORFANAN, a five-year-old, set a new 'world record' for a mile at Brighton, winning the Finnair Brighton Mile Challenge Trophy Handicap in 1 minute 31.1 seconds. Ridden by Tyrone Williams; trained by Paul Howling.

1989 EARLIE FIRES, 42, became the first jockey in the 98-year history of the course to ride 6 winners from 6 rides at Hawthorne, USA.

20 JUNE

1890   Twelve fillies and 8 colts from the Royal Stud at Hampton Court were sold for just over 14,000 guineas - a little more than 700 guineas each.

1894   Landlord of the Half Moon, Dulwich, and owner TOM WORTON had something to celebrate when his 50-1 outsider Victor Wild won the Royal Hunt Cup.

1895   The final racecourse appearance of 1893 Triple Crown winner ISINGLASS - he won the Ascot Gold Cup, bringing his career record to 11 wins and a 2nd place from 12 starts, amassing prize-money of £57,455, a British record which was to survive until exceeded by Tulyar in 1952

1905   KING EDWARD VII was the first Royal to arrive at Ascot races by car.

1942   Breeder of 1976 Grand National winner Rag Trade IAN WILLIAMS born.

1949   All 6 favourites won at Folkestone.

1952   LESTER PIGGOTT rode his first Royal Ascot winner, 100-6 shot Malka's Boy, trained by W. Nightingall, in the Wokingham.

1967   A Royal Ascot double for SCOBIE BREASLEY on Mack Royal in the Coventry Stakes and Reform in the St James's Palace Stakes.

1967   Announcing that shock 100-1 winner of the Grand National FOINAVON was up for sale - a half share of him, at least - the prospectus optimistically claimed that the horse was 'now coming to his best'.

1984   Jockey PAT DAY won 7 races from 8 starts at Churchill Downs. He has twice ridden 6 winners in a day there and 10 times 5 winners on one card, including Derby Day 1989 and 1991.

1986   A tough day at the office for PAT EDDERY. Riding at Royal Ascot he was thrown twice, from Dallas and Live in Hope.

1991   INDIAN QUEEN won the Ascot Gold Cup, the 15th mare to do so - but only the 2nd to do it while pregnant. La Fleche, in 1894, was the first. Indian Queen's resultant foal, a colt by Night Shift, was born on April 19 1992.

1992   MICHAEL ROBERTS, a 100-1 chance for the Jockeys' Championship at the start of the season, rode a treble at Ascot to go 7 clear of reigning champion Pat Eddery. William Hill quoted him as 8-11 odds-on favourite to win the title, which he eventually did.

1992   London-born South African Champion Jockey JEFF LLOYD, 30, became the first jockey to break the 300-winner barrier in that country with a double at Clairwood. His previous best, in 1987-88, was 226.

21 JUNE

1832 The race for the Eclipse Foot was run at Ascot. PRIAM, the 1830 Derby winner, won the prize – one of the hooves of the great Eclipse, set as a snuff box in gold.

1925 Owner CHARLES (ANTHONY BARBARO) ST GEORGE born. Colours: black; white chevron and cap. Among his best horses were Arc winner Rheingold, St Leger winners Michelozzo and Bruni.

1927 Meath, Ireland, trainer BASIL BRINDLEY born. Best horses included Arctic Folly, Listowel Arms and Jubilee Quay.

1939 Mondragon was the 100-8 winner of the 9-runner Irish Derby for jockey Joseph Canty and trainer James Canty.

1940 TV commentator JULIAN (DAVID BONHOTE) WILSON born. Fan of Swindon Town FC. Owner of 1977 Gimcrack Stakes winner Tumbledownwind. Colours: sea green; dark blue seams; quartered cap.

1944 Jockeys JACK MOYLAN and GEORGE WELLS fought out the finish of the Irish Derby twice: first as Moylan, on 4-7 favourite Slide On, prevailed from Wells on 7-2 chance Water Street by a head; then again in the weighing-room when Moylan, taking exception to Wells' riding tactics, floored his rival with a single blow. One of the stewards who fined Moylan £10 was Dermot McCalmont, owner of the horse he had just ridden to victory!

1950 Comic actor, the voice behind many *Spitting Image* puppets and keen punter ENN REITEL born. Amateur rider and owner – best horses Choice of Critics and Foot Prince.

1955 Newmarket trainer ALEX (CHRISTIE) STEWART born. Trained Mtoto.

1961 A record 18 competed for the £7,921 first-prize money in the Irish Derby, Herbert Holmes winning on 33-1 chance Your Highness for trainer Humphrey Cottrill and owner Mrs Stanhope Joel.

1963 TRELAWNY completed the Ascot Stakes–Queen Alexandra Stakes at the same Royal Ascot meeting for the 2nd consecutive season – an unprecedented achievement.

1968 Jump jockey GARY LYONS born.

1982 DAWN RUN, which went on to set a record-winning total for a jumper of £259,740, won a £572 flat race at Tralee for her first victory. She was ridden by her 62-year-old owner Mrs Charmian Hill.

1992 Jockey RAY COCHRANE, whose Epsom Derby mount, Young Senor, had been withdrawn from the race when he refused to enter the stalls, at least managed to get into the traps on his Austrian equivalent mount, Green Foot. However, when the rest of the stalls opened, his didn't and the field went without them. No inquiry was called and the exasperated Cochrane commented, 'Who was the last jockey to ride in two Derbys without getting round in either?'

22 JUNE

1927 KNIGHT OF THE GRAIL (3–1), trained by Ronald Farquharson in Wiltshire, won the Irish Derby ridden by Michael Beary. Six ran.

1928 Leamington Spa trainer WILMER MANN born.

1934 BROWN JACK, ridden by Steve Donoghue as usual, won the Queen Alexandra Stakes for a record 6th successive year, sparking off memorable scenes of celebration. Trainer Ivor Anthony had been unable to watch and had sat under a tree in the paddock.

1948 Epsom trainer PHILIP MITCHELL born. Sent out King's Glory to win the 1982 Lincoln and also trained Peter O'Sullevan's Attivo.

1949 The Aga Khan's Hindoostan (7–1) won the 12-runner Irish Derby, ridden by Rae Johnstone trainer Frank Butters.

1954 Former jump jockey SCOBIE COOGAN born (real name Alan Brian).

1955 Pat's father JIMMY EDDERY rode Panaslipper to win the 13-runner Irish Derby at 4–1. The horse was trained by Seamus McGrath.

1957 Shrewsbury supporter and jockey WILLIAM BRISBOURNE born.

1959 Jockey MICK KINANE born. In 1989 won the Cartier Million and the Arc de Triomphe (Carroll House) – worth a total of £950,000 in just over 24 hours.

1960 Emotional scenes at the Irish Derby, won by 3–1 chance Chamour, ridden by Garnie Bougoure and trained officially by Phonsie O'Brien, who was handling the horse on behalf of his brother Vincent. In May, Vincent had been suspended until November 30 1961 after the stewards of the Turf Club found that 'a drug or stimulant had been administered to Chamour' when that horse won the Ballysax Maiden Plate in April. O'Brien declared: 'I did not drug this or any other horse and I trust my staff.' As Chamour won the Derby Vincent was away fishing. In December he was informed that his sentence had been commuted by six months.

1978 GREVILLE STARKEY won the Ascot Gold Cup on Shangamuzo to become only the 3rd jockey to win the Gold Cup, Derby (Shirley Heights) and Oaks (Fair Salinia) in the same year. Lester Piggott in 1957 and Geoff Lewis in 1971 were the others.

1984 DAWN RUN completed a unique treble of Irish, English and French Champion Hurdles in the same season when winning the Grande Course de Haies d'Auteuil ridden by Tony Mullins.

1989 French trainer Olivier Douieb (42) died of lung cancer. Trained Detroit to win 1980 Arc.

1992 Trainer BILL PREECE celebrated his 100th career win – over four months after the race. His Baluchi was confirmed as the winner of a Ludlow chase run on February 5 after Beau Rose was disqualified. A urine sample had contained a prohibited substance.

23 JUNE

1869 Six lined up for the 4th Irish Derby, won by J. Johnstone's THE SCOUT, ridden by Billy Miller at odds of 7-1.

1875 INNISHOWEN, 2-1 2nd favourite, won the 4-runner 10th Irish Derby under G. Ashworth for Staffordshire trainer Job Toon. It was the first winner trained outside Ireland.

1880 The richest Irish Derby to date, worth £475 to the winner, attracted 11 runners and was won by 100-8 outsider KING OF THE BEES (which actually ran unnamed). Jockey Francis Wynne rode the 1-length winner, trained by Dan Broderick.

1914 Trainer J. J. Parkinson dominated the card at the Curragh, sending out 5 of the 6 winners, 3 ridden by stable jockey Colin Barrett and the other pair by the trainer's son, W. J. Parkinson.

1917 Trainer in America of Hoist the Flag and Slew O'Gold SID WATTERS born.

1920 HE GOES went all the way to win the Irish Derby and 3,400 sovereigns prize-money for owner Captain Henry Whitworth and trainer Joe Butters. Ridden by Fred Templeman, the horse returned 3-1.

1926 English-trained Irish 2,000 Guineas winner EMBARGO added the Irish Derby to his tally. Ridden by Steve Donoghue; 4-5 favourite.

1937 Trainers FRED and MERCY RIMELL were married.

1945 TOM LEADER died aged 66. He sent out 100-1 shot Gregalach to win the 1929 Grand National, having won it in 1927 with Sprig.

1945 PICCADILLY, a 25-1 outsider, was the winner of the 8-runner Irish Derby. Jockey JACK MOYLAN and trainer ROBERT FETHERSTON-HAUGH celebrated their 2nd consecutive win in the race.

1948 With a prize fund of £9,285 the Irish Derby was the most valuable race ever run in that country. The 12-runner race was won by the Aga Khan's 7-2 chance NATHOO for Newmarket trainer Frank Butters, and was ridden by Rae Johnstone on his first Irish appearance. He'd already won the Epsom (My Love) and French Derby (Bey) that season.

1954 ZARATHUSTRA became the longest-priced winner of the Irish Derby, coming home 1½ lengths clear of 10 rivals at odds of 50-1.

1967 Jockey DOUG SMITH rode at Royal Ascot for the last time and went out on a winning note, partnering Spaniard's Mount (100-6) (John Winter) to win the Wokingham. However, his final mount there, Rose of Tralee (Geoffrey Brooke), was beaten in the King's Stand.

1990 SISTER MARY JOY rode Scrubs, the favourite, to win the International Nun Run race held at Trim, Co. Meath.

1992 Trainer SEAN WOODS, aged 26, saddled his first winner with his 4th runner, Sebosan (10-1), in the Tote Credit Handicap at Yarmouth.

24 JUNE

1874   Breeder Sir Tatton Sykes was so little impressed with LILY AGNES that he gave her away to stud groom James Snarry, who must have been delighted today when she won the Northumberland Plate. She became dam of Ormonde, 1886 Triple Crown winner.

1885   He had finished 3rd the day before to The Chicken. He finished behind The Chicken again the next day. But in between, ST KEVIN, ridden by Henry Saunders, won the Irish Derby with The Chicken back in 4th place.

1896   English jockey ALFRED AYLIN won the Irish Derby at his first attempt on 6-1 chance Gulsalberk, trained by Shem Jeffrey.

1914   Trainer JOHNNY OSBORNE, aged 81, sent out The Guller to win the Northumberland Plate from his Brecongill stable at Middleham.

1914   The Atty Persse-Steve Donoghue combination landed the Irish Derby for the second successive year, this time with 3-1 chance LAND OF SONG. Prize-money soared from 1913's record £1,165 to £2,040.

1925   Despite somehow managing to ride in the wrong colours (for which owner the Aga Khan was fined 2 sovereigns) Harry Beasley partnered 5-2 favourite Zionist to a 1^1/2-length Irish Derby victory.

1931   For the first time in ten years a home-trained runner won the Irish Derby. Joseph Canty rode the unbeaten 5-2 winner, SEA SERPENT, for trainer Philip Behan against 5 rivals.

1943   THE PHOENIX, owned and trained by Frederick Myerscough of Dublin, rose to win the 9-runner Irish Derby at 2-5 for jockey Joseph Canty. The Phoenix started at 1-8 for the Irish St Leger - and lost.

1953   PREMONITION (Harry Carr) and CHAMIER (Bill Rickaby) went past the post together in the first Irish Derby photo-finish, the former winning by a head. However, Vincent O'Brien, trainer of 5-4 favourite Chamier, insisted on an objection being lodged on the grounds of boring and 2-1 chance Premonition was disqualified and placed last while Chamier got the race. Premonition's furious trainer, Captain Boyd-Rochfort, refused to run another horse in Ireland - his native land - for over ten years.

1959   Epsom Derby runner-up FIDALGO made amends in the 11-runner Irish Derby, winning by 4 lengths under Joe Mercer.

1960   SHAMROCK STAR equalled the course record at Newcastle for 5 furlongs. Seventeen days earlier he had broken the 5-furlong course record at Redcar, then 6 days later he broke the 6-furlong course record at Liverpool.

1970   BRIGADIER GERARD won on his first appearance - in the Berkshire Stakes at Newbury at 100-7.

1992   Former north-country jump jockey TOMMY FORAN died aged 63.

25 JUNE

1919 First-prize money of £3,450 was on offer for the richest-ever Irish Derby, and it stayed at home when the James J. Parkinson-trained LOCH LOMOND, ridden by apprentice Martin Quirke, won at 3-1 by 6 lengths. Miss Cowhy became the first winning lady owner.

1924 The first dead-heat in the history of the Irish Derby saw even-money favourite HAINE and 3-1 chance ZODIAC sharing the honours.

1930 For the last time a dead-heat was run off. The judge declared RUBY'S LOVE, ridden by Jim Kirby and Lady Scarbrough's WALLOON, partnered by Tommy Lowrey, inseparable at the end of the 7-furlong Berkshire Selling Handicap at Newbury. Ruby's Love won the deciding heat by 3/4 length.

1942 Trainer RICHARD WHITAKER born.

1942 Windsor Slipper, 2-7, cruised to victory in the 13-runner Irish Derby in a record time of 2 minutes 35 seconds. The unbeaten colt went on to land the Triple Crown in the Irish St Leger.

1947 Sayajirao, 3rd in the English 2,000 Guineas and Derby, was evens favourite for the 11-runner Irish Derby, in which he duly obliged by 1 1/2 lengths for jockey Edgar Britt and Newmarket trainer Frederick Lakin Armstrong, known universally as Sam.

1949 CAPTAIN OSWALD MARMADUKE DALBY BELL, the Lambourn trainer who won the 1928 Derby with Felstead, died. Born in 1871 in Australia.

1952 Wantage trainer PAUL BURGOYNE born. Best horse trained Dalmane.

1958 Trainer MICHAEL DAWSON, whose father had ridden 3 and trained 4 winners of the race, sent out Sindon to win the Irish Derby.

1962 Jockey STEVE BUCKTON born.

1977 Robert Sangster-owned THE MINSTREL was the 11-10 winner of the 15-runner Irish Sweeps Derby, partnered by Lester Piggott, trained by Vincent O'Brien. Later, Piggott's stirrup broke as he left the stalls riding Glencoe Lights in a sprint. The jockey fell off his mount at the end of the race. Advised to give up his rides for the rest of the day, Piggott allegedly told the doctor, 'Don't be — silly. I've got to go out there and earn my £14 riding fee in the next race!'

1982 Former Champion Jump Jockey BOB DAVIES retired, having ridden 911 winners during his career.

1989 Former British champion NH trainer MICHAEL DICKINSON sent out his 50th American winner, The Way It's Bin, at Philadelphia Park.

1991 TONY DICKINSON, father of record-breaking trainer MICHAEL, died aged 75. Known as 'The Boss', he became a trainer in 1967.

1991 Trainer RYAN JARVIS died at the age of 77. Began training in 1936. Sent out Front Row to win 1968 Irish 1,000 Guineas.

26 JUNE

1895 PORTMARNOCK (2-5 favourite), ridden by William Clayton, won the Irish Derby by the longest margin ever of 12 lengths over his 5 rivals. Trained by Shem Jeffrey. Jockey Clayton's fortunes later declined and in 1904 he committed suicide at the Curragh.

1935 MUSEUM, the 100-1 winner of the Irish 2,000 Guineas, returned 100-8 as he won the 8-runner Irish Derby. He later collected the Irish St Leger to become the first Irish Triple Crown winner. Steve Donoghue rode him for Curragh trainer John Rogers, who made a clean sweep of all 5 Irish Classics that season.

1954 Jockey TOMMY LOWREY rode his last winner, Florient, at Doncaster. Born 1911. Rode Airborne to win the 1946 Derby.

1965 Singer BING CROSBY was part-owner of Irish Sweeps Derby winner Meadow Court, and to celebrate the Lester Piggott-inspired victory (his first in an Irish Classic) Crosby gave a rendition of 'When Irish Eyes Are Smiling' in the winner's enclosure.

1971 LINDEN TREE (7-4 favourite), ridden by Duncan Keith for trainer Peter Walwyn, took one stride out of the stalls as the Irish Sweeps Derby got underway, swerved out to the left, and stopped dead, leaving 7-2 2nd favourite Irish Ball, ridden by Alfred Gibert for French trainer Philippe Lallie, to win.

1976 JOHANNA MORGAN became the first woman to compete in a British Classic, finishing 14th of 17 behind 5-1 chance Malacate, winner of the Irish Sweeps Derby, riding Riot Helmet.

1982 BUSACO won at Newmarket to give WILLIE CARSON his 2,000th winner in Britain.

1982 STEVE CAUTHEN rode 5 winners at accumulative odds of 11,324-1 at Doncaster, and was 3rd and 4th on his other 2 rides.

1982 Christy Roche rode Robert Sangster's ASSERT win to the Irish Derby for trainer David O'Brien, three weeks after his mount triumphed in the Prix du Jockey Club, becoming the first British-trained horse to complete the double.

1986 Jockey PATRICIA COOKSEY supplanted Diane Crump as most successful female rider at Churchill Downs, USA, when she landed her 80th win at the track.

1991 For the 5th time in 6 years trainer LUCA CUMANI won the Heads Nook Maiden Fillies Stakes at Carlisle, with Shardelisada.

1991 For the 10th time US jockey PAT DAY rode 5 winners in an afternoon at Churchill Downs. He had also ridden 6 in a day on 2 occasions and once set a new record with 7 winners from 8 mounts there.

1992 PAT EDDERY rode a British record of 7 winners in a day: 3 at Newmarket in the afternoon, 4 more at Newcastle in the evening.

27 JUNE

1866 Charles Maidment rode Selim to win the first Irish Derby, at the Curragh, run over one mile 6 furlongs 3 yards. The 5–4 chance, owned by Mr James Cockin, beat 2 opponents.

1900 Twelve went to post for the Irish Derby, won by 6–1 shot Gallinaria by 4 lengths, ridden by amateur rider MR GRAHAM WILDMAN LUSHINGTON (known as Tommy). He was the 2nd and last amateur to win the race. The filly was trained by Dan McNally.

1903 Major Eustace Loder's PRETTY POLLY made her debut, winning by 10 lengths from Lily Langtry's Vergia in the British Dominion two-year-old race at Sandown. Pretty Polly went on to win 22 of her 24 races, including the 1,000 Guineas, Oaks and St Leger.

1919 Trainer MERCY RIMELL born. She won the 1983 Champion Hurdle with Gaye Brief. Before training on her own she had been assistant to her late husband, Fred.

1920 WILLIAM LANE, Champion Jockey in 1902 with 170 winners, and Triple Crown winner on filly Pretty Polly in 1904, died at Tower House, Lingfield – still suffering the effects of a fall at Lingfield in 1904, just two weeks after he had completed his Triple Crown triumph.

1938 Devon trainer SYD COLE born.

1949 Polegate trainer RUFUS VOORSPUY born.

1951 A record turnout of 16 competed for the prize money of £7,081 5s in the Irish Derby, won by 5–2 favourite Fraise Du Bois III. Ridden by Charlie Smirke; trained by Harry Wragg.

1956 TALGO (9–2) set a record time of 2 minutes 30.92 seconds for the Irish Derby in winning the 10-runner race by 6 lengths under jockey Manny Mercer for trainer Harry Wragg.

1960 1991 Arc winner Suave Dancer's trainer JOHN HAMMOND born.

1970 NIJINSKY duly won the Irish Sweeps Derby by 3 lengths as a 4–11 shot is entitled to do, ridden by Liam Ward for Vincent O'Brien. Thirteen ran.

1979 English-born trainer SALLY ANN BAILIE'S Poison Ivory set a world-record time of 1 minute 33 seconds for one mile on turf at Belmont, USA.

1986 DAWN RUN, the only horse to complete the Champion Hurdle-Gold Cup double, was killed when she fell in the French Champion Hurdle at Auteuil. She had run 35 races, winning 21 and amassing record prize-money of £259,740.

1990 PAT EDDERY completed the fastest century by any jockey in Britain since Gordon Richards when landing a double at Kempton. Gordon Richards achieved it on June 17 in 1949.

28 JUNE

1791 A crowd of 40,000 turned up to see George, Prince of Wales, later King George IV, at Ascot, where he reportedly won £17,000 by backing his 20-1 winner of the Oatlands Stakes, Baronet, ridden by Sam Chifney. It was the first big race at the track and was worth 2,950 guineas to the winner in a year when the Derby was worth £1,076 5/-.

1871 MAID OF ATHENS, the 4-6 favourite, won the 3-runner 6th Irish Derby, run for the last time over one mile 6 furlongs 12 yards. Ridden by Tommy Broderick, trained by Pat Doucie. She was the first filly to win the race.

1882 NICHOLAS BEHAN, whose three brothers, William, Jack and Phillie, all trained Irish Derby winners, was the only one to ride one, partnering Sortie to a 5-1 4-length victory over 8 rivals.

1905 FLAX PARK was the 5-1 winner of the 11-runner Irish Derby, holding off the late challenge of unconsidered outsider Velocity, whose connections were invited to explain previous poor performances. Flax Park's jockey, Peter Hughes, had, only the day before, been 'jocked' off Velocity. He was so determined to win that he bought a new whip for the race, and when he pulled up after winning he discovered that only the handle of his stick remained. And people complain about today's riders!

1911 Shanballymore gave jockey JOHN DOYLE his 2nd successive Irish Derby win. The 6-1 chance won by 2½ lengths in a field of 10.

1941 Goole trainer JIM DOOLER born.

1947 Gordon Richards was beaten on 1-20 'certainty' Glendower at Chepstow, and was later mortified to learn that the defeat had cost one fan £20,000. The man always backed Gordon's best ride of the day to win him £1,000.

1950 Visibility Good provided jockey THOMAS WESTON with his final mount. It didn't win.

1957 English trainer in America PHIL GLEAVES born.

1965 Amateur rider SARAH EASTERBY born.

1969 Former hotel pageboy GEOFF LEWIS rode 7-2 2nd favourite Prince Regent to win the 15-runner Irish Sweeps Derby for French trainer Etienne Pollet.

1975 Irish 2,000 Guineas and Epsom Derby winner Grundy stormed to a 2-length triumph in the Irish Derby, for which he was 9-10 favourite, under jockey Pat Eddery.

1990 Jockey ALLAN MCKAY cleared of involvement in a £7 million international drugs ring.

29 JUNE

1769   ECLIPSE won the City Free Plate at Salisbury.

1887   The richest prize in the history of Irish racing, £763, was on offer for the winner of the Irish Derby. A record turn-out of 11 runners went to post and the winner was PET FOX, the 6-1 3rd favourite. Ridden by Terry Kavanagh; trained by Henry Linde, also the owner.

1929   FREDDIE FOX rode 5 winners at Sandown. He went on to finish 2nd in the Jockeys' Championship behind Gordon Richards, but won it the next year. He rode 6 Classic winners. His Derby winners were Cameronian (1931) and Bahram (1935). Died aged 57 in 1945.

1946   Jockey (3rd in 1977 Grand National on Eyecatcher) turned trainer at Pulborough CHRIS READ born.

1951   Larkhill trainer CHRIS WILDMAN born.

1963   RELKO, the 8-11 favourite, was withdrawn not under orders after going lame just prior to the start of the Irish Sweeps Derby, won by 100-7 shot Ragusa, ridden by Garnie Bougoure and trained by Paddy Prendergast. Sixteen ran.

1968   LESTER PIGGOTT and Ribero brought about the sensational downfall of 1-3 favourite (and English 2,000 Guineas and Derby winner) Sir Ivor in the 14-runner Irish Sweeps Derby at odds of 100-6 for trainer Fulke Johnson Houghton and owner Charles Englehard. It was the 2nd successive victory in the race for that combination.

1969   BRIAN TAYLOR rode Don Giovanni to win the Deutsches Derby against 14 rivals.

1974   Peter Walwyn saddled English Prince at 8-1 to win the 13-runner Irish Sweeps Derby. Ridden by Yves St Martin. Beat 12 rivals. Owner of the winner was Vera Hue-Williams, whose husband, Colonel Hue-Williams, owned the runner-up, 11-8 favourite Imperial Prince. The pair collected £90,993 prize-money.

1982   King's Soldier (ridden by Joe Mercer, trained by Peter Walwyn) won a one and a 1/4-mile maiden at Folkestone – but only after a 21-minute delay caused by a flash storm.

1988   MOHAMMED MOUBARAK sent out his first winner as a trainer when Libra's Comet (5-1, Gary Carter) won at Lingfield.

1991   Former trainer-jockey PADDY MORRISEY died, aged 70.

1991   PAT EDDERY set a personal record by riding 19 winners in one week.

1991   A 35-year-old woman was killed when a piece of scaffolding fell from the grandstand at Santa Anita racecourse, USA, during an earthquake measuring 6 on the Richter Scale. The course was being used for training horses.

1992   Former jockey JOHN CARR, who rode some 40 winners, sent out his first winner as a trainer, Here Comes a Star, at Hamilton.

30 JUNE

1897   Tommy Fiely rode 6 winners at the three-day Irish Derby meeting, having ridden only 1 in the season until then. The biggest of them was the Irish Derby on 4–1 favourite Wales for owner-trainer William Parke Cullen. Eight ran.

1916   Northumberland owner-trainer FRANK WALTON born.

1929   Jockey REX HAMEY born. Best horses ridden included Linwell, on which he won the Mildmay Chase at Sandown.

1930   The patrol camera is introduced to British racing, at Newmarket.

1933   Wine importer and owner of the dual Champion Hurdler Sea Pigeon PAT MULDOON born. Colours: McIntyre tartan; red sleeves and cap.

1936   Tavistock trainer GEORGE TURNER born.

1938   Former Bedfordshire trainer CLIVE DREW born.

1947   Trainer of Cozzene and Ogygian JAN NERUD born.

1949   Spigot Lodge trainer CHRIS THORNTON born.

1950   Lambourn trainer PETER HUDSON born.

1962   The inaugural running of the Irish Sweeps Derby attracted a field of 24 bidding to win the £50,027 10s first-prize money. French raider Tambourine II, ridden by Roger Poincelet, won by a short head for Etienne Pollet at odds of 15–2 in a new record time of 2 minutes 28.8 seconds. The winning sweeps ticket, worth £50,000, was won by Melbourne dairy farmer and bookmaker Albert Smith.

1964   NORTHERN DANCER, which went on to become the most important and influential stallion in the world, injured himself while working in preparation for a race at Belmont, USA, and never ran again. He had won 14 and been 2nd in the other 4 of his 18 races. Bred in Canada by E. P. Taylor, he won both the Kentucky Derby, lowering the record time in the process, and the Preakness Stakes. Foaled in 1961.

1979   Epsom Derby winner Troy repeated the performance at the Curragh, winning the Irish Derby by 4l at odds of 4–9. Ridden by Willie Carson; trained by Dick Hern.

1987   MICHAEL DICKINSON, former top English jump trainer, sent out his first American flat winner, Bold Magestrate, at Philadelphia Park.

1990   WILLIE CARSON became only the 3rd jockey this century to ride 6 winners at a single UK meeting when he scored a 3,246–1 accumulator at Newcastle. His other ride, the 3rd race on the 7-event card, finished unplaced. The others to achieve it were Alec Russell (Bogside, 1957) and Sir Gordon Richards (Chepstow, 1933).

1991   The Irish Derby set a new record for the amount bet in Ireland with on-course bookies on a single race when IR£378,000 was wagered on the event, won by GENEROUS.

1 JULY

1931 Epsom trainer MICHAEL HAYNES born. Professional jump and flat jockey from 1946 to 1959, winning the Imperial Cup. As a trainer he sent out Popsi's Joy to win the 1980 Cesarewitch.

1933 Seven Barrows, Lambourn, trainer PETER (TYNDALL) WALWYN born. Won 1975 Derby with Grundy, 1970 1,000 Guineas with Humble Duty and has also won Irish Derby twice. In 1975 he was leading trainer for 2nd successive year with 120 wins worth £373,563. It was the first time a trainer had won 100 or more races in a season since Dobson Peacock sent out exactly 100 in 1932.

1950 Jockey TERRY LUCAS born. Rider of Amyndas and Individualist.

1957 DOUG SMITH completed a 53-hour spell during which he rode at 4 tracks, scoring at Lingfield, Brighton and Wolverhampton, but failing at Longchamp.

1966 Panamanian jockey LAFFIT PINCAY rode his first winner in the USA, Teacher's Art, at Arlington Park. Became leading prize-money winner in the game.

1967 Described by Lester Piggott as the best horse he ever rode, SIR IVOR was beaten first time out at the Curragh, but went on to win 8 of 13 races, including the 1968 Derby.

1967 RIBOCCO (5–2 favourite), ridden by Lester Piggott, ran out the winner by 1 length of the 23-runner Irish Sweeps Derby for trainer Fulke Johnson Houghton and owner Charles Englehard.

1972 The Scobie Breasley-trained 10–1 chance STEEL PULSE was ridden to a 1-length Irish Sweeps Derby victory by Bill Williamson.

1978 SHIRLEY HEIGHTS, 5–4 favourite, won the 11-runner Irish Sweeps Derby, ridden by Greville Starkey and trained by John Dunlop.

1982 Jockey JEFF PEARCE, who injured his neck in a fall at Southwell in October, called it a day. Rode his first winner at Plumpton in February 1972. Born October 6 1947.

1987 MARK JOHNSON sent out his first winner as a trainer when Hinari Video won at Carlisle.

1989 Former jump jockey JACK DELANEY died. Born 1923, rode first winner, Hunting Cap, at Southwell in April 1952. Best horse ridden Bacchus.

1990 SALSABIL, ridden by Willie Carson and trained by John Dunlop, became the first filly this century to win the Irish Derby and the first to complete the 1,000 Guineas, Oaks, Irish Derby treble.

1992 Epsom held its first evening meeting. Richard Quinn rode MAHFIL, 7–4 winner of the first race, the Epsom and Ewell Handicap, for Reg Akehurst.

2 JULY

1730 Treasury records revealed that the manager of the Royal Stud, Richard, Earl of Stafford, was authorised to receive expenses of £10,000.

1921 Former Taunton trainer BETTY KENNARD born. First licence 1967. Best horses trained include El Cardo, All Found, Spider Man.

1924 *Daily Mirror* tipster BOB BUTCHERS, who wrote under the Newsboy by-line, born. He set a record of 43,000 winners, reached in December 1984.

1924 BILLY NEVETT, 6 times runner-up in the Jockeys' Championship between 1933 and 1944, rode his first winner, Stockwood (Dobson Peacock), at Carlisle.

1924 Chairman of the Kenya Jockey Club SIR CHARLES MARKHAM born.

1927 Jockey JOHNNY EAST born. Rider of Much Obliged and Prudent Barney.

1929 The Totalisator was used for the first time in England, introduced at Newmarket and Carlisle. Bookies' odds were better in 4 of the races at each meeting.

1941 Irish trainer JOHN CROWLEY born. As a jockey rode Herring Gull to win the 1968 Irish Grand National. Best horses trained include Ballinacurra Lad, Hippolita.

1942 Former Newmarket trainer who moved to USA (WALTER) NELSON GUEST born. Began training in Denmark in 1968 and boasts winners of Danish Derby, Dutch Derby, Swedish 1,000 Guineas, Danish 1,000 Guineas.

1947 Jockey J. ANDERSON, who had ridden his first winner in 1906, returned from almost 25 years of retirement to partner Gracious Son to victory in the Trial Selling Plate at Carlisle.

1966 An outbreak of swamp fever prevented French challengers from coming over for the Irish Sweeps Derby, which was won by the Frankie Durr-ridden SODIUM, the 13–12 2nd favourite. Trainer George Todd, of Manton House, Marlborough, refused to attend the meeting having vowed, on returning to England after the First World War, that he would never again leave it.

1989 STEVE CAUTHEN won the Irish Derby on Old Vic to complete a unique 4-timer. He had already won the Kentucky, English and French Derbies during his career.

1990 A 4-timer at Wolverhampton for WILLIE CARSON brought his recent record to 25 winners in just 8 days.

Above: Any lingering doubts about Arkle's place among the all-time greats were dispelled after he triumphed by a magnificent twenty lengths in the Gallaher Gold Cup, 7 November 1965 (*Popperfoto*)

Below: Arkle in training, Paddy Woods in the saddle, at Tom Dreaper's stables near Ashbourne, Co. Meath (*Popperfoto*)

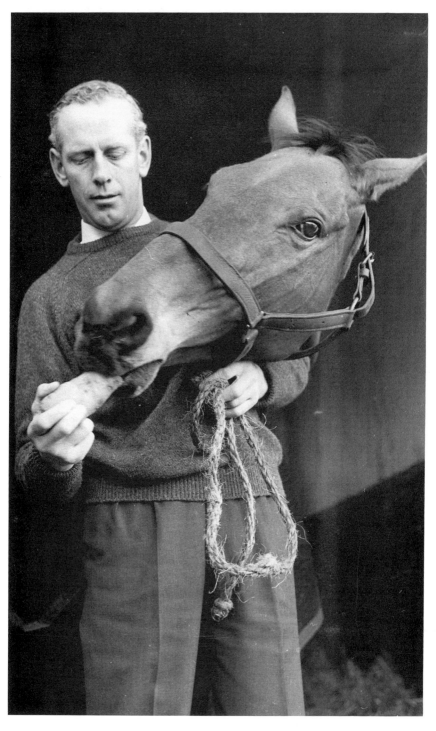

The great Arkle with Jockey Pat Taaffe, photographed in August 1968 (*Popperfoto*)

Above: Lester Piggott, perhaps the most famous jockey of modern times (*Hulton Deutsch*)

Below: As Britain's youngest full-fledged jockey, Piggott, centre, comes through to win the Chesterfield Cup at Goodwood Races, Sussex, 3 August 1951 (*Popperfoto*)

On 23 August 1961, Piggott rode Die Hard to victory in the Ebor Handicap at York, the jockey's third victory in the race in four years (*S & G Press Agency Ltd*)

Simon Sherwood takes Desert Orchid over a hurdle at Sandown racecourse on their way to victory in February 1989. Dessie is arguably the best steeplechaser since Arkle, and certainly the most popular (*Popperfoto*)

Above: Desert Orchid was beaten into third place in the 1990 Cheltenham Gold Cup by 100–1 outsider Norton's Coin (left), ridden by Graham McCourt and owned and trained by Welsh farmer Sirrel Griffiths, and Toby Tobias (right) (*Popperfoto/Reuter*)

Below: Another 100–1 outsider to make history was Foinavon, whose win in the 1967 National was one of the greatest shocks of modern times (*S & G Press Agency Ltd*)

Above: Legendary trainer Vincent O'Brien, 'The Master of Ballydoyle', with actor John Forsythe after Wedding Bouquet's win at the Curragh, 2 July 1989 (*Caroline Norris*)

Below: Vincent O'Brien with brothers Dermot and Phonsie in Limerick, 1950, when over the Christmas race meeting their stables won eight races and Phonsie rode seven winners

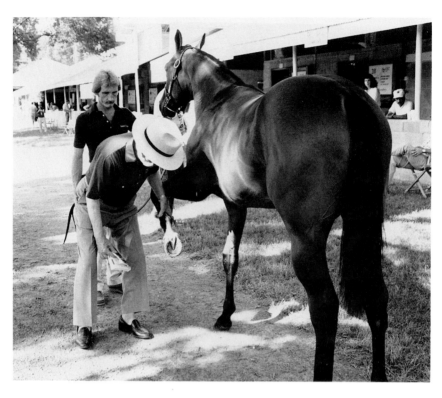

Above: Vincent O'Brien's attention to detail is legendary

Below: Jacqueline O'Brien and camera-shy friend

3 JULY

1770   ECLIPSE benefited from a walkover in the King's Plate at Nottingham.

1909   Owner STAVROS NIARCHOS born. Among his numerous good horses was 1,000 Guineas and Breeders' Cup Mile winner Miesque. Colours: dark blue; light blue cross-belts; striped sleeves; white cap.

1938   Wantage trainer DAVID GANDOLFO born.

1939   PETER O'SULLEVAN opened his first credit betting account – with William Hill.

1952   New York trainer WILLIAM BADGETT JR born. Sent out Go For Wand to win the 1989 Breeders' Cup Juvenile Fillies.

1957   English jockey in Germany STEVE ECCLES born.

1962   Jump jockey JOHN HARRIS born. First winner Mandy's Time at Southwell, December 19 1981. Best horses ridden include Donegal Prince, High Old Time.

1967   Four winners from 4 mounts for GEOFF OLDROYD at Edinburgh's evening meeting: Officer Kelly, Remraf, Cincinatti Kid, Some Tune.

1977   Trainer SAM HALL died in his 61st year. Training from Spigot Lodge he won the Manchester November Handicap in 1950, 1951, 1953, 1955 and 1960 and the Zetland Gold Cup 4 times.

1981   JIMMY BLEASDALE took a fall at Haydock from Maple Queen (later destroyed) which, over ten years later on September 23 1991, forced his retirement. The fall caused him to suffer from blackouts, and a brain scan revealed that brain tissue damaged in the fall was still scarred ten years on, causing blood clots to form. He rode 414 British winners.

1982   First treble for trainer CHARLIE NELSON as Chaste Lady, Maritime England and Wiki Wiki Wheels all won at Bath.

1982   A world record-winning starting price was claimed as two-year-old Anntelle won the Norman Ross Handicap at Canterbury, Sydney at odds of 500–1.

1992   At Hollywood Park, USA, jockey PAT VALENZUELA was riding the Ted West-trained Interwit when he struck the horse with a right-handed whip. The horse ducked sharply into the rail and was killed, while Valenzuela was thrown into a pole. Another horse behind tripped over Interwit and had to be destroyed. The *Racing Post* later reported that West had claimed he told Valenzuela to keep the whip in his left hand and that Valenzuela was being 'sued for negligence by a trainer and owners for his role in the death of two horses in a race at Hollywood Park on July 3'.

4 JULY

1890 America's new Monmouth Park course opened in grounds covering 600 acres. It had a track one and $3/4$ miles around with a one and $3/8$-mile straight course and a 700ft long solid iron grandstand.

1918 Tote Board Chairman LORD WYATT born.

1929 Epsom trainer REG AKEHURST born.

1950 Popular handicapper SUGAR PALM, who won 22 races worth £8,026 in 78 starts, dropped dead at exercise at Weyhill, aged twelve.

1951 Former jump jockey turned Lewes trainer GERRY ENRIGHT born. As a jockey he won the 1977 SGB Hurdle and Kirk and Kirk Hurdle on Kybo, whose name was an acronym for Keep Your Bowels Open.

1954 The undefeated dual Arc winner RIBOT raced for the first time, winning over 5 furlongs at Milan.

1960 Former Sparsholt trainer CHRIS BELL born. First licence 1986.

1972 There was little reason to suspect that the horse who finished 4th in a small race at Aqueduct would go on to prove himself one of the greatest US Triple Crown winners of all, but in 1973 SECRETARIAT achieved just that.

1981 PAUL COOK set a new record by winning at 3 different courses on the same day. He rode Prince's Gate to victory in the 2.15 at Sandown, dashed off to Bath, where he scored on Rammanolie at 5.00pm, then hurtled to Nottingham to win the 7.50 on Pavilion.

1982 Owner EDWARD COURAGE CBE died, aged 75. His chasers included Hennessy Gold Cup winner Spanish Steps. Colours: maroon and yellow halved; sleeves reversed; yellow cap.

1989 Jockey ALLAN MCKAY, free on £250,000 bail accused of a £7 million drugs smuggling offence, rode Bashaq to victory at Folkestone.

1990 South African jockey PIERRE STRYDOM rode 7 winners in 9 races at Newmarket, Johannesburg. Ten days later he rode 7 from 10 at Gosforth Park, Germiston.

1992 KOOYONGA (trainer Michael Kauntze, jockey Warren O'Connor) was the longest-priced winning favourite (7–2) of the Coral Eclipse.

1992 Former jump jockey BRYAN SMART sent out his first Flat winner as a trainer when Sharp Gazelle won at Bath.

1992 Milligram won the Jamaican St Leger to complete a remarkable sequence for trainer Phillip Feanny and jockey Winston Griffiths. The horse won the Derby and 2,000 Guineas for the pair while their Classique won the 1,000 Guineas and Oaks. Griffiths was believed to have become the first jockey to win all 5 of a country's Classic races in one season. Trainer Mick Ryan saddled the winners of all 5 Dutch classics in 1982, all owned by William Nuy. But only 4 were ridden by Terry Cain.

5 JULY

1923 Jockey GEORGE MOORE born. His 4 English Classic wins came on Royal Palace (1967 2,000 Guineas and Derby), Taboun (1959 2,000 Guineas) and Fleet (1967 1,000 Guineas). Also won the Arc on Saint Crespin in 1959. An Aussie, rode first winner at Brisbane on January 1 1940. In 1961 he flew from Australia just to ride Sovrango in the Derby, and finished 4th.

1932 Irish trainer KEVIN PRENDERGAST born. Trained 1977 2,000 Guineas winner and 20–1 chance Nebbiolo. His Nikoli won the 1980 Irish 2,000 Guineas and Arctique Royal the Irish 1,000 Guineas in 1981.

1932 US owner JOE CORNACCHIA, whose company marketed the game Pictionary and who owned 1991 Kentucky Derby winner Strike the Gold, born. Colours: red; white star; white seams on sleeves; red cap.

1956 La Rinconada racecourse, Caracas, Venezuela, opened.

1990 Sandown was named Racegoers' Club Racecourse of the Year for a record 8th time.

1992 PIK KONIG won the Deutsches Derby at Hamburg. It was the last running of the race to be restricted to German-bred runners. It was also the richest race ever run in Germany, with £157,895 prize-money going to the winner.

1993 New Jockey Club rules restricting the use of the whip to five strokes were implemented. Previously up to nine were permitted. Darryll Holland, at Windsor, was the only jockey cautioned on the day, after riding Roxanion to win.

6 JULY

1719 The earliest written reference to racing at Oswestry in Shropshire was on this date. It was discovered in the Chirk Castle accounts and reported: 'Pd my Master's subscription to ye Oswestre Race for this present year to ye hands of Mr James Betton, whose Horse won ye plate . . . £1-1-0.'

1887 Unbeaten Triple Crown winner ORMONDE won the 6-furlong Imperial Gold Cup (later to become the July Cup) at Newmarket on his final racecourse appearance for owner the Duke of Westminster. It was his 16th success in as many outings. His odds were 3-100!

1911 Berwickshire owner-trainer of 1965 and 1966 Grand National runner-up Freddie, REG TWEEDIE born.

1939 Jockey BRIAN TAYLOR born in Southend. Rode Snow Knight to a shock 50-1 Derby victory in 1974. Creole was his first winner, at Yarmouth in 1956.

1941 Jump jockey turned trainer JEFF KING born. Considered by many the best jump jockey never to be Champion. Won Whitbread Gold Cup on Otter Way, 1976. First trainer's licence 1981.

1946 CLOSEBURN and JULIUS won the final 2 races at Stockton. Both were trained by Noel Murless, bred by his wife, Gwendolen, and foaled on the same day.

1965 Jockey JOHN HIGGINS rode his first winner, March Blue, at Chester.

1975 Unbeaten filly RUFFIAN took on Kentucky Derby winner Foolish Pleasure in a match race at Belmont Park, USA. Ruffian was leading when she broke down. She was humanely destroyed and buried in the infield of the track.

1989 US jockey BILL SHOEMAKER made his last appearance in Britain, partnering the Francis Lee-trained Perosini at Haydock. The horse started at 11-4 favourite but finished unplaced. His final mount, Restless Don (6-1) trained by David Chapman, was also unplaced in the final race of the evening, at 9pm.

1990 Trainer JACK BERRY's Distinctly North won at Sandown – to complete his set of winners at all 33 Flat courses.

1992 For the first time a jockey was ordered to contribute towards the legal costs of an appeal hearing. CHRISTY ROCHE lost his appeal against a fifteen-day improper riding ban imposed after an incident in which he was alleged to have hit or attempted to hit apprentice Robbie Skelly with his whip in the Clane Maiden at Naas on June 13 1992. After the hearing in front of the stewards of the Turf Club at the Curragh, Roche was ordered to pay the maximum of IR£5,000 towards the legal costs incurred by the Turf Club in conducting the appeal. He also forfeited his IR£200 appeal deposit.

7 JULY

1829   The first meeting took place at Aintree. The first race, the one and a quarter-mile Croxteth Stakes, was won by Mr Francis's MUFTI.

1886   Partnering the previous year's Derby winner, Fred Archer won on his final July Cup ride as Melton beat Brighton by 3 lengths.

1910   Former owner of Ballykisteen stud SIR IAN HARRIS born.

1925   Owner of the 1974 Cheltenham Gold Cup 7-1 winner Captain Christy PAT SAMUEL born. Also owned dual Colonial Cup winner Grand Canyon. Colours: cerise; gold Maltese Cross, sleeves and cap.

1930   Owner of Perth racecourse LORD MANSFIELD born.

1932   Trainer RON SHEATHER born.

1946   Trainer of Dance Smartly JIM DAY born.

1954   Trainer DAVID MURRAY SMITH born.

1967   LIAM WARD rode 4 winners from 5 mounts at the Curragh.

1989   Eleven jockeys, including Steve Cauthen, Walter Swinburn and George Duffield, refused to race in the 7.10 race at Beverley, saying the bends of the course were in a dangerous condition with water lying on top of firm ground. The race was finally run at 8.29 with only 6 runners and the last 3 races were abandoned.

1990   Police recovered the 220-year-old Richmond Cup race trophy which had been stolen from the home of Penelope, widow of the Marquess of Zetland.

1992   PAT TAAFFE died. Revered as the jockey of the great Arkle, and winner of 6 Irish Grand Nationals. Also won the English Grand National on Quare Times (1955) and Gay Trip (1970). Born in 1930, he was the son of trainer Tom. Retired in 1970 as a jockey and trained with success, producing Captain Christy to win the Irish Sweeps Hurdle, King George VI Chase (twice) and 1974 Cheltenham Gold Cup.

1992   Second favourite O'Donnell's Folly (trained by Alan Bailey and ridden by Danny Wright) collapsed and died of a heart attack after the runners had come under orders for the apprentice race at Pontefract. The race was delayed by twenty minutes but the horse was officially a runner, even though he was dead, as they had come under orders. The winner was 100-1 no-hoper Followmegirls, trained by Mrs A. King and ridden by A. Garth which, it later transpired, had been backed by a punter at Newmarket with an 'away' bookmaker who had laid him the measly odds of 9-2. But the philosophical punter commented, 'I wouldn't have backed it had I known the true price.'

1992   JULIE KRONE, leading US lady jockey, rode in Europe for the first time, winning a race named after her in Taby, Stockholm, Sweden.

8 JULY

1910 Owner DAVID MCCALL born. Owner in partnership of Ile De Bourbon, winner of the King George VI and Queen Elizabeth Diamond Stakes, Coronation Cup, King Edward VII Stakes and many more. Also bred the bizarrely named Purchasepaperchase. Colours: white; scarlet cap.

1947 Former Champion Apprentice (1969) CLIVE ECCLESTON born. First winner August 27 1964 at Carlisle. Amongst the best horses he rode was Pablond.

1962 Former lightweight jockey SIMON GRIFFITHS born. First winner Lunar Wind at Ripon on April 22 1981. Best horse ridden Short Sleeves.

1965 Newmarket became the first British course to use starting stalls.

1981 Jockey JOE BLANKS was fatally injured after his mount, Sleigh Queen, clipped the heels of another runner in the 6-furlong Rock Gardens Maiden Stakes at Brighton and fell. He was rushed to Royal Sussex Hospital but died eight days later, aged 24.

1990 Jockey CARL LLEWELLYN launched a new venture as a publican at The Star, Sparsholt, Wantage – and he claimed to be teetotal!

1992 JULIE KRONE rode in England for the first time, scoring a 46-1 treble at Redcar. Al Karnak won at 2-11 in the race named after her, followed by Gant Bleu (9-1) and 3-1 chance Cockerham Ranger. Reportedly she was not exactly rapturously received by some of the other jockeys.

9 JULY

1839 CRUCIFIX, owned by Lord George Bentinck and ridden by John Day Jr, made a winning debut at 5-6 in the July Stakes at Newmarket, going on to win the 1840 1,000 and 2,000 Guineas and the Oaks before becoming the dam of Derby winner Surplice.

1914 Trainer BILL WIGHTMAN born. Best horses trained include Javata, Privateer, Kingsfold and Halloween, which twice won the King George VI Chase (1952 and 1954).

1916 Cheshire trainer of Roughlyn DOUG FRANCIS born.

1930 Breeder of Whip it Quick ALAN BARRACLOUGH born.

1941 US trainer of Derby winner Quest for Fame BOBBY FRANKEL born.

1950 Trainer RAE GUEST born. As a jockey, he rode his first winner in 1970 in Denmark. He went on to win Danish Derby (twice), Dutch Derby, Calcutta Derby (twice). Best horse trained Aldbourne.

1954 Princely Gift was the great SIR GORDON RICHARDS' final winner, at Sandown, bringing his career total to 4,870 from 21,837 mounts.

1959 Rider of 1983 Grand National winner Corbiere (13-1) BEN DE HAAN born. Also won the Welsh and Norwegian Grand Nationals.

1967 An unnamed Brighton housewife had to search through the garbage after throwing away a jackpot ticket from Kempton. She had been unaware that there was a consolation prize for picking the first 4 winners. Having realised, she managed to reclaim the ticket from the dustbin, and exchanged it for a payout of £711 6s.

1975 CAROLYN EDDERY rode her first winner, Destino, at Doncaster.

1981 JORGE VELASQUEZ scored 6 winners from 6 mounts at Belmont, USA.

1982 BRIAN ROUSE won on all 5 of his rides at Lingfield, for 5 different trainers, at accumulative odds of 170-1.

1990 In the closing stages of the Plumb Centre Handicap at Ripon, Bescaby Boy and It's Me under Ernie Johnson came to blows as they raced to the line. Said Mark Birch, jockey on Bescaby Boy, which drew blood as he clashed heads with It's Me, 'I've never known anything like it.' Bescaby Boy won the race and kept it after a stewards' inquiry.

1992 LESTER PIGGOTT won the July Cup at Newmarket for the 10th time when 16-1 shot Mr Brooks (Richard Hannon) obliged. His first win had come on Vigo (7-2) in 1957.

1992 CHAPLIN'S CLUB won his 24th race, at Redcar, at the age of twelve, and was promptly retired. He raced 160 times and won £144,739 prize-money. He once ran 9 times in 18 days, winning on 7 occasions. Owned by Peter Savill; trained by David Chapman.

10 JULY

1786 Lord Clermont's chestnut colt BULLFINCH (4–1) beat Bustler, owned by Mr Vernon in the first running of the July Stakes at Newmarket, now the oldest race in the world for two-year-olds.

1933 York trainer DAVID CHAPMAN born. Soba, Chaplin's Club and Glencroft, all prolific sprint winners, are among his best horses.

1939 Arundel trainer JOHN (LEEPER) DUNLOP born. Trained Shirley Heights to win 1978 Derby. Other top horses trained include Circus Plume, Habibti, Quick as Lightning, Scottish Rifle, Pitcairn, Salsabil, Shadayid.

1940 Jockey turned valet JOHN BUCKINGHAM born. His big moment as a jockey came in the 1967 Grand National when, lobbing along at the back of the field, taking his time on the unconsidered outsider, Foinavon, he was staggered to see the rest of the field suddenly come to grief. By the time he and Foinavon arrived on the scene they were the only combination able to pick a way through the carnage to jump the fence and go on to land a 100–1 turn-up.

1954 GORDON RICHARDS rode his final mount, Landau, who finished 3rd in the Eclipse Stakes at Sandown. Richards was due to ride in the next race but was thrown by Abergeldie, broke four ribs and retired.

1956 Irish jockey TOMMY CARMODY born. Three King George VI Chase victories – 2 on Silver Buck, the other on Gay Spartan.

1956 Reading trainer IAN COX born.

1956 Jockey PHIL TUCK born. Rode Mr Snugfit into 2nd place in 1985 Grand National and won Cheltenham Gold Cup on Burrough Hill Lad in 1984. At one time one of the most superstitious of jockeys but in 1988 he announced, 'I suddenly thought, it's all daftness.' Once had his backside bitten in public, 'in appreciation', by a waitress who had backed 2 winners he had ridden.

1961 Jump jockey PETER DEVER, who later became a saddler, born.

1965 Jockey RICHARD GUEST born. Partnered Beech Road to victory in the 1989 Champion Hurdle at odds of 50–1.

1982 First-ever treble for jockey BILLY NEWNES. At Lingfield he rode Both Ends Burning, Miguel Clement and Stepout.

1992 Jockey ANTHONY POWELL (33), who suffered hip and other injuries in an accident at Mallow racecourse three years earlier, was awarded IR£29,000 damages and costs in the High Court.

1992 Jockeys Michael Roberts and Jimmy Quinn and trainer Barney Curley survived a plane crash near Chester when the 6-seater Cessna, piloted by ex-policeman Neil Foreman, crashed through hedges, narrowly avoiding trees, and ended up immersed in a water-filled dyke.

11 JULY

1917   Trainer MICHAEL POPE born. First licence 1947. Best horses trained include Luxury Hotel, Golden Leg, Life Sentence. Collected his memories of the sport into a book published by the *Sporting Life* in 1992.

1932   Trainer of American horses John Henry and Bayakoa RON MCANALLY born.

1934   PRINCE ALY KHAN, father of the Aga Khan, rode his own horse Pergomas to win the George Thursby Welter Plate at Salisbury, beating Jack, ridden by the Earl of Carnarvon.

1939   Kelso trainer JOHN 'SWANEE' HALDANE born. Rode professionally for twelve years. First trainer's licence 1981. Best horse trained Border Knight.

1942   Former jockey BRIG ROBSON born.

1957   The AGA KHAN, owner of 5 Derby winners, including 1935 Triple Crown winner Bahram, 6 St Leger winners, 3 2,000 Guineas winners, 2 Oaks winners and 1 1,000 Guineas winner, died in Geneva in his 80th year. The dispersal of his bloodstock interests included the sale of his 1952 Arc winner Nuccio, which went for just under £11,000.

1959   Newmarket trainer IAN CAMPBELL born. First licence November 1982. Best horses trained include Cat's Eyes, Reggae Beat.

1959   Jockey RICKY PUSEY born. Best horse ridden Rose Ravine. Rode for the Queen Mother.

1963   Northern jockey EDWARD GUEST born. Performed well abroad, winning the Norwegian Derby and Oaks. First winner at Hamilton in 1979. Best horses ridden include Wonderful Surprise, Grand Unit.

1983   King Charlemagne won at Epsom to give trainer MARY REVELEY her first flat winner.

1987   HENRY CECIL set record for the fastest 100 winners in a flat season.

1990   WILLIE CARSON rode a 4-timer at Newmarket for his fastest century in 19 seasons.

1992   Trainer CLIVE BRITTAIN and jockey GEORGE DUFFIELD landed their first Irish Classic win when User Friendly became the 8th filly to land the English-Irish Oaks double.

1992   MICHAEL ROBERTS completed his 5th successive century, riding Foolish Heart (10-11) to win at Southwell.

12 JULY

1711 The *London Gazette* carried an advertisement for the first meeting to be run at Ascot Common on August 6 and 7. It was later postponed until August 13.

1888 The first meeting was run at Hamilton Park's new course. The old one had opened in 1782. WILD WEST II, ridden by George Barrett, was the first 'modern' winner, trained by Bob Armstrong.

1939 French trainer ROBERT DE MONY-PAJOL born. Best horses trained included Dictus, Margouillat.

1955 The Royal Ascot meeting got underway, having been transferred from its usual June date because of a rail strike and the official state of emergency proclaimed by the government.

1969 NIJINSKY won on the first appearance of his 13-race career, scoring at 4-11 in the Erne Stakes at the Curragh, ridden by Liam Ward. Trained by Vincent O'Brien.

1972 Jockey DAVID DINELEY rode his first winner, Purple Rock, at Kempton.

1978 WALTER SWINBURN rode his first winner, Paddy's Luck, at Kempton.

1989 Bookie STEPHEN LITTLE accepted what was believed to be the largest bet ever seen at Bath racecourse - £20,000 to win £32,250 on the Guy Harwood-trained Parador, which duly obliged, returning a starting price of 5-4.

1990 US jockey CHIP TERMINI was suspended for 30 days after dropping his towel when he emerged from a shower in the jockeys' room in full view of a 'jockette', at Louisiana Downs.

1992 Trainer DAVID HAYES became the first Australian to win 300 races in a season when he landed a treble at Flemington.

1992 Former trainer TED GODDARD died aged 84. In 1968 he won the Bessborough Stakes with Q.C. and the Queen Alexandra Stakes with Tubalcain, both at Royal Ascot. Born February 18 1908. Rode winners over hurdles pre-war; first licence 1950. Trained prolific 14-race winner Galen. Was a keen amateur boxer.

1992 Racing resumed at Beijing for the first time since the Communists came to power in 1949. Punters bet via lottery tickets. The Kang Xi Cup was won by Inner Mongolia Champion Jockey Za Na.

1992 A crowd of 15,000 turned out to see the first Sunday meeting at Flemington, Melbourne - 3,000 more than their Saturday attendance.

1992 Czech flat jockey JOSEF DOLESJI, 36, broke his neck and died from a last-race fall at Munich, Germany. Six weeks earlier jump jockey HANS STROMPEN had died at Baden-Baden after a heavy fall. These were the first such deaths in German racing since 1971.

13 JULY

1925   Trainer DAVID (TRENCHARD) THOM born. First licence 1960. Best horses included Prince Hansel, Forty Winks, Absent Chimes.

1938   Jockey RON VIBERT born. Best horses ridden include Bold Admiral and Happy Spring. Rode his first winner, Perquisite, in Jersey in 1956.

1958   Trainer JAMES HETHERTON born. Rode as an amateur.

1967   LESTER PIGGOTT won his 3rd Derby of the year. Following the Irish on Ribocco and the German on Luciano he collected the Ulster Harp Derby at Down Royal on Dan Kano, trained by Jimmy Lenehan.

1973   DAVID NICHOLLS rode his first winner, Hunting Tower, at Chester. We're happy to put the record straight here as David's Turf Directory entry lists the year as 1975.

1981   Jockey WILLIE HAYES rode his first winner, Drummer Jess, at Windsor.

1985   Former jump jockey GERRY KELLY scored his first flat win on Always Native at Ayr at the grand old age of 53.

1988   The start of the Ulster Derby at Down Royal was delayed while a flock of sheep was cleared off the track. Outsider of 4 at 6-1, Highland Bud, ridden by R. Quinton for J. Oxx, eventually won.

1990   LESTER PIGGOTT made a sensational comeback, almost five years after officially 'retiring', taking part in an invitation race at Tipperary, a course at which he had never previously ridden. He rode Don Leone in the Silvermines Veteran Riders Stakes, without success.

1991   WALTER SWINBURN became the 2nd jockey (after Willie Carson with 1988 St Leger winner Minster Son) to breed a British Classic winner when Possessive Dancer won the Irish Oaks at the Curragh. He didn't ride it, though – Steve Cauthen was in the saddle.

14 JULY

1919 Former York trainer VIC MITCHELL born. Rode professionally from 1933 to 1963, winning the 1939 Lincoln on Squadron Castle. First trainer's licence April 1 1964. Best horses included Precious Will, Supreme Sovereign.

1927 Owner CHARLIE SPARROWHAWK born. Colours: orange; brown hooped sleeves and star on cap.

1933 Turf Club member LORD WATERFORD born.

1943 Jockey PAT BUCKLEY born. Rode shock 66-1 1963 Grand National winner Ayala. Retired through injury in 1976.

1947 Trainer ANTHONY GILLAM born. Once trained Red Rum.

1950 Irish trainer JOHN OXX born. First licence 1979. Best horses trained include Petite Ile, Orchestra, Eurobird and Green Lucia.

1951 Six-year-old American Triple Crown hero CITATION became racing's first equine millionaire when victory in the Hollywood Gold Cup took his career earnings past $1 million - $1,085,760, to be precise.

1951 Jockey ROBERT HUGHES born. Rode Peter O'Sullevan's Attivo to win the Triumph Hurdle in 1974.

1951 Former Calke Abbey trainer PAT O'CONNOR born. Best horses trained include Hillyway, Toirdealbhach, Barwar.

1955 Two Royal Ascot racegoers were killed by lightning during a violent thunderstorm.

1963 Pat's brother PAUL EDDERY born. Rode 25-1 shot Most Welcome to 2nd place in 1987 Derby.

1965 JOE MERCER rode 4 winners at Yarmouth in the afternoon and 2 more at Doncaster in the evening from a day's total of 10 mounts.

1983 Jockey BILLY NEWNES was saved only by the kiss of life after being pinned down when his mount Silver Venture fell on the gallops.

1990 New England Stud stallion PRECOCIOUS enjoyed a remarkable afternoon when he was responsible for 3 winners in less than half an hour. Bold Starlet won the 4.30 at the Curragh, Sheer Precocity the 4.45 at Chester and Boy Emperor the 4.50 at Ayr.

1992 Owner-breeder JIM JOEL'S will was published. He left estate valued at over £41 million. One of his bequests was a horse to the Queen Mother, who chose his last winner, Keep Talking. The Jockey Club inherited his racing trophies. A total of £10,000 went to British Racing School; £5,000 to Injured Jockeys' Fund. Most went to the Childwick Trust, which Joel set up to give charity to various groups in racing and breeding, particularly the aged and needy.

15 JULY

1940 Former rider of Kingfisher Blue ERIC APTER born.

1945 Doncaster trainer JOHN BALDING born.

1952 Maisons-Laffitte trainer ALAIN BATES born.

1972 SECRETARIAT, the great US horse, won for the first time, at Aqueduct, ridden by P. Feliciano.

1987 JACK VAN BERG trained his 5,000th winner, Art's Chandelle, at Arlington Park, Chicago.

1989 ICONA won the 30th running of the longest-established sponsored flat race, the John Smith's Magnet Cup at York.

1989 The Wonderfuel Gas Handicap at Chester was won by . . . BURNT FINGERS.

1989 Alydaress won the Irish Oaks to make SHEIKH MOHAMMED the first person to own all 4 Irish Classic winners. Shaadi had won the 2,000 Guineas, Ensconce the 1,000 Guineas and Old Vic the Derby.

1989 South African jockey MICHAEL ROBERTS rode his first British 4-timer, at Newbury.

1990 YVES ST MARTIN, 48, rode Chirkpar at the Curragh in the John Dennis Veterans' Race to beat Orbis, ridden by Willie Robinson, 56 (who won the Cheltenham Gold Cup, Grand National and Champion Hurdle). In 3rd place were Legal Legend and Lester Piggott.

1991 LESTER PIGGOTT rode a treble at Killarney on his first visit to the Irish track: Defendant, News Headlines and Classic Trust, all trained by Vincent O'Brien.

1991 Jump jockey SHANE JENNINGS, 25, rode Direct Mail in the Hiskens Chase at Moonee Valley, Melbourne. It finished last of 8 but Jennings was later banned for two years by the stewards for improper practices. He was found guilty of using a hand-held metal object as an 'improper contrivance'. The horse returned with lacerations and grazes on its neck.

1992 Trainer BILLY WRIGHT, 32, grandson of the late Horatio Luro, tested positive for cocaine at Belmont Park. He was subsequently suspended by the New York Racing and Wagering Board. Commented Gale Berg of the NYRWB: 'A steward requested the test, Mr Wright was tested and the test was positive. He was then suspended.'

1992 An 'obscenity' appeared in place of jockey JULIE KRONE'S name during a simulcast of the Matchmaker Stakes at Atlantic City. She was subsequently reported to be filing a multi-million-dollar lawsuit against International Sound and one of its employees. The graphic was apparently seen on track and at all simulcast outlets for two seconds. An employee believed to be responsible was immediately sacked.

16 JULY

1903 The greatest bookmaker ever, WILLIAM HILL, was born in Birmingham. Started by collecting bets from local pubs on his bike. He became the most fearless layer of bets ever seen on a racecourse, and built up a huge credit betting operation, but Hill was initially anti-betting shops. He bred 1949 2,000 Guineas and Derby winner Nimbus, and his 1959 St Leger 100–1 winner Cantelo. Died in 1971.

1926 BOB ARMSTRONG, who had trained the 1st winner at the 1888 opening meeting of the 2nd racecourse at Hamilton Park, did it again when Impress won the 1st race run at the 3rd incarnation of the course, partnered by Joe Thwaites.

1943 MICHAEL CHARLES MORRIS born. An interesting owner, his career was rather brief. The North Devon man listed his Best Horse Owned as Glentino, adding, 'only ran once, injured'.

1948 Jockey DAVID GOULDING born.

1953 A good French horse called Santa Amaro was substituted for a moderate English one called FRANCASAL at Bath. The horse was heavily backed and telephone wires from the course were cut. 'Francasal' won easily at 10–1. However, the perpetrators of the coup were discovered and four men were jailed.

1954 Jump jockey REG CRANK born.

1955 VIMY became the first French-trained winner of the King George VI and Queen Elizabeth Diamond Stakes, trained by Alec Head.

1967 Jockey STEVE WOOD born. Rider of Chaplin's Club.

1967 Former jockey JOE DILLON died aged 82. Joe won the 1903 Irish Derby on Lord Rossmore.

1969 Bad luck dogged WILLIE CARSON on Javatina at Redcar. Set to win the race, Carson had to swerve swiftly to avoid disaster as two dogs raced on to the track. He avoided disaster, but the race was lost.

1990 PAT EDDERY rode 6 winners – 4 at Wolverhampton in the afternoon and 2 at Windsor in the evening – to take his total to 2,815.

1992 Sandown voted Racecourse of the Year by the Racegoers' Club for the 5th successive time, and 10th in all.

1992 Owner PETER SAVILL scored a swift treble with Second Colours (1–3) 3.40 at Hamilton, Night Melody (11–4) 4.05 at Catterick, then Northern Graduate (11–10) 4.10 at Hamilton.

1992 The aptly named MR CONFUSION was reinstated as the winner of the John Smith's Magnet Cup of five days earlier after apprentice jockey Ollie Pears was cleared of careless riding. Mr Confusion had been demoted to 3rd and 2nd-placed Tell No Lies (16–1) promoted to 1st, even though Mr Confusion (8–1) had been found to have interfered with 3rd-placed Steerforth.

17 JULY

1903 A fine field contested the Eclipse Stakes. 2,000 Guineas and Derby winner Rock Sand was 3rd; Sceptre, with 4 Classic victories, runner-up and the winner was the previous season's Derby winner ARD PATRICK.

1930 Owner JAMES MORRISON born. Best horses include Juliette Marny (1975 Oaks 12–1 winner). Colours: dark green; white sash; checked cap.

1932 MICHAEL SCUDAMORE, father of Peter, born. Won Gold Cup on Linwell in 1957, Grand National on Oxo in 1959 and King George VI Chase on Rose Park in 1956. Retired in 1966 after a fall damaged his eyesight and took up training, sending out 1974 Mackeson Gold Cup winner Bruslee. Rode in 16 consecutive Grand Nationals.

1937 Jockey Club member MICHAEL WYATT born. Colours: black; rose pink cuffs, collar and cap.

1941 Former jump jockey ERNIE FENWICK born.

1950 Owner of talented hurdler (Panama Cigar Final) and chaser (Embassy Premier Chase) Border Incident, ANTHONY WARRENDER, born.

1960 Not everyone was happy with the way LESTER PIGGOTT left hot favourite Petite Etoile, 2–5, with too much ground to make up in the straight in the King George VI and Queen Elizabeth Stakes, won by Jimmy Lindley on 100–8 chance Aggressor.

1964 Jockey MARCUS ARMYTAGE, who rode Mr Frisk to win 1990 Grand National and Whitbread Gold Cup, born.

1965 LESTER PIGGOTT won King George VI and Queen Elizabeth Stakes for the first time, on Meadow Court, the 6–5 favourite.

1980 Matilda Cave provided trainer MARK TOMPKINS with his first flat winner, scoring at Kempton.

1990 Trainer BARRY HILLS sacked his stable jockey – his son, Michael. Owners had asked for a different jockey and the philosophical Michael commented, 'I obviously feel let down to some extent.'

1991 Jockey PATRICK MILLINGTON received the heaviest-ever punishment dished out in Ireland for whip offences after Killarney finished 5th at Galway. He received a 28-day ban and IR£500 fine.

1991 Irish trainer WILLIE ROONEY, whose 401 winners as a point-to-point jockey were claimed as a world record, died aged 77. He trained 33–1 shot Bentom Boy to win the 1984 Irish Grand National.

1991 JACK BERRY set a new record for training the fastest 100 winners in a flat season when Our Fan won at Hamilton, beating the previous record, set by Henry Cecil in 1987, by six days.

18 JULY

1911   Rider SIR HARRY LLEWELLYN born. Partnered Ego to finish 2nd and 4th in the Grand Nationals of 1936 and 1937. Also one of the great show-jumpers in partnership with Foxhunter.

1914   Trainer MAJOR VERLY BEWICKE born. As an amateur rider he won the 1938 Territorial Army Cup on Noble Artist at Sandown. Began training in Northumberland in 1947, later moving to Didcot, Berkshire. Sent out Kerstin to win the 1958 Cheltenham Gold Cup and 1959 Hennessy Gold Cup. Also trained 1951 Scottish National winner Court Painter.

1942   Former jockey COLIN MOSS born. First winner Lilac Time at Warwick, May 16 1959. Best horses ridden include Track Spare, Pompous.

1947   There were 18,000 spectators at Britain's first evening meeting at Hamilton Park.

1952   Trainer RICHARD LISTER born. First licence 1980. Best horses trained include Anita's Prince.

1953   Twice (1975–76, 1976–77) champion amateur rider PETER GREENALL born.

1964   SANTA CLAUS, the hottest-ever favourite for the King George VI and Queen Elizabeth Stakes at Ascot at 2–13, was beaten into 2nd place by Nasram II (100–7).

1969   Jockey DERICK STANSFIELD was injured in a fall at Hamilton Park and died two days later. It was the first fatal accident in a flat race in Britain since Manny Mercer's death at Ascot in 1959. Stansfield rode successfully in Kenya and Scandinavia. He was 39.

1989   The last son of the great stallion NORTHERN DANCER was sold for $2.8 million at Keeneland Sales, Kentucky. The son of Mrs Penny was sold to Zenya Yoshida, Japan's leading breeder.

1990   Australian born Hong Kong-based jockey GARY MOORE was banned from all racing for five and a half years and fined almost £100,000 by the Royal Hong Kong Jockey Club after being found guilty of 66 betting-related breaches of the rules of racing. The 38-year-old former French Champion with a home in Italy had been Hong Kong Champion 7 times.

1990   Former jump jockey MICKY HAMMOND saddled his first runner as a trainer, Eladham, which finished 3rd at Hamilton.

19 JULY

1900 Former senior stewards' secretary ROSCOE HARVEY born.

1901 EPSOM LAD (7–1) became the only gelding to win the Eclipse Stakes, but it was a close run thing as Argentinian jockey Pedro Gomez passed the post with his saddle in his hand after it had slipped during the race.

1902 Steward GEORGE MACLACHLAN owned the winners of the first 5 races at Hamilton Park. He had the chance of achieving immortality by owning the 6th and final winner. A contemporary report by Hamilton's clerk of the course at the turn of the century, Brigadier General Sir Loftus Bates DSO, takes up the tale: 'There were only 5 runners but 3 with a chance to win in the 6th race which, of course, he was very keen to win. One of the 3 was a 'stiff 'un' and he had the chance to buy the other 2, but with national caution he would only buy one – and that was the wrong one.'

1919 Racing author PETER WILLETT born.

1935 Former Wiltshire trainer SUE ARMYTAGE born.

1950 American trainer TOMMY SKIFFINGTON born.

1951 LESTER PIGGOTT rode his 100th winner, Wayland, at Bath.

1952 The King George VI and Queen Elizabeth Stakes was run under that name for the first time, at Ascot, and won by Tulyar.

1957 Jockey ALEC RUSSELL went through the card at Bogside's 6-race meeting. His winners were Double Up, Wage Claim, Cligarry, Courtlier, Newton and Roselime. All 6 were for different trainers: Colonel Wilfred Lyde, E. G. Duffy, H. Blackshaw, W. Hide, G. Boyd and E. Carr. Russell, born in 1918, retired after being injured in October 1973.

1959 Kingsclere jockey SHAUN PAYNE born.

1962 WILLIE CARSON rode his first winner, Pinkers Pond, at Catterick.

1967 Jockey GARY MOORE had his first ride in public on Barbentane at Le Tremblay, France.

1972 Jump jockey PAUL MIDGLEY born.

1988 VICTOR MORLEY LAWSON, who rode his first winner at the age of 67, died aged 81. He rode Ocean King to win the Corinthian Amateur Riders' Maiden Stakes at Warwick in October 1973.

1990 STEVE CAUTHEN was fined £1,000 for bringing racing into disrepute after refusing to ride three-year-old Nicholas Payne at Leicester on May 29, having already weighed out. Said Cauthen: 'I did it because it was in my best interests and I would do the same again.'

1991 LUCKY BEN failed to live up to his name at Calder racecourse, Florida. Awaiting the start, he threw jockey Willie Hernandez, bolted straight into the infield lake – and drowned.

20 JULY

1790 The Prince of Wales' PEGASUS won a race in four-mile heats at Winchester.

1914 Winner of the 1903 Triple Crown ROCK SAND died in France, aged fourteen.

1925 Jockey MARTIN MOLONY born. Best horses ridden include Silver Fame and Finnore.

1926 TV commentator JOHN PENNEY born.

1930 Former cock of the north PADDY FARRELL born.

1931 Malton trainer WILLIAM HAIGH born. First licence 1957. Previously NH jockey from 1954 to 1956. Best horses trained include Prince Pecadillo, Kenco, Confluence.

1938 Jockey Club member LORD MCGOWAN born.

1945 Owner of Khan and Highest Trump LORD PETERSHAM born. Colours: Eton blue; chocolate braces.

1953 Lady rider DIANA HENDERSON born. First winner Fire Fairy at Sandown in one and a quarter-mile ladies' flat race. First woman to win under NH rules at Stratford. Wife of trainer Nick.

1953 Lady rider JANE SLOAN born.

1956 Former Lanark trainer JOHN GILLEN born.

1957 French horses finished 1, 2, 3, 4 in the King George VI and Queen Elizabeth Stakes at Ascot. Montanal (1st, 20-1), Al Mabsoot (2nd, 100-7), Tribord (3rd, 100-7), Raphael (4th, 20-1). The winner was ridden by F. Palmer, trained by G. Bridgland.

1959 Newmarket jockey ALLAN MACKAY born. Best horses ridden include Lusitanica, Grand Unit.

1985 STARLITE NIGHT (trained by Henry Cecil, ridden by Paul Eddery) was reckoned such a certainty for a race at Nottingham that no starting prices were returned. The horse finished 5th of 6.

1989 Apprentice jockey JOHN CARR saw the chance of a glorious victory as he partnered Earth Spacer in a race at Catterick. So he went for the line for all he was worth – and the pair passed the post in front – only to stare in disbelief as the rest of the field continued on its way. They had only run 3 furlongs of the one mile 5-furlong race. 'I feel like putting a gun to my head,' said Carr.

1990 US jockey PEDRO ORTEGA, 26, went missing. In August body parts washed up in a garbage bag on the New Jersey shore were identified as his remains. He was believed to have become involved in a drugs conspiracy.

1991 SHANE DYE became the first New Zealand jockey to ride 100 winners in a season in Australia when Beau Channon won at Rosehill. Only 5 other jockeys had ridden 100 winners in Australia in a season.

21 JULY

1841　So thick was the fog at Cheltenham, where the one-mile Sherborne Stakes was being run, that John Chapple on Tupsley thought he had won and pulled his horse up as they passed the winning post. Unfortunately for Chapple, it wasn't the winning post at all, and Sam Rogers on The Currier went past to win. After that the rest of the meeting was abandoned for the day.

1931　Royal jockey-to-be HARRY CARR rode his first winner at the age of fourteen, Knights Folly, at Ayr.

1943　Glamorgan trainer DEREK HAYDN JONES born. Amateur rider from 1959 to 1969. First trainer's licence 1971. Best horses trained include Annie Edge, Melody Time, Parhelion, La Petite Noblesse.

1949　Jockey VIC SOANE born. Best horses ridden include Midnight Fury and Roman Holiday.

1951　CHARLIE ELLIOTT won the inaugural King George VI and Queen Elizabeth Festival of Britain Stakes at Ascot on Supreme Court (100-9) to land record prize-money of £25,322.

1956　Dual Arc de Triomphe winner RIBOT raced in the land of his birth for the first time, winning the King George VI and Queen Elizabeth Stakes at Ascot.

1962　Britain's first Saturday evening meeting was held at Wolverhampton, with a regimental band and a skiffle group entertaining the crowd.

1985　Leopardstown staged the first British or Irish Sunday race meeting.

1990　Prime minister Margaret Thatcher paid her first visit to a flat race meeting, at Newbury.

1990　Cheltenham Gold Cup winner at odds of 100-1 Norton's Coin led a civic parade through the centre of Carmarthen. Said mayor Peter Hughes Griffiths: 'This is the highest award we can give and I am sure it has never gone to a horse before. Norton's Coin has brought honour and a touch of colour to the town.' Trainer Sirrell Griffiths' stable is at Rwyth Farm, Nantgaredig, Carmarthen.

1990　Yellow card! Former England soccer star turned trainer MICK CHANNON was fined £350 by stewards at Ayr for acting in an improper and abusive manner. He was reported after one of his owners was prevented from entering the stable block without a pass.

1990　Lingfield staged trotting as a preliminary to racing.

1991　Derby winning jockey ALAN MUNRO was honoured by the Clan Munro, based at Foulis Castle, Ross-shire, which was founded in 1937 and boasts 1,500 members.

22 JULY

1728 DRUMMER, owned by Capt Hugh Collyer, became the first recorded horse to win a race at Doncaster. Racing probably took place there up to 100 years earlier but no records survive. Third winner on this day was the remarkably named Sweetest When Naked, owned by Mr Clapham.

1920 Owner of Ghofar SIR HUGH DUNDAS born. Also owned and bred Heavenly Note. Colours: white; red spots, sleeves and cap.

1949 Jockey BOB CURANT born. Rode first winner in 1965 at Newbury. Best horses ridden include Nicholas Bill, Khairpour, Heighlin, Home Guard.

1960 Amateur jockey JOHN GREENALL born. Best horses ridden include Youghal, Poker Classic.

1978 SUE DAY became the first lady jockey in New Zealand to win a race against male opposition. She rode Jaws to victory in the South Canterbury Hunt meeting.

1982 'The worst day' of trainer JIM BOLGER's career. 'I took Favourite Niece to Gowran Park. I fancied her and I backed her. She ran a poor race. When I returned home I found the stables on fire!'

1991 PAT EDDERY became only the 5th jockey to ride 3,000 winners in Britain when the aptly named Sure Victory proved just that at Bath – the last leg of a treble, although there was some dispute as to whether the middle leg of that treble, Morocco, was actually the historic winner. Eddery achieved the feat faster than any of the other 4, in 22 years 3 months. Gordon Richards took 24 years, Lester Piggott nearly 27; Willie Carson from July 19 1962 to May 22 1990 and Doug Smith from May 26 1932 until October 21 1965.

23 JULY

1684 Racing was reported as taking place at Doncaster in the *London Gazette*. No records of the meeting survive, however.

1886 The inaugural running of England's first £10,000 race, the Eclipse Stakes, took place at Sandown. Mr H. T. 'Buck' Barclay's BENDIGO was the winner, partnered by Tom Cannon. The horse was trained at Seven Barrows at Lambourn by Charlie Jousiffe.

1945 Trainer HON. GEORGE LAMBTON died, aged 85, just two days after retiring and handing over the reins of his Kremlin House stable, Newmarket, to his son, Teddy. George Lambton trained 13 Classic winners including Sansovino and Hyperion in the Derby and Colorado (1926) in the 2,000 Guineas.

1947 Jockey DENNIS LETHERBY born. Best horses ridden include Caterina, Barwin.

1956 The 'other' STEVE DAVIS, former jump jockey, born. Rider of Jer.

1965 Jockey TONY MULHOLLAND born. Paddy's Dream was his first winner on May 5 1986 at Devon. Best horse ridden Henry Mann.

1977 The Minstrel gave LESTER PIGGOTT his 6th win in the King George VI and Queen Elizabeth Diamond Stakes at Ascot.

1983 The *Sporting Chronicle* racing newspaper closed down.

1985 A record $13.1 million was paid out at Keeneland, Kentucky, by Robert Sangster and his partners for SEATTLE DANCER, which proved practically useless as a racehorse.

24 JULY

1806   The racecourse at Lewes, Brighton, staged a match between 1804 St Leger winner SANCHO, owned by Colonel Henry Mellish of the 10th Hussars, and Lord Darlington's PAVILION for a 2,000-guinea stake. Mellish backed his horse to win £20,000 but Sancho, ridden by Frank Buckle, went lame when in the lead and Sam Chifney Jr brought Pavilion home to win.

1926   Trainer TOMMY GOSLING born. Best horses ridden include Ardent Dancer and Sol Argent.

1948   Newmarket trainer PIP PAYNE born (real name John William Payne). Served his apprenticeship in France and began training there. Best horse trained Medaille d'Or.

1949   Scottish jump jockey DONALD NOLAN born.

1955   Lambourn trainer SIMON CHRISTIAN born. First licence 1984.

1962   Jockey MARK PERRETT born. Bayham Sir Vardon was his first winner at Folkestone on March 17 1980. Won 1985 Topsham Trophy on Smith's Man, 1983 Triumph Hurdle on Saxon Farm, 1989 Mackeson Gold Cup on Joint Sovereignty.

1963   US jockey JAMES BRUIN born in Georgetown, Kentucky. One-time top rider at Turfway Park, River Downs.

1971   Geoff Lewis rode Ian Balding-trained MILL REEF, 8–13 favourite, to a record-breaking 6-length victory in the King George VI and Queen Elizabeth Stakes at Ascot.

1991   Winning owner KEN WHELDON refused to accept the trophy after Doncaster's Yorkshire Metropolitan Property's Selling Stakes because the sponsor's managing director, David Blunt, bid for his horse, Vado Via. Mr Blunt unsuccessfully offered 8,000 guineas, which meant Wheldon had to go to 8,200 guineas to retain the animal.

1992   Trainer Geoffrey Wragg forgot to declare his YOUNG BUSTER for the Mail on Sunday Trophy at the first British Sunday meeting at Doncaster, but the Jockey Club reopened the race for him and other trainers who had also forgotten. Young Buster went on to win the race.

1992   David Swannell MBE, former senior Jockey Club handicapper, collapsed and died aged 73 shortly after giving an address at the Irish Turf Club handicapper Dick Turner's memorial service, taking place near Newmarket. Swannell was responsible for introducing the centralised handicapping system in 1973 and was heavily involved when international classifications were brought in.

1993   Southwell managed to schedule *two* meetings on the same day - a turf meeting in the afternoon and all-weather in the evening.

25 JULY

1769 ECLIPSE won a walkover in the King's Plate at Canterbury.

1786 The second day of the sale by auction of the stud of HRH the Prince of Wales, 'consisting of Stallions, Horses in Training, Brood Mares, Colts, Fillies, Hunters, Coach-horses, Hacks etc.' Two days later the *St James Chronicle* reported, 'The Stud was not sold, but given away, the two-day sale not having amounted to half the sum that was justly expected.'

1899 MP and fraudster HORATIO BOTTOMLEY's Northern Farmer (20-1) won the Stewards' Cup.

1910 Trainer BILL PAYNE born. Father of Pip. Professional jump jockey from 1924 to 1931. Trainer's licence from 1955.

1923 Irish trainer TOMMY SHAW born. Rode as a professional under both codes. First trainer's licence 1957. Trained Zenobia to win the Irish 1,000 Guineas in 1960. Also trained Abadesa, China Clipper and Jongleu.

1928 Owner JIM JOEL had his first flat winner when Black Fly (Percy Whitaker) won at Liverpool. He went on to have 804 more flat winners between then and 1991.

1929 SANDY STRUTHERS born. Owner of 1968 (45-1) Derby 3rd Mount Athos, Oaks runner-up Bonnie Isle and 1970 Ayr Gold Cup winner John Splendid. Colours: grey; pink sleeves; checked cap.

1935 Jockey JEAN DEFORGE born. Best horses ridden included Exbury, Hula Dancer and Diatome.

1936 Bedfordshire permit-holder GEORGE HARTIGAN born.

1941 Swiss owner SVEN HANSON born. His Fair Salinia scored a triple Oaks triumph in 1978, winning the Epsom version, Yorkshire Oaks and Irish Oaks. Colours: blue; white stars; white diamond on cap.

1950 LESTER PIGGOTT rode his first Goodwood winner, Vidi Vici, in the Craven Stakes.

1954 Owner LORD PORTSMOUTH born.

1967 LESTER PIGGOTT rode his 2,000th domestic winner on Peter Walwyn-trained (8-13) Coonbeam at Leicester.

1967 Trainer JOHN DUNLOP saddled his first Goodwood winner, Storm Bird (11-10), in the New Ham Stakes.

1981 Hot favourite Shergar (2-5) won the King George VI and Queen Elizabeth Diamond Stakes at Ascot, by an easy 4 lengths.

1990 JULIE KRONE returned to racing at Monmouth, after having smashed her arm in a fall at Meadowlands the previous November.

1992 Commentator GRAHAM GOODE sponsored the Folks That Live on the Hill Handicap at Southwell to mark his and wife Gill's 21st wedding anniversary.

26 JULY

1920 Former hurdles jockey JOHNNY GILBERT born. In 1959 he rode 10 winners in successive races, a record later equalled by Phil Tuck. Won the Triumph Hurdle on Amazon's Choice in 1959 and the Imperial Cup in 1948 and 1949.

1924 Trainer TOMMY ROBSON born. Twice won Scottish National. Trained 1964 Champion Hurdle winner Magic Court (100-6).

1952 Diorama won at Warwick to give owner CHARLES ST GEORGE his first winner.

1955 Trainer PHILIP HOBBS born. Rode 160 winners as professional jump jockey from 1975 to 1986. Best horses trained include Moody Man.

1958 YVES ST MARTIN rode his first winner, at Le Tremblay.

1961 Jockey NICK ADAMS born. Best horses ridden include March Bird.

1962 Jockey SARA LAWRENCE born. First winner Assured at Hereford, April 1983. Also partnered Honeydew Wonder, Lean Forward.

1973 Golden Hansel won at Limerick to give NIALL MADDEN his first winner.

1975 Nominated by many as the 'Race of the century' (indeed, a book of that name about it was penned by Chris Hawkins), the King George VI and Queen Elizabeth Diamond (inserted for the first time) Stakes at Ascot produced a breathtaking battle between eventual winner Peter Walwyn-trained GRUNDY (Pat Eddery, 4-5) and Bustino (Joe Mercer, 4-1), trained by Dick Hern. The margin of victory for the Derby winner over the St Leger winner was 1/2 length.

1990 CHASE THE DOOR set an unofficial world-record time for a mile, clocking 1 minute 30.9 seconds in the Brighton Summer Cup.

1990 Former Newmarket trainer DICK WARDEN died, aged 82.

1991 PAT EDDERY reached 100 winners for the season for the 18th time when Sun and Shade won at Ascot.

1991 National Hunt trainer BEN WISE died.

1992 Alydeed, 1-20 favourite, was beaten in the Prince of Wales Stakes at Fort Eric, Ontario. Blenburb (24-1) was the winner.

1992 Britain's first Sunday race meeting was held at Doncaster. There was no on-course betting. Mother and daughter Rita and Claire Mason from Mexborough, Doncaster, were the first to pay their £5 admission fees. The attendance was 23,000 - 2,000 more than had been at the Derby. Four-year-old Savoyard won the first race, the 7-furlong Coral First Sunday Race, trained by Michael Jarvis, ridden by Walter Swinburn and returning 36-10 on the Tote. First clear winning favourite was Drum Sergeant (Michael Roberts-J. Parkes) at 34-10 in the 5th race, the Virgin Atlantic Flyer Handicap.

27 JULY

1796 Jockey GEORGE HERRING, rumoured to have once rid⌐⌐n 19 consecutive winners, was killed in a race fall at Hull.

1909 DOWAGER LADY BEAVERBROOK born. Her best horses usually had seven-letter names: 1974 St Leger winner Bustino, Derby runners-up Terimon and Relkino. Owned top sprinter and record gelding prize-money winner Boldboy; Doncaster Cup winner Biskrah. Took up racing following the death of her husband in 1964. Colours: beaver brown; maple leaf green cross-belts and cap.

1910 MAGIC, trained by Felix Leach at Newmarket, pulled off a shock by defeating 1–20 favourite Bayardo by a neck in the Goodwood Cup.

1920 Jockey HARRY SPRAGUE born. Best horse ridden Done Up, on which he won the 1959 Whitbread Gold Cup on his last ride. Done Up was a notably lazy horse and Sprague worked so hard on the horse that he was physically sick following the race.

1923 Former cock of the north JOE SIME born. His first winner had come at Newmarket in June 1941. Won a string of big races such as the Lincoln, Wokingham, Northumberland Plate, Ebor, Cesarewitch, William Hill Gold Cup, Ayr Gold Cup. Retired at the end of 1968.

1943 Peterborough trainer PAM (MARIGOLD) SLY born.

1948 Former Richmond trainer GEOFF CALVERT born.

1955 One of the top post-war fillies, Jim Joel's STAR OF INDIA, won on her debut in the Selsey Maiden Stakes at Goodwood, ridden by Eph Smith and trained by Ted Leader. She won all 5 of her two-year-old races but was unplaced in her only three-year-old start, having been rated at a remarkable 138 by Timeform. Only Windy City, 142 in 1951, was rated higher.

1965 WILLIE CARSON's first Goodwood winner was Osotis in the Charlton Handicap.

1968 ROYAL PALACE gave trainer Noel Murless a 3rd successive victory in the King George VI and Queen Elizabeth Stakes at Ascot, ridden by Sandy Barclay. Busted had won in 1967 and Aunt Edith in 1966.

1974 Filly DAHLIA became the first horse to win two King George VI and Queen Elizabeth Stakes at Ascot. Ridden by Lester Piggott.

1991 Jockey ROGER BROWNE was injured in a fall from a horse at Garrison Savannah, Barbados. He died on August 4.

1992 JULIE KRONE became the first female jockey ever to win a meeting title in New York when she rode a double to take her score to 73 victories from 370 mounts at Belmont Park.

1992 New jockey riding fees were announced for 1992–93. Flat jockeys' basic fees became £54 per ride; NH jockeys £73.70. In 1983–84 the rates were £32 per flat ride; £43.50 under NH rules.

28 JULY

1914   POOR BOY, owned by Solly Joel, by now nine years old, made his 7th successive attempt to win the Stewards' Cup at Goodwood, having finished 2nd 4 times – beaten a neck in 1908 and 1910, 2nd again in 1912 and 1913 – and unplaced in 1909 and 1911. There was no fairytale ending as the horse was unplaced.

1923   Shropshire trainer ARTHUR JONES born. His Merry Deal was one of the few owner-trained winners of the Champion Hurdle (1957).

1924   Jump jockey DEREK ANCIL born.

1932   Hexham trainer WILLIAM GEORGE REED born.

1933   Amateur rider DICK SAUNDERS, who rode Grittar to win the Grand National in 1982 at 7–1 and became, at 48, the oldest man ever to win it, born. He celebrated his National triumph by immediately retiring.

1937   Owner-trainer BRYAN BOUSFIELD born.

1945   Welsh jockey TREVOR ROGERS born. He moved to Germany and rode 39 winners to become Champion in Madras in 1971–72. He can also boast wins in the Deccan Derby at Hyderabad and the Futurity Stakes in Kenya.

1945   Owner ARTHUR BOYD-ROCHFORT born. His Cloonagh won the 1973 Irish 1,000 Guineas and Aldino the Scottish Champion Hurdle. An Ipswich supporter, his colours are Eton blue; black sleeves; checked cap.

1962   Jump jockey KEVIN DOOLAN born.

1973   DAHLIA, Bill Pyers up, equalled Mill Reef's record 6-length victory in the King George VI and Queen Elizabeth Stakes at Ascot.

1973   The first race for lady riders run at Ascot, the 29-runner Cullinan Diamond Stakes, was won by CAROLINE BLACKWELL on Hurdy Gurdy.

1974   Tipster CHARLES LAMB of the *Baltimore News American* selected 10 out of 10 winners at the Delaware Park meeting, a world record.

1982   JOHN FRANCOME, PETER SCUDAMORE and STEVE SMITH ECCLES were all informed that they need not apply for their licences for the forthcoming NH season until August 2, effectively a seven-day suspension. It was revealed that this was because Francome was said to have given the other two £200 each by mutual agreement after riding Donegal Prince to victory in the Schweppes.

1984   French challenger ESPRIT DU NORD, was declared to run in blinkers in the King George VI and Queen Elizabeth Diamond Stakes at Ascot. He arrived at the post without them, and the stewards decided the horse couldn't run and fined trainer John Fellows £200.

29 JULY

1902 Having been taken ill at Sandown Park ten days earlier due to his excessive wasting, jockey JOHN WATTS died. Born in 1861, he rode 19 Classic winners, including 4 Derbys.

1920 Trainer turned journalist and author TIM FITZGEORGE-PARKER born. Among his prolific output of racing books is *The Guv'nor*, a biography of Sir Noel Murless.

1924 Owner LORD WEINSTOCK born. Bred 200th Derby winner Troy. Colours: pale blue; yellow and white checked cap.

1929 Owner DAVID MORT born. His Varingo won the 1979 Coventry Stakes at Royal Ascot. Colours: light blue; red disc; dark blue sleeves; red cap.

1932 Owner ANGELA ABECASSIS born. Her Outpoint won the 1977 Joe Coral Hurdle at Cheltenham. Colours: royal blue; yellow diamond on body and cap.

1935 Jockey GRAHAM MACMILLAN born. Rode his first winner at Hexham, 1955. Best horses ridden included Union Pacific, Credit Call, Tee Cee Bee, Queensberry Lad.

1948 Irish trainer DERMOT WELD born. In 1989 became the first trainer to win over £1 million in prize-money. Has won a string of top races including the Oaks, Irish Oaks, Irish 1,000 Guineas, Irish 2,000 Guineas, Irish Grand National. Best horses trained include Go and Go, Blue Wind, Steel Heart, Kilijaro.

1954 Trainer BILL MOTT born. Best horses trained include Theatrical.

1965 1992 Grand National winner Party Politics' jockey CARL LLEWEL-LYN born. First winner Starjestic at Wolverhampton on March 14 1986. Once listed his favourite recreation as 'eating puddings'.

1967 PAMPALINA (John Oxx–Johnny Roe) won the major prize in the British Isles, the £20,571 Irish Oaks.

1978 WILLIE CARSON rode 4 winners at Goodwood.

1988 Almost Blue (10–1), ridden by John Carroll, won the Molecomb Stakes to give trainer JACK BERRY his first Goodwood winner.

1990 Top Aussie trainer COLIN HAYES retired after 5,329 winners worth AUS$40.7 million prize-money. He was top trainer for 13 consecutive years at Moonee Valley, Melbourne.

1990 Top Aussie jockey PAT HYLAND retired after 35 years and 2,381 winners. He was 2nd on his last ride, Godemus, at Moonee Valley.

1990 GRAEME ROGERSON became the first trainer in New Zealand to send out 100 winners in a season when On the Nose and Grand Coquette won at Ruakaka. He had been stuck on 98 since June 4.

1992 Trainer RICHARD HANNON broke the £1 million prize-money barrier when Son Pardo won the Richmond Stakes at Goodwood.

30 JULY

1714   Turf enthusiast QUEEN ANNE's bay horse Star won a 40-guinea race at York. Three days later she was dead. The new King, George, was not interested in racing.

1840   The heir to the French throne, the DUC d'ORLEANS, won the Goodwood Cup with his Beggarman.

1914   Former steward of the Turf Club LORD KILLANIN born.

1947   FRANK-MORE O'FERRALL gave the first BBC Radio broadcast from Goodwood on the Light Programme, covering just the Goodwood Stakes.

1948   Jockey PAT TAAFFE rode his first double, at Tuam, Co. Galway.

1949   Owner PETER SAVILL born. His Chaplin's Club was a prolific winner.

1959   PETER WALWYN's first Goodwood winner was Enticement in the Lavant Stakes.

1974   RED ALERT won the Stewards Cup, giving trainer Dermot Weld his first win at Goodwood.

1980   DAVID ELSWORTH sent out his first Goodwood winner, Heighlin, in the Goodwood handicap.

1988   Back protectors made mandatory for jump jockeys.

1991   The Hull City AFC Handicap at Beverley was 'won' by 11–1 shot Azubah, ridden by Kieran Fallon and trained by George Moore, only for the race to be declared void because starter John Mangles had got the race under way 1 minute 6 seconds early. He was later fined an undisclosed amount.

1991   Jockey JACK EGAN, former Champion Jockey in Denmark, died aged 59.

1992   German horse ELSURIMO appeared at Goodwood for the Goodwood Cup with jockey Mark Rimmer wearing colours emblazoned with the name of Steigenberger Hotels across his back. Such advertising was in direct breach of Jockey Club rules at a time when the Club was engaged in discussions about allowing jockeys to wear advertising material. The owner of the horse was, not altogether surprisingly, hotel proprietor Mr Steigenberger. Elsurimo finished 6th.

31 JULY

1770 LEONATUS, the Duke of Grafton's five-year-old, entered for a £50 Plate at Huntingdon run in two-mile heats; he ran five, finishing 3rd. Two days later he came out again at Huntingdon, this time in a £50 Plate run in four-mile heats. He ran in five of these: a total of 30 miles raced over 48 hours. He never ran again..

1924 Trainer ALEC HEAD born. First licence January 1 1947. His Lavandin won the 1956 Derby. As a jockey rode Le Paillon into 2nd place in the Champion Hurdle.

1932 Jockey turned trainer ERIC ELDIN born. As a jockey in 1973 he rode Knockroe to break the then record for the Derby course and distance in the Weetabix Wildlife Handicap at Epsom. Rode from 1950 to 1979. Best horses trained include Prowess Prince, Northern Chimes.

1944 Jockey DAVID RICHARDSON, who moved to Germany, born.

1949 A politician with racing interest, ALAN MEALE, born.

1950 Ubiquitous TV commentator, tipster and pundit DEREK THOMPSON born. As an amateur jockey he beat Prince Charles at Plumpton in 1980, riding Classified.

1952 Cheltenham racecourse manager EDWARD GILLESPIE born. A man of impeccable taste, he once used excerpts from a book of mine in his annual Cheltenham fixtures brochure.

1956 GOODWOOD televised for the first time when the BBC showed the Craven Stakes, Stewards' Cup and Bentinck Stakes. Race commentary by Peter O'Sullevan and paddock comments by Clive Graham.

1958 VINCENT O'BRIEN saddled his first Goodwood winner when 1–2 chance Gladness, ridden by Lester Piggott, landed the Goodwood Cup.

1958 Jockey JIMMY FROST born. Won the 1989 Grand National on 28–1 chance Little Polveir, 1991 Champion Hurdle on Morley Street (4–1) and, on same horse, Breeders' Cup.

1959 Trimmer took the Trundle Stakes to give DICK HERN his first Goodwood winner.

1963 Jockey CHRIS RUTTER born. Won 1985 Royal Hunt Cup on Come on the Blues. He rode his first winner, Morwray Boy, on May 6 1984 at Doncaster. Also partnered Polykratis, Sneak Preview.

1964 Jump jockey TIM JARVIS born. First winner Broon Secret, 1981.

1973 TONY MURRAY rode his 500th winner, King Frog, at Goodwood.

1973 Alphadamus won the Spillers Stewards' Cup to give trainer Michael Stoute his first Goodwood winner.

1976 FOOL'S MATE, trained by Henry Cecil, won twice at Glorious Goodwood. He added the PTS Laurels Handicap to the Trundle Handicap he had won four days earlier. He was partnered by Lester Piggott on both occasions.

1 AUGUST

1878   Unbeaten in a career spanning 54 races KINCSEM, the great Hungarian mare, made her only English racecourse appearance, winning the Goodwood Cup.

1898   Large bets were placed on the outcome of races at the Trodmore Hunt meeting, featured in the sporting press. However, once the results had appeared and much money had been paid out by unsuspecting bookies it was discovered that there was no such place as Trodmore. The whole incident was a complete scam.

1920   Owner JACK GOODMAN born. His Team Spirit won the 1964 Grand National. Colours: yellow, red, white and blue; striped sleeves.

1936   Owner NICK ROBINSON born. His Dibidale won the Cheshire, Irish and Yorkshire Oaks and Cracaval won the 1979 Chester Vase. Colours: dark blue with light blue and dark red hoops and armlets; white cap.

1943   Trainer GEORGE PETER-HOBLYN born. Best horses include Rivoli.

1943   Irish trainer DENNIS CORDELL-LAVARACK born in Brazil. Best horses trained include Modest, Snatchingly, Baba Karam and Reet Petite. As Denny Cordell he made a big impression on the sixties pop scene. He was involved in the production of the Moody Blues' first hit, 'Go Now' before making a big breakthrough with Procol Harum's 'Whiter Shade of Pale'.

1945   Racecourse judge SANDRA WILLIAMS born.

1946   Amateur rider DR IAN DAVIES born. Rode first winner Miss Aboyne at Edinburgh on July 9 1990.

1947   Jockey DENNIS ATKINS born. Rode Cancello to win the 1976 Mackeson Gold Cup, run that year at Haydock.

1957   Irish jockey STEPHEN CRAINE born.

1966   Jockey MARK PITMAN, son of trainer Jenny and TV commentator Richard, born. Rode Garrison Savannah to win the 1991 Cheltenham Gold Cup and in the same season finished 2nd in the Grand National, just as his father had done on Crisp.

1974   RAY COCHRANE rode the first of his 8 wins over hurdles on Wanlockhead, at Newton Abbot.

1985   An anonymous punter won £227,812.50 from William Hill after staking 3 £2,000 doubles and a £9,000 treble. The bet made the *Guinness Book of Records*.

1991   A fall from Independent Air at Bangor resulted in jockey SHARRON MURGATROYD breaking her spinal cord.

1992   RUBY TIGER, trained by P. Cole and ridden by T. Quinn, won Goodwood's Nassau Stakes for the second consecutive season, having also won Group races in Italy (twice), US, Germany and Ireland.

2 AUGUST

1803 The first filly to complete the Derby-Oaks double, ELEANOR, beat Fieldfare in two-mile heats at Huntingdon.

1918 Sally Crag, at Newmarket, was the first winner for jockey THOMAS WESTON, born at Dewsbury in 1903. He went on to ride 11 Classic winners.

1927 Trainer FRANK MUGGERIDGE born. First licence 1956. Best horses included Shawnigan, Energy, Soapey Sponge. Also rode under NH Rules from 1945 to 1955.

1928 Former Minehead permit trainer TONY HOBBS born. Best horses included Copper Bar, Redders Boy, No Pardon.

1934 Trainer PETER BEAUMONT born. Rode 1 winner under NH Rules. Best horses trained include J. J. Henry and Jodami, who won the 1993 Cheltenham Gold Cup.

1937 Leicester trainer TOM TRIVETT BILL born. Best horses trained include Cross Master, Northern Bay.

1942 Durham trainer MICHAEL REDDAN born. First licence 1978. Best horses trained included Saintly Lady, Lin Slipper.

1943 Henley-in-Arden trainer JOHN BUKOVETS born. Best horses trained include Essex, Four of a Kind, Honeyman, Sheer Steel.

1947 Racing writer JOHN GARNSEY, Scout of the *Daily Express*, born.

1952 Bloodstock agent JILL LAMB HOLDER born.

1963 Fraxinus took the News of the World Handicap to give trainer BILL WIGHTMAN his first Goodwood winner.

1969 Archer provides trainer JIMMY FITZGERALD with his first winner, at Market Rasen.

1980 Owner and rider ANTHONY ROBINSON died aged 43 after a relapse of the cancer it seemed he had beaten when he saw his horse Tied Cottage win the 1980 Cheltenham Gold Cup, ridden by Tommy Carberry. The horse was later disqualified and, tragically, his trainer Dan Moore also died within months of the race being run.

1985 Jockey KIM TINKLER rode her first winner, Wow Wow Wow, at Edinburgh.

1988 1972 Derby winner ROBERTO died aged nineteen.

1990 Prominent owner SHEIKH FAHAD AL-AHMAD AL SABAH was killed during the Iraqi invasion of Kuwait. Owned Kuwait Tower.

1991 PAUL BARTON became the first former professional jockey to take charge of a meeting as stewards' secretary at Bangor.

1991 It was revealed that a trophy presented by Chepstow racecourse to SIR GORDON RICHARDS after his retirement in 1954, which had gone missing in a 1956 robbery, had been recovered. The trophy was found in a TSB vault in Ashton.

3 AUGUST

1861 *The Airdrie & Coatbridge Advertiser* called for the banning of the annual race fixture at Airdrie as it brought only 'fast youths, fancy men, gamblers, blacklegs and women of easy virtue' to the area.

1941 Four-times Champion Jump Jockey turned top trainer JOSH GIFFORD MBE born. Rode 122 winners in season 1966–67. Sent out Aldaniti to win the Grand National (1981).

1942 Trainer in France CHARLIE MILBANK born.

1946 Jockey MICK WAGNER born. Rider of Philominsky.

1946 French jockey ALAIN LEQUEUX born.

1952 Former jump jockey ROY MANGAN born.

1956 Rider JOEY NEWTON born. Partnered Credit Call.

1958 Former Champion Apprentice (1981) BRYN CROSSLEY born. Rode Latch Spring, Lester Piggott's first winner as a trainer.

1965 WILLIE CARSON lost his apprentice claim on Regal Bell at Redcar.

1966 The following announcement appeared in the *Racing Calendar*: 'Mrs Florence Nagle and Miss Norah Eleanor Wilmot have been granted licences under rule 102 of the rules of racing for 1966.' At last, women were free to train horses with Jockey Club approval. Thus Pat, a winner at Brighton, became the first flat winner to be trained officially by a woman, Norah Wilmot.

1985 The horse that wasn't in a race won it. Bill Watts-trained Handspring was inadvertently left out of the published runners for the Bradford Nursery at Thirsk by Wetherbys. With most of the public therefore unaware that the horse was even running it went ahead and won at odds of 14–1, ridden by Nicky Connorton.

1988 Jump jockey GEE ARMYTAGE revealed a unique claim to fame: she's the only jockey with a sponsored bed! 'I can't imagine what the sponsors expect me to do in such an enormous one – 5ft by 6ft 6,' declared the unmarried Ms Armytage.

1989 Panamanian-born jockey JORGE VELASQUEZ rode his 6,000th winner, Maddie Bumpo, at Arlington International racecourse, US. He became one of 5 to achieve this. The others are Bill Shoemaker, Laffit Pincay, Angel Cordero and Johnny Longden.

1991 Jerry Sung's Auric stables set a record for the most races won by an owner on one card when saddling 7 winners at Bukit Timah, Singapore. All were trained by Teh Choon Beng.

1992 A rarity for punters – a 2-horse race in which they couldn't lose. Jdaayel (5–4) was withdrawn from Ripon's Bouncing Castle Maiden Stakes, leaving 2 runners. Many a Quest won at 4–7 with Tip it In 2nd at 33–1. Rule 4 deductions were 40p in the £, but at that rate punters could have backed both and still made a profit.

4 AUGUST

1825   Two Cossack horses took on 2 English thoroughbreds over 47 miles near St Petersburg. The thoroughbred CHARPER won the race and as a consequence many more were imported, and organised racing (over shorter courses) became a more frequent occurrence.

1900   QUEEN MOTHER born. Colours: blue; buff stripes; blue sleeves; black cap; gold tassel. Her most shattering moment as an owner occurred when Devon Loch fell on the flat with the 1956 Grand National at his mercy, and her greatest moment was when Special Cargo won a thrilling finish to the 1984 Whitbread Gold Cup at Sandown.

1929   Trainer MILES HENRY EASTERBY, universally known as Peter, born. Or was he? When I endeavoured to confirm Mr Easterby's date of birth, for which various dates have been quoted, I was told by his daughter, 'He says he was born on the 4th but Mum is positive it is really the 5th – she says she's seen his birth certificate.' He has 5 Champion Hurdle victories to his credit: Saucy Kit (1967), Night Nurse (1976, 1977), Sea Pigeon (1980, 1981). Night Nurse won Scottish and Welsh Champion Hurdles and Irish Sweeps Hurdle in 1975–76. Also trained Alverton (1979) and Little Owl (1981) to win Cheltenham Gold Cup.

1960   ANNE, DUCHESS OF WESTMINSTER lashed out 1,150 guineas for a three-year-old horse being sold by farmer's wife Mrs Henry Baker. The horse was Arkle, probably the greatest jumper of all time.

1980   SWAYING TREE set off for the Yorkshire Handicap at Ripon, ridden by Eddie Hide, at about 4.30 and finished it, the winner, over an hour later, ridden by Jimmy Bleasdale. The 14 runners got underway as normal, but after 1 furlong of the scheduled 6 a red flag was waved and 6 horses and jockeys stopped. Eight ran on, and Wynbury passed the post in front. At 4.35, though, came an announcement that the race was void. At 4.48 it was announced that there had been a false start. At 5.04 it was announced that the race would be rerun at 5.30. Nine withdrew from the rerun, although Wynbury lined up again. This time, though, the winner was Swaying Tree, one of the 6 who had stopped. In the meantime, original jockey Hide had been kicked by another horse and replaced. Not surprisingly there were many disputes about the payout for this race.

1990   Aussie jockey JEREMY HUSTWITT, 35, became the first of that persuasion to be suspended for testing positive to a drug test after a trace of cannabis was discovered in a urine specimen following a meeting at Belmont Park, Western Australia.

1991   Sizzling Saga (Lester Piggott) was JACK BERRY'S first winner in Germany, scoring at Munich. It was also his first runner there.

5 AUGUST

1839 Jockey JOHN JACKSON, 70, who rode 8 St Leger winners (but no other Classic winners) between 1791 and 1822, died at Northallerton. Normally a respectable man, he once drowned his sorrows in a pub, having lost his job of stable jockey to his trainer, Mr Sykes. Leaving the pub determined to fight Sykes he instead mistakenly set about a passing chimney sweep.

1876 The first meeting took place at Caulfield, Melbourne.

1882 For the 2nd and final time FRED ARCHER rode 6 winners from 6 rides, at Lewes.

1928 Curragh racecourse manager JIM MARSH born.

1932 Jockey GEORGE MILBURN born. Hurgill Lad at Hexham in 1953 was his first winner. He partnered Kerstin and Gentle Moya. He also bred chinchillas.

1934 Jockey WILLIE ROBINSON born. First winner at Navan, 1955. Won the 1963 Cheltenham Gold Cup on Mill House and the Grand National on Team Spirit in 1964 as well as the Champion Hurdle in 1962 on Anzio and 1965 on Kirriemuir. Retired in 1970.

1934 Trainer RODDY ARMYTAGE born. Trainer of Barona, dual Scottish National winner.

1939 Newmarket trainer SUSAN (ELNA) PIGGOTT born. As a jockey twice won the Newmarket Town Plate. Wife of Lester.

1960 Jockey KEVIN DARLEY born. He celebrated his 17th birthday by riding his first winner, Dust Up (9-1), at Haydock. Best horses ridden include Grey Desire, Borushka.

1977 GARY STAHLBAUM had 6 mounts at Fort Eric, Canada, and won on all 6.

1981 JOHN CARROLL rode his first winner, Helvic, at Pontefract.

1984 JERSEY staged the UK's first Sunday race meeting at Les Landes.

1992 Devon and Exeter racecourse was renamed plain Exeter, and ANTHONY COTTRELL, former assistant to his father, Gerald, made a winning start to his training career when Bluechipenterprise won the Bonus Print Novice Chase.

1992 JOHN REID rode 5 winners in a day for the first time – 4 at Brighton in the afternoon and the 5th at Kempton in the evening.

1992 Germany's most successful trainer, HEINZ JENTZSCH, won the highest award ever given to a racing professional in that country when he was presented with the Verdienstkreuz First Class zum Verdienstorden (Order of Merit) at Cologne racecourse. Aged 72, he was 29-times Champion Trainer, saddling over 3,400 winners.

6 AUGUST

1768 The great racehorse Gimcrack, winner 26 times in 36 starts, was beaten at York where he never won, despite the fact that the race which still bears his name today is run there.

1782 DISGUISE, owned by the Duke of Hamilton, won the first race ever staged at Hamilton Park, run in 2 four-mile heats.

1915 Trainer TONY DICKINSON born. Leading point-to-point rider in 1954. Began training in 1967–68 with horses ridden by son Michael.

1922 Air travel pioneer, Jockey Club member and owner SIR FREDDIE LAKER born. Owned Spartan General, Blarney Beacon. Colours: white, red cross-belts; red cap; black hoop.

1926 The first meeting was run at CHEPSTOW. Henri Jelliss rode Conca D'Oro to win the first race, the £200 St Lawrence Selling Plate.

1927 Trainer FRANK CARR born. His Kamundu won 1969 Royal Hunt Cup.

1928 Jockey RAY READERS born. His first winner was Radio Star at Alexandra Park in 1948 and his 100th came on Pigeon Vole, owned by Winston Churchill, who sent him a letter of congratulation.

1929 An unnamed two-year-old gelding by Blink out of Broken Tendril, carrying 123lbs, set a world record time (hand-timed) of 1 minute 6.2 seconds for 6 furlongs at Brighton.

1939 Jockey Club member SIR MICHAEL CONNELL born. Best horses owned include Stuart R., Moon Trip, Kingsbourne Lad. Colours: grey; red cross-belts; green cap.

1941 Former jump jockey JEREMY SPEID-SOOTE born.

1947 Trainer NADINE (DINA) SMITH born. Rode 4 winners under NH Rules as an amateur. Her Shiny Copper won the 1982 Triumph Hurdle.

1955 Rider of 1992 Derby winner Dr Devious JOHN REID born. Also won the Arc de Triomphe in 1988 on Tony Bin.

1956 Trainer DAVID O'BRIEN born. Sent out winners of the English (Secreto, 1984), Irish (Assert, 1982) and French (Assert, 1982) Derbys. Became the youngest trainer of an Epsom Derby winner when Secreto won but gave up in October 1988.

1991 A new Jockey Club rule was introduced permitting race entries to be reopened at the overnight stage when less than 2 overnight declarations have been made.

1992 Saratoga's Racing Hall of Fame admitted 5-times Champion Steeplechase rider Jerry Fishback, Canadian jockey Sandy Hawley, first rider to win 500 races in a season (1973), 1983 Champion three-year-old Slew O'Gold and trainer Scotty Schulhofer.

1992 Former jump jockey CLIVE COX, who rode nearly 100 winners, saddled his first winner as a trainer when Ushba won at Pontefract.

7 AUGUST

1891 Racing was last viewed from the Georgian grandstand at Richmond, Yorkshire. It was built by public subscription in 1775 and in 1991 an appeal to raise money to restore it was launched.

1905 Welsh owner FRANK TYLDESLEY born. Best horses include Winter Rain, Broncho II, Cavity Hunter, Regent Lad. Colours: pale blue; navy cross-belts; green and navy hooped sleeves.

1932 PAUL WRIGHT, headmaster and proprietor of Slindon College, born. It was his proud boast that his was 'the only school to run a National Hunt racing stable'. Bred horses called Slindon, Slindon College, More Slindon under the care of trainer Nicholas Lee-Judson, who doubled up as science master!

1934 Jockey JOHNNY KENNEALLY born. Best horses ridden, Purple Silk, King of Diamonds. Won 8 times over jumps on Red Holly, then named his house after the horse.

1936 Irish owner MICHAEL SMURFIT born. Best horses include Theatrical. Colours: yellow; royal blue epaulets; yellow cap; royal blue star.

1936 Owner JAMES VANNER, whose great-grandfather Charlie Maidment won the Derby twice, born. Best horses include Galahad II, Kalaglow, Haul Knight. Colours: light and dark brown.

1937 Northern jockey PAT MCCARRON born. First big win was 1964 Champion Hurdle on Magic Court. Finished 2nd in consecutive Grand Nationals (1965 and 1966) on Freddie.

1949 French-based trainer JOHN FELLOWS born. Best horses trained include Royal Gait, Arctic Tern, Regal Exception.

1951 Jockey RON HYETT born. First winner, Chepstow 1968; 3rd in the 1980 Grand National on The Pilgarlic; also rode Even Dawn.

1956 Jockey GARY MOORE born. Best horses ridden include Lir, Flying Benny, Reve de Valse.

1961 Jockey WALTER SWINBURN, who rode Shergar to win the 1981 Derby, born. Also won 1986 Derby on Shahrastani.

1964 Jump jockey PETER NIVEN born near Dundee.

1967 LESTER PIGGOTT rode Chestergate (Reg Hollinshead) into 2nd place in a one mile 5-furlong race at Newmarket steering the horse by its mane after the bridle broke just after the start.

1982 Three-year-old SOBA (David Chapman–David Nicholls) won her 8th race of the season by 2½ lengths at Haydock. She won 11 in all.

1986 Riding 11–4 chance AMANTISS at Devon, jockey Anthony Charlton finished first – but the horse finished second. As the pair approached the line, Charlton tumbled out of the saddle and crossed the line a split-second ahead of his horse. The race was awarded to the second horse – named Slip Up!

8 AUGUST

1812 DANIEL DAWSON was hanged in Cambridge having been convicted of poisoning horses to stop them winning races.

1876 FRED ARCHER landed a double at Lambourn, winning on Major Stapylton's Sabrina and Tom Stevens' Miss Croft.

1900 May Race won the Irish Oaks for trainer DAN MCNALLY, who had already won the Irish Derby with Gallinaria.

1927 Trainer MEL STUTE born. Best horses included Snow Chief.

1957 Jockey turned Cumbria trainer JOHN (LENNOX) GOULDING born. Rode Astral Charmer to win the 1981 Scottish National.

1967 Owner Len Coville's claim that Schweppes Gold Trophy winner HILL HOUSE could have made his own cortisone was finally accepted by the stewards of the National Hunt committee and no further action was taken against him, trainer Ryan Price or jockey Josh Gifford.

1970 WILLIE SHOEMAKER rode his 6,000th winner, Shining County, at Del Mar.

1982 Owner Craig B. Singer issued a writ against the Jockey Club. His filly Cairn Rouge finished 2nd to Vayrann (15-2) in the previous October's Champion Stakes and the winner failed a post-race dope test. However, after owner the Aga Khan's experts argued that the colt could have produced his own anabolic steroids the stewards of the disciplinary committee allowed the result to stand. Singer's argument was that Vayrann broke the rules and should be disqualified. The result in the history books is still a win for Vayrann.

1990 Trainer JACK BERRY became the first northern handler for 58 years to score 100 winners in a season when Heaven-Leigh-Grey won at Brighton. Berry won a £100 bet at odds of 50-1 with Graham Lisle of Leeds. Dobson Peacock in 1932 had been the last northern trainer to reach a ton.

1990 FULKE JOHNSON HOUGHTON-owned and -trained Akdam won for the 4th time at Kempton, thus collecting a £100,000 bonus, but as the race was a claimer Johnson Houghton lost the horse.

1991 Snooker star ALEX 'HURRICANE' HIGGINS was arrested at Uttoxeter racecourse for alleged threatening and abusive behaviour.

1991 BILL WIGHTMAN, aged 77, Britain's longest-serving trainer, had to face the stewards for the first time since taking out a licence in 1937 when his Divine Pet won at Brighton. They asked for an explanation of the 12-1 shot's improved form and accepted the answer that the horse needed firm ground.

1992 MICHAEL ROBERTS landed his first British 6-timer on Mamdooh, Our Occasion and Amwag at Newmarket plus Yenoora, Lys and Five Islands at Lingfield's evening meeting.

9 AUGUST

1916   Former Chepstow permit-holder BILL GILLOW born.

1937   Racecourse commentator JEREMY BRANFOOT born.

1937   Owner MICHAEL POLAND born. Colours: black and white diabolo; halved sleeves; red cap. Best horses include Midnight Air, King's Loch.

1939   Owner TONY BUDGE OBE born. Colours: yellow; red epaulets; hooped sleeves; hooped cap. Best horses include Danish Flight, Rock City.

1939   Racing took place for the last time at Derby with the £500 Peveril of the Peak Plate going to Lady Ludlow's MORWELL, ridden by Sam Wragg for trainer Captain Ossie Bell's Lambourn stable. The Hartington Plate was void – no runners were declared, which perhaps explains why the course ceased to exist.

1942   Trainer IAN WARDLE born. Best horses trained include Jimmy Miff, Rowe Residence, Czarist.

1947   The Tote takings of £31,550 at Phoenix Park were an Irish record, as was the £8,652 invested on the Phoenix Plate.

1963   Jockey MARK DWYER born. Won 1985 Cheltenham Gold Cup on Forgive 'n' Forget and 1993 Gold Cup on Jodami.

1964   Wantage jockey JIMMY DUGGAN born. Rode Aonoch to win 14 races. Also partnered Amarach.

1967   Jockey turned William Hill PRO DAVID HOOD, who rode winners for Stan Mellor, born.

1991   SPY IN THE SKY became the first racehorse foaled in Barbados to race in Britain. The Richard Hannon-trained two-year-old finished 14th of 21 at Newmarket behind winner X My Heart.

1992   Champion Trainer of Malaysia and Singapore JOHNNY KOK was suspended for three years (later reduced to six months) after his sprinter Giltedged III tested positive to Etorphine ('Elephant Juice', a stimulant) after it won the Jubilee Stakes at Bukit Timah, Singapore. He was later banned for a further six months when Star of Today won on October 10 and Salute For Me was 2nd on October 11, reportedly for the same offence. Kok, who claimed he was being set up, announced that he would retire and become an owner.

10 AUGUST

1711 Jonathan Swift wrote in his diary, 'Dr Arbuthnot, the Queen's favourite physician, went out with me to see a place they have made for a famous horse race tomorrow, where the Queen will come.' 'A place' was Ascot; the Queen, Anne.

1940 Trainer JOHNNY LIMB, who moved to Kenya, born.

1944 Racing writer, specialising in breeding, TONY MORRIS born.

1947 Sherborne trainer BILL TURNER born.

1950 LORD ASTOR's High Stakes scored his 34th win from 50 starts when he landed the one and a half-mile Rotherham Stakes at Pontefract, taking his owner's prize-money over the £20,000 mark.

1951 Jockey JOHN CURANT born.

1965 Arkansas-based jockey MICHAEL EARL SMITH born in New Mexico. Twice within seventeen days in January 1992 he rode 6 winners in a day at Aqueduct.

1965 MIKE SMITH, jockey of Fourstars Allstar, born.

1966 Jump jockey SIMON HODGSON born.

1981 Heather Can won at Sligo to give jockey GEORGE MERNAGH his first winner.

1985 Tremulous at Haydock was trainer BARRY HILLS' 1,000th flat winner in Britain.

1991 M. Tebbutt partnered LIVING IMAGE, trained by W. Jarvis, to win the Bonusprint Hcp at Redcar at 6–1 – the last of owner Jim Joel's 805 flat winners since 1928.

1991 *Weatherby's General Stud Book* celebrated its 200th anniversary. Volume 1 of the book, the world's first national stud book, was produced in 1791 by James Weatherby.

1991 Jockey John Lowe rode 11–2 shot KAWWAS, trained by William Holden, to win the 11-runner You Can't Beat Heat Handicap at Southwell – the first Flat turf race run at the track.

1991 VANESSA DE CARRERE, a four-year-old mare, 'won' Arab racing's most prestigious event, the Dubai International, at Kempton Park, only to become the 3rd consecutive winner to fail a post-race drug test. In 1989 French-trained Dida Cherie did likewise and in 1990 the appropriately named Dutch-trained Drug also failed.

1992 MICHAEL ROBERTS rode a treble at Windsor, in the process reaching 150 winners in Britain for the first time in his career.

1992 SIR ANDREW LLOYD WEBBER was on song when he paid 39,000 guineas at Doncaster Sales for the five-year-old Russell Dalus, with only one race (2nd in a bumper at Hereford) to his credit.

11 AUGUST

1711 Racing took place at Ascot for the first time, watched by Queen Anne plus courtiers. £558 19s 5d had been spent on clearing the course to provide 'the round Heath on Ascott Common' and a further £15 2s 8d was paid to mark it out with painted posts. Seven went to post for the first event: Doctor, Have At All, Teague, Dimple, Flint, Grey Jack and Grim, but history does not appear to have recorded which of them won.

1894 Popular and successful jockey TOMMY CORRIGAN, who had a career total of 239 winners to his credit, died after falling from his mount Waiter during the Caulfield Grand National Steeplechase. His funeral went down in folklore when his cortège took 30 minutes to pass the massive crowds.

1933 Former Irish Champion Jump Jockey TOS TAAFFE born. Younger brother of Arkle's jockey, Pat, and of amateur jockey Willie. In 1959 Pat rode Zonda to win the Irish Grand National, and Tos was 2nd on Knightsbrook.

1942 Jockey JEAN-CLAUDE DESAINT born. Best horses ridden included Riverman and Comtesse De Loir.

1947 Owner of 1988 Grand National winner Rhyme 'n' Reason JULIET REED born. Colours: pink; purple stars; purple cap with pink star.

1953 Trainer of Old Applejack HOWARD JOHNSON born.

1956 Jockey WILLIE HIGGINS born. Rode Primula Boy to win 1979 Ayr Gold Cup.

1961 Jump jockey and optician ANDY ORKNEY born.

1961 Irish jockey NIALL BYRNE born.

1987 Former England soccer international FRANCIS LEE scored another success – training his first winner on the flat. Two-year-old Foilinski obliged at Beverley.

1991 LESTER PIGGOTT won the Swedish Derby at Jagersro on Tao. He'd last won it in 1958 on Flying Friendship.

1992 Red Rum's trainer, GINGER MCCAIN, was fined £1,250 by the Jockey Club's disciplinary committee for failing to pay the correct wages to his stable staff.

12 AUGUST

1941   Trainer DENIS MCCARTHY, handler of Federal Trooper, born.

1960   Jockey NIGEL TUTTY born.

1960   Irish jockey BRENDAN SHERIDAN born. Partner of Perris Valley.

1960   Newmarket trainer GRANT EDEN born.

1967   Her Majesty's HOPEFUL VENTURE won for the 4th time in 5 starts when scoring by 5 lengths in the Oxfordshire Stakes at Newbury.

1988   Lambourn jockey PAUL CROUCHER was killed in a car crash. Classified was his first winner on May 5 1981 at Plumpton and on December 8 1984 he rode a treble at Nottingham. Among the best horses he rode was Mr Frisk.

1988   KLUTE, touted as the fastest horse in the world, but which had never competed on a racecourse, was trounced over 5 furlongs in a match at Haydock by the Jack Berry-trained So Careful.

1989   The QUEEN's first runner in the US for 35 years, Unknown Quantity, won the Grade 1 Arlington Handicap at 10-1, ridden by Jorge Velasquez, at Arlington International, Chicago. It was Her Majesty's first American winner.

1989   The Jack Berry-trained O. I. Oyston helped to raise money for charity when he was released into a field divided into squares, which had been raffled off, to leave his droppings in the winning square. O. I. Oyston kept the punters waiting for 40 minutes before relieving the tension, and himself! Winner BOB HEATHCOTE donated the £1,000 prize to the Royal Manchester Children's Hospital.

1989   Former Newmarket trainer BILL MARSHALL celebrated his imminent 71st birthday by sending out Coo-Bird to win the Barbados Derby. His own horse Valial was 2nd.

1990   Jump jockey ANDY ORKNEY won a chase at Pyatigorsk, USSR, and then finished 4th, with colleague Marcus Armytage in 3rd place, in the Russian Grand National on the same card.

1991   Trainer JIM BOLGER sent out 5 winners from 5 runners at Gowran Park for a 196.5-1 accumulator.

13 AUGUST

1711   QUEEN ANNE watched at the new course at Ascot Common, whose first race had taken place two days earlier, as the 5-runner Queen's Plate was run. Jonathan Swift, the writer, attended and noted that the Queen was 'dressed like a man' in a long riding coat and waistcoat. However, Swift was late to arrive as 'everybody's coach had gone'.

1737   A horse race took place between two contestants from Tyler's Ferry to the Bridge at Hackney Marsh. There was a notable difference about this event, though - the horses were swimming and didn't have jockeys.

1888   Racing first took place at Wolverhampton's Dunstall Park course. The first race winner, Silver Spur, was ridden by Tommy Loates who had won the last race at the previous Wolverhampton course, Broad Meadows.

1919   The great American horse MAN O'WAR was defeated for the only time in his career - by the aptly named Upset, which he subsequently beat 6 times.

1922   Owner JOHN SUMNER born. Loup Cervier won 11 times for him and Royal Marshall II was the 1974 Hennessy and 1976 King George VI winner. Colours: green; yellow sleeves; white cap.

1924   Bishop Auckland trainer DENYS SMITH born. Became a trainer in 1961 and sent out Red Alligator to win the Grand National in 1968. In the same year he was leading trainer with 55 winners worth £37,944. Dual purpose, he also sent out the winners of the Lincoln and William Hill Gold Cup. Other good horses trained include Foggy Bell, Royal Prerogative, The Grey Bomber.

1925   Trainer JOHN (HUYSHE) WEBBER born.

1932   Jockey DEREK MORRIS born. Best horses ridden included Sacarole.

1950   Jockey PETER BROGAN, rider of Avondhu, born.

1958   Former Champion Amateur rider (1980–81) PAUL WEBBER born. Partner of Tower Bird.

1964   Jump jockey RICHARD DENNIS born.

1964   Jockey JONATHAN ADAMS born.

1967   Jockey TIM SPRAKE born.

1982   Trainer DAVID O'BRIEN saddled his first winner in England when Pas De Seul (Pat Eddery) won the Hungerford Stakes at Newbury.

1985   Hi-Tech Leader was EDDIE HIDE's 2,591st and last British winner as an active jockey, at Nottingham.

1992   DALE BAIRD, holder of the world record for training most winners, saddled his 6,000th success, Irish Laser, at Mountaineer Park, West Virginia.

14 AUGUST

1865 The first meeting took place at Eagle Farm, Queensland, Australia.

1918 Trainer BILL MARSHALL born. Awarded the DFC while serving as a fighter pilot during the Second World War. Dual purpose trainer. Made a name for handling grey horses: Grey Mirage, My Swanee and prolific sprinter Raffingora were among them. Narrowly escaped death in an air crash on the Sunday before Royal Ascot in 1972. Rescued by jockey Joe Mercer. Later moved to Barbados.

1938 Newmarket trainer MICHAEL JARVIS born. Rode 3 winners under NH Rules. Won 1989 Arc with Carroll House. Farmed the Grand Criterium International d'Ostende, winning it 9 times. Best horses trained include Petong, Tudor Music, Green God, Beldale Flutter, Totowah.

1940 Owner of Chico, Peteona and Rising Falcon LADY MARY MUMFORD born. Colours: sky blue; white seams; scarlet cap.

1946 Haydock resumed racing for the first time since the war.

1950 Trainer of King Credo STEVE WOODMAN born.

1952 Trainer in France TONY CLOUT born.

1967 JOE MERCER fractured his spine in a fall at Folkestone.

1982 LESTER PIGGOTT rode his 4,000th domestic winner on 1-3 favourite Ardross in the Geoffrey Freer Stakes at Newbury.

1982 JO BERRY, wife of trainer Jack, won the amateur riders' race at Wolverhampton for the 4th time in as many attempts.

1986 Catterick staged a Christmas meeting. Santa Claus was there to see 6 races with titles such as the Christmas Morning Nursery, Stuffed Turkey Handicap and Queen's Speech Stakes. It was switched to August, having been abandoned because of bad weather during the festive season.

1987 MARTIN PIPE completed a record-breaking run of training 7 consecutive winners at Devon and Exeter.

1991 Weight problems caused jump jockey TOM MORGAN to retire.

1992 MARK PERRETT rode his first winner on the Flat at the age of 30, more than twelve years after starting out as an apprentice with Guy Harwood. Better known as an NH jockey.

1992 Newcastle United striker MICK QUINN's Mighty Miss Magpie, trained by Mick Channon, won at Southwell, and another former England international, Francis Lee, also trained a winner on the card, Must Be Magical. The Southwell meeting also featured three harness races on which the on-course Tote turnover was £2,606, compared with £17,163 on the horse racing.

15 AUGUST

1720   Racing resumed at Ascot after a six-year gap following the death of Queen Anne.

1825   Racing was held at Broad Meadows, Wolverhampton, eccentric gambler Jack Mytton's EUPHRATES winning the feature event, the three-mile Darlington Cup. Wolverhampton races were moved to Dunstall Park in 1888.

1863   The first race meeting at Saratoga, USA, was concluded. The track became known as 'the favourites' graveyard' – Champions Man o'War, Gallant Fox and Secretariat all met with shock defeats here. Huge gambler John 'Bet a Million' Gates was said to have lost $400,000 at one meeting.

1930   EPH SMITH, brother of Doug, rode his first winner, Red Queen, at Windsor. He went on to ride until 1965, scoring 2,313 winners, including Blue Peter, the 1939 Derby and 2,000 Guineas winner. Found dead in 1972 – a verdict of death by misadventure was recorded. He left £141,798.

1935   Gloucester trainer GRAEME ROE born.

1939   Trainer ROSS FENSTERMAKER born.

1943   Trainer CAPTAIN MARK SMYLY born.

1947   New York trainer SUE ALPERS born. First winner 1982.

1950   Keen amateur rider the PRINCESS ROYAL born.

1954   Arab horse jockey ROBERT BLYTH born.

1962   Amateur rider TRACEY BAILEY born.

1962   Jockey KIM TINKLER born.

1967   SCOBIE BREASLEY rode a hat-trick at Windsor on Dear Mama, Wippip and Onward.

1972   The unbeaten BRIGADIER GERARD, the hot favourite, was defeated for the only time in an 18-race career, finishing 2nd to Roberto. Winning jockey Braulio Baeza was specially flown in from USA, and started at 12–1 for the Benson & Hedges Gold Cup run at York.

1989   CRICKET BALL became the first horse to win a Group race for the 4th consecutive year when he won the Prix de Meautry at Deauville. Gerald Rose rode the John Fellows-trained six-year-old.

1992   Sunderland-born ANDY LAKEMAN rode his first winner on his first ride in public, Flashy's Son, at Ripon.

1992   Amsterdam-based businessman DAVE SPENCER flew over to England to see his two-year-old Palacegate Episode run at Newbury. Arriving at the airport with no luggage he was strip-searched by immigration officers, who also checked every note of currency he had with him. 'They'll have a lot more to check on the way back,' declared Spencer after his pride and joy won the St Hugh's Stakes.

16 AUGUST

1731   The bodies of three robbers (Joseph Askwith and Richard and John Freeman) who had been hung that morning were cut down to enable racegoers to have an uninterrupted view of the racing at York, where Lord Lonsdale's MONKEY won both heats of the 100 guineas King's Plate.

1912   Trainer CAPTAIN HENRY RYAN PRICE born. He died 74 years later on his birthday. In between he carved out a career as one of the greatest of all jump trainers, winning virtually every big race in the book. And not content with that, he also, from 1970 onwards, turned out many top flat race winners. His jump triumphs included What a Myth's 1969 Cheltenham Gold Cup, Kilmore's 1962 Grand National and 3 Champion Hurdles Clair Soleil (1955), Fare Time (1959) and Eborneezer (1961). He won the Schweppes Gold Trophy 4 times. On the flat his Ginevra won the 1972 Oaks and Bruni the 1975 St Leger.

1915   Owner PADDY BURNS born. Best horses include Red Sunset, Park Appeal, Park Express. Colours: white; red stars; green cap.

1933   Jockey JOCK WILSON born. Best horses ridden include Polyfoto, Tribal Chief.

1955   Jockey COLIN BROWN born. Best horses ridden included Desert Orchid, Combs Ditch, Floyd, Sabin du Loir, Barnbrook Again.

1957   Former jump jockey CHRIS FAIRHURST born. Best horses ridden include Sharp Song. Son of trainer Thomas.

1957   Former jump jockey turned saddler MARTIN PEPPER born. Best horse ridden Ruckley.

1989   Sixteen-year-old chaser KEN'S LAKE almost pulled off a 200-1 sensation when it finished runner-up at those odds in a 5-runner chase at Devon.

1990   Jockey turned trainer MENIN MUGGERIDGE sent out a winner with his first runner over jumps, 33-1 shot Swingtime Belle (W. Irvine up) at Newton Abbot.

1991   Former soccer international FRANCIS LEE scored his first racecourse hat-trick as a trainer when Charly Pharly, Killy and Sir Arthur Hobbs all won at Haydock.

17 AUGUST

1869 A crowd of 40,000 turned up to see the first day's racing at Ballybrit, Galway.

1898 The first flat meeting took place at Folkestone.

1899 Born in 1845, trainer ROBERT PECK died at Scarborough. He handled 4 Classic winners, including Oaks and St Leger winner Marie Stuart who did the double in 1873, and Derby winner Doncaster in the same year. Trained at Russley Park, near Lambourn. Thanks to the profits from his astute tilts at the ring he was able to retire from training at the age of 36.

1932 Former jump jockey ALAN HONEYBONE born. First winner 1947. Best horses ridden include Le Jacobin.

1935 JOHN BIGGS of the Racehorse Owners' Association born.

1942 Delightfully named bloodstock agent TOTE CHERRY-DOWNES born.

1954 Jockey ANTHONY WEBBER born. Human and horse chiropractor by trade. Best horses ridden include The Snipe, Hard Outlook.

1955 CAMARERO lost for the first time, after having won an astonishing 56 successive races in Puerto Rico.

1959 Jockey GRAHAM MCCOURT born. Pulled off one of racing's great sensations when he partnered 100-1 shot Norton's Coin to victory in the 1990 Cheltenham Gold Cup.

1964 Newmarket jockey KEVIN BRADSHAW born.

1974 MICHAEL WOOD rode his first winner, Mary Mod (17-2), at Ripon.

1978 Pretty Cute gave LORNA VINCENT her first winner - the first NH victory by a professional lady rider in Great Britain - at Devon & Exeter.

1991 For the first time in twenty years of training EDDIE HARTY managed to book Lester Piggott to ride for him. Sha's Dream (12-1) duly won the 6-furlong Tattersalls Auction Race at the Curragh.

1992 The Tote announced that the £9,540.40 dividend it had declared two days earlier for the Placepot at Newbury should really have been £4,659.20 after it found a £1.10 bet in a Fulham betting shop which hadn't been added to the pool.

18 AUGUST

1916 Owner PEARL LAWSON JOHNSTON OBE born. Best horses include Cry of Truth, Integrity. Colours: white; pink sash and cap.

1929 Owner DAVID HORTON born. Best horses include Celtic Shot, Clutterbuck, Clay Duck. Colours: pink; silver sleeves; pink and mauve hooped cap.

1931 Irish-based owner BERTRAM R. FIRESTONE born. Among his best horses were champion US two-year-old Honest Pleasure, Kentucky Derby runner-up General Assembly, Irish 2,000 Guineas winner King's Company, Breeders' Cup Turf winner Theatrical. Colours: green; white diamond frame (back and front); green and white diamonds on sleeves; green and white quartered cap.

1940 Newbury trainer CHARLES JAMES born.

1940 Irish owner-trainer JOHN MULHERN born. Best horses trained include Galmoy, Friendly Alliance, Wolf of Badenoch. Racing colours: red with white question-mark back and front; quartered cap.

1948 Twelve-year-old youngster LESTER PIGGOTT rode his first winner, The Chase (10–1), at Haydock in the Wigan Lane Selling Plate.

1955 Wantage trainer JAMES BENNETT born.

1956 Leading US rider DEAN KUTZ born. Had a kidney transplant in 1985.

1961 Jockey ROSS ARNOTT born.

1965 Jockey GER LYONS born.

1975 PETER SCUDAMORE had his first ride in public, finishing unplaced on Stellemon on the flat at Leicester.

1980 GEORGE DUFFIELD earned a place in the *Guinness Book of Records* when he partnered two-year-old Spindrifter to win the Leicester City Football Club Stakes at Leicester – the 11th consecutive victory he had chalked up on the horse that season in its 12 appearances. The one time it was beaten C. Nutter had ridden.

1981 WILLIE CARSON fractured his skull following a fall from Silken Knot at York.

1989 Trainers IAN SEMPLE (Good Mood at Perth) and HENRIETTA KNIGHT (The Grey Gunner at Bangor) both won with their first winners as trainers.

1991 Wonder horse ARAZI cruised to a 3-length win in the Prix Morny at Deauville.

1992 Forty-four years after riding his first winner as a twelve-year-old schoolboy, LESTER PIGGOTT rode one of the best of his career as he steered Rodrigo De Triano to victory in York's Juddmonte International Stakes at York at 8–1. Owner Robert Sangster said it was 'the first time in 25 years' that Lester had asked for advice on how to ride a horse.

19 AUGUST

1931   Jockey WILLIAM (LEE) SHOEMAKER was born near Fabens, Texas, a premature arrival. His grandmother is said to have incubated him in a shoebox. Went on to become the most successful jockey of all before being paralysed in a car crash.

1934   Bookmaker JOHN BANKS – 'betting shops are a licence to print money' – born.

1938   Jockey FRANK NASH born. Rider of Drinny's Double.

1962   Irish jockey DONAL MANNING born.

1967   PAT EDDERY's first mount, True Time, finished last at the Curragh.

1982   Even money favourite SHARPO completed a consecutive hat-trick of wins in the William Hill Sprint Championship at York, ridden this time by Steve Cauthen and in the previous two runnings by Pat Eddery at 14-1 in 1981 and 3-1 in 1980. Trained by Jeremy Tree.

1982   Permit trainer GAIL HARRISON saddled her first winner, 50-1 chance Taras News, at Devon and Exeter.

1988   LESTER PIGGOTT's wife, Susan, was badly injured in a fall on the gallops.

1992   LESTER PIGGOTT, MICHAEL HILLS, PHILIP ROBINSON and GEORGE DUFFIELD were all aboard a plane to York which missed colliding with an RAF jet by 'about 2ft'. In March 1993 an official report revealed that the Piper air taxi carrying the jockeys was almost sliced in two by a Tornado because of blunders by air traffic controllers. Nonetheless Duffield went on to ride User Friendly to victory in the Yorkshire Oaks.

20 AUGUST

1739 DICK TURPIN, the highwayman, was put to death at York's Knavesmire hours before racing began and Smallhopes won the King's Plate.

1770 ECLIPSE continued to frighten off the opposition. The King's Plate at York was the horse's 3rd consecutive walkover.

1817 The scheduled date for the first day's racing at a new course – Wormwood Scrubs. Six days earlier an objection by the Army killed off the project.

1824 Lord George Bentinck's OLIVE raced 4 times at Goodwood in one afternoon. It was unplaced in the first race and dead-heated with Swindon in the next. The two ran off over the same three-quarter-mile course, but it was another dead-heat, requiring another run-off. This time Olive won.

1853 The Betting Houses Act became law, suppressing the hundreds of betting offices – reputable or otherwise – that had sprung up.

1860 NAT FLATMAN, the first ever Champion Jockey (in 1846 and for the next 6 seasons), died at the age of 50. He left £8,000 and was buried under the tower of All Saints Church, Newmarket. He rode 10 Classic winners, the first of which was Preserve.

1925 Racing journalist, author, owner, trainer and rider IVOR HERBERT born. In 1957 he saddled Linwell to win the Cheltenham Gold Cup, although it was credited to his head lad, Charlie Mallon, as the stewards of the National Hunt Committee had ruled that Herbert's activities as a racing journalist precluded him from being a public trainer.

1943 Former editor of the *Sporting Chronicle* turned spokesman for the Betting Offices Licensees' Association TOM KELLY born.

1952 Jockey IAN JENKINSON born. Partner of Sin Y Sin, Only for Jo.

1959 New York trainer RICHARD ARTHUR DESTASIO born.

1966 Fifty-five of the 66 licensed jockeys riding boycotted a meeting at Accra, Ghana, because the Accra Turf Club had refused to accede to their request to slaughter a sacrificial cow at the 6-furlong bend of the course. Eleven accidents had taken place there and the jockeys wanted to appease the fates. The riders were banned, and no cow was provided.

1967 Jockey ROD GRIFFITHS born.

1991 TERIMON led from the front to pull off a 16–1 shock win in the 6-runner Juddmonte International Stakes at York.

1992 LYRIC FANTASY became the first two-year-old for 36 years and the first-ever filly of that age to win the Keeneland Nunthorpe Stakes at York. Ridden by Michael Roberts; trained by Richard Hannon.

21 AUGUST

1846 The Gimcrack Stakes was run for the first time at York. The winner was ELLERDALE, owned by Captain Harcourt, ridden by Tommy Lye, trained by Tom Dawson at Middleham's Tupgill Stable.

1897 Well-fancied two-year-old SABINE QUEEN finished unplaced in the Londonderry Plate at Leopardstown. The advertised distance of the race was 5 furlongs and owner Lt Col F. F. McCabe lodged an objection on the grounds that the course was too short. McCabe took his battle to the Turf Club. It was subsequently discovered that the course was indeed 100 yards short. Leopardstown were fined and forced to correct the distance for future races.

1918 Trainer DERMOT 'BOGGY' WHELAN born. First licence, 1955.

1971 The Queen Mother's horse MASCARA won at Baldoyle, Ireland.

1971 Then the world's most expensive yearling ($510,000), CROWNED PRINCE, trained by Bernard Van Cutsem, made his debut at Newmarket. Starting at 2-7 he finished 6th.

1985 ALAN MUNRO rode first winner, Sentimental Roses, at Yarmouth.

1989 DARAKAH, a chestnut filly, trained by John Benstead at Epsom, made her 'debut' at Windsor. It turned out that she was in fact MUARIJ, a chestnut filly also trained by Benstead and owned by Sheik Hamdam Al Maktoum, also the owner of Darakah. Muarij, who was really Darakah, had already raced 4 times, winning once. Said Sue Williams of the Jockey Club: 'The form of the two fillies will be swapped.'

1990 PAT EDDERY came within inches of death when, as he rode Batshoof to the start of a race at York, a car 'emerged from the car park as we were cantering across the middle of the course and missed us by an inch, no more'.

1991 JACK BERRY saddled his 128th winner of the season, breaking his own previous record, when Food of Love won at York.

1991 A punter in William Hill's Sunderland branch won £163,884.16 for £81.50. The bet involved 8 selections. Seven of them won, but the other, Jet Ski Lady, was second at York, beaten in a photo-finish and failing to prevail after an inquiry.

1992 Irish Champion Jockey CHARLIE SWAN felt a little better after having a five-week suspension reduced to one following a bizarre incident in Australia. Punters in Victoria were reckoned to have lost some AUS$350,000 (£140,000) after Swan took the wrong course on 6-4 favourite and clear leader King Taros in the Hot Shot Steeplechase, part of an International Jockeys Challenge. Afterwards Swan, who was fined $500, commented, 'I like Australia and Australians. I hope to come back to make up for the mistake.'

22 AUGUST

1822   The first recorded organised race meeting in Germany took place at Bad Doperan.

1832   DENNIS COLLINS, a former sailor, was found guilty of high treason and sentenced to be 'hanged, decapitated and quartered' (they liked to make sure in those days!) for the offence of throwing a stone at King William IV at Ascot races. The King reprieved him and he was transported to Australia.

1856   BLINK BONNY, whose owner-trainer was William I'Anson of Malton, won the Gimcrack Stakes at York. The next season the great mare completed the Oaks–Derby double. Later she became the dam of Derby winner Blair Athol.

1970   PAT EDDERY rode his first 5-timer at Haydock. He was still an apprentice at the time.

1989   A racegoer laid out total stakes of £205,000 on 3 races at York – and ended the day exactly level. He lost £90,000 on Cacoethes, 2nd at 4–9; won £50,000 for £25,000 on Zalazl, then collected £40,000 profit from a £90,000 wager on Weld.

1990   STEVE SMITH ECCLES rode Spofforth to win at Fontwell, his 8th winner from as many rides during the jump season to date.

1991   KLASSY BRIEFCASE, which had come from USA to challenge for the Nunthorpe Stakes, had a wasted journey, finishing last behind winner Sheikh Albadou.

1992   A bizarre accident put jockey WALTER SWINBURN out of action for several weeks. He was knocked over by someone running down the street as he emerged from a Newmarket restaurant. Swinburn apparently fell backwards and hit his head on the kerb.

1992   MARTIN PIPE'S son David, aged nineteen, rode his first winner under rules when Passed Pawn, trained by Dad, won at Hereford.

23 AUGUST

1770   ECLIPSE was a slightly warm favourite – 1-20 – for a Subscription Plate race run over four miles at York, which he duly won by a distance.

1926   Preston trainer CAPTAIN JAMES HUME WILSON born. Best horses trained include Profilic, Marshalla, Crofter's Cline.

1942   Cumbria trainer ROGER FISHER born. Best horses trained include Ekbalco, Aonoch, Flarey Sark, Ballydurrow, Run and Skip.

1942   Jockey GRANT CANN born. Best horses ridden include What a Myth.

1955   Gloucester trainer CHRISTOPHER BROAD born.

1957   Irish jockey THOMAS MCGIVERN born. First winner Watties Grove at Leopardstown in 1974. Best horse ridden For Auction.

1960   Newmarket trainer WILLIAM HAGGAS born.

1966   MRS LOUIE DINGWALL became the third woman to be granted a trainer's licence, following Florence Nagle and Norah Wilmot.

1980   Jockey STEVE DAWSON rode his first winner, Queen Kate, at Windsor.

1982   WILLIE RYAN rode his first winner, Will George, at Windsor.

1986   PHIL TUCK rode the first of a run of 10 consecutive winners, the last coming on September 3. The record is 12, set by Gordon Richards in October 1933.

1986   Mega-punter TERRY RAMSDEN stood to win a staggering £8.5 million from a £10,000 win treble he had placed. Lack a Style won at 16-1 at Newmarket and Cry for the Clown, 4-1 at Windsor, but Miss Milveagh, 9-1, was caught and beaten close home by Remain Free, a 20-1 shot, also at Windsor.

1990   Willie Carson said, 'He could prove himself the fastest horse in the world' after riding the Dick Hern-trained DAYJUR to win the 5-furlong Keeneland Nunthorpe Stakes at York, setting a new course record of 56.16 seconds, which smashed the old one by over a second.

1991   MARTIN PIPE and PETER SCUDAMORE had the first 5 winners on the 6-race card at Devon: Nordic Delight (4-9), Arabian Sultan (2-9), Refute (2-5), Takemethere (4-11), The Blue Boy (2-5). In the last race their Ever Smile was 5-6 favourite but finished 2nd, beaten by the appropriately named 15-8 chance Frosty Reception (trained by John Baker, ridden by Nigel Coleman). Baker was sending out his 5th winner from as many runners that season.

1992   The ashes of legendary gambler ALEX BIRD were scattered at Haydock Park racecourse, where he had scored many of the biggest wins of his early career.

1992   West Country amateur JOHN FARTHING, who rode 80 winners, died aged 57.

24 AUGUST

1684   CHARLES II attended the races for the last time, an event captured in the only recorded engraving of the monarch at the races. It was created by Francis Barlow in 1687, two years after the King's death, and titled 'The Last Horse Race Run before Charles the Second of Blessed Memory by Dorsett Ferry'.

1796   HAMBLETONIAN, Sir Charles Turner's famous horse, met defeat for the only time in his 22-race career when he ran out of the course in a sweepstake of 100 guineas at York. Otherwise, he won the 1795 St Leger, two Doncaster Cups and a famous match against Diamond in 1799 over four miles 1 furlong 138yds for 3,000 guineas at Newmarket in front of a vast crowd. He went on to sire over 140 winners.

1830   KING WILLIAM IV attended his first race meeting since succeeding to the throne, at Ascot, and had a winner in the first race – The Colonel. Later in the afternoon his Frederica also won.

1915   Scottish trainer WILF CRAWFORD born. Trainer of Dunrobin, Mirval.

1946   Former jump jockey DAVID MUNRO born.

1949   Irish jockey GABRIEL CURRAN born. In 1977 he partnered 20–1 shot Nebbiolo to win the 2,000 Guineas. Also won Irish 2,000 and 1,000 Guineas.

1956   Jockey ALLEN WEBB born. Best horse ridden Young Arthur.

1968   DR FAGER, aged four and carrying 134lbs, set a world-record time (other than hand-timed) when clocking 1 minute 32.2 seconds for one mile at Arlington Park, USA.

1969   English jockeys took the honours in Norway's Norsk Derby as Frankie Durr rode runner-up and favourite Polar Sea behind winner Lord Lark (partnered by Brian Taylor), owned by the country's CROWN PRINCE HARALD and his wife. The colt was a wedding-day present from the Norsk Jockeyklub.

1988   The 1965 Grand National winner JAY TRUMP put down, aged 31.

1990   WILLIE CARSON moved up to 3rd on the all-time list of British jockeys when a double at Newmarket took his total of winners to 3,112, 1 better than Doug Smith but still behind Sir Gordon Richards and Lester Piggott.

1991   MICK CHANNON sent out Affair of State (12–1) to win the Tattersalls Breeders' Stakes at the Curragh.

1991   As the Russian coup took place, BOLD RUSSIAN became one of the most topical of all tips. Willie Carson duly obliged on the 100–30 shot in the Beefeater Gin Celebration Mile at Goodwood for Barry Hills.

25 AUGUST

1804 ALICIA THORNTON took on her brother-in-law CAPTAIN FLINT, who was secretly in love with her, in a public race at York for a side-stake of 500 guineas. A crowd of 100,000 turned out to see Alicia, riding Vinagrillio, beaten by Thornville over four miles. Alicia's husband, Colonel Tom Thornton, refused to pay up, and Flint later horse-whipped him (someone should turn this story into a mini-series!). Alicia went on to challenge the top jockey of the day, Frank Buckle, to a match – which she won.

1875 LILY AGNES won the Ebor at York for James Snarry.

1909 A British military force in Tibet organised a race meeting, complete with a steeplechase and Army Cup, which took place in front of a bemused crowd of Nepalese, Tibetans and four important Lamas.

1917 Dual Welsh Grand National-winning trainer EARL JONES born. Best horses trained include Forty Secrets, Honey End, Tasco, Trespassing, Pattered.

1922 Trainer RAY LAING born. Best horses include Roaring Riva.

1928 Lambourn trainer DAVID HANLEY born. Jockey from 1942 to 1958.

1928 Jockey FRANK BARLOW born. Won the Champion Stakes on Narrator in 1954 and 2,000 Guineas on Gilles de Retz in 1956.

1934 Owner-trainer of Lyford Cay and True Lad BILL SWAINSON born.

1944 Former Champion Lady Rider SANDY BROOK born.

1961 Racing writer and Champion of the punters via the National Association for the Protection of Punters MARK COTON born.

1978 Formulate won the Waterford Candelabra Stakes to give MICHAEL ROBERTS his first Goodwood victory.

1988 JIMMY EDDERY, twice Irish Champion Jockey and father of jockeys Pat and Paul, died aged 64.

1989 Stable lass MELODY TOWN was leading Cotton on Quick round the parade ring at Goodwood for trainer Alan Bailey, when it was discovered that Dewi Williams, jockey of Damaskeen in the Oakley Handicap, wasn't qualified to ride. Melody was called upon to ride, and duly got home by half a length.

1992 GAY KELLEWAY, the only woman to ride a Royal Ascot winner, landed her first win in 5 years when John Rose won at Brighton, trained by her father Paul.

26 AUGUST

1880 Top northern jockey JOHNNY (THE OLD PUSHER) OSBORNE won the Gimcrack Stakes for the 9th and final time on Simnel.

1918 Owner DICK HOLLINGSWORTH born. Best horses include Ark Royal, Hermes, Buoy, Sea Anchor. Colours: crimson; silver braid.

1925 Former Champion Jockey OTTO MADDEN, now an owner and trainer, sent out his Chapeau, ridden by that season's Champion, Gordon Richards, to win York's Ebor by 3 lengths from Highbrow, piloted by future Champion Jockey Tommy Weston.

1935 Jockey BOBBY BEASLEY born. Won the 1959 Cheltenham Gold Cup on Roddy Owen and 1960 Champion Hurdle on Another Flash, but as his grandfather Harry won the Grand National twice, his Uncle Tommy 3 times and his father-in-law Arthur Thompson once, this was the race he really wanted. In 1961 Nicolaus Silver achieved that ambition for him.

1939 FULKE WALWYN'S first winner as a trainer was Poor Duke (Bruce Hobbs) at Buckfastleigh.

1967 JOHN EDWARDS saddled his first winner, Mons Badonicus, at Hereford.

1974 An audacious coup almost paid off when Gay Future won at 10–1 at Cartmel. The horse had been coupled with 2 of trainer Anthony Collins' declared runners in doubles and trebles, but the other 2 were non-runners, leaving all the money relying on Gay Future. It was reckoned that over £250,000 was involved. Some of it was paid out at once, some withheld once the bookies' intelligence system smelled a rat. Scotland Yard investigated the coup and two men, one of them Collins, were charged with conspiracy to defraud bookmakers. Both were found guilty, fined £1,000 and ordered to pay £500 towards prosecution costs.

1977 ERNIE JOHNSON, riding Courjet at Newmarket, was thrown against a post when the horse swerved and ran off the course. He broke a leg, injured his shoulder and was out for the rest of the season.

1988 STEVE CAUTHEN fell from Preziosa at Goodwood, sustained concussion and missed the rest of the season.

1989 The Trade Union NALGO sponsored the card at Market Rasen with race titles such as the Help Your National Health Service Hurdle.

1991 RON SMYTH, a trainer for 44 years, announced that he planned to retire at the end of the season.

27 AUGUST

1771 Racing was staged at Hereford for the first time, reported the Sporting Calendar. '50 sovereigns was run for by 4yos.2 mile heat won by Mr Foley's bay horse.'

1879 ISONOMY (who would sire Triple Crown winner Isinglass) won the Ebor Handicap carrying 9st 8lbs for jockey Tom Cannon and trainer John Porter, coming home 8 lengths clear of Knight Templar.

1888 Racing was held for the first time at Leopardstown. It was not an instant success - in fact, after problems dealing with the crowds, transporting them and catering for them, it seemed that the first meeting might also be the last. One sporting paper published the following 'obituary': 'Sacred to the memory of Leopardstown - finally and brutally strangled at birth by gross incompetence, bungling and mismanagement - August 27 1888.'

1921 CHARLIE SMIRKE rode in public for the first time, finishing 3rd on King George at Gatwick. He was fourteen.

1945 Former jockey and trainer TOM CANNON died aged 73. He rode 33 winners between 1887 and 1889 and sent out 288 winners on the flat worth some £94,000.

1948 Jump jockey turned trainer ANDY TURNELL born. Rode shorter than almost any other jump jockey, but to good effect: he won the Massey Ferguson Gold Cup on Arctic Bow (1972), Hennessy on April the Seventh (1975) and the Mackeson on Bruslee (1974). He trained Maori Venture to win the 1987 Grand National.

1949 Jockey GEORDIE MAWSON born. Best horse ridden Spanish Steps.

1960 Last meeting held at Buckfastleigh, Devon.

1964 Jockey CLIVE ECCLESTON had his first winner, at Carlisle.

1966 MRS ANNE BIDDLE became the first of her sex in Ireland to be granted a licence to train.

1977 DERMOT WELD trained 5 winners at Tralee.

1990 STEVE SMITH ECCLES failed to take his run of consecutive winners into double figures when Vision of Wonder finished 2nd at Plumpton. However, his next mount, Spofforth, won.

1990 LANFRANCO DETTORI became the youngest jockey since Lester Piggott in 1955 to ride 100 winners in a season. The nineteen-year-old did it on Line of Thunder at Chepstow and beat Lester, who achieved his first ton ten days short of his twentieth birthday. Dettori wasn't to reach that landmark until December 15.

1990 New trainer FERDIE MURPHY saddled 3 winners from 5 runners on his first day. Sibton Abbey, John O'Dee and Gee-A all won at Huntingdon, ridden by Declan Murphy.

1991 Dual Derby winner GENEROUS was syndicated for nearly £8 million.

28 AUGUST

1890 On Monmouth Park's straight course of one and $^3/_8$ miles, top US four-year-old SALVATOR was lined up for an unusual race against the clock in a bid to smash the then mile record of 1 minute 39$^1/_4$ seconds. He was 2–5 favourite to beat the clock and, carrying 110lbs and partnered by Martin Bergen, he duly clocked 1 minute 35$^1/_2$ seconds.

1928 Trainer HERBERT HANDEL born. Best horses trained Royal Toss, Coolera Prince.

1939 Scottish owner of Transworld and Junius SIMON FRASER born. Colours: white; black and orange quartered cap.

1943 Jockey TOMMY CAREY rode 5 consecutive winners at Ascot, and made it 6 when partnering the first winner at the next meeting on September 11.

1943 Leading lady jockey 3 times ELAIN MELLOR born.

1947 England soccer star and owner EMLYN HUGHES born. His 100–1 outsider Wayward Scot fell in the 1979 Grand National.

1959 Jump jockey MARK RICHARDS born. Best horses ridden include Hawkbarrow, Cruising Altitude.

1964 Jump jockey TIM WOOLLEY born.

1967 Jump jockey JAMIE OSBORNE born. Won Hennessy Gold Cup on Arctic Call in 1990. Also partnered Aldino and Young Snugfit.

1967 RED RUM (Tim Molony–Derek Morris) prevailed in the nursery handicap at Warwick in a photo-finish.

1972 ROGER WERNHAM rode his first winner, Pharaoh's Call, at Chepstow.

1982 The most expensive publicly purchased horse in training in Britain, $3.3 million SHAREEF DANCER, made a winning debut for Michael Stoute, ridden by Walter Swinburn at Newmarket.

1989 Former Champion Jump Jockey JONJO O'NEILL landed his first treble as a trainer when Roliad, Master Lamb and Ben Ledi all won at Cartmel.

1989 In the Prix du Mont-Canisy at Clairefontaine, France, Alfred Gibert, riding Timely Column, was run away with after his reins broke during the race. CASH ASMUSSEN, forfeiting his chances on Glenetive, rode after Gibert and brought his horse under control, saving the jockey from serious injury. Later Asmussen was honoured by a national TV station for making 'the year's most sporting gesture'.

1992 Newmarket jockey ALLAN MACKAY was out of action for two weeks after injuring his hand while washing up!

1805   A race whose conditions were advertised as being restricted to those who had been caused to pay out at least £200 in 'adverse litigation' was run at Tralee, Ireland. It was run for a plate donated by 'the Gentlemen of the Profession of the Law in the County of Kerry', and was won by a Protestant clergyman, REV. MR DENIS of Wicklow.

1918   Owner SIR JOHN ASTOR born. Best horse owned Coronation Stakes winner Cut Above. Colours: light blue; pink sash.

1923   FLINT JACK, a six-year-old gelding, became the first horse to win the Ebor twice, for trainer Ossie Bell, ridden by H. Gray at 10–1.

1931   Chairman of United Racecourses SIR EVELYN DE ROTHSCHILD born.

1937   Stud owner SONIA JORGENSEN born.

1939   Clerk of the scales GRAHAME WELCOME born.

1941   US trainer of Unbridled (1990 Breeders' Cup Classic winner) CARL NAFZGER born.

1941   US trainer JOE CANTEY born. Best horses include Cox's Ridge, Temperance Hill.

1950   Jockey EDWARD HIDE had his first ride, on Copper Wire, at Birmingham.

1957   US jockey JERRY BAILEY born. Best horses ridden include Hansel, Black Tie Affair. On the latter he won the 1991 Breeders' Cup Classic.

1963   Jockey PETER HILL born. Best horses ridden include Madraco.

1967   Leading US jockey JOE JOHNSON born in Owensboro, Kentucky. Height 5ft 1in. Taught to ride by elder brother, jockey Patrick.

1981   A first Goodwood training success for GEOFF LEWIS as Hollow Heart wins the Drawing Room Stakes.

1982   MICK RYAN-trained Boxberger Speed completed the Dutch Triple Crown, winning the St Leger at Dunduigt.

1988   Conditional jockey VIVIAN KENNEDY broke his neck in a fall at Huntingdon and died two days later.

1992   A Newmarket treble took MICHAEL ROBERTS past £1 million in British win prize-money.

1992   The Sarah and Mike Gull Handicap Hurdle at Southwell was named in honour of the couple, who had married that afternoon. The bride, bridegroom and guests were photographed in the winner's enclosure after Nun's Jewel won the race.

30 AUGUST

1771 HEREFORD staged its second-ever meeting. Lord Chedworth's bay WEAZLE 'won easy' over heats of four miles, reported the *Sporting Calendar*.

1825 Sporting annals reported a match at Maghull, ten miles from Liverpool: 'Equestrians thronged to the scene of action and for more than a mile the road from Liverpool to Maghull might be seen crowded with horse and foot.'

1922 Owner-breeder HERMIONE COURAGE born. Best horses included Smart Tar.

1939 Mountain-climbing owner-trainer CLIVE HOLMES born. Best horses trained include Clearly Bust, Cocaine and Master Nibble, which he also owned. Colours: black; white sleeves; light green cap.

1953 Dual World Amateur Rackets champion and owner of Gentle Gypsy, Lammastide and Straight Through JOHN PRENN born. Colours: royal blue and emerald green check; royal blue sleeves; checked cap.

1966 Jockey JULIE BOWKER born. Partnered Crofter's Cline.

1969 MICHAEL ROBERTS survived an objection to win his first race on Smyrna at Scottsville, Natal, South Africa. He was fifteen.

1969 HENRY CECIL saddled his first Goodwood winner, Rohays, in the Wills Embassy Mile.

1972 The previous year's Derby winner, MILL REEF, fractured his near foreleg while exercising at Kingsclere. Superb veterinary attention saved him for stud duties.

1981 WILLIE SHOEMAKER partnered the great John Henry to victory in the first million-dollar race, the Arlington Million in Chicago.

1982 Jump jockey GEE ARMYTAGE rode her first winner, Applante, at Southwell.

1983 SPARK CHIEF, trained by Frank Durr, clocked the fastest ever electronically recorded time for 5 furlongs – 53.7 seconds – at Epsom (equivalent to almost 42mph).

1983 TYRONE WILLIAMS' first winner was Going Going at Epsom.

1991 CHICMOND (16–1) won the Solario Stakes at Sandown to give trainer Sir Mark Prescott his first Group winner in Britain.

1991 SIR IVOR, 1968 2,000 Guineas and Derby winner, retired from stud duty.

1991 French-trained ZINO, the 1982 2,000 Guineas winner, died of colic.

31 AUGUST

1928 Twenty-one-year-old CHARLIE SMIRKE's mount, Welcome Gift, was left at the post at Gatwick. It was a hot favourite and the Jockey Club called an inquiry. Smirke's licence was withdrawn, and it was 5 years before he was allowed to ride again. In fact, Welcome Gift went on to acquire a reputation for dwelling at the start of his races. Smirke returned in 1934 and rode Windsor Lad to win the Derby.

1937 Owner JOHN HAYTER born. His Roland Gardens won 1978 2,000 Guineas. Colours: red and white diamonds; black sleeves and cap.

1940 Newmarket trainer PAUL KELLEWAY born. As a jockey he won the Cheltenham Gold Cup on What a Myth (1969) and the Champion Hurdle on Bula in 1971 and 1972. Best horses trained Swiss Maid, Donegal Prince, Miss Boniface, Star Way.

1962 MYRDDIN LLOYD THOMAS, better known as Taffy, rode his first winner, Weather Way, at Hurst Park.

1965 The jockey son of Yves, ERIC SAINT-MARTIN, born.

1968 SIR GARY SOBERS backed 3 winners – Gipsy Bridge, Mycropolis and Jubilation – which all won at 10-1, 20-1 and 4-1. Then he went out to bat and celebrated by hitting 6 sixes in one over off Glamorgan's Malcolm Nash.

1978 PETER SCUDAMORE rode his first winner, Toby Balding-trained Rolyat, over hurdles at Devon.

1982 JACK BERRY saddled his 100th winner when eight-year-old Bri-Eden (George Duffield) won a handicap sprint at Epsom.

1990 Leading Italian jockey MARCO PAGANINI died. On August 25 he had fallen from Massimina at Grosseto in the Premio Mulina, a 5-furlong handicap, during a floodlit meeting. He rode 1,036 winners and was Champion in 1986–87.

1992 The Jockey Club's new overnight declaration of jockeys system, OJOCS, opened to receive bookings for meetings a week hence, and JOHN REID was the first jockey to use it.

1992 Ten-year-old Manhattan Boy won at Plumpton for the 11th time.

1992 HIGH LINE, who sired 22 European Group winners, died aged 26.

1992 Yorkshire farmer STEPHEN SWIERS was the first British-born jockey for ten years to win the amateur riders' derby, the Moet & Chandon Silver Magnum at Epsom, riding Statajack, a 5-1 chance.

1992 MAXINE JUSTER beat rivals from 8 other countries to win the European Ladies' Championship, staged in Vienna and Bratislava.

1992 Three ex-English horses finished 1, 2, 3 in the $1 million Pacific Classic at Del Mar, USA. The winner was former Barry Hills inmate MISSIONARY RIDGE, followed home by ex-Guy Harwood Defensive Play and ex-Dick Hern Claret.

1 SEPTEMBER

1913 American trainer WOODFORD (WOODY) CEFIS STEPHEN born at Stanton, Kentucky. Trained 1974 Kentucky Derby winner Cannonade and 1982 Belmont Stakes winner Conquistador Cielo.

1930 GOLDEN MILLER, later to win 5 Cheltenham Gold Cups, made his debut, unplaced at 25-1, in the Farnsfield Hurdle at Southwell.

1936 Former Newmarket jockey CHARLIE 'JOCK' GASTON born.

1936 Trainer COLIN CROSSLEY born.

1939 PADDY BRODERICK born. Partnered Night Nurse to a string of wins including the Champion Hurdle (1976, 1977), Irish Sweeps Hurdle (1975), Welsh and Scottish Champion Hurdles.

1942 Owner PAUL GREEN born. His Very Promising won the 1986 Mackeson Gold Cup. Also owns Carvill's Hill. Colours: light blue; dark blue diamond on body and cap.

1947 Somerset trainer JIM OLD born.

1957 Trainer STEPHEN CRAINE born.

1961 The Horserace Totalisator Board and the Horse Race Betting Levy Board created.

1961 Champion Jockey in South Africa JEFF LLOYD born.

1965 The shock winner of the Seaton Handicap at Devon at 20-1, JUNGLE STUDENT, collapsed and died of a heart attack after passing the post, while beaten favourite GALATEA, who had earlier fallen, galloped on riderless before also collapsing and dying of a heart attack.

1988 A manufactured surface was used at an American meeting for the first time. They raced on Equitrack at the inaugural meeting of the Remington Park, Oklahoma track.

1990 The most successful Scottish flat race trainer of modern times, GEORGE BOYD, died at the age of 83. He won the 1961 2,000 Guineas with 66-1 chance Rockavon, the only Scottish-trained horse to win an English Classic.

1992 One of Australia's most popular jockeys, NOEL BARKER, died in hospital twelve days after a fall in a race trial at Randwick, Sydney. Aged 30, he was once Champion Jockey in Hong Kong and his wife Kelly said she would scatter his ashes at Sha Tin racecourse. However, the Royal Hong Kong Jockey Club would not permit this: 'The local feelings on such matters are very strong.'

1992 ANTOINETTE 'TIDDLER' ARMES, aged 23, became the first woman apprentice to ride a winner over the Derby course, on Incola (Henry Candy), in the Steve Donoghue Apprentice Handicap at Epsom. On the same card YOSHIBA OKABE became the first Japanese rider to win at Epsom when Shrewd Partner (13-2) won the Chalk Lane Handicap.

2 SEPTEMBER

1917 Irish trainer CLEM MAGNIER born. Best horses handled include Cavaliero, Overshadow, Albergo, Top Twenty, Just a Game.

1935 The world's most successful trainer, D. (DARRELL) WAYNE LUKAS, born in Wisconsin. In 1987 he sent out 343 winners which collected over $17,000,000 prize-money. In 1978 he had only 6 horses. His Winning Colors won the 1988 Kentucky Derby and Steinlen the 1989 Arlington Million. Trainer of more Breeders' Cup winners than anyone else.

1942 Hampshire trainer MICHAEL MADGWICK born.

1947 Former jump jockey JOHN 'JINKS' JAMES born.

1949 Newmarket trainer WILLIE MUSSON born. Best horses trained include Ore, Roaring Riva, Broughton Bay, Ash King.

1953 Derby winner PINZA was found to have developed an injury and was retired to stud. The horse gave Gordon Richards his first and only success in the race earlier in the year.

1955 Somerset trainer JACQUI THORNE born. Best horses trained include Imperial Champagne.

1969 Lewes trainer TOM MASSON died aged 71. He sent out 33-1 shot Kami to be 3rd in the 1947 Grand National while his Pindaric won the 1962 Lingfield Derby Trial, only to fall in the real thing.

1975 ROCHE NOIRE (9-2) at Brighton gave JOE MERCER his 2,000th winner as a jockey.

1978 DULCIFY, who went on to win the Victoria Derby, AJC Derby and W. S. Cox Plate in Australia, began his career with a 300-1 win at Morphetville, Adelaide.

1990 Born in South Africa, and once the richest man in his adopted country of Australia, ROBERT HOLMES A'COURT, owner of 1984 Melbourne Cup winner Black Knight, died aged 53.

1991 Martell announced they were to sponsor the Grand National in a £4 million package.

3 SEPTEMBER

1770 ECLIPSE scared off the opposition again and had a walkover for the King's Plate at Lincoln.

1889 The first day's racing took place at Koln, Germany.

1932 Jockey MICK BATCHELOR born. Won Scottish National on Fincham in 1960. Best horses ridden include Dovecote.

1941 Burton-on-Trent trainer BARRY MORGAN born.

1982 Levy Board Chairman LORD PLUMMER opened the new £2.5 million stand at Haydock.

1986 Jump jockey PHIL TUCK completed a sequence of 10 consecutive winners, equalling Johnny Gilbert's record set in 1959, riding even money favourite, Doronicum, at Southwell.

1987 Cnoc Na Cuille won at Worcester to give PRINCESS ANNE her first winner over fences, at odds of 7–2, in the Droitwich Handicap Chase. Trained by David Nicholson.

1990 1977 Derby winner THE MINSTREL was put down in Kentucky.

1992 LESTER PIGGOTT was presented with his first grandson when eldest daughter Maureen, wife of Newmarket trainer William Haggas, gave birth to her second child, a boy weighing almost 9lbs.

1992 Ex-jump jockey RICHARD ROWE saddled his first flat winner as a trainer when L'Uomo Classics won at Salisbury.

1992 Irish born STEPHEN HILLEN, 22, became Britain's youngest trainer after being granted a flat licence.

4 SEPTEMBER

1826 MARKSMAN won the Yeomen's Plate at Ashford, Kent, losing the first two and a half-mile heat of the event but winning the next 2. This was a remarkable achievement as Marksman was certainly eighteen years old, and possibly even nineteen, at the time. Various reports mention both ages, although there appears to be no other claim for a horse to have won a race aged nineteen or older.

1894 Owner JIM JOEL born. Real name Harry Joel Joel. His Maori Venture won the Grand National in 1987 and Royal Palace won the Derby and 2,000 Guineas in 1967, with Picture Play winning the 1,000 Guineas in 1944. Colours: black; scarlet cap.

1919 Trainer HARRY BLACKSHAW born. Successful jockey under both codes. Rode Pappatea to win 1948 Northumberland Plate and also won both the Danish and Swedish Derbies.

1933 Jockey ROY EDWARDS born. Won the 1967 Champion Hurdle on Saucy Kit.

1933 Jockey STAN HAYHURST born. Won the 1958 Cheltenham Gold Cup on Kerstin.

1935 Jump jockey DAN O'DONOVAN born.

1945 Racing resumed at York following the war, during which time the course had been a prisoner-of-war camp.

1958 Jump jockey JOHN LOVEJOY born. Partnered Jugador.

1967 GEORGE and DENNIS WARE were found guilty of running a ringer in a point-to-point event earlier in the year. The verdict was not a surprise as one of the horses involved in the case had a large star on his head, and the other was unmarked.

1982 Five winners from 5 rides was PAT EDDERY's score at Leopardstown.

1987 STOCK HILL LASS won for the 3rd time in a season at Kempton to land a £50,000 bonus prize.

1990 TIMELESS TIMES won at Pontefract to equal the record of 16 wins as a two-year-old currently held by The Bard (1885) and Provideo (1984). The horse failed to exceed the record.

1992 1991 Arc de Triomphe winner SUAVE DANCER was retired.

5 SEPTEMBER

1862 Trainer T. S. DAWSON completed a run of 7 successive victories in races at the 2-day Ayr meeting with horses he both owned and trained. Four of the races were won by his horse Tommy Jones.

1899 Tod Sloan rode DEMOCRAT to win the Champagne Stakes at Doncaster. Another rider - Field Marshal Lord Kitchener - was given the horse when its ability abated to use as his charger when Commander-in-Chief in India.

1908 Trainer MATT FEAKES born. Jump jockey from 1927 to 1946. Best horses trained King's Bench, Tudor Jinks, Eagle Lodge.

1909 Impresario and former owner LORD DELFONT born. He once explained why he ceased to be an owner: 'When a jumper I had wouldn't take a fence, the trainer seriously told me the horse would need a psychiatrist. I knew that was enough, and got out.'

1928 Former senior steward of the Turf Club LORD HEMPHILL born.

1934 Trainer BOB HARMAN born. Handler of Orchard Park.

1945 CHAMOSSAIRE (11-2), ridden by Tommy Lowrey, won the last wartime substitute St Leger run at York. Trained by R. Perryman.

1957 Champion point-to-point rider JENNY PIDGEON born.

1966 LESTER PIGGOTT rode the first 5 winners at Warwick.

1981 SHEIKH ALI ABU KAMSIN had received the trophy for his Migrator's win in the Garrick Jubilee Handicap Hurdle at Stratford before Samuel Morshead objected on behalf of 3rd-placed Space Ship. The winner was demoted to 3rd, the runner-up Sir Eamon was awarded the race, Space Ship was moved up to 2nd and the trophy had to change hands.

1989 All 4 runners in the Chilton and Windlestone Working Men's Club Handicap Chase at Sedgefield either fell or refused at the final fence. Jockey ANDY ORKNEY remounted Grange of Glory - which had landed literally on top of the fence - after dragging him off it, and the 5-4 favourite went on to win by a distance.

1990 MICK CHANNON's first double at one meeting when Lorna Vincent won on Dear Miff and Golden Scissors at Fontwell.

1990 TIMELESS TIMES was 3rd at York in an attempt to break the record of 16 two-year-old wins.

1992 MARY REVELEY reached the 50-winner mark for the first time when Corn Lily (10-1, ridden by Darren Moffat) won the Hambleton Cup at Thirsk. This made her only the 3rd trainer in Britain to score a half-century in consecutive flat and jump seasons. First was Denys Smith in the 1969-70 jumps and 1970 flat season; then Peter Easterby did it in the 1977-78 jump and 1978 flat season. He went on to achieve the feat in 7 consecutive seasons in all.

6 SEPTEMBER

1854   1,000 Guineas winner VIRAGO won the three-mile Warwick Cup with Oaks winner Mincemeat finishing last of 4.

1893   THOMAS LOATES rode 40–95 favourite Isinglass to victory in the 7-runner St Leger to complete the Triple Crown for the horse. Isinglass created a new prize-money record of £57,285 during his career, £5,300 of which he gained from this victory.

1899   MORNINGTON CANNON won the St Leger on the John Porter-trained Flying Fox, 2–7 favourite, which defeated 5 opponents with the minimum of fuss in completing the Triple Crown.

1911   Jockey TOMMY LOWREY born at Ryton-on-Tyne. Rode Chamossaire to win the 1945 St Leger and took the 1946 Derby and St Leger on the grey Airborne.

1936   Former trainer PAUL SMYTH born.

1949   York jockey MARK BIRCH, former Cock of the North, born. Best horse ridden Sea Pigeon.

1990   TAKENHALL won at York for jockey DALE GIBSON, breaking his run of 102 consecutive losers.

1990   SIMON SHERWOOD sent out his first runner as a trainer, Murphy, to win at Newton Abbot.

1991   WILLIE CLARK, at 69 the oldest active jockey, rode for the final time, at Charles Town, USA. He began his career in 1945 and rode 1,143 winners from 10,631 mounts.

1991   Perfect Circle gave WALTER SWINBURN his 1,000th winner in Britain, at Kempton.

1991   Former trainer TOM CORRIE died aged 73. He trained Champion Hurdler Comedy of Errors to win 4 flat races. Began training in 1958.

1991   Having jumped the final fence at Sedgefield, SKOLERN (ridden by J. Callaghan) looked all over the winner – until More Swag, coming the other way, suddenly charged towards him, causing jockey Callaghan to fall and leaving Lawrence Mullaney on Nishkina to claim a highly improbable victory.

1991   A two-year-old making his debut at Del Mar, USA, rejoiced in the name of Honk a Wanker. It finished 5th.

1992   GAY KELLEWAY became the first non-American female to ride in the Arlington Million, finishing last on her father's John Rose. She was also the first jockey to ride wearing a jockey-cam, a 4-inch camera mounted on the rider's helmet to give TV viewers a jockey's-eye view of the action.

7 SEPTEMBER

1764 Jockey JOSEPH ROSE completed a tough stint when riding Bachelor at Manchester. The previous day he had ridden Young Davy at Richmond, Yorks, and the day before that had piloted Favourite at Lincoln – all this by commuting between meetings on his own horse, carrying his racing saddle on his back. No private helicopters in those days!

1892 1,000 Guineas winner and Derby runner-up LA FLECHE, ridden by John Watts, won the 11-runner St Leger at odds of 7–2 for trainer John Porter.

1898 WILDFOWLER (10–1) won the 12-runner St Leger ridden by Charles Wood for trainer Sam Darling, both of whom landed their 2nd successive win in the event. Jeddah, 5–6 favourite, was 2nd.

1930 GORDON RICHARDS (no relation), who trains out of fourteenth-century Greystoke on the edge of the Lake District, born. Trained Grand National winners Lucius (1978) and Hallo Dandy (1984), and Titus Oates won the Massey Ferguson and King George VI in 1969.

1932 American trainer of Spectacular Bid BUD DELP born.

1932 Four of the first 5 home in the St Leger were owned by the AGA KHAN. Winner Firdaussi, runner-up Dastur, 4th-placed Udaipur and 5th-placed Taj Kasra were all trained by Frank Butters.

1967 Garage proprietor, bus-driver, part-time post-mistress and now at last an official trainer LOUIE DINGWALL gained her first victory since the Jockey Club officially permitted women trainers when Denis Ryan rode Olympic Boy to a 33–1 triumph at Folkestone.

1969 Jump jockey JOHNNY LEHANE was found dying in a Devon hotel aged just 34. He won the Irish Grand National on Gold Legend in 1958. His nickname was 'Tumper', due to his willingness to 'tump' either man or horse should he deem it necessary.

1970 WILLIE SHOEMAKER passed John Longden's previous all-time record of 6,032 winners at Del Mar on Dares J.

1980 Apprentice WALTER SWINBURN, aged nineteen, was taken on by Michael Stoute.

1989 Former jump jockey JOHN DOWLING died aged 57. Born on August 22 1932. First winner, Joe's Ginger, at Ludlow on October 21 1954.

1990 Coincidence backers were in no doubt as to the good thing of the day at Kempton, where a Spitfire flypast took place to commemorate the Battle of Britain shortly before the running of the Spitfire Handicap. The race was won by 11–2 chance BLUE AEROPLANE.

1992 JOHN BOTTOMLEY of Yorkshire was the first trainer to miss the newly inaugurated OJOCS (overnight declaration of jockeys) deadline when he failed to declare a jockey for Swynford Flyer at Leicester.

251

8 SEPTEMBER

1820 The biggest field yet, 27, turned out for the St Leger, won by 7–1 chance ST PATRICK, ridden by R. Johnson.

1897 The Sam Darling-trained 1–10 favourite Galtee More, which had won the Derby, was regarded as a certainty for the St Leger. Charles Wood, returning to the saddle this season after being warned off for ten years, duly rode him to a 3/4-length victory and thus the Triple Crown against just 4 opponents.

1941 Top French jockey YVES ST MARTIN born. First Classic winner in Britain was Monade in the 1962 Oaks and he also won the 1963 Derby on Relko. Sassafrass was his first Arc winner in 1970 and he repeated the victory on Allez France in 1974.

1955 Meld's St Leger victory made CAPTAIN CECIL BOYD-ROCHFORT the first trainer to earn total winnings in excess of £1 million.

1955 A yearling called BALLYMOSS fetched 4,500 guineas at Doncaster, bought by Vincent O'Brien for American owner J. McShain, a builder. The horse was bred at the Naul stud, Co. Dublin, by Richard Ball, known as 'The Poet' owing to having once published a volume of verse. The horse went on to become the record European prize-money earner and then landed the 1958 Arc, having been runner-up in the 1957 Derby. He also won the Irish Derby and became the first Irish-trained colt to win the St Leger.

1956 Carrick-on-Suir trainer PAT FLYNN born. Best horses trained include Virginia Deer, Cheap Display, Maiden Fair, Mons Mark.

1959 Jump jockey JOHNNY GILBERT rode 10 consecutive winners between this date and September 30 to set a record only Phil Tuck has ever equalled among jump jockeys. Only Gordon Richards, with a run of 12 in October 1933, has ever exceeded it on the flat.

1960 Jump jockey GRAHAM BRADLEY, who won the 1983 Gold Cup on Bregawn, born. Also partnered Wayward Lad, Kildimo.

1970 The last meeting took place at John McCririck's favourite course, Alexandra Park.

1990 DAYJUR (Willie Carson–Dick Hern) became the first sprinter to complete the King's Stand–Nunthorpe–Ladbroke Sprint hat-trick when winning the latter at Haydock.

1991 Wonder horse ARAZI boosted his reputation with an easy win in Longchamp's Prix de la Salamandre.

1992 Burooj won at Lingfield to complete 49-year-old WILLIE CARSON's 21st century of winners in 22 seasons. A fall in Milan in 1984 prevented the clean sweep.

9 SEPTEMBER

1754 DRIVER, owned by Mr Lamego, won the Give and Take Plate at Maidenhead in a 3-heat event, ridden by a different jockey in each one. Thomas Brett fell during the first heat and was replaced by David Newcomb,who rode so badly that he was in turn replaced by Thomas Arnold. Arnold rode the horse to win.

1817 Jockey RICHARD GOODISSON, who rode the first three Oaks winners in 1779, 1780 and 1781, died at Newmarket. He was reputed to always carry £500 in cash with him after being refused a credit bet for that amount on a horse that had won.

1868 Tom Chaloner rode 100–30 joint favourite FORMOSA to victory in the 11-runner St Leger.

1882 Racing took place for the first time at Newcastle's High Gosforth Park. Jump racing was introduced there in 1951.

1891 COMMON, 4–5 favourite, ridden by George Barrett and trained by John Porter, won the 9-runner St Leger, completing the Triple Crown in the process.

1896 It was 66–1 bar 2 as the 7 runners in the St Leger lined up, and indeed 2–11 favourite PERSIMMON, the Derby winner, owned by HRH Prince of Wales, won from 6–1 2nd favourite Labrador. The winner was the last of John Watts' 5 Leger successes and was trained by Richard Marsh.

1911 Kent trainer ALBERT NEAVES born. Best horses trained include Certain Justice, Do or Die, All Promise.

1944 Pink Floyd guitarist and owner ROGER WATERS born.

1966 Newmarket jockey ABIGAIL PEATE born.

1991 KNOWN RANGER, five-year-old half-brother to Reference Point, equalled the world record of 1 minute 32.4 seconds for a mile on turf at Belmont Park, USA.

1992 For the first time a race was run over 6¹/₂ furlongs at Doncaster. The EBF Fillies Nursery Handicap was won by STEVE CAUTHEN and MICHAEL STOUTE with Falsoola.

1992 Gaelic Frolic won at Exeter for trainer PETER CUNDELL, giving him his 400th winner. The trainer also sent out his first, Irish Word, at Exeter.

10 SEPTEMBER

1879 French horse Rayon D'Or, owned by COMTE DE LAGRANGE, who had also owned Triple Crown winner Gladiateur, won the 17-runner St Leger, ridden by Jem Goater, joint favourite at odds of 3-1.

1884 Thirteen ran in the St Leger, won by John Watts on THE LAMBKIN.

1890 The St Leger was won by the George Dawson-trained Oaks winner MEMOIR (10-1), ridden by John Watts.

1906 Newmarket trainer HUMPHREY COTTRILL born. Trained Narrator, which won the 1954 Champion Stakes at 20-1 and 1955 Coronation Cup at 100-30.

1922 JOHN OSBORNE, who rode 12 Classic winners, including the Derby on Pretender in 1869 and 6 2,000 Guineas winners, died aged 89. He was still training successful horses at the age of 81, when The Guller won the Northumberland Plate.

1942 The government announced that because of the war it was 'unable to sanction NH racing' any longer. It was January 1945 before it returned on a regular basis.

1961 Jockey STAN MOORE born. Best horses ridden Ardross, Neblin.

1965 GEE ARMYTAGE born. One of the few women to ride in the Grand National, she partnered the aptly named Gee-A in 1988. Landed a double at the 1987 Cheltenham Festival on The Ellier (Kim Muir Memorial Challenge Cup) and Gee-A (Mildmay of Flete Hurdle).

1969 The Fulke Johnson Houghton-trained RIBOFILIO, already beaten favourite in three Classics - the 2,000 Guineas, Derby and Irish Derby - was again 11-10 market leader in the St Leger. But once again even Lester Piggott could not win on the horse, which finished 1½ lengths second to the Ron Hutchinson-partnered Intermezzo.

1972 The great French mare ALLEZ FRANCE made her debut ridden, as she would be throughout her career, by Yves St Martin. She won the Prix de Toutevoie at Longchamp.

1977 ZULU GOLD returned odds of 400-1 when winning at Cheltenham (Cheltenham in Adelaide, that is).

1981 Jump jockey MALCOLM BATTERS announced his retirement from the saddle - to take up deep-sea diving.

1982 Highly rated jumps trainer BOB TURNELL died aged 67. His Pas Seul won the Gold Cup and Salmon Spray the Champion Hurdle.

1988 WILLIE CARSON rode Minster Son to win the St Leger with particular delight as he also bred the horse, trained by Neil Graham.

1989 Racing began at Taipa Island, Macau, where 2,500 were locked out as £1.5 million was bet on the Tote.

1992 Channel 4 announced that it was dropping live coverage of the Arc de Triomphe in favour of Italian soccer.

254

11 SEPTEMBER

1711   *The Post Boy* carried an advertisement for a race to be run 'on 9th October next on Coleshill Heath, Warwickshire, a plate of 6gns value. The winning horse to be sold for £10, to carry 10st weight if 14 hands high, if above or under to carry or be allowed weight for inches. Also a plate of less value to be run for by asses'.

1867   A dozen runners lined up for the St Leger. Tom Chaloner rode filly ACHIEVEMENT to victory at 7–4, beating 6–5 favourite and Derby winner The Hermit into 2nd place.

1872   The St Leger was won by 8–1 chance WENLOCK, ridden by Charlie Maidment, against 16 rivals.

1878   Fourteen went to post for the St Leger, one fewer than had been intended: jockey F. Sharpe, who would have ridden Yagar, broke his leg in a preliminary canter when he was kicked by another of the runners. FRED ARCHER won for the second successive year, bringing Lord Falmouth's 5–2 favourite, the Oaks winner Jannette, home in front. The same owner's Childeric was runner-up, the second consecutive year he had owned the first 2.

1889   Fred Barrett rode 8–13 favourite and Derby winner DONOVAN, trained by George Dawson, to win the 12-runner St Leger by an easy 3 lengths from Miguel. Donovan, owned by the Duke of Portland, won 11 of his 13 outings as a two-year-old.

1895   The Mathew Dawson-trained SIR VISTO, ridden by Sam Loates, was the 9–4 favourite winner of the 11-runner St Leger.

1917   French owner of Arc winner Allez France, DANIEL WILDENSTEIN, born. Writer of 50 books on art, he has owned top horses such as All Along (1983 Arc winner), Pawneese, Flying Water, Crow, Sagace, Epervier Bleu and Pistolet Bleu. Colours: royal blue; light blue cap.

1936   Irish jockey TOMMY MURPHY born. Won Irish 1,000 Guineas on Lady Capulet in 1977. Best horse ridden Alleged.

1941   Wantage trainer PAUL COLE born. Trained Generous to win 1991 Derby at 9–1 and his Snurge won the 1990 St Leger. Also trained Bint Pasha, Ibn Bey, Ruby Tiger, John de Coombe and Bel Byou.

1944   Cheshire trainer MICK LAMBERT born. Best horses include Fine Sun.

1954   Jump jockey RICHARD LINLEY born.

1991   FARFELU, ridden by Simon Whitworth, fell in the Portland Handicap at Doncaster, two years after a similar fall in the same race forced Paul Cook to retire.

12 SEPTEMBER

1843 Second-place money was doubled to £200 and the 3rd saved his stake, for the first time, as 9 went to post for the St Leger, won by NUTWITH (Job Marson) at 100-7. Connections collected prize money of £3,070 4s 6d. Derby winner Cotherstone was second.

1855 Unusually, an objection was made to one of the 12 St Leger runners even before the race had taken place. It was on the grounds that the owner was in default for bets, but the stewards disallowed the objection. The race was won by 40-1 outsider SAUCEBOX.

1877 Fred Archer won his first St Leger, on Lord Falmouth's Derby winner Silvio, the 65-40 favourite, which defeated 13 opponents.

1888 JACK ROBINSON won his second successive St Leger on Lord Calthorpe's Oaks winner Seabreeze. Trainer Mr Jewitt also scored for the second successive year. The winner was 5-2 2nd favourite.

1894 Mornington Cannon was on board shock 50-1 St Leger winner THROSTLE. Even Throstle's owner, Lord Arlington, had despaired of her, actually trying to give her away at one stage – the prospective recipient couldn't be bothered to collect her!

1900 The Prince of Wales' DIAMOND JUBILEE, 2-7 favourite, completed the Triple Crown by winning the St Leger, ridden as usual by stable lad Herbert Jones, and trained by Richard Marsh.

1917 Owner of dual Champion Hurdler (1971 and 1972) Bula CAPTAIN BILL EDWARDS-HEATHCOTE born.

1934 Naas trainer PADDY OSBORNE born. Best horses include Deep Idol.

1954 Jump jockey CHRIS JONES born. Best horse ridden Cantlie.

1966 Former jockey TIM BROOKSHAW, who broke his neck in a fall at Liverpool in 1963, but taught himself to walk and ride again, had his first success as an owner with What a Yarn at Wolverhampton.

1981 Derby winner SHERGAR was only 4th of 7 behind 28-1 chance Cut Above in the St Leger.

1985 GREVILLE STARKEY rode 5 winners at Salisbury.

1990 The publisher's idea of promoting DICK FRANCIS's latest novel by sponsoring a race in its honour at Plumpton hit a snag when only 1 horse was declared for the race, making it hardly an appropriate vehicle to support the new title – *Longshot*.

1990 Artist MAX BRANDRETT was fined £1,200 and ordered to pay £2,000 compensation after forging Lester Piggott's signature on paintings of the maestro on Teenoso. Piggott himself instigated the action.

1991 Champion Hurdler MORLEY STREET just failed to win the Doncaster Cup when Great Marquess hung on for victory.

1992 George Duffield rode Oaks winner USER FRIENDLY (7-4 favourite) to victory in the St Leger for trainer Clive Brittain.

13 SEPTEMBER

1682 A large crowd gathered at Leasowe in Cheshire to see the DUKE OF MONMOUTH ride in a race worth £60, which he duly won on Young Whiteley, his own horse.

1842 Jockey TOMMY LYE had bet £200 on his St Leger mount, Blue Bonnet, an 8-1 chance which won the 17-runner race. But he gave the filly such severe punishment in the process that trainer Tom Dawson never hired him again and the horse never won again.

1848 Surplice, ridden by Nat Flatman, won the 9-runner St Leger at 9-4 at the 2nd attempt. The runners had first all set off without any indication from the starter, for which all the jockeys were fined.

1865 GLADIATEUR won the St Leger at 8-13, ridden by H. Grimshaw, becoming the first and only horse to win the Triple Crown plus the Grand Prix de Paris. Before and after the Leger an objection to Gladiateur was made on the grounds that he was older than three.

1871 Filly HANNAH, which had won the 1,000 Guineas and Oaks, completed a Classic treble when she was 2-1 winner of the St Leger.

1876 Lord Dupplin's 2,000 Guineas winner Petrarch, ridden by Jem Goater, won the 9-runner St Leger.

1882 Fred Archer won his 4th St Leger on the 40-1 outsider Dutch Oven.

1942 SUN CHARIOT (9-4) established a record when she won the St Leger, giving the Royal colours 4 of the 5 Classic winners. Sun Chariot also won the 1,000 Guineas and Oaks (ridden in all three by Gordon Richards), while Big Game (Richards) took the 2,000 Guineas. Both were leased from the National Stud by King George VI.

1947 Jockey GERRY FAULKNER born. Partnered Supermaster.

1950 Fifteen-year-old JOE MERCER rode his first winner, Eldoret, at Bath.

1959 Jockeys ALAN HILL and KEVIN RAYMONT born.

1989 Three jockeys were injured when MADRACO fell in the Portland Handicap at Doncaster. Ray Cochrane broke his collarbone, Ian Johnson hurt his lower spine and Paul Cook fractured his right foot, right thumb, two ribs and broke his collarbone. Madraco, ridden by Cook, broke his off-hind fetlock in the incident, 2½ furlongs out, when he put his foot in a hole and fell, bringing down Johnson on Pendor Dancer and Cochrane's Tolo.

1992 English Derby winner Dr Devious just got the better of Irish Derby winner St Jovite in the Champion Stakes at Leopardstown.

1992 GIANFRANCO DETTORI, who started his career with a winner for Sergio Cumani 31 years earlier, bowed out with a double on Only Royale and Inner City for that trainer's son, Luca, at San Siro, Milan. He was Italian Champion 13 times. His 'retirement' was short-lived – he was back in action a fortnight later.

14 SEPTEMBER

1725 A 'ladies' plate' was run for by female riders on Ripon Heath, Yorkshire.

1841 WILLIAM 'GLORIOUS BILL' SCOTT won his 4th successive St Leger on Satirist at 6-1, beating Derby winner Coronation.

1853 WEST AUSTRALIAN (6-4 favourite), owned by Mr John Bowes, created history by becoming the first Triple Crown winner as he added the St Leger to the 2,000 Guineas and Derby. Trained at Malton by John Scott and ridden by Frank Butler.

1864 10 contested the St Leger, won by 2-1 favourite Blair Athol, the Derby winner, ridden by Jim Snowden.

1881 Iroquois (2-1 favourite) was FRED ARCHER's 3rd St Leger winner, beating 14 opponents, including Voluptuary, which finished last but went on to glory in the 1884 Grand National.

1887 Temperamental 4-1 favourite KILWARLIN, trained by Mr Jewitt, stood stock still as the 8 other runners in the St Leger set off, losing a good 150 yards. However, William 'Jack' Robinson's mount gradually made up ground and prevailed by 1/2 length.

1919 Jockey TIM MALONY born. Champion Jump Jockey for 5 consecutive seasons from 1948 to 1952, he won the Champion Hurdle from 1951 (Hatton's Grace) to 1954 (3 straight wins for Sir Ken).

1950 Leading American jockey CHARLES WOODS JR, in the top six on the all-time list at Churchill Downs, born in Louisville, Kentucky.

1959 America's new Aqueduct track opened with Willie Shoemaker riding Four Lane, trained by T. M. Waller to win the first race.

1975 Great French mare Allez France won for the 13th and last time, in the Prix Foy at Longchamp.

1977 Jockey MARK RIMMER's first winner was Flying Empress (12-1) at Yarmouth.

1983 MELD, the 1955 Triple Crown winner, died in Ireland at the age of 31 - a record for longevity among English Classic winners.

1985 JOHN FRANCOME's first runner over jumps as a trainer, Crimson Knight (7-2), ridden by Steve Smith Eccles, fell at the 3rd last at Worcester and later died.

1989 WELD won the Doncaster Cup at 1-5 to become Lord Howard de Walden's 400th winner as an owner, and his 35th Group race winner.

1991 After 2 furlongs of the St Leger the field was confronted by a 35-year-old man, Alan Davis, and an eight-year-old boy sitting on the course. The field managed to swerve past them. TOULON, ridden by Pat Eddery, went on to win at 5-2 for trainer André Fabre.

1992 SURPRISE OFFER won at Bath to give Richard Hannon his 1,000th British flat winner.

15 SEPTEMBER

1835 QUEEN OF TRUMPS became the first Oaks winner also to win the St Leger, beating 10 opponents and starting at 11-8.

1840 Having been left in a false start, 7-4 favourite Launcelot (ridden by William Scott) won the 11-runner St Leger - but only courtesy of runner-up Maroon, 4-1, ridden by J. Holmes. Lord Westminster owned both and 'declared to win' with the favourite, causing Holmes to prevent his mount from taking the lead.

1842 Known as 'The Pride of Northumberland', the great mare BEE'S-WING won the Doncaster Cup for the 4th time.

1875 Craigmillar (100-15) beat 12 opponents to win the St Leger.

1880 Derby winner Bend Or, 8-11 favourite, was a disappointment in the St Leger, finishing unplaced to Robert the Devil.

1886 FRED ARCHER landed his 6th and final St Leger victory on the Duke of Westminster's Ormonde, completing the Triple Crown.

1910 Doyen of racing writers RICHARD BAERLEIN of the *Guardian*, who called his house Shergar, born.

1930 Oxfordshire trainer JOHN BOSLEY, whose Eyecatcher was 3rd in the Grand National of 1976 and 1977, born.

1935 Curragh trainer JOHN MURPHY born.

1949 Irish trainer ARTHUR MOORE born. Best horses include Royal Bond, Drumgora, Fredcoteri, Venture to Cognac, Weather the Storm.

1956 Champion Irish Amateur from 1985 to 1989 WILLIE MULLINS born.

1970 Mrs Hauksbee won the Plantation Stakes to give jockey PAT EDDERY his first Goodwood winner, while trainer GUY HARWOOD achieved his with Early Session in the Harroways Stakes.

1979 STEVE CAUTHEN chalked up the 1,000th win of his career when he won at Doncaster - on a horse called Thousandfold.

1984 LESTER PIGGOTT rode Comanche Run, the 7-4 favourite, to a neck victory in the St Leger for trainer Luca Cumani. Piggott set a record of 28 Classic victories, overtaking Frank Buckle's 27.

1989 For the second time in three days a horse fell without apparent reason at the Doncaster St Leger meeting. The oldest Classic was abandoned for only the second time since 1776 (and the previous time, 1939, was because of war). BILLY NEWNES was the jockey to fall, from Able Player, in the first race of the eve of St Leger card. The race was rescheduled for Ayr on September 23.

1990 SNURGE became the first maiden since 1913 to win the St Leger, scoring at 7-2, ridden by Richard Quinn for trainer Paul Cole.

1990 Doncaster stewards waited for 7 minutes before announcing a stewards' inquiry into the Prix Vincennes Nursery. They later disqualified 'winner' Jenufa and awarded the race to Tiber Flow.

16 SEPTEMBER

1822 A remarkable St Leger took place. To say that THEODORE was unfancied is an understatement: jockey John Jackson, upon learning that he was to ride the horse, reportedly burst into tears and declared, 'What! Ride such a cripple as that?' The horse was lame and one layer struck a bet of £1,000 to a walking stick about the 200–1 shot. Theodore promptly shocked everyone by beating his 22 rivals for trainer James Croft, who was also responsible for 2nd, 3rd and 4th (Violet, Professor and Corinthian) in the 23-runner event.

1834 Derby winner and 10–12 favourite PLENIPOTENTIARY finished last but one in the 11-runner St Leger, and was later proved to have been poisoned. Touchstone, 50–1, emerged the winner.

1863 Despite being left at the post and an estimated 50 lengths behind the leaders at one stage – and being freely offered at 50–1 at that point – LORD CLIFDEN, the 100–30 favourite, ridden by John Osborne, came through to win the 19-runner St Leger and the £4,975 prize-money for Lord St Vincent.

1885 THE BARD set a new record with a 16th success as a two-year-old in the Tattersall Sale Stakes for trainer Martin Gurry of Newmarket.

1925 Former Irish prime minister and owner CHARLES HAUGHEY born. Best horses include The Chaser (8 victories), Miss Cossie (6), Aristocracy (5). Colours: black; blue sash and cap.

1927 1928 Champion Hurdler and 6 times winner of the Queen Alexandra Stakes BROWN JACK made his hurdling debut, finishing 3rd at Bournemouth over one and a half miles.

1931 Sheriff Hutton trainer GERRY KELLY born.

1941 Jockey TOMMY CARBERRY, who rode L'Escargot to win the 1970 and 1971 Gold Cups and the 1975 Grand National, born.

1945 Trainer ROD SIMPSON, famous for his flamboyant dress sense, born.

1955 Irish Champion Jump Jockey JOE BYRNE born.

1966 Jockey TYRONE WILLIAMS born. Best horse ridden, Hawkley.

1972 MERIEL TUFNELL won her 3rd race of the season (on Hard Slipper at Newbury) in the 11th of 12 ladies' races to become the first ever Champion Lady Jockey on the flat.

1981 Five winners out of 7 mounts for LESTER PIGGOTT at Yarmouth.

1982 PAUL COLE celebrated his 500th training success in his 15th season as Brandon Creek (Richard Quinn) won at Brighton.

1989 Two horses trained by RON O'LEARY failed to arrive for racing at Bangor. It was reported that the horsebox carrying them had gone to the seaside town of Bangor, instead of the racecourse at Bangor-on-Dee. The trainer himself claimed the box had broken down . . .

17 SEPTEMBER

1711 Ascot began its second ever meeting with just one race: a plate of 50 guineas for which 3 runners went to post.

1839 The first St Leger dead heat saw 4–7 favourite CHARLES XII and 13–1 chance EUCLID pass the post together in the 14-runner event. The former won the run-off by a head, ridden by William Scott.

1845 THE BARON (F. Butler) was the 10–1 winner of the 15-runner St Leger. For the first time the jockeys drew lots for position at the start and went off without a hitch in two ranks.

1851 SIM TEMPLEMAN rode 12–1 chance Newminster to defeat 17 opponents in the St Leger.

1856 Derby winner Ellington (8–13 favourite) was unplaced as WARLOCK, 12–1, ridden by Nat Flatman, beat his 8 rivals in the St Leger. Later in his career, in 1857, Warlock beat Fisherman, winner of 67 races, in the Queen's Plate at York.

1862 Ridden by Tom Chaloner, 100–30 chance THE MARQUIS beat 14 rivals to win the St Leger. His reward was to be sold to Russia.

1925 Owner of dual Welsh Grand National winner Bonanza Boy STEPHEN DUNSTER born. Colours: pink; white stars; purple armlet; pink cap with white star.

1939 Newmarket trainer (MICHAEL FREDERICK) DAVID MORLEY born. Best horses trained include Calaba, Sesame, Havanus.

1940 Former Champion Apprentice (1958) PETER BOOTHMAN born.

1956 VICTORIA 'TOCKIE' MCKIE born. Owner-trainer of Risk a Bet. Also owned Man of Europe. Colours: green; yellow sleeves; white cap.

1958 Jockey MAXINE JUSTER born. Champion Lady Jockey 1986. Won Ascot Ladies' Diamond Race in 1983, 1986 and 1989.

1963 Springmount at Fontwell was GUY HARWOOD's first winner as a trainer.

1973 Tracona, at Wolverhampton, was jockey WILLIE HIGGINS's first winner.

1979 Tina's Gold at Wolverhampton was jockey NICKY CARLISLE's first winner.

1989 Previously unbeaten 2,000 Guineas and Derby winner NASHWAN was beaten for the first time, in the Prix Niel at Longchamp, into 3rd place behind Golden Pheasant and French Glory.

1992 The QUEEN recorded a personal best when Zenith won at Beverley to become her 23rd home-bred winner of the season.

1992 The National Stud's bid for Derby winner Dr Devious was turned down by owner Sidney Craig.

1992 RICHARD HANNON sent out his first French winner, Central City, at Maisons-Laffitte.

18 SEPTEMBER

1794 The Mayor of Doncaster staged a public burning of gaming tables which had been proliferating at the racecourse. At the races BENINGBROUGH, the 2–1 winner of the previous day's St Leger, won the Gold Cup.

1827 After 7 false starts the Hon. E. Petre's filly MATILDA, 11–1, beat Derby winner Mameluke into 2nd place to win the 26-runner St Leger, ridden by Jem Robinson.

1835 Having won the St Leger three days earlier, QUEEN OF TRUMPS was rated a certainty for her next race, the Scarbrough Stakes at Doncaster, for which she was duly installed at 1–10 favourite. She looked sure to win as she cruised to the front with 100 yards to run, when a large dog suddenly appeared on the course, causing the horse, ridden by Tommy Lye, to swerve dramatically. Ainderby nipped through to win the race and £2,000 for her owner, Captain Frank Taylor, from a bet he'd placed. Legend has it he was so grateful to the dog that he found its owner, bought the pooch and gave it a life of luxury.

1838 The smallest field since 1802 turned out for the 7-runner St Leger. DON JOHN cruised to a 12-length victory in a record time of 3 minutes 17 seconds for jockey William Scott.

1850 VOLTIGEUR, ridden by J. Marson, won the 8-runner St Leger, starting at 8–13 following his Derby victory. However, he had to beat Russborough in a run-off following a dead-heat to take the honours.

1861 1,000–15 outsider CALLER OU, ridden by Tom Chaloner, came out on top in the St Leger, beating favourite and Derby winner Kettledrum into 2nd place. The winner won 51 of 101 races.

1931 Dual purpose trainer MICK O'TOOLE born. His Davy Lad won the Cheltenham Gold Cup in 1977. Also trained Faliraki, Dickens Hill.

1940 OGDEN PHIPPS born. Chairman of USA Jockey Club, and owner of 1980 1,000 Guineas winner Quick As Lightning.

1948 FREDDIE MAXWELL sent out his first winner (of 425) as a trainer, Dance Away (Davy Jones), at Bogside.

1968 RED RUM made his NH debut after 10 flat races of which he had won 2½ (one dead-heat). He finished 2nd at Cheltenham.

1975 GRAHAM MCCOURT rode his first winner, Vulrory's Kid, at Ascot.

1982 GEORGE DUFFIELD won the last 4 races at Catterick.

1989 Credit bookmakers H. Backhouse ventured into sponsorship at Bath, by awarding a prize for the best turned-out owner!

1991 AIDEN WALL rode Release the Beast to win at Dundalk carrying 10st 4lbs. Just nine days earlier the same combination had won at Roscommon, when the jockey had reportedly weighed 11st 6lbs.

19 SEPTEMBER

1801 1799 St Leger winner COCKFIGHTER took on highly rated SIR SOLOMON in a famous 500 guineas match over four miles. The undefeated Cockfighter was odds-on but beaten by 1½ lengths.

1826 For the first time the St Leger was run over the distance of one mile 6 furlongs 132 yards, over which it still takes place today. TARRARE (20-1) won under George Nelson for Lord Scarbrough against 26 opponents.

1913 Trainer WILLIE ROONEY born (Trench House, The Pegger).

1924 Former trainer (DOROTHY CYNTHIA) MONICA DICKINSON born. Handled Silver Buck, Browne's Gazette, Wayward Lad.

1930 Owner of Go South REX JOACHIM born. Colours: white; purple chevron on sleeves and cap.

1937 Wantage trainer MICHAEL HINCHCLIFFE born. Best horses include Westway Lad, Cutting Wind, Premier Charlie, Induit.

1942 Owner VALERIE SHAW born. Best horses include Milliondollarman, Proverity. Colours: yellow; McAlpine tartan sleeves.

1967 DOUG SMITH rode 2 winners at Yarmouth - the 2nd, Geoffrey Brooke-trained Monte Carlo, was the 20,000th ride of his career.

1978 Gay God won at Hereford to give jockey PHIL TUCK his first success in a chase.

1989 ALASTAIR LIMONT MBE, senior veterinary surgeon, retired after 41 years of service to Epsom, Kempton and Sandown.

1991 Jockey JOHN LOWE rode his 1,000th British winner, Lobinda (3-1), at Beverley.

1991 US jockey CHARLES WOODS JR recorded his 2,000th career win, at Turfway.

1992 STEVE CAUTHEN rode Mashaallah to win the Irish St Leger as British horses finished 1, 2, 3 and 4.

1992 LOCHSONG (10-1) completed a unique treble when she won the Ayr Gold Cup, run on a Saturday for the first time in 189 years, to add to her Stewards' Cup and Portland Handicap victories. Ridden by Francis Arrowsmith; trained by Ian Balding; owned by J. C. Smith.

1992 The Town Council Novices Chase at Market Rasen was won by CORRUPT COMMITTEE, ridden by A. Tory!

1992 VINCENT O'BRIEN saddled the winner of the Smurfit National Stakes at the Curragh for the 15th time when Fatherland was partnered to victory by Lester Piggott.

1992 Britain's youngest trainer, 22-year-old STEPHEN HILLEN, based at Corse Lawn, near Cheltenham, sent out his first winner, 25-1 shot Dr Lechter, at Catterick.

20 SEPTEMBER

1819 It took over two weeks to sort out who had won today's St Leger. The 19-runner race was 'won' by James Ferguson's Antonio, a 100–3 chance, but 5 runners missed the start and the stewards ordered a rerun. Only 10 lined up for that, with Antonio absent. This time W. Scott rode Sir Walter to victory. An appeal was made to the Jockey Club who, on October 4, announced 'the stewards should not have allowed a second race' and awarded the spoils to Antonio.

1825 A record 30 came under orders for the St Leger, with Bill Scott riding the 11–4 favourite MEMNON to victory. There was so much interest in the result that the news was rushed to London by carrier pigeon, and to Manchester by a team of dogs!

1836 ELIS dumbfounded bookies who had fielded against him in the St Leger by winning the 14-runner race by 2 lengths at 7–2, after 3 false starts. Rumours that Elis wouldn't even make it to the course were squashed when trainer John Kent Sr transported the horse from Goodwood to Doncaster, some 250 miles, in a van drawn by relays of post horses. The horsebox had been invented.

1926 FRED WINTER born. Champion Jockey and Trainer, and the first jumps trainer to win over £100,000 for his patrons in one season, 1973–74. Son of flat jockey turned trainer, he broke his back in a fall at Wye in 1947 and was out for a year. Battled back and became Champion Jockey in 1952–53, 1955–56, 1956–57, 1957–58. Won Gold Cup on Saffron Tartan (1961) and Mandarin (1962). Won the National on Sundew (1957), Kilmore (1962), Champion Hurdle on Clair Soleil (1955); Fare Time (1959); Eborneezer (1961). Retired in 1964 and was first jump jockey to receive CBE. Applied to become an assistant starter and was turned down! As a trainer he sent out Midnight Court to win the 1978 Gold Cup; Jay Trump (1965) and Anglo (1966) to win the National and Bula (1971 and 1972) and Lanzarote (1974) to win the Champion Hurdle.

1950 LESTER PIGGOTT, aged fourteen, lost his apprentice allowance when riding Zina to victory at Brighton.

1951 COLIN ASTBURY born. Champion Jump Jockey of 1977 – in Norway.

1976 JIM BOLGER sent out his first winner as a trainer when Peaceful Pleasure scored at Roscommon.

1989 DIANE CLAY, reigning Champion Lady Jump Jockey with 12 wins in 1988–89, announced her retirement, aged 25.

1989 After 31 years' training at Malton, PAT ROHAN sent out his last British runner, 25–1 shot Integrity Boy, which finished 2nd to Kildonan at Beverley. He left Britain to train in Bahrain.

1989 Ayr was first British course to install sectional timing facilities.

21 SEPTEMBER

1812 OTTERINGTON, a 100–1 outsider, won the 24-runner St Leger.

1818 REVELLER was the 7–2 winner of the 21-runner St Leger for jockey Bob Johnson and owner Mr Peirse. Reveller went on in 1822 to prevent Dr Syntax from winning the Preston Cup for the 8th year in succession.

1830 SAM CHIFNEY, who never managed to win the St Leger during his illustrious career, finished runner-up for the 4th time, on Priam, behind winner Birmingham, which was ridden by Patrick Connolly.

1923 Dinkie, Dumas and Marvex triple dead-heated for the Royal Borough Handicap at Windsor.

1929 Scottish owner–trainer HELEN (BOGLE) HAMILTON born. Best horses include Peaty Sandy, Nuits St Georges, Hold Off, Lord Provost.

1930 Trainer of triple Grand National winner Red Rum, DONALD 'GINGER' MCCAIN born. Masterminded his greatest triumphs from his yard tucked behind a garage in Southport.

1946 Raceform race-reader ALAN AMIES born. Went into the folklore of tipsters by backing a 200–1 winner!

1950 LESTER PIGGOTT rode his first Ascot winner, Tancred.

1951 American Champion Jockey EDDIE DELAHOUSSAYE born.

1957 Former Jump Jockey BRIAN REILLY born. Rode 7 winners from 9 rides in November 1978. Best horse ridden Scoggy.

1968 BILL RICKABY, who won 3 classics including Sweet Solera in the 1961 1,000 Guineas and Oaks, rode a winner on his final ride, Silver Spray, at Newmarket. Reached rank of major during the war.

1989 WILLIE CARSON complained that he was beaten on Aradu at Lingfield in the Creative Design Advertising Handicap when his mount shied away from an advertising hoarding!

1991 The 3-runner Nalgo Novice Chase at Market Rasen saw Sudbrooke Park fall at the 10th, bringing down Vantard. Cairncastle refused, leaving the remounted Vantard in the lead. Vantard fell at the 12th. Cairncastle now refused for a 2nd time, then a 3rd. Meanwhile jockey Mark Sharratt remounted Vantard yet again and went on to win.

1991 French-trained 3–1 chance 5-year-old TURGEON (Tony Cruz) beat favourite Patricia in the Irish St Leger.

1992 Madagans announce sponsorship of 1,000 Guineas until 1995.

1992 Trainer LEE BONG-RYE jumped from the roof of his apartment block in Anyang, South Korea. He had been questioned by police in connection with rigged races and was the second trainer to commit suicide – Choi Yon-Hong hung himself at a golf range – as the investigations continued.

22 SEPTEMBER

1778   For the first time the St Leger, now in its 3rd year, was actually run as the St Leger Stakes and it took place, also for the first time, on Doncaster Town Moor, run over two miles. It was won by GEORGE HERRING (sometimes Hearon) on 5-2 chance Hollandaise.

1789   JOHN MANGLE was deprived of a 4th consecutive St Leger victory when he came home 1st on Zanga, only to be disqualified for jostling. The race was awarded to the favourite, filly Pewett.

1817   EBOR (25-1) beat hot favourite Blacklock into 2nd place in the St Leger, for jockey Bob Johnson and owner Mr Peirse. Eighteen ran.

1879   Reported the *Birmingham Daily Post*: 'No less than fourteen summonses, we are told, were issued on the third instant against persons charged with betting on the racecourse at the last Warwick meeting, and the open and wholesale manner in which the proceedings were conducted by some of the offenders would seem to show that the law against betting had no real terrors for them.'

1911   Owner MRS ENID BOUCHER born. Her chaser Killiney won 14 of 19 races before having to be destroyed at the age of seven at Ascot in April 1973 as a result of a fall. Colours: tangerine and white (halved); tangerine and white hooped cap.

1925   Leading US trainer JOHN TAMMARO born in Baltimore.

1940   Trainer MARY (CHRISTIANA) REVELEY born.

1944   Amateur jockey, owner and actor FRAZER HINES, of TV soap *Emmerdale*, born. Owner of Escapism and Joe Sugden.

1951   EDDIE HIDE rode the first of over 2,500 winners, Ritornello, at Chepstow.

1954   US Champion Jockey DARREL MCHARGUE born.

1966   TERRY BIDDLECOMBE rode 5 winners from 5 mounts at Ludlow.

1975   MICHAEL WIGHAM rode his first winner, Highland Jig, at Leicester.

1989   JOHNNY BURNS watched the Ayr Gold Cup yet again, never having missed one since first watching it in 1920, when his jockey brother Tommy 'T.P.' Burns won it on 6-1 chance Forest Guard, which Johnny trained.

1990   PAUL COLE became the first trainer to complete the English-Irish St Leger double in the same season when his Ibn Bey, aged six, became the oldest horse to win a Group 1 race in Ireland. Cole had won the English Leger with Snurge and Ibn Bey completed the first clean sweep of Irish Classics by British trainers since 1956.

1992   LESTER PIGGOTT rode his first Nottingham double since his 'retirement' party there seven years earlier. His winners were Snowy River and Jumaira Star. The former was his first ride for Jon Scargill and that trainer's 50th flat winner.

23 SEPTEMBER

1777 BOURBON, ridden by John Cade, won the second running of the St Leger, run over two miles, returning odds of 3-1 in a 10-horse race.

1788 The first properly organised race meeting to take place in Middlesex was held on the marshes at the bottom of Green Street, Enfield.

1800 Champion became the first horse to land the Derby–St Leger double when Frank Buckle partnered the 2-1 chance to Doncaster victory.

1811 SOOTHSAYER, 13-2, won the record 24-runner St Leger.

1906 Jockey CHARLIE SMIRKE born in Lambeth. He rode 11 Classic winners including 4 Derbys.

1936 Trainer GERALD 'TOBY' BALDING born. His Little Polveir (1989) and Highland Wedding (1969) both won the Grand National while Beech Road (1989) and Morley Street (1991) were his Champion Hurdlers and Cool Ground his 1992 Gold Cup winner.

1939 Wantage trainer MATTHEW MCCORMACK born.

1944 JEREMY GLOVER, trainer of 1987 (Balthus) and 1989 and 1992 (Rambo's Hall) William Hill Cambridgeshire winners, born.

1948 Possibly the hottest favourite ever to lose a race in Britain, ROYAL FOREST, 1-25 for the Clarence House Stakes at Ascot, was beaten by 33-1 chance Burpham.

1975 L'ESCARGOT, the first horse since Golden Miller to complete the Gold Cup–Grand National double, raced for the last time, finishing 2nd at 12-1 in a three-mile chase at Listowel, Ireland.

1980 BOB CHAMPION rode his first winner in England for sixteen and a half months after beating cancer when Physicist scored at Fontwell. It was Josh Gifford's 500th winner as a jump trainer.

1989 For the first time, one of the 5 Classics was run in Scotland. Ayr hosted the St Leger, moved from Doncaster after a series of falls caused the abandonment of the meeting. The Henry Cecil-trained 6-4 chance Michelozzo, ridden by Steve Cauthen, was the winner.

1989 Champion American lady jockey JULIE KRONE was involved in an altercation with fellow jockey Joe Bravo during and after a race at the Meadowlands, New Jersey. She whacked him with her whip after he crowded her. She was later suspended for fifteen days and fined $500 while he was suspended for five days and fined $250.

1989 American jockey CHRIS ANTLEY was removed from all his mounts at Belmont Park. He later announced that he would be seeking help for his 'substance abuse' problem.

1990 The Jockey Club announced that 2 runners at the St Leger meeting, Bravefoot (W. Hern) and Norwich (B. Hills), were doped with a 'relatively quick acting tranquilliser'. Both were beaten – the former was favourite, the latter joint favourite.

24 SEPTEMBER

1793 Coincidence backers, if such existed in those days, must have cashed in as the horse with the same name as the year, NINETY THREE, was the 15-1 winner of the 8-runner St Leger under jockey William Peirse.

1795 Owner SIR CHARLES TURNER dominated the three-day St Leger meeting, winning the race itself with Hambletonian, 4-6, on the first day. He also landed all but 1 of the 7 events which were held over the 3 days, missing out only in the Corporation Plate, won by Capsicum. On this day his Beningbrough won a £100 Plate.

1805 COLONEL MELLISH enjoyed his 2nd consecutive St Leger victory as his Staveley, 5-1, won the 10-runner race ridden by John Jackson.

1837 Jockey GEORGE FORDHAM, who went on to ride 16 Classic winners, born in Cambridge. He weighed just 3lbs 10oz when winning the 1852 Cambridgeshire on Little David, for which feat he was given a Bible and a gold-mounted whip. Died in 1887.

1930 Former jump jockey LARRY MAJOR born. Best horse ridden Siracusa.

1949 NORMAN MCINTOSH rode first winner, Highland Clan, at Hamilton.

1951 RICHARD BURRIDGE, scriptwriter and owner of Desert Orchid, born.

1959 Open Goal at Perth gave ARTHUR STEPHENSON his first winner as a licence-holding trainer.

1967 TOM TAAFFE, father of Pat and Tos and trainer of 1958 Grand National winner Mr What, died.

1977 English-born trainer SALLY ANN BAILIE became the first woman trainer to win a $100,000 stakes race when Tequillo Boogie won the New York Breeders' Futurity at Finger Lakes. Five years later she became the first woman trainer to win a $200,000 stakes when Fast Gold won the Pegasus at Meadowlands.

1981 BARONET and HERON'S HOLLOW passed the post together at Ascot. Judge Michael Hancock placed Baronet (B. Rouse) 1st, and bookies and the Tote paid out. Thirty minutes later the result was reversed, with Heron's Hollow (B. Raymond) being given the decision.

1982 BILL SHOEMAKER rode 2 winners at Ascot, beating Lester Piggott in a match on Prince's Gate, then partnering Rose Du Soir to victory in a one and a quarter-mile handicap.

1990 Filly PAS DE REEF was brought down during a race at Hamilton - by a golf ball from the adjacent golf course. Jockey Michael Wigham said: 'It must have wedged in her foot.'

1992 Trainer NIGEL TWISTON-DAVIES sent out a 454-1 4-timer at Perth.

1992 Japanese rider TAKESHI TAMANOI, 20, died of injuries suffered during a fall six days earlier, the 17th jockey fatally injured in Japan since 1954.

25 SEPTEMBER

1766 The first running of a, if not the, Doncaster Cup took place in four-mile heats of 4 runners. CHARLOTTE came out on top after 3 heats. The six-year-old was owned by Lord Hamilton.

1792 A 5th St Leger victory for jockey JOHN MANGLE. He brought Lord Hamilton's Tartar home clear of 10 rivals at amazing odds of 25-1, taking into account that combination's record in the race.

1793 Mr John Hutchinson's OBERON achieved a feat remarkable even for those days, when horses were less mollycoddled than today, winning the four-mile Doncaster Stakes at 4-1 and then, just an hour later, also winning the four-mile Gold Cup at 2-1, defeating useful opponents including the previous day's St Leger winner, Ninety Three, who was 3rd.

1804 An eventful St Leger saw Vesta fall, seriously injuring jockey Spencer; Sir Bertrand fell and Witchcraft also came down. SANCHO, 2-1 favourite, beat the other 7 who managed to stay upright.

1815 Filho De Puta (which apparently means son of a whore in Portuguese) was the even-money winner of the 15-runner St Leger, ridden by John Jackson.

1849 A meeting at Kelso consisted of 1 race – and that was a walkover. The beneficiary was ELTHIRON, the uncontested winner of the Produce Stakes.

1878 SIR BEVYS won for the first time in his career at Newmarket, and went on to win the Derby the next season.

1922 Jockey TONY GRANTHAM born. Partnered Monaveen, Gay Donald.

1944 Former jockey GILLIAN KELLEWAY born.

1951 Newmarket trainer DI HAINE born.

1951 Jockey PETER MADDEN born. Partnered Fireside Chat.

1954 Jockey CRAIG SMITH born. Best horses ridden include Bawnogues, Scot Lane.

1960 Lambourn trainer JOHN HILLS born. Rode 21 winners as an amateur. Best horses trained include Carol's Treasure, Guest Performer.

1962 Jockey turned trainer MICHAEL HAMMOND born. Best horses ridden include Ballydurrow, Alkepa.

1971 Jockey SEB SAUNDERS born.

1989 BBC Radio 2 listeners were startled to hear an announcement during a sports bulletin that the 2,000 Guineas and Derby winner NASHWAN was to run in the Champion Hurdle! The next bulletin corrected the announcement – to Champion Stakes.

1992 BROUGH SCOTT broke a losing run of over 20 years' standing when he won for the first time since 1971 on 9-1 chance Kitaab in the Shadwell Estates Handicap Private Stakes at Ascot.

26 SEPTEMBER

1781 No member of the St Leger family ever won the Classic race founded by sportsman Lt General Anthony St Leger, and on this day Mr St Leger's brown colt and Colonel St Leger's brown filly (both unnamed) were also-rans behind winner Serina, ridden by Richard Foster. No odds were recorded.

1814 William gave the DUKE OF HAMILTON his 7th St Leger victory in a race of which it was said that 'more roguery was practised by transactions relative to the race previous to the time of running than was ever known'.

1848 Jockey BILL SCOTT died, aged 50, at Highfield, Malton. He rode 19 Classic winners. Scott's last words were recorded as follows: 'There's three things I can confess to. Since I was 21 I have been drunk almost every night; I never sold a race, which is more than some can say; and I never kissed a lass against her will.' Contemporary records suggest that the second of those claims was somewhat suspect.

1927 Champion Hurdler-to-be BROWN JACK won for the first time over those obstacles, at Wolverhampton.

1933 GORDON RICHARDS reached 200 winners in a season for the first time when he won on Nevertheless at Newmarket.

1954 Cheshire jockey SEAMUS O'NEILL born.

1956 Lambourn trainer BRYAN SMART born.

1957 TOBY BALDING sent out his first winner, Bowerchalke, at Ascot.

1959 MANNY MERCER, who rode Happy Laughter to win the 1953 1,000 Guineas and Darius to win the 1954 2,000 Guineas, died after being thrown by Priddy Fair at Ascot. Born 1930, elder brother of Joe Mercer.

1963 Jump jockey VICKI HARRIS born. Best horses ridden include Kasu.

1968 The great jumper MILL HOUSE gained his 17th and last victory, winning the Somerset Chase at Wincanton.

1982 The QUEEN completed the purchase of West Ilsley Stables from Sir Michael Sobell and son-in-law Lord Weinstock. The deal was believed to have been financed by the sale of Her Majesty's filly Height of Fashion to Sheikh Hamdan for an estimated £1.4 million.

1990 ANN BOLEYN lost her head when she threw jockey Steven Porter, who ended up in hospital after she crashed through the rails at Brighton on the way to the start, galloped across the course and ended up at Roedean school for girls being fed bread by pupils.

1991 RAVINELLA, the 1988 winner of the English and French 1,000 Guineas, died at stud while in foal to Nashwan.

27 SEPTEMBER

1780 JOHN MANGLE partnered 5–2 St Leger winner Ruler, beating 6 others for owner Mr Bethell.

1785 COWSLIP, no odds recorded, ridden by George Searle, won the 4-runner St Leger.

1791 Young Traveller, who won the Gold Cup at the same meeting, landed the St Leger at 3–1. In the Cup he beat former Leger winners Spadille, Ambidexter and Pewett.

1796 AMBROSIO, 4–5, won the St Leger for Mr Cookson, ridden by John Jackson. The next day the horse was beaten in the Gold Cup.

1803 Benjamin Smith rode the first of his 6 St Leger winners when Remembrancer was a 5–4 all the way winner against 7 opponents.

1813 Run over one mile 6 furlongs 193 yards for the first time, the St Leger suffered 10 false starts before 11–5 favourite ALTISIDORA, ridden by John Jackson, defeated 16 opponents.

1894 The original Aqueduct track opened in Queen's, New York. Just 700 people and 6 bookies turned up.

1894 The previous season's Triple Crown winner ISINGLASS started at 2–5 for the first running of the Jockey Club Stakes and carried 10st 2lbs to beat French challenger Gouvernail by 2 lengths.

1901 US jockey LESTER REIFF, who had been English Champion in 1900 with 143 winners, was beaten by a head on De Lacy by his brother John, riding Minnie Day, at Manchester. The stewards reported Lester to the Jockey Club, who subsequently withdrew his licence and warned him off.

1926 BOB LYALL enjoyed a good day at Market Rasen, riding 4 winners and a runner-up. When he died his ashes were scattered near the winning post at the track.

1932 Trainer JOHN BLUNDELL born. Best horses include Sam Da Vinci.

1946 American trainer DARRELL VIENNA born.

1949 Jockey turned top sculptor PHILIP BLACKER born. Rode Pollardstown to win the 1979 Triumph Hurdle.

1966 Trainer Lt Colonel WILFRED LYDE, in business since the end of the Second World War, announced his retirement.

1992 Having 'retired' two weeks earlier, GIANFRANCO DETTORI suddenly turned up to ride again at the Capanelle, to bid Roman racing fans farewell, as he had won his first race there in 1961. Born in 1941, he rode Bolkonski (1975) and Wollow (1976) to win the English 2,000 Guineas. Father of Frankie.

1992 MIOCAMEN became the highest-earning Italian-trained thoroughbred when he won Italy's Gran Premio Merano Forst, taking his earnings to a total of L2.2 billion (just over £1 million).

28 SEPTEMBER

1779 TOMMY, even money, ridden by George Lowry, won the 10-runner 4th St Leger.

1784 OMPHALE, ridden by John Kirton, beat 6 rivals in the St Leger.

1790 GEORGE SEARLE won his 3rd St Leger on Mr Goodricke's 5-1 chance Ambidexter, defeating 8 opponents.

1802 JOHN SINGLETON JR partnered Orville to a 5-1 victory in the St Leger, beating 6 others. The 26-year-old jockey died just three months later.

1870 FRED ARCHER rode his first winner under Jockey Club rules, Athol Daisy, at Chesterfield.

1928 Trainer LEONARD JOHN 'JACK' HOLT born. Best horses included Sweet Monday, Argentum, Quortina, Epsom Imp.

1932 Fire destroyed the members' stand at Kempton, and with it many of the course's records. The course remained closed until May 1933.

1932 Jockey PADDY COWLEY born. Partnered Motel, Royal Toss, Look.

1973 Jockey JOSEPH MARSHALL died in his home town, Brighton, aged 65. He rode 33-1 shot Trigo to win the 1929 Derby.

1982 Owner EDWIN JOHNSON caught a flight to Peru – and missed seeing his first winner for 20 years as La Perricholi came in at Nottingham.

1985 CHESTER's county stand, originally built in 1899, burned down.

1990 Ray Barratt, riding RUDDA CASS at Redcar, was suspended for 8 days for excessive use of the whip. Two days earlier, he had been suspended for 4 days at Pontefract for the same offence on the same horse. On August 29 Gary Hind had been suspended for 3 days for improper use of the whip – on the poor Roy Robinson-trained Rudda Cass.

1991 American challenger Forty Niner Days finished 5th in the Queen Elizabeth II Stakes at Ascot. Selkirk won the race.

1992 Owners KEN HIGSON and BARNEY CURLEY protested at what they described as Fontwell's 'despicable' prize-money by withdrawing 9-4 favourite Across the Card and 2-1 favourite Torwada at the 'off'. Both owners and jockeys Gary Moore and Jason Twomey were fined £1,200 each.

1992 On what was meant to be the final day of flat racing on turf at Wolverhampton Steve Cauthen rode the last winner, 9-1 shot Iota, in the West Midlands Handicap.

1992 CHRISTINE GOULANDRIS, 44, whose occupation is described as 'racehorse owner', listed by *Business Age* magazine as the wealthiest woman in Britain, with a £290 million fortune. She is married to millionaire head of Heinz, Tony O'Reilly, and has horses with François Boutin. Owned Priolo, winner of top French races in 1990-91.

29 SEPTEMBER

1721 A race took place at Annapolis, Maryland, for which the first prize was eight silver spoons and the 2nd four of the same.

1788 One of the best colts of his day, ESCAPE, made his debut, winning a match against Feenoli at Newmarket. Escape, sold by the Prince of Wales for 95 guineas to Mr Franco, was named when his owner exclaimed 'Oh, what an escape!' on being told by his groom that the horse had been extricated after kicking out in his box, and embedding his fetlock in its woodwork. The horse was re-purchased two years later by the Prince of Wales for 1,500 guineas.

1879 W. R. BROCKTON had a good day at Market Rasen, winning 3 of the 4 races and finishing 3rd in the other – even though he rode only 2 horses all day. He won 2 races on Moorhen then 1 on Hopeless (a complimentary name!) before finishing 3rd on the same horse in the final event of the day.

1920 Somerset trainer LES KENNARD born. Best horses included Cantlie, Highland Abbe, Stradivarius, Walnut Wonder.

1922 Trainer (BURNUP) ROY CAMBIDGE born. Best horses include Roaring Wind, Java Fox.

1923 Owner SHIRLEY TAYLOR born. Her best horses include Alleged and Try My Best. Colours: straw; salmon slashes and chevrons.

1937 Trainer JOCK SKILLING born.

1948 Six Dorothy Paget-owned, Fulke Walwyn-trained, Bryan Marshall-ridden horses ran at Folkestone. Five of them won: Legal Joy, Langis Son, Jack Tatters, Endless and Loyal King. The 6th, Loyal Monarch, was beaten by 1/2 length in the last race.

1951 Lancashire trainer JUDY EATON born. Best horses include Palm Cross, Harley.

1965 Point-to-point rider–trainer TRELAWNEY HILL born.

1967 Ascot's first charity day was run in aid of the St John's Ambulance, and featured the course's first sponsored flat race, the 5-furlong Joynson Commodity Stakes, won by So Blessed (5-1), ridden by Frank Durr and trained by J. Thompson.

1984 Robert Williams rode 8 winners from 10 rides at Lincoln, Nebraska.

1984 Met Officer won at Market Rasen to open the career account of jump jockey SIMON COWLEY.

1989 SHEIKH HAMDAM AL-MAKTOUM owned all 6 runners turning out for the one and a quarter-mile Shadwell Estate Sweepstakes at Ascot. The race was run to raise money for charity and the riders were 6 ex-jockeys currently working for Channel 4. The winner was 8-11 favourite Wabil, ridden by Jimmy Lindley; 2nd was Polemos, 7-1 (Bill Smith); 3rd Hateel (Lord Oaksey), at 8-1.

30 SEPTEMBER

1923 Trainer of Arc winner Allez France, ANGEL PENNA, born.

1925 Owner of Super Cavalier, Super Sunrise and Russian George JACK MAXWELL born. Colours: black and white; yellow cap.

1937 London *Evening Standard* racing writer and gourmet CHRISTOPHER POOLE born.

1948 Tarporley trainer MARTIN COUSINS born.

1950 Jockey CHRIS LEONARD born. A globe-trotter who rode successfully in India, Ireland, Holland, Belgium and Germany.

1958 Meath trainer SUZANNE FINN born. The first woman elected to the Irish Racehorse Trainers committee.

1959 JOHNNY GILBERT set a winning sequence record for a jump jockey of 10 consecutive winners, having ridden the first on September 8.

1961 Northampton amateur jockey JULIA 'TIK' SAUNDERS born. Claimed an extraordinary collection of recreations in the 1990 *Directory of the Turf*: wrestling, hang-gliding, skiing and stamp-collecting.

1962 A week before he was due to partner Val De Loir in the Arc, jockey GEORGES CHANCELIER was killed in a car accident. Partnered by J. P. Boullenger, the horse eventually finished 3rd in the race.

1978 STETCHWORTH reared up and nearly threw jockey Taffy Thomas as the runners came under orders for the first race at Redcar. Thomas hung on and the combination romped home. After the race gun-shot marks were found on Stetchworth's rump – it transpired that he had been shot at by youths hidden in long grass.

1982 English-born trainer SALLY ANN BAILIE became the first woman to train a $200,000 stakes race winner when Fast Gold scored at Meadowlands in the Pegasus Stakes.

1984 GEORGE RHODES picked 7 winners in his 5p ITV 7 bet and landed world record odds of 1,670,759–1, which put him into the *Guinness Book of Records*. His winnings came to £86,056.42, and I had the pleasure of visiting his Aldershot home to present him with his cheque from William Hill. In answer to the inevitable question, 'What will you do with the money?' the retired businessman said, 'Buy a new Rolls-Royce – mine is getting on a bit'!

1989 Former jockey–trainer KEN GETHIN died aged 78.

1990 BILL SHOEMAKER trained his first graded stakes winner when Baldomero won the Golden Harvest Handicap at Louisiana Downs.

1992 BLYTON LAD (6–1), owned by John and Jenny Addleshaw, won the Rous Stakes at Newmarket for the 3rd consecutive year, each time with a different trainer: John Balding in 1990, William Pearce (1991) and Maurice Camacho (1992).

1 OCTOBER

1765   The Marquis of Rockingham's BAY MALTON beat Lord Bolingbroke's GIMCRACK in a match for 1,000 Guineas at Newmarket. Gimcrack later twice avenged that defeat and raced until the age of twelve, winning 26 of his 36 races.

1885   Mr Robert Vyner's MINTING was slightly fancied to win the Produce Stakes at Newmarket, starting at 100-1 *on* to defeat his 2 rivals. Ridden by Fred Archer, the horse scrambled home by 3/4 length from Charioteer. Trainer Mat Dawson still considered his charge unbeatable, but suffered a rude awakening when Minting was defeated by Ormonde in the 2,000 Guineas. A trifle miffed, Dawson stormed away from the course and retired to bed, where he sulked away the remainder of the meeting.

1891   W. SHARP became the first New Zealand jockey to ride 6 winners in a day when he achieved that feat at Kurow.

1901   The reigning Champion Jockey, American LESTER REIFF, was warned off by the Jockey Club, who decided that he had stopped a horse, De Lacy, at Manchester, so that his brother Johnny might win on Minnie Dee for American politician owner 'Boss' Croker.

1934   Channel 4 commentator and racing historian–author, JOHN TYRREL born.

1943   Fife permit-holder JANE WEIR born.

1947   Newmarket dual purpose trainer HUGH COLLINGRIDGE born. His Buzzard's Bay won the 1982 Royal Hunt Cup. Also trained Cuvee Charlie, Va Toujours.

1947   Owner-breeder of top chaser Pearlyman WILLIAM JENKS born. Colours: dark blue and black stripes; hooped cap.

1949   Thirsk trainer LYNDA RAMSDEN born.

1958   Newbury trainer MARK USHER born. Best horses include Mystery Ship, Valley Victory, Portogon.

1979   GORDON W. RICHARDS saddled 5 winners at Carlisle.

1990   Trainer MICHAEL HAMMOND sent out his first treble – Choice Challenge, Azusa and Tignanello – at accumulative odds of 76-1 at Carlisle.

1991   WILLIE CARSON rode the first 5 winners at Newcastle – Aasff, Perjury, Lord Oberon, Subsonic, Najeb – a 539-1 accumulator.

2 OCTOBER

1911 Racing first took place at Laurel, Maryland, USA.

1939 Owner of Polly Peachum and Able Albert ANNE HENSON born. Colours: emerald green; white cross-belts; scarlet cap.

1951 GORDON SUMNER born – better known, perhaps, as Sting, formerly of pop group Police. He went on to own a useful horse called Sandalay. He told me he'd been encouraged to become an owner by a group of builders working on his home.

1952 Leading US trainer STEVE PENROD born in Lexington, Kentucky. Began training in 1981 for Claiborne and Cherry Valley farms.

1954 Champion Jockey of Norway in 1979 PAUL HAMBLETT born. Best horses ridden include Optia.

1965 Irish jockey TOMMY STACK rode his first winner, New Money, at Wetherby.

1972 PAT ROHAN finally landed his 500th winner as a trainer when Persian Palm won at Wolverhampton. He had been waiting since August 4 to reach the milestone.

1981 BBC TV dropped the 'triella' bet. Punters had had to predict 1st and 2nd in correct order in 3 consecutive races.

1990 Pioneer woman jump trainer MRS POSY LEWIS died aged 83. Her father, Captain Morel, was one of the founders of Chepstow racecourse.

1990 Veteran owner FRANK HILL, 87, celebrated the 114th winner of his owning career, Saysana at Brighton. However, racegoers were astonished to see him at the races, since the *Daily Telegraph* had recently printed his obituary! Frank first became an owner in 1922 and his best horses included Be Patient, Be Cautious, Acrobatic. Colours: petunia; gold sleeves; green cap.

1991 DARREN O'SULLIVAN rode Karakter Reference, trained by his uncle Roland, to win the Park Course Handicap Chase, the first race run on Cheltenham's new Park course.

1991 Geoff Wragg-trained Young Senor (14–1) landed a £500,000 bonus by winning Newmarket's Highflyer Stakes.

1992 All 5 runners in the Keilder Marketing Group Handicap Chase at Hexham took the wrong course and ended up on a spur of the track which is used only on the final circuit of the chase course. Jockey Lorcan Wyer, riding Chain Shot, was the first to realise and he shouted to all the other riders, who eventually retraced their steps, taking varying amounts of time to do so. Eventually 3–1 chance Spree Cross, ridden by Kenny Johnson, crossed the line first, but Johnson and all 4 of the other jockeys were fined £100 each.

3 OCTOBER

1810   A bay filly, MARIA, owned by W. R. Johnson, raced an astonishing twenty miles in winning a race. The race, the Fairfield Jockey Club Purse of $500, at Richmond, USA, attracted 5 runners and produced 2 dead-heats in a row before it was necessary to run 3 further four-mile heats to produce a winner.

1922   Three-times Champion Apprentice KEN MULLINS born.

1933   GORDON RICHARDS rode the 5th race winner at Nottingham (Barnby), he then rode all 6 winners at Chepstow the next day and the first 5 on the next to set a new record of 12 consecutive winners.

1934   Mr THEO WEST of Louth put up a staggering 33lbs overweight in partnering Cornafulla at Market Rasen. He had wagered that he would complete the course and, weighing out at 13st 2lbs, he managed to do it, and to finish in 3rd place.

1946   King Penguin won at Ludlow. Nothing too odd about that, except that jockey DICK BLACK and trainer JOHN DE MORAVILLE had agreed to form a partnership when they met in a German prisoner of war camp, and this was their first winner.

1951   Jockey turned agent JOHN SUTHERN born. Twice rode the winner of the Belgian National. Best horses ridden include Gembridge and Jupiter.

1954   Ridden by the oldest jockey in the race and trained by the youngest handler, SICA BOY won the Arc de Triomphe. Rae Johnstone, nearly 50, was the jockey and Pierre Pelat the trainer. The horse was beaten in each of his remaining 3 races, but the F25 million plus entry fees Arc prize-money must have been a consolation.

1957   Newmarket jockey MARK BANNER born.

1960   Carlisle trainer ZOE GREEN born. Best horse trained All Night Long.

1963   After inquiries which had lasted since the French-trained RELKO won the Derby earlier in the year, an announcement in the *Racing Calendar* finally declared that the stewards had 'found no evidence that would justify a disqualification of Relko'. The inquiries had centred around 'a substance other than a normal nutrient present in the horse'. The affair caused considerable ill-feeling in France.

1981   BARONET, the winner in 1978 and 1980, finished 2nd in the Cambridgeshire behind 50-1 Clive Brittain-trained Braughing, ridden by Steve Cauthen.

1981   The PRINCE OF WALES enjoyed his first success as an owner when Richard Linley rode the Nick Gaselee-trained Good Prospect to victory at Chepstow.

1992   Jeremy Glover trained the William Hill Cambridgeshire winner for the 3rd time as 9-2 favourite RAMBO'S HALL landed his 2nd victory in the race, ridden by Dean McKeown.

4 OCTOBER

1770   ECLIPSE ran his final race, and although this 21st victory in as many races was another walkover, hordes of people turned out to cheer the great horse for the last time. He went to stud at Clay Hill, near Epsom, in 1771 at a fee of 50 guineas, and sired the winners of 862 races worth £158,047.

1866   Jockey HENRY GRIMSHAW, who rode Gladiateur to win the 1865 Triple Crown, was killed aged just 25 when the trap he was driving home to Newmarket after racing overturned in the dark.

1871   Trainer JOHN SCOTT died. In 46 years at the Whitewall Stable at Malton he sent out an amazing 16 St Leger winners, 5 Derby winners, 7 2,000 Guineas winners, 9 Oaks winners and 4 1,000 Guineas winners. Born in 1794, at Chippenham near Newmarket.

1945   Newmarket trainer GAVIN PRITCHARD-GORDON born.

1953   LA SORELLINA (odds of 65-4) became the first filly since Corrida in 1937 to win the Arc de Triomphe. The dam of both winner and runner-up Silnet was Silver Jill.

1959   LYCASTE II became the first runner trained by a woman, Sweden's Miss Brita Strokirk, to compete in the Arc de Triomphe. The Swedish Oaks winner was partnered by Joe Mercer and finished 18th of 25 at 120-1, behind 17-1 winner Saint Crespin (ridden by George Moore, trained by Alec Head, owned by Prince Aly Khan). Saint Crespin dead-heated with the Jean Fabre-ridden Midnight Sun, but Moore objected for bumping and later was awarded the race.

1964   One million francs plus 78 per cent of entry fees was the reward for PRINCE ROYAL II's 16-1 Arc de Triomphe win (partnered by Roger Poincelet, trained by George Bridgland).

1970   NIJINSKY (Lester Piggott) suffered his first defeat, going down in the Arc de Triomphe to the Yves St Martin-partnered 19-1 chance Sassafrass.

1981   ANDY TURNELL rode Jupiter to win the Norwegian Grand National.

1986   *Morning Star* newspaper racing tipster Cayton (Alf Rubin) tipped 4-9 shot Suhailie to win a 3-horse race, which it did. Nothing too remarkable about that – except that it broke a run of 57 consecutive daily losing nap selections.

1989   SECRETARIAT, an all-time great of US racing, was put down aged 19 at Claiborne Farm, Kentucky. He won the 1973 Triple Crown.

1991   Midlands trainer STAN PALMER died aged 77.

1992   ARAZI, whose reputation had become slightly tarnished, came back to form with a win in the Ciga Prix du Rond-Point at Longchamp, on the same day as Subotica (trained by Andrew Fabre, ridden by Thierry Jarnet) won the Arc for France.

5 OCTOBER

1933 GORDON RICHARDS completed his record 12 consecutive winners, begun on October 3 at Nottingham. The 12th winner was an unnamed filly by Hurry On in the Hughes–Morgan Nursery. In 1958 Rhodesian Pieter Stroedel reportedly rode 12 in a row at Bulawayo.

1939 Owner, trainer, lapsed priest, punter, self-styled punters' champion and general maverick of the racing world BARNEY CURLEY born.

1950 Gallops were littered with broken glass at Maisons-Lafitte when a stable lads' strike raged for three days before the Arc de Triomphe was due to take place. One head lad was kidnapped by strikers and locked up, but eventually tempers cooled and the Arc went ahead.

1952 LESTER PIGGOTT had his first ride in France, finishing unplaced on Bagnoles de L'Orne in the first race at Longchamp on Arc day. In the big race the sixteen-year-old Piggott rode Oise into 10th place of the 18 starters. Winner was Nuccio (74–10), which never won again despite 5 attempts as a five-year-old in 1953.

1958 BALLYMOSS (ridden by Scobie Breasley and trained by Vincent O'Brien) won the Arc de Triomphe at odds of 39–10, the first Irish winner of the race. The win took his total earnings at the time to £98,650 – surpassing the previous record of prize-money won by an English or Irish horse, £76,417, held by Tulyar.

1969 PARK TOP, ridden by Lester Piggott, was 2nd in the Arc de Triomphe behind the Bill Williamson-ridden winner Levmoss.

1991 PETER NIVEN rode the first 5 winners at Kelso and was offered the ride on the favourite in the last. However, stewards refused to allow the switch, so Graham McCourt kept the ride and his mount, Rawan, duly won. Niven, whose winners were Go Tally-Ho, Local Customer, Ambuscade, The Maltkin and Danza Heights, could have become the first jump jockey to go through the card.

1991 The first 3 home in the William Hill Cambridgeshire were, for the first time, all trained by women. Mary Reveley's 10–1 chance Mellottie was the winner, from runner-up High Premium (14–1), saddled by Lynda Ramsden, who also sent out 3rd-placed Vague Dancer, 40–1. Twenty-nine ran.

1991 ARAZI galloped away with the Grand Criterium at Longchamp. He was a 1–5 chance to land his 6th straight win, and did so for jockey G. Mosse by 3 lengths. After the race, owner Allen Paulson, mildly impressed, commented: 'Arazi is not just the best horse I have ever owned – he's the best horse anyone has ever owned.'

1992 SUE CAUSTON, aged 35, made her contribution to racing history when she became the first woman member of a starting stalls team.

6 OCTOBER

1867 THOMAS LOATES, Champion Jockey in 1889, 1890 and 1893, was born in Derby. He rode 6 Classic winners, including 1893 Triple Crown winner Isinglass. Rode 222 winners in 1893.

1897 Alabaman owner and US racing's grand old man FRED HOOPER born. His Hoop Jr won the Kentucky Derby.

1935 WILLIAM ANDERTON, whose Russian Winter won 18 races, born. Colours: white; red cross of Lorraine; red and white checked cap.

1935 Jockey Club mouthpiece DAVID PIPE born.

1941 Trainer GAVIN HAVARD HUNTER born. Best horses include Chummy's Special, Penmarric, Shangamuzo, Krayyan.

1947 Newmarket trainer JEFF PEARCE born.

1948 Jockey MICK GOREHAM, who partnered Royal Prerogative, born.

1949 COL MATT J. WINN, generally credited with making the Kentucky Derby one of the greatest races in the world (he was Churchill Downs president from 1938 to 1949), died aged 88. He witnessed the first 75 Derbys.

1956 Forty-year-old US jockey EDDIE 'BANANA NOSE' ARCARO and his 29-year-old countryman SAM BOULMETIS, with 5,500 US winners between them, were given acclimatising rides in the Prix des Fortifications. They were in France to ride in the Arc but had never ridden at Longchamp before. Banana Nose fell and Boulmetis finished 3rd. The next day Arcaro rode Career Boy into 4th place in the Arc while Boulmetis was 9th on Fisherman.

1957 OROSO was the shock winner at 52–1 of the F40 million plus entry fee prize-money of the Arc de Triomphe, ridden by Serge Boullenger, who was serving his military service in the French army at the time, and trained by D. Lescalle.

1963 For the final time the Arc de Triomphe was started without starting stalls. EXBURY, 36–10 2nd favourite, trained by G. Watson and ridden by J. Deforge, was the 2-length winner for owner M. Le Baron Guy de Rothschild, who collected F900,000 plus 78 per cent of the entry fees. Exbury never raced again, having won 8 of his 16 races and won a European record £156,161 in prize-money.

1965 GARY CARTER, twice Champion Apprentice, born.

1989 A mystery punter lost £100,000 backing 4 consecutive beaten odds-on favourites at Hexham. He watched his selections lose at 4–5, 2–5, 1–4 and 1–4, and then flew off in a helicopter.

1991 SUAVE DANCER, ridden by Cash Asmussen and starting at 37–10 for trainer J. Hammond, won the 14-runner Arc de Triomphe. Derby winner Generous was a distant 8th, despite starting 9–10 favourite.

The unique William Hill Man *v.* Horse *v.* Mountain Bike Marathon, held every year in e Welsh village of Llanwrtyd Wells. A human runner has yet to win, despite a potential prize of £14,000 (*Tim Moss*)

Four views of women in racing

posite, top: Geraldine Rees, riding Cheers, negotiates the Chair fence at the 1982 Grand National and becomes the first woman to finish the race (*S & G Press Agency Ltd*)

Opposite, centre: Miss S. Lawrence, daughter of commentator John Oaksey, is thrown from The Yomper after clearing the last jump in the Triumph Hurdle at Cheltenham, 13 March 1986 (*Popperfoto/Reuter*)

Opposite, bottom: Julie Krone smiles aboard Colonial Affair after winning the 125th elmont Stakes at Belmont Park, New York State, on 5 June 1993 and becoming the first woman to win an American triple crown race (*Popperfoto/Reuter*). No woman has yet ridden a British Classic winner

Above: A more traditional image of ladies at the races (*Popperfoto/Reuter*)

The Grand National has always been disastrous for some

Opposite, top: 1954's eventual winner Royal Tan, ridden by Bryan Marshall, only just manages to avoid a collision at the first fence (*S & G Agency Ltd*)

Opposite, centre: R. Evans takes a dive on Proud Percy at the Chair fence during the 1973 race. On the right is Princess Camilla, ridden by Ron Barry (*S & G Agency Ltd*)

Opposite, bottom: Some of the jockeys who fell at the first fence during the 1951 National (including now-famous novelist Dick Francis, centre) watch the rest of the race (*S & G Agency Ltd*)

Above: Danger of another sort awaited Arthur Thomson, seen here being led in on Sheila's Cottage after their victory in the 1948 National. Shortly afterwards, the horse bit his finger off (*S & G Agency Ltd*)

Above: Miss Dorothy Paget leads in Golden Miller, ridden by Gerry Wilson, after their victory in the 1934 Grand National (*S & G Agency Ltd*)

Below: Miss Paget attending the races. She was known for betting in telephone number it was not unusual for her to put £10,000 on one of her horses. She used to sleep during the day and rise at night, and was so famous for her honesty that one bookmaker allowed her to bet on races that had already been run

bove: Robert Sangster, one of the most important owners in the world, seen here with trainer Vincent O'Brien (*Caroline Norris*)

Below: Charles O'Brien – following in the hoofprints of his father?

Above: National Hunt trainer Jenny Pitman, the first woman to train a Grand National winner, who listed her hobby in *Directory of the Turf* as 'watching Dallas'

Below: Martin Pipe, record-breaking jump trainer, who demonstrated his versatility when Balasani won at Royal Ascot in 1993 (*Bob Thomas Sports Photography*)

7 OCTOBER

1816   EPPERSTON, owned by Lord Queensberry, won the first race held at Edinburgh racecourse. It was a four-mile event run in 3 heats.

1937   Lancaster trainer JACK BERRY, the first to carry commercial advertising on his horsebox, born in Leeds. He has a propensity for red shirts. Now a prolific producer of winners, among them Touch Boy, Paris House, O. I. Oyston, Bri Eden, Clantime.

1944   Somerset trainer ALLAN DUNN born.

1949   The QUEEN's first runner, Astrakhan (Willie Smyth–Tommy Burns), finished 2nd in Ascot's Sandwell Stakes.

1951   TANTIEME, 17–10 favourite, again ridden by Jacques Doyasbere, trained by François Mathet and owned by François Dupré, won the Arc de Triomphe for the second successive year.

1956   RIBOT won his 16th successive race and 2nd successive Arc de Triomphe at odds of 6–10. Enrico Camici rode as usual. Ribot was retired undefeated after this race.

1956   Jump jockey WILLIAM JAMES LANGRISHE BUTCHARD born.

1962   Six Classic winners from 5 countries were among the 24 runners in the Arc de Triomphe. None of them won, though, as 40–1 outsider SOLTIKOFF, ridden by Marcel Depalmas, won by a length.

1978   Hong Kong's Sha Tin track staged its first meeting. The course was built on 250 acres of land reclaimed from Sha Tin Bay.

1981   BOB CHAMPION rode his 400th winner, Lumen, at Cheltenham.

1989   CASH ASMUSSEN won 5 races, including 4 Group events (in itself a record) and was 2nd twice, at Longchamp.

1989   Trainer ROGER CURTIS sent out Androbote to win the Isle of Wight Stakes at Goodwood at 100–1. His Stargaze once won at the same odds.

1989   Jockey DEAN MCKEOWN won the Cambridgeshire on 15–1 shot Rambo's Hall to celebrate his daughter Hayley's second birthday. On the day she was born he rode a double at York.

1991   A triple-heat occurred at Belmont Park, USA, when Scorecard Harry (Herb McCauley), Space Appeal (Zoltan Varga) and Cafe Lex (Chris Antley) proved inseparable in the 6-furlong race. It was the first triple dead-heat in New York since 1944.

1992   At York, Fetchinni collapsed and died in the stalls prior to the off of the Micklegate Selling Stakes. The horse came under orders so was officially a runner. Fetchinni was trained by A. Bailey and, incredibly, the last time a similar situation occurred, on July 7 at Pontefract, it had been another Bailey horse, O'Donnells Folly, which had died in the stalls. Trainer Bailey himself had suffered a heart attack earlier in the year.

8 OCTOBER

1936 West Auckland trainer NORMAN CHAMBERLAIN born. Best horses included Queen's Lane, Aucklander and Gipsy Rambler.

1939 Legendary owner, trainer and gambler ROBERT SIEVIER, whose self-trained Sceptre won 4 Classics and was 4th in the Derby in 1902, died aged 79. In 1902 he became the first owner-trainer to head the list of winning owners with £23,686. He ran a paper called the *Winning Post* in which he poked fun at and made more sinister allegations about racing figures of the day. Further investigations should be directed towards the *Autobiography of Robert Standish Sievier*, published in 1906. Colours: black; gold facings and sleeves; red cap.

1940 Flat jockey DES CULLEN born. Forced to retire in 1977 on the advice of the Jockey Club neurologist. First winner Tudor Flash at Newmarket in April 1958. Won the Stewards' Cup on Sky Diver (1967), Ayr Gold Cup on Somersway (1974) and the Cambridge-shire on King Midas in 1971, the year in which he rode his personal best 45 winners. Became a jockey's valet.

1950 TANTIEME, a 5–2 chance ridden by Jacques Doyasbere, trained by François Mathet and owned by François Dupré, won the Arc de Triomphe by 1 1/2 lengths from 11 rivals.

1961 Sir Winston Churchill's High Hat, ridden by Duncan Keith, finished 4th in the Arc de Triomphe at odds of 60–1. The race was won by Enrico Camici on MOLVEDO. The 18–10 chance was trained in Italy by A. Maggi, who brought in NF600,000 plus 78 per cent of entry fees. Molvedo was sired by the great Ribot.

1963 Durham jump jockey KEVIN JONES born. Best horse ridden The Thinker. Won Top Conditional Jockey award 1984.

1967 BILL PYERS rode Topyo for trainer Mick Bartholomew to land a shock 81–1 Arc de Triomphe victory. But a bigger shock was in store for jockey Pyers, who ended up in prison after a TV viewer recognised him as the man who had driven the car that had collided with her vehicle fifteen months earlier. Pyers had failed to attend a court hearing about the matter and was jailed in his absence for three months. He spent several days behind bars before the matter was resolved.

1991 WALTER SWINBURN was about to pass the post in front on 3–1 favourite Hamanaka in the Settrington Maiden Fillies Stakes at Redcar when his saddle slipped and he fell, breaking his wrist and collarbone. The race went to 10–1 shot Manbaa, ridden by Richard Hills. Swinburn had first broken his collarbone on July 17, when he was thrown from Sharling at Yarmouth.

9 OCTOBER

1889 Signorina (4–6) won the Middle Park Stakes and was later mated with a horse called Chaleureux, because eccentric Italian CHEVALIER GINISTRELLI thought the two were in love. He must have been right, for their offspring, Signorinetta, won the Derby and Oaks.

1948 Jockey IAN WATKINSON born. Rode Sea Pigeon to win the 1977 Embassy Handicap Hurdle and 1978 Fighting Fifth Hurdle.

1949 Somerset trainer GERALD HAM, who is also a pig farmer, born.

1951 Newmarket jockey MARK GILES born. Best horse ridden Lastcomer.

1955 RIBOT (ridden by Enrico Camici) won at odds of 88–10 to become the first Italian (even though he was born in Britain) Arc de Triomphe winner since Crapom in 1933.

1955 LESTER PIGGOTT achieved his first victory in France, riding Patras to a 3-length victory in the Prix St Moran at 17–1.

1959 Irish jockey KEN MORGAN born.

1966 BON MOTT III, ridden by Freddie Head and trained by Willie Head, won the Arc with Lester Piggott back in 8th on Aunt Edith.

1968 On the same day that former Gold Cup winner Mill House fell in his last race, at Ludlow, his great rival ARKLE'S retirement was announced by owner the Duchess of Westminster. He was injured in his last race, when beaten by Dormant on Boxing Day 1967.

1982 Three-year-old sprint ace SOBA (D. Nicholls–D. Chapman) won her 11th race (out of 14) of the season.

1990 Two-year-old SACQUE smashed the all-age record time for 5 furlongs at Folkestone, beating the record of 58.5 seconds by 0.1 second.

1991 Former jockey MIKEY HEATON-ELLIS, who was paralysed in a fall at Huntingdon in 1981, was granted a trainer's licence.

1991 Former jump jockey BRYAN MARSHALL died, aged 75. Rode consecutive Grand National winners for Vincent O'Brien: Early Mist (1953) and Royal Tan (1954). Champion Jockey in 1947–48 with 66 winners. Forced to retire through injury in 1954 with over 500 winners to his credit. Became a trainer.

1991 DARRYLL HOLLAND set a post-war record of 76 winners in a season for an apprentice when Merryhill Maid won at York.

1992 RICHARD HANNON sent out Brigante Di Cielo to win at 20–1 at Ascot, where his Bold Pursuit in the Mayflower Apprentice Stakes made him the first flat trainer to have 1,000 runners in a season.

1992 Belmont Park witnessed success for a number of their senior owners: 82-year-old Thomas Mellon Evans' Pleasant Tap won the Jockey Club Gold Cup, 85-year-old Paul Mellon's Sea Hero won the Champagne Stakes and 95-year-old Fred Hooper's Roman Envoy won the Kelso Handicap.

10 OCTOBER

1866   WILLIAM BLENKIRON of Middle Park stud at Eltham, Kent, put up £1,000 to support the Middle Park Stakes at Newmarket, won in the first running by The Rake (4–1), ridden by Jack Loates.

1943   Irish jockey DESSIE HUGHES born. Enjoyed the 1977 Cheltenham Festival, riding Davy Lad to win the Gold Cup, Tip the Wink to win the Arkle Challenge Trophy and Mac's Chariot to victory in the Lloyds Bank Champion Novice Hurdle. Also partnered Monksfield to win the 1979 Champion Hurdle.

1944   Trainer MAURICE CAMACHO of Malton, North Yorkshire, born. His Clear Cut won the 1975 Mackeson Gold Cup.

1947   Royston trainer JOHN (RENFIELD) JENKINS born. Best horses trained include Ayyabaan, Great Light, Beat the Retreat, Wing and a Prayer.

1949   Monave'en (owned jointly with the then Princess Elizabeth) was the Queen Mother's first winner, scoring at 3–10 favourite over fences at Fontwell, ridden by Tony Grantham for trainer Peter Cazalet. It was the first horse to win for a Queen of England for 235 years, since Queen Anne's Star.

1959   Newmarket trainer CONRAD ALLEN born. He trained the first flat winner on an all-weather track in Britain when Niklas Angel won at Lingfield in October 1989.

1959   Leyburn trainer MARK JOHNSTON born.

1960   Newmarket trainer MICHAEL LEOPOLD WENTWORTH BELL born.

1973   PETER WALWYN's Deliverance won the Founder's Plate at Lingfield, the stable's 84th win of the season, beating Captain Charles Elsey's post-war record. Walwyn ended up with 87 winners in all.

1974   Jockey SANDY HAWLEY rode 7 winners from 9 rides at Woodbine, Canada. He did the same thing on May 22 1972.

1989   Trainer LES HALL died aged 82. His big successes included 50–1 outsider Ashurst Wonder in the 1954 Stewards' Cup.

1989   Top National Hunt sire RELKINO, sixteen-year-old son of Derby winner Relko, died at the Conduit Stud.

1990   PAT EDDERY landed a 1,028–1 York 5-timer – all for different trainers.

1991   Trainer JACK BERRY ended an uncharacteristic run of 19 days without a winner when Fylde Flyer scored at York at 13–2.

1992   South African jockey MICHAEL ROBERTS declared that he planned to take out British citizenship during 1993.

1992   RICHARD DUNWOODY won the Breeders' Cup Chase on Jonathan Sheppard's Highland Bud, which also won in 1989.

11 OCTOBER

1877   Jimmy Ryan-trained Springfield (11–8) won the first Champion Stakes, beating Derby winner Silvio by a length. Run at Newmarket.

1887   Jockey GEORGE FORDHAM died, aged 50, with 16 Classic winners to his credit. He became Champion Jockey in 1855 and only surrendered the championship twice up to 1871. Continued wasting probably contributed to his early death.

1932   Former Middleham and Hong Kong trainer ERIC COLLINGWOOD born.

1933   Irish jockey TOMMY KINANE born. Rode Monksfield to win the 1978 Champion Hurdle, beating Sea Pigeon and Night Nurse.

1946   Jockey PETER ENNIS born. Partnered Young Ash Leaf.

1949   Owner of 1985 Gold Cup 4th-placed Drumadowney LADY VESTEY born. Colours: dark blue; emerald green seams; dark blue cap.

1953   Former wife of John and amateur rider MIRIAM FRANCOME born.

1956   Jockey TREVOR WALL born. Best horse ridden Cashew King.

1965   Jump jockey RUSSELL GARRITY born. Best horses ridden include Sword Beach.

1977   Rockeater (4–1 favourite) won at Redcar to give GREVILLE STARKEY his 1,000th British win.

1981   Bookmaker Herbert King, operating as Jack Warner, deliberately flouted the law to bet in public on a Sunday, taking bets on the Newmarket Town Plate to demonstrate to the Jockey Club and the government that there was a demand for Sunday racing with betting. The police turned a blind eye. 'Warner' took £1,000 and divided his profits between the New Astley club and the Injured Jockeys' Fund.

1990   Evry-based FREDDY PALMER, who rode Phil Drake to win the 1955 Derby, announced his retirement from training.

1990   LESTER PIGGOTT was granted a full Flat licence by the Jockey Club, and the 54-year-old was set for a sensational comeback, having officially retired on October 29 1985.

1992   Czech-trained QUIRINUS won the Martell Velka Pardubicka in Pardubice, Czechoslovakia, ridden by Josef Brecha. The race was interrupted by animal rights protesters as the runners approached the 3rd fence. The protesters had already delayed the start by 30 minutes. They were objecting to 'The Taxis', a massive fence 1.5m high and 8ft wide with a 7ft ditch.

1992   Twenty-two-year-old jockey KENT DESORMEAUX fell from Judge Hammer at Hollywood Park, sustaining 14 hairline skull fractures, haemorrhaging and hearing loss. He returned to the saddle on January 22, winning on his first ride back.

12 OCTOBER

1837 Jockey THOMAS LYE won the first race at Northallerton on Alzira, having won on Abraham Newland and Modesty at far-off Edinburgh just the day before – and he didn't have a private plane to make the journey in.

1894 ROBERT SHERWOOD died, four days after suffering a fit. As a jockey he rode a French Derby-Oaks double on Jouvence in 1853 and in 1855 partnered Wild Dayrell to win the Epsom Derby. As a trainer he had two Classic successes: St Gatien in the 1884 Derby (dead-heat) and the 1889 Oaks with L'Abbesse de Jouarre.

1920 US equine superstar MAN O'WAR ran his 21st and final race, winning the Kenilworth Park Gold Cup at Kenilworth Park by 7 lengths.

1959 Jockey NICKY CARLISLE born. Won the Ayr Gold Cup on So Careful for Jack Berry in 1988. Also partnered Hello Cuddles, Ashal.

1968 Jockey DARREN BIGGS born. Partnered Chelsea Girl.

1981 Grand National winning jockey BOB CHAMPION married Jo Beswick.

1982 CHAPLIN'S CLUB won for the first time, on his 6th appearance. He started 9-4 favourite and was ridden by John Reid over 5 furlongs at Folkestone. Before retiring in July 1992, Chaplin's Club was to race 114 times, winning 24 races, being placed 38 times and picking up £146,665.70, as well as becoming one of the most popular handicappers in training.

1989 PETER SCUDAMORE broke his own record for the fastest 50 jump winners in a season when he rode In-Keeping to win at Wincanton.

1991 The Toby Balding-trained MORLEY STREET became the first horse to win two Breeders' Cup Chases, and only the 3rd to win two Breeders' Cup races of any description, after Miesque, which twice won the Mile (1987 and 1988) and Bayakoa, which won the Distaff in 1989 and 1990.

1991 Trainer JOHN GOSDEN scored his second treble at York – Kansk (W. Carson, 7-4), Go Executive (M. Roberts, 8-1), and King Athelstan (Carson, 6-4) – within three days, thus passing the half a million prize-money mark in Britain.

1992 Jockey RICHARD QUINN reached 100 winners in a season for the first time when Young Ern (6-1) won at Leicester. He had been stuck on 99 for 53 rides.

1992 The PRINCESS ROYAL officially opened Jackdaw's Castle, a £1.8 million training complex in the Cotswolds which became the new base for David 'The Duke' Nicholson.

13 OCTOBER

1857 A triple dead-heat took place between the inseparable PRYORESS, EL HAKIM and QUEEN BESS in the Cesarewitch at Newmarket. Before a run-off of the race was arranged, bookmaker George Hodgman organised of a gambling coup. Having observed that jockey Tankersley had given 30-1 chance Pryoress a less than perfect ride, he rapidly arranged for owner Richard Ten Broeck to engage crack rider George Fordham, then plunged in to back the new combination. The Fordham-partnered Pryoress beat El Hakim by a length.

1923 Owner MARGARET 'HEPPY' WALTON born. Best horses include Scottish National winner Mighty Mark.

1925 Occasional racegoer MARGARET THATCHER born. Clement Freud named a horse after her memorable remark, Weareagrandmother.

1927 The first meeting took place at Arlington Park, US.

1941 Dorchester permit trainer DR DAVID CHESNEY born.

1951 Ascot was televised for the first time as KING GEORGE'S Good Shot, ridden by Gordon Richards, won the Tankerville Nursery Stakes.

1953 Jockey JOHN MATTHIAS born.

1953 Top US jockey PAT DAY born. Among the biggest successes of his career was Easy Goer's 1989 Belmont Stakes victory.

1982 One time star two-year-old in 1978, but a disappointment later, TROMOS died in Kentucky aged 6.

1984 Nine-year-old American superstar horse JOHN HENRY won at Meadowlands to bring his earnings to a record $6,597,947.

1989 Friday the thirteenth proved unlucky for trainer JONJO O'NEILL when Hit the Ceiling slipped up on the flat when leading at Carlisle. Then his Roliad broke down badly when going well, and Ben Ledi had to be withdrawn before the start of the race. There was one gleam of sunshine, though, when Paco's Boy won the last for Jonjo.

1990 The last meeting took place at Phoenix Park. WILD JESTER won the last race, the Irish Independent Handicap, ridden by Christy Roche. The course was 88 years old.

1991 ZELEZNIK, a Czech-trained chaser, won the gruelling Velka Pardubicka in Czechoslovakia for an amazing 4th time at the age of thirteen in the 101st running of the testing marathon event.

1991 RICHARD HANNON saddled Fair Crack (13-2) and Autocracy to finish 1st and 2nd in the Goffs Million at the Curragh to take his European earnings past £2 million.

1992 GEOFF LEWIS collected a £90,000 gamble when the appropriately named Dare to Dream landed the 40-1 bet he had taken at the beginning of the season that he would send out 50 winners. The previous season he had allegedly won £100,000 for 40 winners.

14 OCTOBER

1671   KING CHARLES II rode his first winner as a jockey at Newmarket in the Town Plate, and remains the only reigning monarch to ride a winner.

1862   WILLIAM CHIFNEY, who trained 5 Classic winners and was the elder son of Samuel Chifney, died in poverty at the age of 76, despite having earned £18,000 in bets when winning the 1830 Derby with his own horse, Priam.

1885   ORMONDE made his first racecourse appearance. The colt, which would go on to win the 1886 Triple Crown, scored in the Post Sweepstakes at Newmarket.

1886   Few each-way bets were staked on Ormonde, as the talented colt was backed down to 1–100 for the three-runner Champion Stakes which he duly won.

1908   WILLIAM BEHRENS born. Owner–breeder of 28–1 1973 St Leger winner Peleid. Colours: dark blue; chocolate sleeves; white cap.

1941   Hampshire trainer JOHN BRIDGER born. Trained the horse which couldn't, or wouldn't win, Amrullah.

1946   Moody Blue, owner and breeder JUSTIN HAYWARD born.

1956   Jockey CHRIS GRANT born. Was 2nd in the 1986 Grand National on 66–1 shot Young Driver, runner-up again in 1988 on Durham Edition and yet again on the same horse in 1990. 'Mr Nearly' also occupied the runner-up slot in the 1987 Cheltenham Gold Cup on 25–1 chance Cybrandian.

1960   BRENDAN POWELL born. Won 1988 National on Rhyme 'n' Reason.

1960   Trainer WILLIAM JARVIS born.

1967   The first jump meeting took place at Teesside Park. King Tarquin won the first race, the Harold Dawson Handicap Hurdle, at 6–1. Ridden by G. Lee; trained by G. Vergette.

1972   BRIGADIER GERARD won on his final racecourse appearance, the Champion Stakes. The 1–3 favourite, ridden by Joe Mercer for Dick Hern, was owned and bred by John Hislop and ran in his wife's name. He won 17 of 18 races from 5 furlongs to one and a half miles, and collected £212,319 in prize-money.

1978   Dukery was trainer NICKY HENDERSON's first winner at Uttoxeter.

1989   Three-year-old HAWKSTER, carrying 121lbs, set a new world record of 2 minutes 22.8 seconds for one and a half miles at Santa Anita Netlon turf course.

1991   LESTER PIGGOTT celebrated the end of his first comeback year with a victory on Claret at Leicester.

1992   Ingenuity (14–1) won at Redcar to give the QUEEN her 24th winner of the season. Her previous best year had been 1957.

15 OCTOBER

1946 Sussex trainer JAMES BRYAN SAYERS born. Best horses trained Hoorah Henry, Bigee.

1948 Sussex jockey ROGER ROWELL born. Best horses ridden include Avec Moi and Brantridge Farmer.

1950 Marlborough jockey MICHAEL KETTLE born. Best horses ridden included Roy Bride.

1950 Pop star and owner CHRIS DE BURGH born. His best racehorse Missing You was named after one of his hit records.

1980 JONJO O'NEILL rode 5 winners from 6 mounts at Wetherby.

1982 One of the all-time unexplained performances saw Dick Hern-trained, Willie Carson-ridden, highly touted GORYTUS trail home last of 4 despite starting 1–2 favourite in the Dewhurst Stakes at Newmarket.

1982 JOHN DUNLOP enjoyed his 1,000th success in sixteen years as a trainer when John Lowe rode Prince Elo to win at Catterick.

1984 NEEDLES, who won the 1956 Kentucky Derby, died aged 31, the 2nd greatest age ever recorded for a winner of that race.

1990 LESTER PIGGOTT rode Lupescu – his first comeback mount some five years after his official retirement. The horse was beaten in a photo-finish and he drew a blank on both of his other rides at, inevitably, Leicester. At the same meeting Walter Swinburn rode 5 winners and was then asked, 'Are you worried about Lester's return?' by a radio announcer.

1991 LESTER PIGGOTT rode Shafouri (9–2) into 2nd place in the Lester Piggott All-aged Stakes at Chepstow. The race was won by Afif, 11–2, ridden by D. Harrison.

1992 User Friendly's owner BILL GREDLEY called for a one-day strike of owners on November 2 in protest at the government's deductions from betting. He later withdrew the call when the authorities showed displeasure.

16 OCTOBER

1804 CHANCELLOR, owned by Lord Cassillis, won the first running of the Ayr Gold Cup - then contested over two heats of two miles - beating 2 opponents. He then competed in the Ayr Subscription of £50, consisting of four heats of four miles, and finished second. Chancellor had completed over 20 miles, carrying 8st 10lbs, in a single afternoon.

1920 Owner JOSEPH MCGRATH born. Best horses include Allangrange, Levmoss. Colours: maroon bird's eye; maroon cap.

1920 GORDON RICHARDS' first mount, Clockwork, was unplaced at Lingfield.

1921 Paul Mellon's trainer in USA, MACK MILLER, born.

1940 Owner of Sylvan Barbarosa DAVID JOHNSON born. Colours: green; orange sleeves; white hoop and cap.

1957 Scottish jockey SANDY DUDGEON born. Best horses ridden include Gayle Warning, Peaty Sandy.

1973 VICTOR MORLEY LAWSON won the Corinthian Amateur Riders' Maiden Stakes on Ocean King at Warwick. It was his first win, and he was a mere 67-year-old stripling, setting a new record for the oldest jockey to record a debut victory.

1976 After DERRINGO finished 6th at 6-1 in the Highflyer Handicap at Newmarket, owner Marcos Lemos declared that Willie Carson would no longer ride his horses: 'Of all the things I could have been fired for,' declared Carson. 'Usually people criticise me for trying too hard.' Lemos had been upset that Carson was leaving trainer Clive Brittain for Dick Hern, replacing Joe Mercer, the Queen's jockey.

1989 A fire at stables at Randwick racecourse, Sydney, killed 11 racehorses worth AUS$1 million.

1990 LESTER PIGGOTT rode the first 2 winners of his comeback at Chepstow: 4-6 chance Nicholas, trained by his wife, and 11-1 shot Shining Jewel.

1991 Derby winner GENEROUS was retired to Banstead Manor stud.

1992 The latest two-year-old 'wonder horse', ZAFONIC, won the Dewhurst Stakes and became hot favourite for the 2,000 Guineas.

17 OCTOBER

1919   Joint breeder of Formulate and Kalaglow GEORGINA PHILLIPS born.

1919   Vet, former Arsenal, Derby and Cardiff soccer star, TV and radio broadcaster on racing, and owner WYN GRIFFITHS born. Best horses owned include Tanwen, Gwynfi Ni, Megwen. Colours: royal blue; yellow armlets; pink cap.

1962   Top US jockey PAT VALENZUELA, partner of Sunday Silence, born.

1966   DENYS SMITH sent out his 100th winner as a trainer - Wife's Choice - ridden in a handicap hurdle at Southwell by Terry Biddlecombe.

1967   Jockey JONATHAN LEECH born.

1967   Jockey BILL PYERS, who had ridden Topyo to victory in the Arc de Triomphe just nine days earlier, was languishing in a French prison after a TV viewer watching the race accused him of being a hit and run driver. It took him three weeks to extricate himself from the mess.

1970   NIJINSKY'S career ended in defeat as he started 4–11 favourite for the Champion Stakes only to finish 2nd to 100–7 winner Lorenzaccio, ridden by Geoff Lewis and trained by Noel Murless. Nijinsky won 11 of his 13 races and was twice runner-up. He had earlier won the 2,000 Guineas, Derby and St Leger, but was runner-up to Sassafras in the Arc. He won £246,132 in England and Ireland; F480,000 in France.

1989   An earthquake hit the San Francisco area, causing slight damage at Bay Meadows and Golden Fields racecourses.

1990   PAT EDDERY reached a career best 198 winners for a season - and went on to total 209.

1991   ANGEL CORDERO joined Bill Shoemaker and Laffit Pincay in the 7,000-winner club when Don't Cross the Law won at Belmont Park. That's without including his 258 winners in Puerto Rico.

1992   The legend continued as Lester Piggott rode Rodrigo De Triano to victory in Newmarket's Champion Stakes by a neck from Lahib.

1992   Not the best day trainer SUE BRADBURNE of Fife ever enjoyed. Of the 5 horses she had running at Kelso, Ayia Napa and Dante's Inferno were pulled up; Stagshaw Belle unseated her rider at the first and was injured; Off the Bru finished last and a vet's certificate was produced for Rogany, which did not run.

18 OCTOBER

1917   A match race at Laurel, Maryland, pitted 1917 Belmont Stakes winner HOURLESS against OMAR KHAYYAM, the Kentucky Derby winner, over one mile. Hourless won by a length.

1937   New York trainer FRANK ALLEN ALEXANDER born.

1938   Sixteen-year-old apprentice DOUGIE MARKS rode Brescia to win at Newcastle.

1939   A 2-day meeting at Newmarket, including a 2-division Cambridgeshire, won by Gyroscope (100-6) and Orichalque (25-1), began. It was the first racing since it was announced on September 4 that racing would be abandoned for the year. There were only twelve more days' racing – at Newbury, Newmarket, Manchester, Thirsk and Stockton – allowed.

1945   The first French raider since 1940, PRIAM II, went close to winning the Champion Stakes at Newmarket, but was beaten by 2,000 Guineas winner Court Martial, 4-1 favourite.

1947   ELI BENDON, a contemporary of Fred Archer who had ridden winners in England, France and the US, died aged 86.

1952   The Washington DC International was run for the first time, taking place at Laurel Racecourse, Maryland. In 1954 it became the first race outside Britain in which a runner had carried Royal colours when the Queen's Landau competed.

1955   Champion (1987) amateur point-to-point jockey MIKE FELTON born.

1958   Former (1978-79) Champion Amateur Jockey GEORDIE DUN born.

1966   Newmarket trainer HENRY CECIL married Sir Noel Murless's daughter, Julie, now a trainer in her own right.

1966   AURIOL SINCLAIR became the first woman officially to train a double when Ladino and Golden Gloves won at Folkestone.

1975   ALLEZ FRANCE raced for the 2nd time in England – again in the Champion Stakes, as in 1973 – and again finished runner-up.

1978   DAVE GALL rode 8 winners from 10 mounts at Cahokia Downs, Illinois.

1991   DR DEVIOUS, who was to win the 1992 Derby, won the Dewhurst Stakes at Newmarket, ridden by Willie Carson.

1991   Petite-D-Argent won at Newmarket to give ALAN MUNRO his first century of winners.

1991   SHEIKH MOHAMMED paid a reported $8.5 million to owner Allen Paulson for a half-share in Arazi.

1992   PAUL COLE's Snurge won the Rothmans International in Canada, getting the race after the disqualification of Wiorno. The day before Cole's Zoman had won the Budweiser International ($750,000) at Laurel, Maryland, ending a 23-year drought for British raiders.

19 OCTOBER

1914 Owner-breeder-trainer of 1982 Grand National winner Grittar FRANK GILMAN born. Colours: mauve and white hoops; quartered cap.

1915 Trainer of Lochranza JOE CARR born. Rode successfully under NH Rules from 1936 until he fell at Ludlow in May 1940, and lost his right leg above the knee as a result. Also trained Salmon King, Remraf, Sufi, Mountain King.

1932 HARRY WRAGG was thrown from Donatia in a race at Newcastle. His right leg was smashed and doctors only just managed to avoid amputation. He returned to action early the next season.

1932 Former Champion Amateur rider (1971-72) BILL FOULKES born.

1953 Female jockey JOANNA MORGAN born. Best horses ridden include Baby Brew.

1964 Twice Champion Jump Jockey RON BARRY, now an Inspector of Courses, rode his first winner, at Ayr.

1988 Former Irish Champion Jockey MARTIN QUIRKE died aged 89. Rode 9 Irish Classic winners including Soloptic in the 1,000 Guineas and Oaks in 1929, and Salisbury in the 2,000 Guineas. Set a record of 86 winners in 1923, which stood until 1972, when Johnny Roe beat it.

1989 SUPER TONY completed an unusual double at Hexham. He won a handicap chase on a walkover – as he had done the last time he'd been entered there.

1989 The Buckenham Selling Stakes at Newmarket made history when the photo-finish of the race was the first ever to be displayed in public in colour. It revealed that Sister Sal had beaten Gabbiadini by $^1/_2$ length; the two were 5-1 joint favourites.

1989 A crowd of 15,000 people – 5,000 more than the previous record – watched BILL SHOEMAKER ride his first winner in Australia on Cosign in the Moe Cup at Moe, Melbourne.

1990 GENEROUS, 50-1, was the longest-priced winner in the 115-year history of the Dewhurst Stakes at Newmarket. Trained by Paul Cole and ridden by Richard Quinn, the horse won the Derby in 1991.

1990 JACK BERRY equalled the 1905 record for winners by a Northern trainer – 124 by William Elsey – when Time for the Blues and Doublova won at Catterick.

1991 DANCING BRAVE, the European champion of 1986, was sold to Japan.

1992 MICHAEL ROBERTS broke Gordon Richards' record of 1,000 domestic rides in a season when in action at Folkestone on his 1,001st, the unplaced Aalu.

20 OCTOBER

1841   CATHERINA set a British record by winning her 79th race at Leek, Staffordshire. She ran 176 times between 1832 and 1841 and was unplaced as 3rd favourite in the 1833 Oaks.

1915   Warwickshire owner–trainer MICHAEL MARSH born. He trained his own Larbawn to win the Whitbread Gold Cup in 1968 and 1969.

1917   THOMAS WESTON, who went on to ride 11 Classic winners, rode in public for the first time on Black Crag at Stockton.

1923   American champion ZEV, ridden by Earl Sande, defeated English Derby winner PAPYRUS trained by Basil Jarvis and ridden by Steve Donoghue, in a $100,000 match at Belmont Park, USA, winning by 5 lengths. Papyrus' cause certainly was not helped by the unsuitable shoes with which he was fitted.

1930   Former trainer JOHN BOOTH born.

1936   Argentinian-born trainer in New York ALFREDO CALLEJAS born.

1945   Overcrowding at Worcester racecourse resulted in the collapse of a Tote building, and 25 spectators were injured.

1952   Worcester trainer MARK CASTELL – who boasts a BA Honours (Economics) – born.

1957   NEALE DOUGHTY, who rode Hallo Dandy to win the 1984 Grand National, born.

1957   Swindon trainer ADRIAN CHAMBERLAIN born.

1964   The QUEEN MOTHER celebrated her 100th winner over jumps when Bobby Beasley rode the Jack Donoghue-trained Gay Record to victory at Folkestone.

1990   Sizzling Saga gave trainer JACK BERRY a new record score for a Northern trainer in one season of 125 when winning at Catterick.

1990   Two-year-old Timeless Times, already the winner of 16 races so far during the season, went to Laurel, USA, in a bid to land a record 17th in the Futurity at the Maryland track. But the Bill O'Gorman-trained youngster was out of luck, finishing last of 13.

1990   PETER ALAFI rode his 2,218th winner on Noveka at Gelsenkirchen-Horst to equal the record number of winners for a German-based jockey, held by Otto Schmidt.

1990   MORLEY STREET travelled from Britain to win the $250,000 Breeders' Cup Steeplechase by 10 lengths at Belmont Park.

1992   GEORGE DUFFIELD, aged 45, completed his first century of winners when Two Left Feet won at Chepstow, trained by Sir Mark Prescott. This brought his career total to 1,652, and made him the only jockey to have ridden so many without ever becoming Champion. Later Duffield raced over hurdles in the Flat Versus Jump Jockeys' Challenge Hurdle, won by flat jockey Michael Hills on Silver Age.

21 OCTOBER

1791 Having been beaten the day before when favourite, the Prince of Wales' horse Escape, won at long odds at Newmarket. A stewards' inquiry was held and the Prince was told that 'if Chifney were suffered to ride the Prince's horses, no gentleman would start against him'. The controversial Chifney was suspected by many of pulling the horse in the first of the 2 races. The Prince stood by his much-maligned rider and refused ever to race at Newmarket again.

1925 Swiss-based owner GERRY OLDHAM born. His Lucero won the 1950 Irish 2,000 Guineas while Irish Derby winner Talgo was also an Arc runner-up, as was Salvo. Fidalgo too won the Irish Derby and was runner-up in both the Derby and St Leger. Colours: chocolate and white hoops; white cap.

1936 Trainer OWEN O'NEILL born. Dual purpose jockey who rode around 100 winners. Best horses trained include Model Pupil, Stormy Prospect, Christian Schad, Mole Board.

1939 Former jockey DINAH NICHOLSON born.

1954 Jockey GERRY NEWMAN born. Best horses ridden include Captain Christy, Bright Highway, Chinrullah, Chorelli.

1965 DOUG SMITH took his British total of winners to 3,000 when he rode a double at Newbury on Soft Collar and As Before.

1966 Northern jockey RODDY LAPPIN born. Best horses ridden include Miss Primula. First winner, Gay Meadow, at Thirsk, April 27 1984.

1981 RICHARD QUINN rode his first winner, Bolivar Baby (Paul Cole), at Kempton.

1985 GARY 'THE ANGRY ANT' BARDWELL rode his first winner, Beech-wood, at Hamilton.

1991 Trainer LORD JOHN FITZGERALD announced he was to quit Newmarket to start training in Germany.

1992 Jasoorah, trained by Alec Stewart, won at Chester to make MICHAEL ROBERTS only the 5th jockey to ride 200 winners in a domestic season.

1992 Jockey Club member TOMMY WALLIS died aged 69. Owned Cash Desire, Grand Military Gold Cup winner of 1962. Colours: white; royal blue hoop on body.

22 OCTOBER

1855 OVERREACH, UNEXPECTED, GAMESTER and LADY GOLIGHTLY ran a quadruple dead-heat in a £10 sweepstake for two-year-olds at Newmarket.

1945 Newmarket trainer MICHAEL STOUTE born in Barbados, where his father was Commissioner of Police. Twice won the Derby, with Shergar in 1981 and Shahrastani in 1986. Fair Salinia (1978) and Unite (1987) have won the Oaks for him; Shadeed (1985) and Doyoun (1988) won the 2,000 Guineas and Musical Bliss (1989) the 1,000 Guineas.

1950 Jockey GARY OLD born. Best horses ridden include True Song.

1964 BILL SHOEMAKER rode his 5,000th winner, Slapstick, at Aqueduct.

1982 TONY MURRAY rode his 1,000th career winner on Guy Harwood's Northern Adventure at Doncaster.

1984 The Breeders' Cup unveiled its permanent trophy: a 1,850lb bronze and marble reproduction of the Torrie horse, an ecorche or flayed horse designed by the sixteenth-century sculptor Giambologna.

1992 Japan acquired Classic winners DR DEVIOUS ($6 million) and RODRIGO DE TRIANO ($6.2 million) for stud duty.

23 OCTOBER

1927 Jockey Club member and owner of Master Eye, winner of 21 races, MILES GOSLING born.

1928 Hertfordshire trainer ALAN BLACKMORE born. Trainer of Silent Echo.

1935 Racing writer CHARLES BENSON born.

1950 Turkish Jockey Club founded with headquarters in Istanbul.

1955 Arc winner RIBOT won Italy's Premio Del Jockey Club by an impressive 15 lengths.

1962 Newmarket-based jump jockey ROSS CAMPBELL born.

1966 There was controversy at Cologne's Preis Von Europa when Russian horse Anilin got the nod over Salvo, ridden by Joe Mercer and trained by Harry Wragg. There was no photo-finish available and Mercer was convinced he had won.

1987 LESTER PIGGOTT was jailed for tax offences.

1989 After controversy over safety, a new look Becher's Brook was unveiled at Aintree. The ditch had been raised by 30ins and the slope on the landing side levelled off. The fence remained 4ft 10ins high, but the drop to the water became 8ft. The ditch is 15ins deep. The area beyond the fence was widened to enable horses to jump straight ahead. Changes to the Mildmay course were also unveiled.

1990 LESTER PIGGOTT rode 4 winners from four rides for Vincent O'Brien at the Curragh: Legal Profession, Passer By, Fairy Folk and Classic Minstrel.

1990 WALTER SWINBURN rode 100 winners in a season for the first time when Lilian Bayliss scored at Chester.

1990 PAT EDDERY joined Fred Archer (8 times), Tommy Loates (1893) and Sir Gordon Richards (12 times) when he rode his 200th winner of the season, Miranda Jay at Chepstow. It was the first time the feat had been achieved since 1947.

1991 The new Jockey Club ruling on walkovers, introduced in July, was implemented for the first time when ARTHUR STEPHENSON re-entered Palm Reader to take on Old Applejack in the Durham Handicap Chase at Newcastle. All the other 7 5-day entries were also invited to re-enter. Old Applejack, 6-4, beat 1-2 favourite Palm Reader. On October 21 1992 the pair met again in the same race – with the same outcome.

1991 STEVE CAUTHEN completed his 10th consecutive century of British winners when Knifebox won at Chester.

1992 Racing at Newbury was abandoned after 6 of the scheduled 7 races 'because of a spillage of aviation fuel on the course' after a light aircraft carrying racegoers back to Hampshire crashed on to the Flat course. The occupants of the plane were not seriously injured.

24 OCTOBER

1826 Horses belonging to eccentric owner (he would saddle up and ride a pet bear and once allegedly set fire to his nightgown to cure himself of hiccups) 'MAD' JACK MYTTON, who even named his son after his best horse Euphrates, came up for sale at an auction. Best price was 860 guineas for Longwaist, by Whalebone, while a two-year-old bay colt by Sceptre fetched just 43 guineas.

1851 ST HELIER, ridden by Tom Olliver, who won 3 Grand Nationals, won the Grand Annual Free Handicap Chase at Hereford by 8 lengths.

1876 The four-year-old ROSEBERY completed the Autumn double, winning the Cambridgeshire, despite carrying a stone more than in the Cesarewitch. He was owned by brothers James and Sidney Smith, who cleaned up to the tune of £250,000 over the two races.

1906 Owner of 1971 Grand National winner Specify, holiday camp supremo SIR FRED PONTIN, born.

1938 Former jockey turned trainer PAUL TULK born.

1939 Bedfordshire trainer MICHAEL BANKS born. First licence 1974.

1942 Jockey (ALFRED) TONY KIMBERLEY born. He won the Barbados Guineas on 4 occasions.

1947 The first dead-heat under Jockey Club rules recorded by the camera occurred at Doncaster, when PHANTOM BRIDGE and RESISTANCE shared the honours in the 5-furlong Beechfield Handicap.

1953 Impney caused a major upset when he defeated 1-7 favourite SIR KEN at Uttoxeter to break that horse's run of 16 consecutive victories.

1966 Northern jockey MARK GILES born.

1974 Brighton jockey GARY LEE MOORE's first winner was Jamie's Cottage at Plumpton.

1981 NIGEL COLEMAN rode his first winner, Walmari, at Stratford.

1982 Former trainer PERCY VASEY died aged 92. Sent out over 300 winners from his Wetherby base, headed by Trimbush in the Doncaster Cup and Mad Carew in the Manchester November Handicap. The Vasey family are among the oldest racing families in the land and his grandfather was a trainer as early as 1855.

1988 Jockey PETER SCUDAMORE completed the fastest 50 winners in a jump season on Wolfhangar at Fakenham.

1988 LESTER PIGGOTT was released from prison, just over a year after being jailed for tax offences.

1992 SUPER IMPOSE, trained by Lee Freedman, became the biggest earner in the Southern Hemisphere when he won the $1.7 million W. S. Cox Plate at Moonee Valley, Melbourne, to take his career earnings to $5,659,358.

25 OCTOBER

1852   WEST AUSTRALIAN made the first of 10 racecourse appearances by finishing 2nd at Newmarket. Improved to win all of the other 9 and became the first winner of the Triple Crown, in 1853.

1881   American-bred FOXHALL completed the autumn double when he won the Cambridgeshire, ridden by Jack Watts for owner American financier J. R. Keene.

1927   Owner BRENDA DAVIS born. Her Mon Fils won the 1973 2,000 Guineas. Also owned Son Fils, Son of Silver, Mendip Man.

1934   1979 Champion Jockey JOE MERCER born. Partnered Brigadier Gerard in all his races, including the 1971 2,000 Guineas. Also rode Highclere (1974) and One in a Million (1979) to win the 1,000 Guineas; Oaks successes Ambiguity (1953) and Provoke (1965) and Bustino in 1974 to win the St Leger.

1937   Owner DAVID STODDART born. His High Havens won 10 chases.

1942   American racing writer DAN FARLEY born.

1947   Ireland's first triple dead-heat was recorded when COLOMB'S KINGDOM, HISWAY and LILTING LADY proved inseparable for 2nd place at the Curragh.

1948   New York trainer DENNIS BRIDA born.

1949   HARRY STRAUS, the American who invented the Totalisator, died in a plane crash in Maryland.

1967   The last meeting took place at Le Tremblay, France, expropriated by President de Gaulle for a new sports stadium.

1968   RIBOFILIO, who had become a great favourite with the bookmakers, finished his career in the St Simon Stakes, for which he started favourite and was unplaced. He had started favourite in no fewer than 4 Classics – the English 2,000 Guineas, Derby and St Leger and the Irish Derby – and been beaten in the lot.

1979   HEYWOOD HARDY (Joe Mercer) was the last of Ryan Jarvis's 1,010 winners in Britain when scoring at Newbury.

1985   STEVE SMITH ECCLES rode his 500th winner, Dhofar, at Newbury.

1986   TONY MURRAY rode his final British winner, Jupiter Island, in the St Simon Stakes at Newbury.

1990   Jockey STEVE PERKS was fined £150 at Pontefract – for changing his boots. The trouble was he'd already weighed out in the original pair to ride Grace Card, on which he finished last.

1992   Flamboyant racecourse tipster PRINCE MONOLULU was remembered when relatives and admirers attended a celebration on what would have been his 111th birthday at the pub bearing his name in Maple Street, London. Abyssinian Monolulu died in 1965 and was best known for his appearances at Epsom and his cry of 'I gotta horse'.

26 OCTOBER

1924 LT-COLONEL SIR JAMES SCOTT, owner of Big Venture and Proud Pathan, born. Colours: black; white cross-belts; black and green quartered cap.

1925 Jockey–trainer BOBBY BREWIS born. Trainer of Candy II, Solo Call, Carpril, Whinstone Hill, Carno.

1933 Having been refused a licence for over five years after an incident when a horse he was riding took no part in a race, jockey CHARLIE SMIRKE, by now 27, resumed his career on Equidistant at Newmarket.

1941 Official handicapper BILL PATON SMITH born.

1942 Thirsk trainer SUE BRAMALL born. Best horses include Shilgrove Place, Castle Vennon, Pearl Merchant.

1950 Rider of 1987 King George VI Chase winner Nupsala ANDRE POMMIER born.

1955 LESTER PIGGOTT completed his first century of winners in a season when Ragd won at Newmarket, ending up 3rd behind Doug Smith, with 103 winners in all.

1963 BROUGH SCOTT rode his first winner over hurdles, Arcticeelagh, in the Monmouth Handicap Hurdle at Chepstow.

1966 PERSIAN WAR, later to win 3 Champion Hurdles, won on his hurdling debut at Ascot.

1982 Jockey TOM GRANTHAM rode his first winner, Peyton Pearl, at Plumpton.

1986 PATRICIA COOKSEY became the first female rider to partner a stakes race winner at Churchill Downs when she guided Bestofbothworlds to victory in the Pocahontas.

1989 Jump trainer MARTIN PIPE broke his own record for the fastest 50 winners in a season with Walk of Life at Wincanton. It took him until October 28 the previous season.

1989 JOHN KENNY MBE died aged 74. Manager of Stratford racecourse and owner of Milford Grove, which won 11 races during the 1970s.

1991 LESTER PIGGOTT won Italy's Gran Criterium at San Siro, Milan, on Alhijaz, for trainer John Dunlop.

1992 Trainer CHARLIE NELSON quit the game after his last runner, Awesome Power, won at Lingfield.

1992 Dawn Grant, wife of jockey Chris, died tragically of cancer.

1992 The terms of the Wysall Stakes at Leicester made it somewhat surprising that trainer Paul Cole had entered his RUN DON'T FLY. With 1lb allocated for each £500 won in 1st-place prize-money, Run Don't Fly, which had picked up £91,154, would have had to shoulder 21st 3lbs!

27 OCTOBER

1870 Preakness won the first stakes race run at Pimlico racecourse, USA. Three years later the Maryland Jockey Club honoured the colt by naming a race over one and a half miles for him. The race became part of the coveted American Triple Crown, along with the Kentucky Derby and Belmont Stakes, but Preakness's own future wasn't too bright. The horse went to stud at the Duke of Hamilton's in England. His temper was apparently as bad as that of the irascible Duke himself – who shot him in a fit of anger.

1939 Owner LORD DUNRAVEN born. Best horses include Cheval.

1943 Trainer MEL BRITTAIN born. Best horses trained include Grey Desire.

1945 Irish trainer ANDY GERAGHTY born. Best horses include Destriero.

1946 EL LOBO won a handicap at Bay Meadows, San Francisco. Five days earlier he had become one of the first 2 racehorses (Featherfoot travelled with him) to fly to a meeting when he arrived from Los Angeles. The plane's pilot, Major William Hicke, backed El Lobo, and set a new trend for transporting horses in this manner.

1951 Former jockey ANNE COCHRANE, wife of jockey Ray, born.

1955 Jockey COLIN HAWKINS born.

1963 Jump jockey PENNY FFITCH-HEYES born.

1967 Jump jockey PHILIP BARNARD born. First winner Bellagio, in 1985.

1989 Jump trainer MARTIN PIPE saddled 6 winners from 7 runners at 3 meetings – 4 winners at Devon, and 1 each at Hereford and Newbury.

1990 LESTER PIGGOTT produced Royal Academy with a dramatically timed late run to snatch the Breeders' Cup Mile at Belmont Park, worth $450,000 to winner, which was trained by Vincent O'Brien. In the Breeders' Cup Sprint WILLIE CARSON was set to win on Dayjur (Dick Hern), but the horse jumped a shadow as it came to the line and lost out by a neck to Safely Kept, 12–1.

1990 For the first time in the UK all 4 runners for a race, the Racing Post Trophy at Doncaster, were supplemented runners – all the original entries withdrew. Steve Cauthen rode Peter Davies, 2–1 favourite, to win.

1991 TURGEON, which had previously won the Irish St Leger, added the French (Prix Royal Oak) equivalent at Longchamp to his record.

1992 Former jockey and trainer DERMOT BROWNE was disqualified for ten years by the Jockey Club. He was found to have breached six rules of racing, including giving information to a bookmaker in return for monetary reward. Browne, amateur riders' champion and a professional jump jockey before taking up training in January 1990, was exonerated on charges relating to his being aware of the doping of Norwich and Bravefoot at Doncaster in September 1990.

28 OCTOBER

1864   GEORGE FORDHAM won 6 races on the 9-race card at Newmarket.

1935   Five rides, 5 winners for jockey JIMMY KING at Churchill Downs, USA.

1942   Moreton-in-Marsh trainer SALLY GILL born. Broke her back in a fall hunting in November 1985 and was confined to wheelchair. Best horses trained include Mr Mole, Eventime.

1944   Wantage trainer HENRY CANDY born. Trained Time Charter to win the 1982 Oaks at 12-1. Learned his trade in Sydney and Chantilly. First big win Ascot Stakes with Kambalda in 1974. Other top horses include Wind and Wuthering, Master Willie.

1950   Owner of Towcester racecourse LORD HESKETH born.

1950   Former Champion Amateur Jockey (joint 1975-76) GEORGE JONES born. Best horses ridden include Roc Imp.

1951   Jockey DICK MARSHALL born. Best horses ridden include Philominsky, on which he won the 1976 Northumberland Plate.

1958   Kildare trainer DREW MCMILLAN born. Best horses trained Kamakasi, Seul Etoile.

1958   Jockey CHARLES SPARES, who rode Arctic Prince to win the 1951 Derby, died in his 41st year.

1958   Leading US jockey PATRICK JOHNSON born in Owensboro, Kentucky. Rode his first winner on January 24 1981 at Tampa Bay.

1970   After 10 flat races and 24 over hurdles, RED RUM made his chasing debut and finished 3rd under Tommy Stack in a novice chase at Newcastle.

1973   Great American equine superstar SECRETARIAT raced for the last time, winning the Canadian International Championship on turf at Woodbine, ridden by E. Maple. Secretariat won 16 of his 21 races, winning $1,316,808. Won Triple Crown in 1973.

1981   SIR RANDLE FEILDEN died aged 77. He was one of racing's greatest administrators, responsible for the introduction of starting stalls, camera patrols and regular dope-testing. As an owner his colours were light and dark blue check; light blue sleeves and cap.

1989   LADY WINNER won the Martha Washington Handicap at Laurel, ridden by Kent Desormeaux, who went on to set a record of 597 winners in a season - or did he? Lady Winner was disqualified and placed last, but in March 1990 she was reinstated by the Maryland Racing committee. Then in January - 1991, a circuit court in Baltimore upheld the original disqualification.

1989   HIGHLAND BUD won the Breeders' Cup Steeplechase by 10 lengths.

1992   The National Stud announced the purchase of a half-share in Arc winner SUAVE DANCER.

29 OCTOBER

1875   The first running of the Dewhurst Stakes took place at Newmarket. Run over 7 furlongs with £300 prize money put up by Mr Tom Gee, owner of the Dewhurst stud at Wadhurst in Sussex. Hungarian-bred KISBER was the 10–1 winner and went on to win the Derby.

1881   Hartford, Connecticut, jockey DANNY MAHER was born. He won the English Championship in 1908 (139 winners) and 1913 (115). In 1910 he was retained by Lord Rosebery for £4,000. Rode 9 Classic winners including Rock Sand (1903), Cicero (1905) and Spearmint (1906) in the Derby.

1886   FRED ARCHER rode his 2,748th and last winner when two-year-old Blanchard won at Newmarket for owner Lord Falmouth. Ten days later he was dead.

1911   Owner SIR PHILIP OPPENHEIMER born.

1923   TV racing commentator and wine merchant KEN BUTLER born.

1926   PHAR LAP, greatest of Australasian horses, foaled in New Zealand.

1927   Trainer GEORGE FAIRBAIRN born.

1961   Former Champion Amateur Jump Jockey (1981–82 and 1982–83) DERMOT BROWNE born.

1966   English jockey in France GUY LANDAU born. Partnered Lean Ar Aghaidh into 3rd place in the Grand National, and to win the Whitbread Gold Cup in 1987.

1975   STEVE SMITH ECCLES rode his first winner, Ballysilly, at Market Rasen.

1983   DESERT ORCHID won for the first time in a novice hurdle race at Ascot.

1985   LESTER PIGGOTT 'officially retired' from UK race-riding at Nottingham, taking his tally of British winners to 4,349 on Full Choke.

1988   English-bred JIMMY LORENZO, ridden by Graham McCourt, won the third running of the $250,000 Breeders' Cup Steeplechase at Fair Hill, Maryland.

1990   Trainer JIM BOLGER set a new record with 138 wins in one year in Ireland when Latin Quarter scored at Galway, breaking the previous record set by Senator Jim Parkinson in 1923.

1991   Very Dicey finished 3rd at Salisbury, the last runner of trainer RON SMYTH's career, which spanned 45 years. He was Champion Jump Jockey in 1941–42 and won the Champion Hurdle 3 times on Seneca (1941), Forestation (1942) and National Spirit (1948).

1992   SET FREE, the only brood mare of the century thus far to produce 3 Classic winners in Britain, put down at the age of 28. She spent her career at the Fonthill stud in Salisbury and produced Juliette Marny (1975 Oaks), Julio Mariner (1978 St Leger) and Scintillate (1979 Oaks).

30 OCTOBER

1845 The first recorded example of a triple dead-heat was reported from Newmarket.

1856 Three-year-old colt Fisherman landed a record-breaking 23rd win in a single season, scoring from 4 furlongs to 3 miles. Owned and trained by Tom Parr, the horse went on to win 22 races during 1857, and 21 in 1858.

1903 One of the biggest gambling coups of all time was successfully landed when HACKLER'S PRIDE won the Cambridgeshire, netting connections the equivalent of £10 million. Backed down on the day from 8-1 to 9-2, the horse had been laid out for the race all season by the 'Druids Lodge Confederacy', which operated from the Druids Lodge stable on Salisbury Plain where Jack Fallon was the trainer. Their exploits are discussed in detail in Paul Mathieu's *The Druids Lodge Confederacy*.

1944 Owner HEATHER ALWEN born. One must assume that 'Yeoman' is her lucky name, considering that her best horses have borne names like Sir Percy Yeoman, Reggae Yeoman, Yeoman Metro, Noble Yeoman, Bold Yeoman, Wily Yeoman, Charlton Yeoman (yes, she supports Charlton) and Steel Yeoman. Colours: yellow; red chevrons.

1945 Wokingham trainer CON (CORNELIUS AUGUSTUS) HORGAN born. Sent out Western Dancer (20-1) to win 1985 Ebor Handicap.

1949 Former Royal jockey BILL SMITH born. Rode Comedy of Errors to win the 1973 Champion Hurdle and Tammuz to win the 1975 Schweppes Gold Trophy for the Queen Mother. Was nearly lost to racing when he quit the game to work in Moss Bros!

1967 Jockey MICHAEL MARSHALL born. First winner April 1987.

1981 FULKE WALWYN had a field day when all six runners from his stable won - 4 of them at Kempton, 2 at Devon.

1984 A total of 77 horses were pre-entered for the 7 inaugural Breeders' Cup Championship races.

1989 Lingfield staged Britain's first all-weather meeting on their new Equitrack surface and 7-2 favourite NIKLAS ANGEL, ridden by Richard Quinn and trained by Conrad Allen, won the first race on the 12-event card - the William Hill Stakes.

31 OCTOBER

1765 Great owner the DUKE OF CUMBERLAND died. His stud included Herod, a great sire, and the famous Eclipse, then just eighteen months old. Cumberland's death at the early age of 44 was due to 'excessive corpulence' and the effects of an old war wound.

1791 CASH became the first yearling to compete on a British racecourse when he beat a three-year-old which was conceding 3st in a match at Newmarket. Five days later, now renamed Ariel, and with a new owner, the horse ran and won again on the same course. Yearling racing was banned in 1860.

1920 The jump jockey best remembered for the inexplicable collapse of the Queen Mother's Devon Loch when the 1956 Grand National was at their mercy, DICK FRANCIS OBE, born. He was Champion Jockey in 1953–54 with 76 winners. He retired in 1957 and then began writing a so far unbroken string of bestselling novels.

1943 Dual purpose Malton trainer JOHN BOTTOMLEY born.

1945 GORDON RICHARDS became the first English jockey to ride 3,000 winners.

1947 EDGAR BRITT rode his 100th winner of the season, joining Gordon Richards, brothers Eph and Doug Smith and Billy Nevett. It was the first time for 48 years that 5 riders had completed a century.

1948 Irish trainer WILLIAM ROPER born. Best horses include In the Dock, Cabinet Meeting, Elevate, Kinky Lady (mixing those names into a different order might be interesting).

1950 York-based jockey JOHN LOWE, former Cock of the North, born.

1958 Owner–rider of hunter-chaser Eliogarty CAROLINE ROBINSON born.

1982 TONY MURPHY, believed to be the brains behind the celebrated Gay Future coup, died in his home town of Cork, aged 52.

1987 American jockey CHRIS ANTLEY rode 9 winners – 4 at Aqueduct and 5 more at The Meadowlands, New Jersey.

1990 Australian jockey MALCOLM JOHNSTON was ordered to pay a damages claim plus interest of AUS$121,490, plus his own costs and those of Glenn William Frazer, an apprentice jockey who was injured in a fall during a 1989 race and sued for damages. He had suffered a broken thigh and back injuries. Johnson had to sell his house. He was found negligent in the way he handled his mount, which crossed 2 horses, forcing them into Frazer's mount.

1991 RAY COCHRANE rode 100 winners for the 5th consecutive season when Navarra (10–1) won at Newmarket.

1992 LESTER PIGGOTT broke his collarbone and two ribs, and wound up in intensive care, after falling from the fatally injured Mr Brooks in the Breeders' Cup Sprint at Gulfstream Park, Florida.

1 NOVEMBER

1947 American MAN O'WAR died at the age of 30. Odds-on in every race he ran, losing just one of 21, he won a total of $249,465.

1949 Jockey STEVE (S.A.) TAYLOR born. Partnered Nerak.

1953 Jockey DAVID DINELEY, Champion Apprentice in 1976, born.

1966 MICHAEL SCUDAMORE, father of Peter, took the fall that finished his career as a jockey, from Snakestone at Wolverhampton, breaking his jaw, the top of his palate and his cheekbone. His eyesight was also affected. Rode Linwell to win the Cheltenham Gold Cup in 1957, and Oxo to win 59 National.

1975 ALLEZ FRANCE, the great French star, finished unplaced in the last of her 21 races, on dirt at Santa Anita, USA. She won 13 races in all, including the 1974 Arc.

1977 After 99 years trainer Etienne De Mestre's record of 5 Melbourne Cup winners was beaten in the 117th running of the race when Adelaide handler BART CUMMINGS produced the previous season's runner-up, Gold and Black (7-2 favourite) to beat 23 rivals. John Duggan won in a 3,200m race record of 3 minutes 18.4 seconds.

1984 DAWN RUN won for the first time over the larger obstacles in the Nobber Chase at Navan, ridden by Tony Mullins at 4-5.

1984 PROVIDEO set a new record, landing his 16th win as a two-year-old at Redcar. The Bard also won 16 in 1855 but included a walkover. Provideo ran 3 more times as a three-year-old, without winning, and was retired to stud.

1985 DESERT ORCHID won his first chase, the Woolea Lambskin Products Novice Chase at Devon, ridden by Colin Brown at 4-5.

1986 A Breeders' Cup record crowd of 69,155 attended the 3rd running of Breeders' Cup Championship at Santa Anita Park and wagered $15,410,409 on the day's races, establishing a North American single-day on-track handle record. Census won the inaugural running of the Breeders' Cup Steeplechase at Fair Hill Race Course, Maryland, bringing his career earnings to $439,000.

1988 FLORENCE NAGLE, the first woman officially recognised as a trainer, died aged 94.

1989 Southwell staged the first day's jump racing on an artificial surface, Fibresand. ZULU (Jonothan Lower–Martin Pipe) won the first race.

1991 A double on They All Forgot Me and Salamander Joe at Stratford took Richard Dunwoody's career total of winners to 500.

1992 One of racing's few centenarians, owner SIR MICHAEL SOBELL, celebrated that landmark, still a member of the Jockey Club. His Troy won the 1979 Derby and in 1983 Sun Princess landed the Oaks–St Leger double.

2 NOVEMBER

1877   SIR AGA SULTAN MUHAM SHAH, the 3rd Aga Khan, was born in Karachi. A great breeder who, when he died on July 11 1957, had 65 broodmares in France, 90 horses in training at Chantilly and another 85 broodmares at Sheshoon stud in Ireland.

1936   Alexdream (Harry Blackshaw) gave RYAN JARVIS the first of 1,010 wins as a trainer with a victory at Birmingham.

1939   Lambourn jockey BRIAN HENRY born. Rider of Martial Law, Janeat.

1939   Jockey JOHN 'KIPPER' LYNCH born. Partnered Olwyn, Tromos.

1954   Jockey ALAN BROWN born.

1963   Jockey PATRICK FARRELL born. Won 1984 Schweppes on Ra Nova.

1985   PEBBLES (trainer Clive Brittain; jockey Pat Eddery) won her final race, the Breeders' Cup Turf, at Aqueduct, no doubt boosted by her diet supplement of a pint of Guinness a day. The prize of £775,862 took her winnings to a record £1,182,140, beating Teleprompter's previous best for a British-trained horse.

1989   Royal trainer DICK HERN, confined to a wheelchair following a hunting accident in 1984, was named Man of the Year by the Royal Association for Disability and Rehabilitation.

1990   Personal form books compiled by Phil Bull, founder of Timeform, were sold at auction for £18,000. They covered 1935 to 1989, the year in which he died, aged 79.

1991   BRADBURY STAR became the first horse to benefit from the Jockey Club rule designed to prevent matches and walkovers when he won at Warwick for Josh Gifford, who had once withdrawn him, only for the race to be reopened when only 2 declared to run from the original 23 entries.

1991   New company Sportscast began beaming live racing coverage to Britain's pubs and clubs by showing action from Wolverhampton.

1991   DANCE SMARTLY won the Breeders' Cup Distaff at Churchill Downs to pass Lady's Secret as racing's all-time leading female money-earner with $3,083,456.

1991   It just might have been the most astonishing performance anyone had ever seen on a racecourse before or since. But no one who witnessed what the unbeaten two-year-old ARAZI (21–10 favourite) did to his 13 rivals in the Breeders' Cup Juvenile over 1 mile 110 yards at Churchill Downs could ever forget the scintillating manner in which Pat Valenzuela brought the horse through to pick off rival after rival, going round one, past another, inside another, to eventually cruise home by 4 lengths.

1992   FRANKIE DETTORI and RAY COCHRANE both reached 100 winners for the season, at Newcastle.

3 NOVEMBER

1841 LOTTERY, the best chaser of the day, was asked to carry 13st 6lbs over four miles at Newport Pagnell. He still started 4–5 favourite, but was beaten into 2nd place.

1864 Three-year-old LANTERN won the 4th Melbourne Cup at 15–1 carrying 6st 3lbs on a heavy track. Next day trainer S. Mahon pulled the horse out to run again and he won the Victoria Derby by 6 lengths. Thus Lantern became the only horse ever to have won the Melbourne Cup before the Derby. Not content with this famous double, connections produced him for a 3rd consecutive race on November 5, and he won the one-mile Publicans' Purse by 3 lengths, having been left 100 yards at the start.

1982 EDDIE HIDE's 2,500th winner was Chrome Mag at Edinburgh.

1989 Racegoers at Bangor had to make do without closed circuit TV and the stewards without camera patrol film after the camera crew went to Bangor, North Wales, instead of Bangor-on-Dee.

1990 WILLIAM HASTINGS-BASS was fined for failing to allow Royal filly Chestnut Tree to run on her merits at Newmarket, the first time one of the Queen's horses had been found guilty under the non-triers' rule. The fine was £300 and apprentice Dale Gibson was fined a similar amount. The horse was 5th in the EBF Balaton Lodge Maiden Fillies' Stakes.

1990 A double with Nordic Surprise and Elementary at Down Royal gave trainer JIM BOLGER a record 121 winners in an Irish flat season.

1990 Australian DAVID HAYES, having trained for just three months, broke the world record for the number of Group or graded race winners in one day when he sent out 6 at Flemington, Melbourne: Raise a Rhythm, Wrap Around, Beachside, Planet Ruler, Better Loosen Up and Mount Olympus. They won a total of £375,000.

1991 FRANKIE DETTORI's plane dash from Churchill Downs to Saint-Cloud paid off as he rode his first French winner on John Gosden trained Susurration.

1992 For the first time ever the same trainer won 3 of Australia's top races with three different horses in one year: LEE FREEDMAN had already won the AUS$1 million Caulfield Cup with Mannerism and the AUS$1.7 million W. S. Cox Plate with Super Impose before today landing the AUS$2 million Melbourne Cup with Subzero.

1992 SUBZERO won the Melbourne Cup, but betting turnover on the race dived to AUS$1.76 million (£0.8 million) from AUS$2.6 million (£1.2 million) the previous year. However, Hong Kong punters invested a record £6.7 million on the event at Happy Valley, where they were allowed in free to watch it on a giant screen.

4 NOVEMBER

1886 FRED ARCHER was beaten in his last race, on the strongly fancied Tommy Tittlemouse at Lewes.

1908 Irish-bred JERRY M., which four years later the Grand National, landed the Becher Chase at Aintree for Bob Gore's Findon stable.

1930 Great Australasian horse PHAR LAP won the Melbourne Cup – despite an attempt to shoot him on his way back from morning exercise.

1933 GORDON RICHARDS equalled Fred Archer's record of 246 winners in a season when El Senor won at Thirsk. He waited a further five days to break the record.

1967 The Peter O'Sullevan-owned BE FRIENDLY won the Vernons Sprint Cup for the 2nd successive season at Haydock, ridden by Scobie Breasley for trainer Cyril Mitchell.

1967 As the flat season came to an end owner JIM JOEL topped the lists with 34 winners worth £120,952 and his cousin Stanhope was 2nd with 26 victories and £64,118 first-prize money. Top trainer was NOEL MURLESS with 60 victories and £256,899 prize-money, who beat Sir Gordon Richards (30 wins, £62,507 prize-money) into 2nd. LESTER PIGGOTT was top jockey with 117 wins.

1972 Trainer SAM ARMSTRONG (real name Frederick Lakin), who trained a winner at every flat course, sent out his last 2 runners. Both of them, Rag and Ismaquehs at Haydock, were winners.

1975 Think Big (33-1), ridden by Harry White, gave trainer BART CUMMINGS his 5th win in the Melbourne Cup to equal the record of Etienne de Mestre. The same combination had won the previous year at 12-1. Part-owner of the horse was Tunku Abdul Rahman, former prime minister of Malaysia.

1976 NICK GASELEE achieved his first winner as a trainer when Timerah won at Newbury, ridden by Bill Smith.

1979 Absalom, ridden by Lester Piggott, won the Premio Chiusura in Milan to give trainer RYAN JARVIS his last winner.

1981 Malza, ridden by Steve Jobar, gave JIMMY FOX his first winner as a trainer in a handicap hurdle at Wincanton.

1982 Starawak won at Redcar to bring CLIVE BRITTAIN's 1st-place career earnings as a trainer to over £1 million.

1984 The first Sunday meeting took place at Churchill Downs, USA. A crowd of 8,971 turned up and wagered $1,167,593.

1989 The 6th Breeders' Cup Championship, at Gulfstream Park, attracted a Florida record attendance of 51,342. In a thrilling Breeders' Cup Classic, SUNDAY SILENCE upset Easy Goer by a neck to earn Horse of the Year honours. The event was simulcast to 149 outlets across US and Canada.

5 NOVEMBER

1831 SQUIRE GEORGE OSBALDESTON won himself £1,000 after proving that he could ride 200 miles in less than 10 hours on circuits of the round course at the Newmarket Houghton meeting. He used 29 horses in completing the 200 miles in 8 hours 42 minutes.

1831 FRANK BUCKLE, who rode 5 Derby winners, had his final mount on Colonel Udny's Conservator, 50 years to the day that he joined Mr Vernon's stables at Newmarket.

1928 Saxon House trainer CATH WALWYN born.

1935 LESTER PIGGOTT born at Wantage.

1950 FULKE WALWYN sent out 4 winners at Stratford, all owned by DOROTHY PAGET: Albany Street, Prince of Denmark, Buck Skin and Semeur.

1955 A record 166 runners competed on a 6-race card at Windsor. The previous highest turn-out had been 157 at Leicester in 1949.

1963 MALCOLM REID, aged 81, from Adelaide owned 25-1 shot Gatum Gatum (Aboriginal for boomerang), the Melbourne Cup winner ridden by Jim Johnson and trained by Graeme Heagney.

1968 RAIN LOVER, ridden by J. Johnson, won the Melbourne Cup by 8 lengths in a record time of 3 minutes 19.1 seconds. Trained by Mick Robins, the horse returned 7-1 and beat 25 opponents, collecting AUS$51,100 for owner Clifford Reid. Robins, a novice trainer whose first runner in the race this was, became so excited during the race that he fell down the steps of the trainers' stand.

1969 The first running of the Lionel Vick Memorial Steeplechase at Newbury paid tribute to the jockey who had died in a car crash in May aged 45. He had retired after being severely disabled and paralysed following a fall at Sedgefield in 1951, and was one of the early forces behind the Injured Jockeys' Fund.

1980 NIGEL TINKLER rode his first winner, Just Jet, at Wolverhampton.

1988 A Breeders' Cup record crowd of 71,237 attended the 5th running of the Breeders' Cup Championship at Churchill Downs, Kentucky. PERSONAL ENSIGN won the Breeders' Cup Distaff by a nose and retired undefeated in 13 career starts. GREAT COMMUNICATOR won the Breeders' Cup Turf to become the first gelding to win a Breeders' Cup flat race.

1991 Trainer BART CUMMINGS landed his 9th Melbourne Cup victory when 3-1 favourite Let's Elope survived a stewards' inquiry. Even if it had gone the wrong way runner-up Shiva's Revenge, also trained by Cummings, would have provided some consolation.

1992 ROD SIMPSON sent out Walk the Beat, his final runner from Deja Vu stables at Foxhill, Wiltshire, to win at 6-1 at Edinburgh.

6 NOVEMBER

1935   Jockey Club member and owner of Carrigeen Hill, winner of 13 chases, NIGEL CLARK born. Colours: black; yellow cross-belts; star on cap.

1938   Former Champion Amateur rider (1961–62) TONY BIDDLECOMBE born.

1942   York trainer DONALD LEE born. Best horses trained include Misty Spirit.

1948   French trainer (CHRISTIANE) CRIQUETTE HEAD born. Her Three Troikas won the Arc in 1979; Ma Biche the 1,000 Guineas in 1983. Also trained Ravinella, Bering, Sicyos.

1970   RED RUM won a chase for the first time, scoring at 100–7 in the Town Moor Novice Chase at Doncaster ridden by Tommy Stack.

1990   BILL SHOEMAKER's father, 'B. B.', died aged 81.

1991   ARAZI was operated on to treat an arthritic knee in Lexington, Kentucky. The operation was reported to be a success.

1992   1969 Derby winner BLAKENEY was put down at the National Stud aged 26.

7 NOVEMBER

1861 The first running of Australia's major race, the Melbourne Cup, took place. It was won by a horse which walked 475 miles in 28 days to get to the racecourse at Flemington for the two-mile event. ARCHER, from New South Wales, was ridden by J. Cutts for trainer-owner Etienne de Mestre at 6–1. First-prize money was £710; 17 ran and 4,000 watched. Archer returned the next year, walking again – and won again, this time as 2–1 favourite.

1873 FRED ARCHER rode Sterling to win the Liverpool Autumn Cup. The owner, Thomas Roughton, rewarded him with a present of a short-barrelled gun to mark the occasion. It was the weapon with which Archer would ultimately take his own life.

1922 JANE PILKINGTON born. Stow-on-the-Wold owner-trainer of triple Golden Hurdle winner at Cheltenham Willie Wumpkins. Colours: black; white spots; cerise cap. The 1979, 1980 and 1981 victories of Willie Wumpkins were a real family affair – Mrs Pilkington's son-in-law, Jim Wilson, rode the horse.

1928 Trainer of 1970 Ascot Gold Cup winner Precipice Wood ROSEMARY LOMAX born.

1938 Trainer IAN (ANTHONY) BALDING born in New Jersey. Rode 70 winners under rules as an amateur. Younger brother of Toby. First licence 1964. Trained Mill Reef, winner of the 1971 Derby, Eclipse, King George VI and Queen Elizabeth Stakes and Arc de Triomphe.

1955 The first lady jockey to complete the course in the Grand National (on 66–1 shot Cheers, 8th and last in 1982) GERALDINE REES born.

1962 Australian jockey NEVILLE SELLWOOD, who rode Larkspur to win the 1962 Derby in which 7 horses fell, was killed when riding the inappropriately named Lucky Seven in the Prix de la Hezière at Maisons-Laffitte. The horse fell and rolled on to the jockey, who was at the time leading rider in France with 102 winners.

1981 King Hustler (John Francome) was NICKY HENDERSON's 100th winner as a trainer when scoring at Chepstow.

1989 New Zealand jockey Shane Dye, aged 23, rode Tawrrific to win the Melbourne Cup in a record 3 minutes 17.1 seconds.

1992 RICHARD DUNWOODY rode 5 winners at 1 meeting for the first time, at Chepstow.

1992 Trainer JOHN GOSDEN took the honours in the last big race of the flat season, the William Hill November Handicap, when 10–1 chance Turgenev beat 11–4 favourite and stable companion Daru.

1992 MICHAEL ROBERTS rode his final winner of his first championship season when Branston Abby won at Doncaster to bring his total to 206.

av. rides per season.   476.

" winners "   "   162

34%

8 NOVEMBER

1884 STEVE DONOGHUE, Champion Jockey from 1914 to 1923, born in Warrington. Rode 14 Classic winners. Won 4 Derbys in 5 seasons from 1921 to 1925, missing out only in 1924. Retired as a jockey in 1937 but wasn't successful as trainer. Died March 23 1945. His son Patrick won the 1926 Lincolnshire on King of Clubs.

1886 FRED ARCHER, perhaps the greatest jockey ever, took his own life at the age of 29. After a career of 17 years, during which he was Champion Jockey 13 times and rode 2,748 winners from 8,084 mounts, he left estate worth £60,000.

1910 Trainers FULKE WALWYN and his twin sister HELEN JOHNSON HOUGHTON were born at Wrexham, Denbighshire. Peter Walwyn is a first cousin. Helen married flat race trainer Gordon Johnson Houghton, whose career was cut short by his premature death but their son, Fulke Johnson Houghton, trained great horses such as Ribero and Rose Bowl. Helen was the first woman to be responsible for the training of a Classic winner when Gilles De Retz won the 1956 2,000 Guineas, but since the Jockey Club did not officially recognise women trainers until 1966 the 50-1 winner was credited to Charles Jerdein. She handed over to son Fulke in 1961 and in 1977 became one of the first 3 women elected to the Jockey Club. Fulke Walwyn trained 4 Cheltenham Gold Cup winners: Mont Tremblant (1952), Mandarin (1962), Mill House (1963) and The Dikler (1973). His Team Spirit won the 1964 Grand National. Anzio (1962) and Kirriemuir (1965) won the Champion Hurdle for him.

1933 GORDON RICHARDS broke Fred Archer's record of 246 winners in a season when he rode Golden King at Liverpool, his 247th in a season which netted him 259 winners. In 1947 he rode 269.

1955 Jockey ROGER WERNHAM born. Rode Peter O'Sullevan's Attivo.

1981 Former jump jockey TIM BROOKSHAW died, aged 52, from injuries sustained in a fall a week earlier. He was Champion Jockey in 1958-59 with 83 winners.

1986 JAYNE THOMPSON, 21, fell at the first in a novice hurdle race at Catterick and died six days later from her injuries. She was the first female jockey killed on a British track.

1989 No starting price was returned for a 14-runner handicap at Southwell during the first all-weather meeting at the track. Starting price reporters said that only one bookmaker was displaying a full list of odds and no market was ever formed. Admiralty Way (paid £9.80 on the Tote) won the one-mile artificial surface Starling Handicap. Crystal Pool was the winner of the 1st race at 13-2.

1991 Corn Lily was PETER NIVEN's 300th winner, at Market Rasen.

9 NOVEMBER

1883 HARRY BEASLEY rode Too Good to win the City Cup at Liverpool. Eight years later Beasley won the Grand National on Come Away and, incredibly, in 1935 at the age of 85 he became the oldest man to win a race when winning the Corinthian Plate at Baldoyle.

1916 Jockey DANNY MAHER, winner of 9 Classics, died aged 35 in the US having squandered much of his money in an ill-advised investment in a New York hotel. Born in Connecticut, USA, he was Champion Jockey in England in 1908, 1913 and champion in the US in 1898.

1928 Dual Derby winning trainer (Spearmint, Spion Kop), PETER (VALENTINE PURCELL) GILPIN died in his 70th year. Also trained the great Pretty Polly, winner of the 1,000 Guineas, Oaks and St Leger.

1942 MATT CURRAN, rider of Vulpine and Dim Wit, born.

1963 Manchester racecourse held its final meeting.

1985 JOE MERCER rode Bold Rex to a 20–1 victory in the William Hill November Handicap at Doncaster, his last mount before retiring.

1986 Jockey FRANKIE DETTORI broke his duck by riding a winner at Turin.

1989 RICHARD DUNWOODY partnered Desert Orchid for the first time. Together they won a 2-horse race against Roll a Joint at Wincanton.

1991 ANOTHER CORAL won the Mackeson Gold Cup. Trainer David Nicholson put the victory down to his request to the jazz band entertaining racegoers between races to stop playing as his horse went down to the post – the chaser loathed music.

1991 GERALDINE REES, the first woman to complete the Grand National, rode her first winner on the flat when I Perceive, trained by Francis Lee, was a 20–1 winner at Doncaster.

1991 New trainer CHARLIE EGERTON had a winner with his first runner when Torrent Bay won a chase at Windsor.

1992 It is doubtful who celebrated MICHAEL ROBERTS' first flat jockey championship the most excitedly: the South African rider, who had clocked up 206 victories, or the agent who booked his rides, Graham Rock, who had helped himself to a now legendary £100 pre-season bet with William Hill at odds of 100–1 about Roberts' title chances. Richard Hannon's 147 winners for £1,780,014 prize-money saw him top of the lists, with Lady Champion Jockey honours going to LYDIA PEARCE, with 12 victories.

10 NOVEMBER

1868 Owner and gambler the MARQUIS OF HASTINGS died, aged 26. He had lost an estimated £102,000 betting against Hermit in the 1867 Derby, and just before he died he said, 'Hermit's Derby broke my heart. But I didn't show it, did I?'

1926 Jockey turned trainer FRANK DURR born. The Liverpudlian rode his first winner in 1944 at Pontefract. His Classic winners were Mon Fils (1973) and Roland Gardens (1978) in the 2,000 Guineas and Sodium (1966) and Peleid (1973) in the St Leger. Best horses as a trainer (first licence 1979) were Ahonoora, Another Realm, Noalto.

1930 Twice Champion Amateur rider – 1955–56 (joint) and 1956–57 – BOB MCCREERY born. First winner 1949. Won 1953 Welsh Grand National on Stalbridge Rock.

1935 Controversial racing writer JAMES UNDERWOOD born.

1940 Jockey PETER JONES born. Partnered Fortina's Palace.

1947 GORDON RICHARDS rode Twenty Twenty at Leicester to break his own record of 259 wins in a season. He ended up with 269.

1948 Owner ROBERT WALEY-COHEN born. Best horses include Rustle, The Dragon Master. Colours: brown; orange sleeves; quartered cap.

1984 The inaugural Breeders' Cup Championship was run before 64,254 at Hollywood Park, California. Chief's Crown won the first Breeders' Cup Championship race; the Breeders' Cup Juvenile and long shot WILD AGAIN won the Breeders' Cup Classic in a thrilling stretch duel with Slew O'Gold and Gate Dancer. It was not long before the first disqualification in a Breeders' Cup race took place, when Fran's Valentine, a 74.8-1 outsider, finished 1st in the 2nd event, the Breeders' Cup Juvenile Fillies, only to be disqualified for interference. The race was handed to 2nd-placed OUTSTAND-INGLY, ridden by W. Guerra. EILIO, the winner of the 3rd race, the Breeders' Cup Sprint, was retired after his victory to go to stud but he died four weeks later following surgery for colic.

1986 SIR GORDON RICHARDS died, aged 82, having won 4.870 races from 21,837 rides. Knighted in 1953 for services to racing. Champion Jockey an incredible 26 times. He rode 14 Classic winners but won the Derby only once, on Pinza in 1953.

1992 BARBARA HOLLAND of Corals was voted the first female *Racing Post* Betting Shop Manager of the Year.

11 NOVEMBER

1874   The last meeting was held at the Thameside course at Reading. The last race went to FLASH, trained by his owner Tom Stevens at Chilton on the nearby Berkshire Downs.

1904   The great chaser MANIFESTO ran his last race at the age of sixteen. Winner of 2 Grand Nationals and placed in 4 more, he was unplaced at Liverpool in the Valentine Chase.

1911   Trainer JACK WAUGH born. His Matador won the 1956 Stewards' Cup under a then record weight for a three-year-old of 9st 2lbs, while Sanlinea was 3rd in the 1950 St Leger. He was something of a Royal Ascot specialist: French Fern won the 1960 Ribblesdale Stakes, Light Harvest the 1956 Wokingham and Amerigo the 1957 Coventry Stakes. Also trained Oncidium. Retired in 1970.

1953   DAVID DINELEY, Champion Apprentice in 1976, born.

1955   PAPPA FOURWAY, one of the best post-war sprinters, won the 8th race of his three-year-old career – appropriately enough Manchester's The Tetrarch Stakes, named after probably the fastest horse ever to race in Britain. Pappa Fourway, trained by William Dutton, had cost just 150 guineas.

1958   Arc de Triomphe winner and record English and Irish prize-money winner BALLYMOSS ran his final race in the Washington DC International at Laurel Park, USA. In an eventful race Ballymoss was baulked and jostled but managed to finish 3rd. That brought his career earnings to £107,166, overhauling Ribot's European record of £106,515.

1959   Jump jockey turned trainer RICHARD ROWE born. First winner 1978. Best horses ridden include Kybo, Royal Judgement.

1968   All 5 of trainer KEN OLIVER's runners won at Wolverhampton – all ridden by Barry Brogan.

1975   Seven horses started as 8–1 co-favourites for the Blackburn Nursery at Haydock in a field of 22. The winner was the Richard Fox-ridden HARGRAVE ROGUE, one of those 8–1 shots, trained by D. Thom.

1989   GREVILLE STARKEY rode for the last time in his active career in Britain, on Osric, unplaced in the William Hill November Handicap at Thirsk, which was won by Firelight Fiesta. Starkey rode 1,989 British flat winners plus 3 over the sticks, and rode London Gazette in the 1964 Champion Hurdle.

1991   The flat season ended with Pat Eddery Champion for the 9th time, with 165 winners.

12 NOVEMBER

1878 A riot took place at Shrewsbury race meeting. First, welshing bookies were attacked by aggrieved punters, then an organised mob from Birmingham rushed the paddock, evidently determined to murder the course security man – an ex-Sergeant Ham – and to rob wealthy leading bookies. Ham was knocked unconscious, but a group of racing patrons saved the day by fighting off the invaders.

1886 Newmarket closed down for the day to pay tribute to the great FRED ARCHER, whose funeral was taking place. It was a cold, wet day and the shops put up their shutters and blinds. A tribute was written by poet Edgar Lee: 'Farewell, best jockey ever seen on course/Thy backers weep to think by Fate's decree/The rider pale upon his great white horse/Hath beaten thee.'

1931 Jockey CLIFF PARKES born. First winner 1952. Best horses ridden include Dawn Watch, Welsh Border, Violetta.

1935 Stratford trainer JAMES WEST born.

1948 Lead vocalist of pop group Hot Chocolate and owner of Grand National runner Gainsay ERROL BROWN born.

1948 MISS GRILLO, aged six and carrying 118lbs, set a world-record time of 4 minutes 14.6 seconds for two and a half miles at Pimlico, USA.

1959 A record 171 runners turned out for a 6-race card at Manchester.

1988 The PRINCESS ROYAL fell at the first when riding Canon Class at Windsor in a handicap chase.

1988 Rats chewed through a mains cable and scuppered the entire Tote system at Huntingdon.

1991 STEVE SMITH ECCLES became the 9th post-war jockey to ride 800 winners when Norman Conqueror won at Wolverhampton. The others? Peter Scudamore, John Francome, Ron Barry, Stan Mellor, Jonjo O'Neill, Bob Davies, Terry Biddlecombe and Fred Winter.

13 NOVEMBER

1889   The Foston Selling Plate at Derby was declared void after the whole field got lost in the thick fog covering the course and ended up running round the back of a cricket pavilion. Two of the runners crashed into a set of hoardings.

1897   TOD SLOAN rode Phenomenon to win the Carandini Starting Machine Plate, for which the field was sent off using the contraption of that name. The rest of the races on the Liverpool card were started by the traditional flag. Not until 1965 did stalls come into common use in Britain.

1938   The trainer of 1967's shock 100–1 Grand National winner Foinavon, JOHN KEMPTON, born. Kempton was so sure that Foinavon had no chance that he was at Worcester with another of his horses, which also won.

1941   Former Champion Amateur Jockey COLIN PLATTS born.

1943   Sedgefield trainer JOHN WADE born.

1945   Trainer JACK PAYNE died, aged 57.

1958   Jockey STUART SHILSTON born. Best horses ridden include Crimson Embers.

1990   Irish trainer PHILIP MCCARTAN killed in a road accident, aged 33.

1992   PETER NIVEN rode a 5-timer at Ayr, 4 of his winning mounts trained by Mary Reveley.

14 NOVEMBER

1917   Shrewsbury trainer TOM CORRIE born. He trained Boonah and Comedy of Errors, which won 4 times on the flat for him.

1927   Top Aussie trainer BART CUMMINGS (full name James Bartholomew) born, in Gleneig, South Australia.

1948   Owner and amateur rider PRINCE CHARLES born. Colours: scarlet; royal blue sleeves; black cap.

1960   Chepstow jockey GRANVILLE DAVIES born. Partnered Grey Dolphin to win 10 races in a season.

1964   Jockey LORCAN WYER born. First winner was Champion Prince at Navan in 1984. Best horses partnered include Nohalmdun.

1973   Captain Mark Phillips wed Princess Anne – and bookmakers were almost cleaned out by coincidence backers as Windsor's Royal Wedding Handicap Chase was won by ROYAL MARK.

1978   PETER SCUDAMORE rode Majestic Touch for John Yardley at Ludlow to score his first win over fences.

1984   OLIVER SHERWOOD saddled his first winner, The Breener, at Newbury.

1987   A 'pick six' pool of $1,190,876 had built up at Churchill Downs, and 28,396 turned up at the track in an effort to win it. Three lucky winners eventually pocketed $396,958.60 each.

1989   The third all-weather race meeting in Britain was abandoned – because of the weather! Fog made it impossible to race at Southwell.

1989   JAMES LAMING, who claimed to have invented an ultrasonic 'stun-gun' which could 'stop' horses (including the Greville Starkey-ridden Ile De Chypre), was found guilty of a drug plot.

1992   CARL LLEWELLYN rode Tipping Tim to win the Mackeson Gold Cup for trainer Nigel Twiston-Davies.

1992   Three men died and 12 were critically injured after a terrorist attack on James Murray's starting-price betting office in Old Park Road, Belfast.

15 NOVEMBER

1873 Literally a 'run for gold' took place at Ocean View Park, San Francisco, when a race of four-mile heats was run for a prize of $20,000 in pure gold, a prize which created a huge stir with the financial panic going on at the time. Four top horses contested the event and up to 15,000 people turned up to watch, gambling $100,000 on the outcome. The popular California-based champion THAD STEVENS came out on top.

1883 PERDITA II, which would produce Derby winners Persimmon and Diamond Jubilee for the Prince of Wales, won the Chesterfield Nursery at Derby.

1911 Racing writer BILL CURLING, once Hotspur of the *Daily Telegraph*, born.

1915 Jump jockey DICK BLACK born. Won the 1947 Cheltenham Gold Cup on Fortina while still an amateur.

1940 Jockey MARCEL DEPALMAS born. Partnered Soltikoff, Blabla.

1945 Former Champion Jump Jockey (1976-77 and 1974-75) turned trainer TOMMY STACK born. Rode Red Rum to win the 1977 Grand National. Training base, Thomastown Castle, in Ireland.

1945 Trainer (RALPH) BILL STUBBS born. Best horses include Pit Stop, Bay Hero, Carriageway. Moved to Sweden.

1946 Trainer PETER DAVIS born. Best horses include Princess Hecate, Black River.

1984 Leading US jockey PAT DAY rode 6 winners from 7 mounts at Churchill Downs. Hot Derby (10.2-1), Upper Action (7.2-1), Requa (4.2-1), Seldon Still (4.8-1), Native Delight (3.6-1) and Lanny (6.6-1). His other mount, 7-1 chance Flying Trophy, finished 3rd.

1988 Hurdler Cometti Star made history by becoming the first horse to be entered for a race under the new 5-day entry system.

1989 PETER SCUDAMORE equalled John Francome's record of 1,138 winners on Regal Ambition at Worcester.

1990 LESTER PIGGOTT rode a comeback winner at the Ippodromo, Livorno, Italy. Ghilly Du was the winner, and the crowd was 3 times up on normal.

1990 ALYDAR, runner-up to Affirmed in the 1978 US Triple Crown, was destroyed after fracturing a hind leg in a stable accident which left Lloyds of London facing a $50 million payout.

1992 The first-ever Sunday jump meeting took place at Cheltenham, where the 1st race, The Racegoers Remittance Man Amateur Riders' Chase, run over three miles 1 furlong, was won by SIBTON ABBEY, ridden by Mr Paul Murphy and trained by F. Murphy. The attendance was approximately 15,000.

16 NOVEMBER

1940 Trainer of Hard Outlook ANDREW WATES born. First licence 1968. Former president of the Racehorse Owners Association.

1941 Former amateur rider turned publisher SIR RUPERT MACKESON born.

1942 Bognor Regis trainer RONALD O'SULLEVAN born.

1942 WILLIAM FISHER HUNTER CARSON OBE born. Champion jockey 5 times: 1972, 1973, 1978, 1980 and 1983. Won the Derby on Nashwan (1989), Henbit (1980) and Troy (1979).

1946 HARRY WRAGG celebrated his final day as a jockey by riding a treble on Tiffin Bell (7–4), Aprolon (7–4) and Las Vegas (20–1) in the Manchester November Handicap. He rode 1,762 winners from 11,658 British races.

1947 Director of the Société d'Encouragement, and less than enthusiastic advocate of British bookmakers, LOUIS ROMANET born.

1948 US jockey MIKE McDOWELL born in Jeffersontown, Kentucky. Rode first winner at Hawthorne in 1965. Height 4ft 9ins.

1957 MANDARIN won the first Hennessy Gold Cup, run at Cheltenham, with Gold Cup winner Linwell behind him. The race moved to Newbury in 1960.

1982 Jockey CARROLL GRAY must have reflected that the fates were against him. Having failed to ride a winner since New Year's Day the previous year, and having broken a leg in consecutive seasons, he took a fall from Sue Lark at Haldon and punctured a lung.

1989 A sad 'first' when filly Batu Pahat, trained by Bill Turner, had to be put down after hitting a hurdle at the 3rd last in the opening race at Lingfield's first-ever all-weather hurdles meeting.

1990 Probably the greatest modern thoroughbred, NORTHERN DANCER, was put down at the Northern Stallion Station, Maryland, USA, at 6.20am, aged 29. The 1964 Kentucky Derby winner had sired the winners of 99 European pattern winners from 605 foals. Three of his sons won the Derby: Nijinsky (1970), The Minstrel (1977) and Secreto (1984). His son El Gran Senor finished 2nd in the 1984 race.

1991 JENNY PITMAN saddled 8 runners for the Grunwick Decade Celebration National Hunt Flat Race at Warwick – a third of the 24-strong turn-out. However, the best she could manage was 2nd place with Mailcom, runner-up behind the David Nicholson-trained Carobee.

1992 Jockey MICHAEL BOWLBY announced his retirement to concentrate on his horse-bedding business. He rode his first winner, Emperor Napoleon, at the age of 28 in 1983 at Bangor. Won the 1989 Whitbread Gold Cup on Brown Windsor.

17 NOVEMBER

1950 Amateur jockey WILLIE DIXON born.

1956 Jockey BILLIE NEVETT rode his final winner, Setting Star, at Manchester. Four times runner-up to Champion Jockey Gordon Richards, he had 3 Derby winners to his credit: Owen Tudor (1941), Ocean Swell (1944) and Dante (1945).

1959 Former Champion point-to-point rider JOHN BRYAN born.

1964 Former Champion Lady point-to-pointer LUCY CROW born.

1965 Jump jockey TONY QUINN born. Rode his first winner on Measure Up, at Sedgefield in 1985. Best horses ridden include Battlefield Band.

1990 LESTER PIGGOTT rode a comeback winner in France: Bashful Boy, at Parc Borely, Marseilles.

1990 Stallion NORTHERN DANCER was buried at his birthplace, Windfields Farm in Canada, close to the barn he occupied at the start of his career.

1990 CHRISTY ROCHE equalled Michael Kinane's record of two years' previously when he rode Topanoora to victory at Leopardstown, his 113th winner of the season.

1991 William Hill advertised odds of 33-1 about MOUNAMARA winning the next year's Champion Hurdle. They were surprised that no one was interested in taking the odds, until someone pointed out that sadly the horse had died several months earlier!

18 NOVEMBER

1914   Trainer KEN CUNDELL born. Best horses trained included Stalbridge Colonist, which won 4 hurdles races and 13 chases, including the 1966 Hennessy Gold Cup, in which he became one of the few horses to lower Arkle's colours. First licence 1947. Also trained Zucchero, March Past and Tancred. Dual purpose stable. Retired at the end of the 1974 season, handing over to son Peter.

1914   Trainer BOB TURNELL, father of twins Andy and Robert, born. Trained Pas Seul to win the 1960 Cheltenham Gold Cup and Salmon Spray, 1966 Champion Hurdler. Also trained Bird's Nest, The Laird, Rondetto, April Seventh.

1915   Trainer RON SMYTH born. As a jockey he was Jump Champion in 1941–42 and won 3 Champion Hurdles. He began training in 1947. From his Clear Height stable at Epsom he sent out 33–1 chance Patient Constable to win the Stewards Cup in 1966 and Flash Imp to win the 1975 Great Metropolitan. Other good horses trained include Boxer, Blarney Beacon, Tremblant.

1930   Jockey TOMMY CARTER born. Partnered My Beau, Songedor.

1936   Lincolnshire trainer BASIL RICHMOND born.

1943   Jockey DAVID SUNDERLAND born. Partner of Lictor.

1967   Then an apprentice, TONY MURRAY rode his first Irish winner, Marcia's Mark, trained by Paddy Norris, at Leopardstown.

1975   William Hill announced that they were to take over York's Nunthorpe Stakes, a 5-furlong sprint, and rename it the William Hill Sprint Championship. SHARPO won the race 3 times, in 1980, 1981 and 1982.

1981   The winners board looked rather repetitive when ROY DAVIES won at Worcester on Milliondollarman, then HYWEL DAVIES on Rogairio – then GRANVILLE DAVIES on Santoss.

1982   JOHN FRANCOME completed the fastest 50 of a jump season when he landed a treble at Kempton, beating Jonjo O'Neill's record, set on December 5 1978.

1988   Listed as dead in the official scratchings published two days earlier, We're in the Money ran at Ascot in a Novice Hurdle. On the same day English River, who was listed in the form book as having died after falling in a previous race, ran at Nottingham. A case of two dead certs?

1989   PETER SCUDAMORE set a new record for the number of winners ridden by a jump jockey when Arden won at Ascot to give him his 1,139th success. Scu passed the record total of John Francome.

1992   Barnstaple trainer JOHN HILL celebrated his first treble as Tendresse, Golden Klair and Klairover won at Southwell for a 377–1 hat-trick.

19 NOVEMBER

1913   Trainer RYAN JARVIS born. Won the 1952 Stewards Cup with Smokey Eyes, and the 1968 Irish 1,000 Guineas with Front Row. Also trained Absalom, Dred Scott.

1918   Trainer AURIOL SINCLAIR born. Best horses trained include Magic Boy, Wilhelmina Henrietta, Simian, Avec Moi, Magic Boy.

1939   English trainer in Canada ROGER ATTFIELD born.

1955   Trainer JOHN SHEARMAN born. Best horses included Hunter's Delight, Daring Glen.

1956   Jump jockey TED WAITE born. First winner 1976. Best horses include Shock Result.

1965   Ascot staged its first sponsored race, the Kirk and Kirk Handicap Chase, won by RUPUNUNI, ridden by H. Beasley.

1973   Owner Mrs Mirabel Topham sold Aintree racecourse to property developer Bill Davies for £3 million.

1979   WAYWARD LAD, which by the time he retired had won more prize-money than any jumper except Desert Orchid, won on his racecourse debut, landing the Stoughton Novice Hurdle at Leicester.

1982   Only 362 spectators – the lowest on record – turned up in awful weather at a meeting at Ayr.

1991   Stewards at Newmarket racecourse in South Africa were alerted to an unusual race-rigging attempt when the turf was deliberately cut short along the complete length of the outside rail, evidently to enhance the chances of RINGELMAN, the odds-on favourite for the valuable sprint race taking place there. The stalls were moved and Ringelman was beaten into 2nd place.

1992   It was announced that SHEIKH MOHAMMED had bought Allen Paulson's half-share in Arazi, who had been retired to stand at Dalham Hall for £20,000.

20 NOVEMBER

1899 Northampton boot manufacturer's son HERBERT RANDALL, then an amateur, defeated crack American jockey Lester Reiff in the Stonelight Plate at Warwick. Randall rode an unnamed gelding by The Weaver and was sufficiently encouraged by his success to turn professional shortly afterwards. He went on to enjoy Classic success on Sceptre, winning the 2,000 Guineas, 1,000 Guineas and Oaks on her. Born in 1877 he retired at the outbreak of the First World War.

1947 Leopardstown racecourse manager TONY CORCORAN born.

1948 Racing writer and former SIS presenter IAN CARNABY born.

1954 Bloodstock agent TEDDY BECKETT born.

1962 Jump jockey SIMON COWLEY born. Something of an intellectual, he has a BA from Oxford and held the position of president of the Oxford University Turf Society. Has also been known to ride the odd horse, including Mole Board.

1990 ALIYSA was disqualified from first place in the 1989 Oaks. Trainer Michael Stoute was fined £200 and ordered to pay the costs of the legal and scientific advisers retained by the disciplinary committee. Snow Bride, the runner-up, was awarded the race. The affair centred around the Aga Khan's filly having a prohibited substance, hydroxy-camphor, in her system. The Aga Khan, though, refused to accept the verdict and launched a series of thus far unsuccessful counter-actions.

1991 Australian jockey GARY MURPHY rode Mercator to win the Ballarat Cup at a course near Melbourne. He was so pleased that he announced he would buy the entire crowd of 13,000 a beer! He probably meant one between them. Chaotic scenes ensued in the bars.

1991 ARAZI won the inaugural Horse of the Year commendation in the Cartier Awards.

1992 The BBC announced it was scrapping the racing-based series *Trainer*.

21 NOVEMBER

1936   Chester-le-Street trainer PETER LIDDLE born.

1938   Jockey BRIAN JAGO born.

1943   Jockey ROBERT ALNER born.

1949   CORONACH, winner of the 1926 Derby and St Leger, died in New Zealand, aged 26. Won £48,225 in stakes.

1950   Seven-year-old gelding BISTOR went mad after winning a hurdles race at Fontwell and savaged trainer Bill Marshall.

1978   Lucky backers who backed GOLD AND RUBIES at Churchill Downs could afford to buy gems of their own – it returned a record for the track of $246.80 for $1.

1979   Sea Lane gave the unknown PETER SCUDAMORE his first winner as a professional at Worcester.

1987   A Breeders' Cup Championship crowd of 57,734 watched as FERDINAND defeated Alysheba by a nose after a thrilling duel in the 4th Breeders' Cup Classic at Hollywood Park. The colt's performance earned him Horse of the Year honours. Total 1987 Breeders' Cup wagering of $36,014,720 set an all-time North American single-day betting mark.

1988   The *Sporting Life* was banned in Dubai after it carried an article about the Arab influence on British racing.

1988   Jump jockeys were allowed a 1lb weight allowance to compensate them for having to wear body protectors.

1988   Former jockey and trainer DEREK LESLIE died aged 59. Won 173 races as a jump jockey between 1949 and 1961 and trained from 1967. Best horses trained include Easter Island, Lilac Star.

1990   EQUINOCTIAL (A. Heywood), trained by N. Miller, won the 10-runner Grant's Whisky Novice Handicap Hurdle at Kelso, returning a British record winning starting price of 250-1. A punter at a William Hill branch in Chester-le-Street placed a £10 each-way bet on the horse and on-course bookie Alex Farquhar (known as Macbet) laid a £1 each-way bet at 300-1.

1990   The Bank of Ireland, which had announced a three-year deal to sponsor the Champion Hurdle from 1991, increasing the value of the race to £120,000, pulled out of the deal.

1991   A plan to turn Wolverhampton into Britain's first floodlit racecourse by January 1993 was announced. It didn't make it.

1991   Trainer MICHAEL OLIVER, whose West Tip won the Grand National, handed in his licence.

1992   Aintree held its first jump meeting (apart from the National meeting) for twenty years. A crowd of 11,301 saw KILDIMO win the Crowther Homes Becher Chase.

22 NOVEMBER

1910 American owner of 1990 Grand National winner Mr Frisk LOIS DUFFEY born. Colours: red and green quarters; yellow sleeves; red cap.

1922 Owner CHRIS BARBER-LOMAX born. His Pee Mai won 13 races, Panglima 6 and Pandu 5. Colours: dark green; orange disc and cap.

1928 Breeders' Cup mastermind JOHN GAINES born.

1930 FREDDIE FOX and Gordon Richards went into the final day of the flat sea on level pegging. Richards won the November Handicap on Glorious Devon to go ahead but Fox took the title by winning the 4th and 5th races.

1938 Owner ANTHONY PILLER born. His Mummy's Pleasure and Mummy's Treasure both won 6 races. Colours: gold; green sleeves; gold armlets; green cap with gold stripe and peak.

1947 GORDON RICHARDS rode his 269th winner of the season, Campanelle, at Lingfield, a record which has yet to be broken.

1949 Newark trainer ROBERT HARTOP born. Best horses trained include Golden Vow, Pax, Celtic Cracker. Specialises in homeopathic treatment of horses.

1950 North Yorkshire trainer MICHAEL ELLERBY born. First licence 1982. Best horses trained include Cape Farewell, Cottage Leas, Travel Home.

1956 Irish trainer NEIL MCGRATH born. Best horses trained include Stepaside Lord, Soluce, Fiery Celt, Photo Copy, Molly. Once listed his favourite recreation as 'sleeping', but as he also scuba-dives it would be advisable not to combine them.

1958 Trainer of Lingfield specialist Rapporteur CHARLES (CLARE) ELSEY born. His father Charles won the Oaks and St Leger with Pia (1967) and Peleid (1973).

1966 MERRYMAN II, winner of the 1960 Grand National, collapsed and died at the age of fifteen while hunting.

1990 Irish trainer DENIS CULLEN, 46, died in Dublin after suffering a brain haemorrhage earlier in the week.

1990 US jockey PAT DAY rode Screen Prospect to win the Falls City Stakes at Churchill Downs – the 5,000th win of his career. To commemorate the achievement, the track donated $5,000 to a local hospital and children's hospital fund.

23 NOVEMBER

1951   The Fulke Walwyn-trained MONT TREMBLANT was beaten 6 lengths by Rose Park in a novice chase at Sandown, only to come out and win the Cheltenham Gold Cup later that season.

1967   Newmarket jockey RON HILLIS born. First winner 1983. Best horses ridden include Roubayd.

1973   FULKE WALWYN sent out his first winner for the Queen Mother, Game Spirit, at Newbury.

1989   Racing at Haydock was put back by 55 minutes because one of the two ambulance crews required by Jockey Club regulations refused to work during a national ambulance dispute. Another eventually arrived.

1989   Jockey BRIAN ROUSE revealed his secret weapon to combat the 'kickback' effect of all-weather tracks – a stocking over his face.

1990   RICHARD DUNWOODY completed the fastest 50 of his career on Another Coral at Newbury.

1991   The winner of the 1975 Cheltenham Gold Cup, TEN UP, was put down aged 24.

1992   Jockey RICHARD GUEST broke his left leg in a fall at Wolverhampton.

24 NOVEMBER

1875   HANNAH, winner of the 1871 Triple Crown of 1,000 Guineas, Oaks and St Leger, died after having slipped twins.

1906   Trainer of Citation JIMMY JONES born.

1950   The QUEEN MOTHER celebrated the first win of a horse running in her own name when Manicou (trained by Peter Cazalet, ridden by Tony Grantham) won over fences at Kempton in the Wimbledon Handicap Chase at 5-4.

1955   Owner of Rely on Guy and dabbler in cricket IAN BOTHAM born.

1971   Puerto Rican-born New York jockey JOHN VELAZQUEZ born.

1972   MICHAEL EDDERY, brother of Pat, suffered an accident while riding Grimsby Town in a hurdle race at Newcastle. Tragically, his leg had to be amputated.

1989   Top US lady jockey JULIE KRONE fractured her left arm in a fall at Meadowlands.

1989   The *Racing Post* revealed that the Queen Mother's favourite chaser, SPECIAL CARGO, supposedly a gelding, was thought to have got a mare pregnant. He had been turned out with the mare, On the Hill, and several other geldings. The speculation was that Special Cargo was actually a 'rig' - a horse in which one of the testicles has not descended.

1990   JULIE KRONE became the first female rider to win in Japan.

1990   Five runners set off in the Steel Plate and Sections Novice Chase at Newcastle, but they all came to grief on the way round. TROPENNA (Tim Reed) was finally remounted to win for trainer John Goulding.

1991   PAT DAY set a new North American record for Stakes victories in a single season when he took his total to 58 on Blacksburg in the Hawthorne Juvenile. He thus exceeded the record set by Jorge Velasquez in 1986 and equalled in 1990 by Craig Perret.

1991   American raider GOLDEN PHEASANT, ridden by Gary Stevens, won the Japan Cup from French-trained Magic Night.

1992   Racing in Hong Kong was suspended as a result of a virus epidemic.

25 NOVEMBER

1907 Owner RAYMOND GUEST OBE born. His Sir Ivor won the 1968 Derby while L'Escargot won two Cheltenham Gold Cups and the Grand National. He is the only owner to complete that treble. Also won Derby with Larkspur. One-time US Ambassador to the Republic of Ireland. Colours: chocolate; pale blue hoops and cap. Died December 1991.

1916 Tipster ALF RUBIN, Cayton of the *Morning Star*, born.

1926 Owner DONALD FAIRBAIRN born. His Stock Hill Lass won 3 races at Kempton, winning a £50,000 bonus in the process. Also owned Stock Hill Lad. Colours: emerald green and royal blue check; green sleeves; green cap with blue star.

1926 Taking advantage of the absence of Gordon Richards, out since May with tuberculosis, TOMMY WESTON rode his final and 95th winner of the season (Lord Derby's Schiavoni at Manchester) to clinch the jockeys' title.

1941 Cirencester trainer MICHAEL HENRIQUES born.

1945 Jockey JOHN BRADBURNE born. Partnered General Chandos.

1967 Racing suffered a total shutdown as a result of an outbreak of foot-and-mouth disease, and only resumed on January 5 at Sandown. The last winner before the closedown was Pony Express, 9–1 winner of Newbury's 3.35, the Speen Novice Hurdle, ridden by G. Robinson, trained by Fulke Walwyn.

1988 CASH ASMUSSEN became the first jockey to ride 200 winners in a season in France when he won on Forest Angel at Maisons-Laffitte.

1990 The Japan Cup at Fuchu was run in front of a reported crowd of 164,328 – a record paying attendance which gambled 22,508 million yen (£90 million) on the Cup alone. The race was won by Better Loosen Up, from Australia.

1991 DAVID HAYES completed the fastest-ever century of winners by an Australian trainer (and quite possibly the fastest achieved anywhere) when he landed a treble at Sandown, Australia. The first of the 3, What a Budget, completed the ton. The Aussie season had begun on August 1.

1992 DESERT ORCHID's life was at risk following an emergency operation for a twisted gut. He survived.

26 NOVEMBER

1880 An extraordinary sequence of 9 races in 2 months – of which she finished 1st in 8 – came to an end for 5-1 1878 Irish Derby winner MADAME DUBARRY when she won the Manchester November Handicap at odds of 12-1. Two days earlier she had won the November Cup, also at Manchester. On November 5 she had won over two miles at Lincoln, but was unplaced there the day before. On October 13 she won at Newmarket, following an earlier victory (later disqualified) at Perth over 9 furlongs on October 1. Prior to that she had won over one and a quarter miles at Perth on September 30 and at Ayr on September 28, and over one and a half miles at Manchester on September 25, when the sequence had begun. Owned by north of England man Charles Perkins.

1908 American owner of Buckpasser, Boucher and Easy Goer OGDEN PHIPPS born. Colours: black; red and white striped cap.

1943 Preston trainer ERIC ALSTON born. Best horse trained Stack Rock.

1949 MARTIN MOLONY rode 5 winners at Navan's jump meeting.

1951 Jockey BOB MANN born. Best horses ridden include Flash Imp.

1966 STALBRIDGE COLONIST upset the odds on hot favourite Arkle in the Hennessy Gold Cup at Newbury.

1988 Jump jockey CHRIS WARREN, aged 25, returned from a 5-week lay-off with a broken collarbone to partner Allied Force at Newbury in a novice hurdle. The horse fell at the first. Warren was thrown off – and broke his collarbone.

1989 The first Sunday meeting in New Zealand took place at Tauherenikau.

1989 New Zealand mare HORLICKS, a six-year-old, set a new world record of 2 minutes 22.2 seconds in winning the Japan Cup in Tokyo.

1989 HUGO DITTFACH, 53-year-old German-born jockey and a top rider in Canada for 33 years, rode his 4,000th winner, at Greenwood Park, Toronto, and promptly retired.

1991 DESERT ORCHID was beaten at Huntingdon by Sabin Du Loir.

27 NOVEMBER

1865   Trainer RICHARD DAWSON was born in Ireland. He went on to send out 8 Classic winners from Whitcombe and Newmarket in England, including Derby winners Fifinella (1916), Trigo (1929) and Blenheim (1930), while he also handled the blindingly fast filly Mumtaz Mahal. Was 3 times leading flat trainer – in 1916, 1924 and 1929 – and in the last year won 58 races worth £74,754. A humourless man, he sported a drooping moustache and a pince-nez.

1897   American rider TOD SLOAN, who popularised the 'monkey up a stick' style of riding in Britain, rode 4 winners at Manchester on the final day of the season. He rode 254 winners from 801 mounts in England, but was eventually deprived of his licence for disregarding the rule forbidding jockeys to bet. He died in the charity ward of a Los Angeles hospital in 1933, aged 59.

1902   Breeder of 1990 Arc de Triomphe winner Saumarez ELISABETH LONGTON born. Owner of 12-times winner Nearly New. Colours: black; black and red striped sleeves; black and red checked cap.

1912   Owner LORD HOWARD DE WALDEN born. His Lanzarote won the 1974 Champion Hurdle and Slip Anchor won the 1985 Derby. In 1931, while in Germany, he knocked down a man whilst driving a car – it was Adolf Hitler!

1949   TOM WALLS, owner, trainer and renowned actor, died aged 66. He trained his own April the Fifth to win the 1932 Derby.

1957   Leading American trainer GREG FOLEY born in Somerset, Kentucky. Won his first title as a trainer when becoming top man at Churchill Downs in spring 1991.

1968   Middleham jump jockey JASON CALLAGHAN born. Best horse ridden Sharpsong.

1990   LESTER PIGGOTT rode Dear Doctor to victory at Maisons-Laffitte, his first French winner since launching his comeback.

1990   After a selling race at Newton Abbot, 3rd-placed BORE HILL PRINCESS and riderless THRINTOFT collided. The former was knocked over along with jockey Dale McKeown and both horses later collapsed and died.

28 NOVEMBER

1929 RAYMOND HITCHCOCK, owner of Royal Hunt Cup winner Fear Naught (1978), born. Colours: orange and pale blue quarters; pale blue cap.

1938 Former jump jockey ANDY ANDREWS born.

1941 Owner of Tartan Tailor DAVID STEVENSON born.

1947 Amateur jockey DAVID EVATT born. Rode his first winner, Braganza, on February 24 1968. Best horses ridden include Inch Arran (for the Queen Mother), Dark Highway, Shawnigan.

1948 England soccer international and breeder of Jamesmead and Ghofar turned successful trainer MICK CHANNON born.

1952 Curragh trainer MICHAEL GRASSICK born. First licence 1977. Best horses trained include Alder Rose, Bell Tower, Dóchas, Quiet Thoughts.

1983 Leading New York apprentice jockey ERIC BEITA died as a result of a gunshot wound suffered a week earlier. A memorial award in his honour, to be presented to the leading apprentice on the NY circuit, was instituted and was won in its first year by Declan Murphy.

1988 Royston trainer WILLIE STEPHENSON died aged 76. Cousin of Arthur Stephenson. At the age of sixteen he rode Niantic to dead-heat in the Cambridgeshire. As a trainer he sent out Oxo to win the 1959 Grand National and Arctic Prince to win the 1951 Derby. His Sir Ken ran up a hat-trick of Champion Hurdle wins from 1952 to 1954.

1989 JONJO O'NEILL, having overcome cancer himself, handed a cheque for £225,000 for Cancer Research to Professor Derek Crowther of Christies Hospital, Manchester. He raised the money over an eighteen-month period. Jonjo said, 'In the darkest days when I was very low I vowed I'd do something to help.'

1990 At the very moment her father officially became prime minister, ELIZABETH MAJOR was x-raying a sedated racehorse at a vet surgery near Abbots Ripton, near Huntingdon. Elizabeth was at the time studying at the Animal Health Trust.

1992 Silver ring bookies went on strike at Newbury in protest at the poor facilities in their enclosure. The silver ring was moved following the completion of the course's new Berkshire Stand to a site 1½ furlongs before the winning post. Said Liphook bookmaker Frank Morrad, 'There were no official spots for us to pitch up and bet from. We cannot see the finish.'

1992 Adrian Maguire rode the longest-ever priced Hennessy Cognac Gold Cup winner, SIBTON ABBEY at 40-1, for trainer Freddie Murphy at Newbury.

29 NOVEMBER

1928 Former Hampshire trainer NEVILLE DENT born. First licence 1956. Best horses trained include Basking, Turkish Bandit.

1932 Trainer STEVE DI MAURO born. Best horses trained include Wajima, Dearly Precious.

1939 Irish owner of King's Chorus and bloodstock agent LIAM SPRING born. Colours: white; blue braces; white cap.

1944 Breeder of Novel Dancer and Tolomeo JAMES EGAN born.

1956 East Ilsley trainer MARTIN FETHERSTON-GODLEY born. First licence 1986. Best horses include Toshair Flyer, Super Trip, Where's the Money.

1966 ANDREW PARKER BOWLES won on his first mount over fences, the Fulke Walwyn-trained Brown Diamond at Warwick.

1991 Respected racing writer ROGER MORTIMER died, aged 82. Wrote the exhaustive *History of the Derby Stakes*.

1992 CHARLIE SWAN broke Martin Molony's Irish record of 92 NH winners in a calendar year, established in 1950. He rode Atone (Bunny Cox) to land his 93rd winner, at Fairyhouse.

30 NOVEMBER

1891 Owner, breeder, amateur rider and racing administrator SIR HUM-PHREY DE TRAFFORD born. His 4–9 favourite Alcide won the 1958 St Leger and Parthia (10–1) the 1959 Derby, ridden by Harry Carr.

1916 Royal jockey (WILLIAM HENRY) HARRY CARR born, at Clifton near Penrith. Partnered Meld to win the 1955 1,000 Guineas, Oaks and St Leger. Won the Derby on Parthia in 1959.

1929 COOLE paid £341 2s 6d for 2s (10p) (odds of 3410 1/4–1) on the tote at Haydock – a record return which was won by Catherine Unsworth of Liverpool.

1933 Racing writer and historian RICHARD ONSLOW born.

1943 Carlisle trainer JOHN DIXON born.

1946 Jockey GEORGE DUFFIELD born. Set a new record when winning 11 consecutive races on one horse, Spindrifter. Became the first to manage the feat this century in 1980.

1949 Newmarket trainer JOHN SHAW born. Best horses include Wylfa.

1953 Jump jockey JEFF BARLOW born.

1960 Jump jockey ALAN JONES born. First winner 1981.

1963 MILL HOUSE and ARKLE, two of the greatest of chasers, clashed for the first time, in the Hennessy Gold Cup. Mill House won but never again got the better of his great rival, who made a bad jumping mistake and finished 3rd.

1964 JOSH GIFFORD fell from Reverando at Nottingham, breaking his right thigh, and was out for the remainder of the season. On his return he managed to break his leg again in a car accident and was out for 14 months. His next winner was on January 28 1966 at Windsor.

1985 JOHN FRANCOME sent out his first winner as a trainer when 25–1 chance That's Your Lot won at Sandown, ridden by Steve Smith Eccles.

1988 Findon trainer DIANE OUGHTON died at the age of 62.

1989 MELODY TOWN, aged seventeen, became the first woman to ride a winner on Lingfield's Equitrack course – Beechwood Cottage.

1989 American jockey KENT DESORMEAUX set a world record for a single season's victories when he won the 5th race at Laurel, USA, his 548th of the year, eclipsing Chris McCarron's record.

1990 JIM JOEL, aged 96, saw his Book of Gold and Coruscate both win at Sandown. The former beat the Queen Mother's Furry Knowe into 3rd after which the two veteran owners (she was 90) took tea together.

1990 LESTER PIGGOTT rode on an all-weather track in Britain for the first time, failing to trouble the judge at Southwell.

1 DECEMBER

1936   Trainer ROBIN BLAKENEY born. Best horses trained include Barmer, Bold Argument, Mellie. First licence 1971.

1939   Jockey JACKY TAILLARD born. Partnered Miss Dan, Infra Green.

1947   Jockey NIGEL WAKLEY born. Rode his first winner in 1969 at Newton Abbot. Best horses ridden include Royal Toss, Indianapolis, All Found, Mr Straight.

1957   Former Champion Lady point-to-point rider LUCY GIBSON born.

1989   Jockey ALEX GREAVES rode her first winner, Andrew's First, at Southwell. On May 31 1991 she became the first woman jockey in Great Britain to ride out her claim as she landed a double on Love Jazz (11-10) and Mac Kelty (10-1) at Goodwood.

1989   The AGA KHAN resigned his honorary membership of the Jockey Club because of his 'strong opposition' to the Club's current drugs-testing procedure.

1990   Leading French jump trainer HENRI GLEIZES died aged 78.

1990   The mare SINZINBRA was responsible for 4 runners on the same day: Young Snugfit, Peanut's Pet and Cashew King at Sandown and Snuggle at Nottingham. Young Snugfit was the only winner of the four.

2 DECEMBER

1921 Owner PAM SMART born. Best horses include Crimson Embers and Rose Ravine. Colours: turquoise; black braces; cerise cap.

1923 Trainer MARTIN TATE born. Rode 25 winners under NH rules. Best horses trained include Bawnogues, Cullen Piro T.

1940 Trainer JONATHAN SHEPPARD born. Best horses include Flatterer, Highland Bud.

1941 West Ilsley jockey BRIAN PROCTER born.

1961 Jockey (THOMAS) RICHARD QUINN born in Stirling. First winner 1981. Champion Apprentice 1984. Won St Leger on Snurge in 1990. Other top horses ridden include Ibn Bey, Ruby Tiger, Bint Pasha.

1964 Dual purpose jockey WILLIE HAYES born. First winner 1981. Best horses ridden include Cree Bay.

1970 JOHN FRANCOME rode his first winner at the age of seventeen, Multigrey, at Worcester. It was also his first mount.

1990 French jockey FREDDIE HEAD, aged 43, made his debut over jumps at Auteuil, riding Avaleur for trainer David Smaga, to commemorate the 100th anniversary of the birth of his grandfather, Louis. Head finished 2nd.

1990 Teleretta won in Macau but subsequently tested positive to caffeine. Singapore trainer WILLIAM CHUA was disqualified for twelve months.

1992 Flying filly LYRIC FANTASY, owned by Lord Carnarvon, was sold for 340,000 guineas at the Newmarket sales to Paul Shanahan of Ashtown House stud, who said he purchased her for a 'Kuwaiti consortium'.

1992 African Chimes, ridden by Emma O'Gorman, won for the 8th time in the flat season, in the Julius Caesar Claiming Stakes at Southwell, equalling Plan Ahead's total for the season and giving African Chimes' trainer BILL O'GORMAN the most prolific (or joint) winner of the season for the 4th time in his career - a record. Abdu won it with 9 wins in 1978, Provideo with 16 in 1984 and Timeless Times, also with 16, was his other winner.

3 DECEMBER

1791   Although evening racing is generally believed to have started at Hamilton Park in 1947, a meeting took place at Baltinglass, Ireland, on this day, with 4 heats of three miles each being run for the Silver Cup given by the Countess of Aldborough. The *Irish Racing Calendar* reported: 'The last heat was not over at six o'clock when lights were erected at each corner of the course, to direct the riders.'

1915   KIT PATTERSON, former clerk of the course at Ayr and Carlisle, born.

1947   Owner BILL CAMERON born. Best horses trained include Lady Murfax, Bye Bye Baby. Colours: royal blue; red and gold quartered cap.

1949   Irish Champion Jockey CHRISTY ROCHE born. Won the Irish Derby on St Jovite in 1992 when that horse beat Epsom Derby winner Dr Devious by 12 lengths. Rode Secreto, 14–1, to win the 1984 Derby.

1969   The QUEEN MOTHER'S 200th winner over jumps, Master Daniel, won at Worcester for jockey Richard Dennard and trainer Peter Cazalet.

1973   Former Kentucky Derby winner Count Fleet died aged 33, the greatest age ever recorded for a winner of that race, which he won way back in 1943 as one of its hottest favourites ever at odds of 2–5.

1988   THE DRAGON MASTER was the 100–1 winner of a novice chase at Sandown. Owner-trainer Robert Waley-Cohen's wife put £100 on the horse.

1988   1983 Grand National winner CORBIERE was put down aged thirteen after suffering circulation problems. Named after a Jersey lighthouse.

1990   MAGOMED TAKOV became the first Russian jockey to win a race in Britain, partnering Macho Man at Kelso during an international challenge event, the Maxwell Motors Glasnost Handicap Hurdle.

1992   Trainer (WILLIAM) ARTHUR STEPHENSON died, aged 72. He spent his whole training career at Crawleas Farm, Bishop Auckland. Won the 1987 Cheltenham Gold Cup with The Thinker. First licence 1959. In 1969–70 he became the first NH trainer to saddle 100 winners. Trained Supermaster to win 34 races. On the Flat his Rapid River won the 1972 Gimcrack Stakes and in the same year, Tudenham won the Middle Park Stakes. 'Little fish are sweet' was his explanation for often concentrating on smaller events.

4 DECEMBER

1930 Comedian and owner RONNIE CORBETT born.

1933 Chairman of the Racegoers' Club, TONY FAIRBAIRN, born.

1939 US owner MARSHALL W. JENNEY born. Best horses owned include Flamenco, River Mist. Bred Mrs Penny, Danzig. Colours: sapphire blue; emerald green cross-belts, white sleeves and cap.

1946 Newmarket jockey RAY STILL born. First winner 1966. Best horses ridden include Big Hat, Heave To.

1956 Jockey HYWEL DAVIES born. Partnered Last Suspect to a 1985 50-1 Grand National shock win. First winner 1977. Best horses ridden include Celtic Ryde, Ghofar, Barnbrook Again. Once listed his favourite recreation as 'sleeping'.

1963 Irish jockey KEVIN O'BRIEN born.

1963 Former Champion jump jockey Tim Brookshaw broke his back in a fall at Liverpool. He was runner-up to Oxo in the 1959 Grand National on Wyndburgh after losing his stirrup leathers.

1967 Former trainer HUGH BARCLAY, grandfather of jockey Sandy, died aged 81. Trained near Lockerbie. At Perth in 1949 he sent out 3 winners, ridden by his sons Hugh, Andrew and John.

1973 Jump jockey JEFFREY BARLOW got off the mark with a double when Quintus and Capuchin both won at Huntingdon.

1990 The AGA KHAN announced that he was to withdraw all his horses from British racing as a protest against the decision to disqualify Aliysa as the 1989 Oaks winner.

1990 Champion NH jockey PETER SCUDAMORE, out of action through injury, attended Buckingham Palace to receive the MBE.

1990 LESTER PIGGOTT collected the first ban of his comeback, at St Cloud. He was found guilty of not riding 3rd-placed Lady Isis to full potential. He was stood down for four days.

1991 HENRY CECIL sent out his first all-weather winner when Citiqueen won the Macbeth Maiden Stakes at Southwell.

1991 LORNA VINCENT (81 jump winners) rode her first flat winner when Grog - trained by Mick Channon and backed from 25-1 to 6-1 - won on the all-weather at Southwell.

1992 Three Court of Appeal Judges found that the Jockey Club decision to disqualify the Aga Khan's 1989 Oaks 'winner' Aliysa was not subject to judicial review.

5 DECEMBER

1911 ISINGLASS, the 1893 Triple Crown winner belonging to owner-breeder MP Harry McCalmont, died at Cheveley Park Stud.

1912 Owner–breeder of Homing and Swiftfoot LORD ROTHERWICK born. Colours: light blue; white sleeves; quartered cap.

1919 Jersey-based owner of Crews Hill and Secret Society LORD MATTHEWS born. His Twigairy won 19 races. Colours: emerald green; yellow and green quartered cap.

1932 LORD SCARBROUGH, owner of Valentinian, born. Colours: sky blue and white stripes; white cap.

1947 Thirteen-year-old Schubert, a winner there before the war, returned to Worcester to win the three-mile Kingham Handicap Chase, ridden and trained by Cliff Beechner. -

1950 Jump jockey ALLAN DICKMAN born. Best horses include Scorton Boy, Polar's Laddie.

1953 Northumberland trainer and Newcastle Gosforth rugby player BRIAN MCLEAN born. Best horses trained include Jack of Clubs, Worthy Knight.

1960 Jockey SIMON ANDREWS born. First winner 1978. Best horses ridden include Newnham, Private Audition, Golden Casino.

1963 Jockey TOM GRANTHAM born.

1969 Jump jockey STUART FOSTER born.

1978 Three times on his morning radio programme, which included a racing bulletin, Terry Wogan announced that Newton Abbot races were abandoned because of freezing fog. This was news to clerk of the course CARL NEKOLA, who had to quickly ring the BBC and explain that they - and he - had been victims of a hoax. The meeting went ahead, but the crowd was much smaller than might have been anticipated.

1991 Owner HENRY SENN, whose Seattle Rhyme had been made ante-post favourite for the next year's Derby, died aged 67. His best horses had been Princess Athena and Young Turpin. Colours: white; yellow seams and cap.

1991 The BBC announced that the racing series *Trainer* would return for a second series despite mixed reviews.

1992 MARTIN PIPE saddled the first 3 home in Chepstow's Rehearsal Chase, in which Run for Free beat Miinnehoma and Bonanza Boy.

6 DECEMBER

1920 Former BBC racing commentator PETER DIMMOCK born.

1921 Trainer WILLIAM JARVIS died. His Ravensbury was second in the 1893 2,000 Guineas, Derby and St Leger, to Isinglass on each occasion, and his Cyllene (6-4), ridden by S. Loates, won the 1899 Ascot Gold Cup.

1922 Irish trainer DANIEL KINANE born. Best horses trained include Kilmore, Forest Rock.

1928 Provocative racing writer and former *Sporting Life* editor MONTY COURT born. His 'Court Circular' column has been known to raise a few hackles!

1936 Devon trainer DAVID BARONS born. Best horses include Bootlaces and Play School. He still believes that the latter was 'got at' before the Cheltenham Gold Cup. His Seagram won the Grand National in 1991 at odds of 12-1 for owner Sir Eric Parker and jockey N. Hawke.

1959 Jockey BILLY NEWNES born. Won the 1982 Oaks on Time Charter (12-1), owned by R. Barnett and trained by Henry Candy. Rode his first winner in 1978.

1989 Two-year-old filly TEXAS BLUE ran 9th of 14 in the Cromwell Lock Stakes, the 1.10 at Southwell, then turned out for the very next race, the Trent Nursery Handicap, at 1.40. She finished last of 13. Ridden both times by S. Maloney and trained by Mel Brittain.

7 DECEMBER

1924 Devon trainer GERALD COTTRELL born. First licence 1971. Best horses trained include Young Inca, Governor General, Ever Sharp, Roman Prose, Gallant Hope.

1948 Director of Animal Health Trust DR ANDREW HIGGINS born.

1960 Jump jockey BILLY WORTHINGTON born. Best horses ridden include Deadly Going.

1964 Newmarket jockey RICHARD LINES, who moved to Australia, born.

1967 The eagerly awaited sale of highly fancied Observer Gold Cup winner VAGUELY NOBLE took place at Park Paddocks, Newmarket. There was high excitement as the horse was bought for a record 136,000 guineas on behalf of plastic surgeon Robert Franklyn. It went on to win the Arc de Triomphe and become a top sire.

1983 CHRIS BROWNLESS rode On Leave to win at Carlisle. His next winner, Candy Cone, at Hexham, did not arrive until March 21 1992. In between he had retired to assist handler Bobby Brewis, who trained his comeback winner.

1984 Trainer DICK HERN broke his neck in a hunting accident in Leicestershire.

1985 FULKE WALWYN saddled his 200th winner at Cheltenham, Arctic Stream, 2-1, in the Fred Withington Novice Chase, ridden by K. Mooney.

1989 FORBES SPIRIT made an unfortunate piece of history when he became the first horse to fall on Lingfield's Equitrack. The Paul Howling-trained runner later died.

1991 PETER NIVEN set a record by riding 5 winners for the 2nd time in a season, at Doncaster. His other mount was 2nd. He had first achieved the feat at Kelso.

8 DECEMBER

1921 Malton trainer BILL (CHARLES WILLIAM CARLTON) ELSEY born. First licence 1961. Won the St Leger with Peleid (28-1, Frankie Durr up) in 1973 and the Oaks with Pia (100-7, Eddie Hyde up) in 1967.

1935 San Isidro racecourse, Argentina, opened.

1937 FULKE WALWYN rode French Mandate to win the three-mile Pegasus Handicap Chase at Gatwick, where the course consisted of part of the current airport.

1942 Salisbury trainer JAMES FOX born. Rode over 100 winners as a jockey, including Red Candle, winner of the 1973 Hennessy Gold Cup. Best horses trained include Hill-Street-Blues, Fortune Cookie, Friendly Henry.

1945 Irish jump jockey JOHN LYNN died in hospital, having suffered a crashing fall from his mount Red World at Southwell the previous day. He was 38.

1947 Limerick trainer MICHAEL HOURIGAN born.

1953 Vincent O'Brien-trained triple Cheltenham Gold Cup winner (in 1948, 1949 and 1950, ridden all three times by Aubrey Brabazon) COTTAGE RAKE ran his last race, finishing 3rd, ridden by Dick Francis in the three-mile Shrewsbury Chase at Wolverhampton. He was fourteen.

1970 Jump jockey STEVE HAZELL born.

1975 Trainer BERNARD VAN CUTSEM, born 1916, died. His only Classic winner was 1972 2,000 Guineas winner High Top. He also handled top filly Park Top. In 1971 he had in his yard world-record purchase ($510,000) two-year-old Crowned Prince, which failed to achieve its potential.

1992 Aintree clerk of the course JOHN PARRETT died, aged 45.

9 DECEMBER

1926   Owner NORMAN ROLFE born. Best horse owned Jigsaw Boy.

1929   Former Australian prime minister and racehorse owner BOB HAWKE born.

1939   Burton-on-Trent permit trainer RICHARD PERKINS born.

1949   PRINCE REGENT, the greatest chaser of the 1940s and reckoned by trainer Tom Dreaper to be nearly as good as Arkle, raced for the final time, falling in the Blindley Heath Chase at Lingfield.

1952   Jockey PHILIPPE PAQUET born. Best horses ridden include Trepan, Nureyev, April Run.

1961   ARKLE saw a racecourse for the first time and ran 3rd in a £133 maiden plate at Mullingar, returning 5-1 and ridden by M. Hely-Hutchinson.

1961   The QUEEN MOTHER landed a treble at Lingfield when Laffy (evens), Double Star (4-1) and The Rip (8-13) all won.

1967   Jump jockey ROGER MARLEY born. Partnered the best horse he has ridden, Nohalmdun, to victory at Doncaster on his 21st birthday. Also associated with Antinous, Yaheeb.

1989   Jump jockey STUART SHILSTON retired at the age of 31 after riding Slightly Gone at Towcester, the same track at which he had ridden his first winner, Mr Linnet, in 1976. He rode 131 winners in all.

1989   Run for Free held the record time for a two-mile hurdle at Cheltenham, 3 minutes 56 seconds, for precisely 1 hour 10 minutes before CRUISING ALTITUDE clocked 3 minutes 55.4 seconds.

1992   An ordinary two-mile hurdle race took longer than a Grand National to run at Haydock after the runners mistakenly missed out the 2nd hurdle, which ground staff had closed off. The field completed nearly a full circuit of the track before being warned that they would have to return to the missed-out flight and jump it, otherwise the race would be voided. They went back and virtually restarted. Richard Dunwoody eventually won on MIGHTY MOGUL, in 12 minutes 19.6 seconds.

10 DECEMBER

1924 The man who launched Belmont Park racecourse, USA, AUGUST BELMONT II, died.

1937 Owner DAVID OLDREY born. His Oats (10–1) was 3rd in the 1976 Derby, Crozier won 13 times and Halsbury (14–1) won the Cesarewitch. Colours: red; white sleeves; black and white quartered cap.

1944 Former Champion Amateur Jockey 1963 and 1964 STEVE DAVENPORT born. First winner 1961. Best horses ridden include Eternal.

1950 Lambourn trainer NICKY HENDERSON born. Responsible for triple Champion Hurdle winner See You Then. Also handled top horses Zongalero, The Tsarevich, Brown Windsor, Remittance Man. First licence 1978.

1954 MANDARIN, who would become one of the best-loved chasers of all, winning over £50,000 in prize-money and landing the Hennessy and Cheltenham Gold Cups in 1961–62, made his racecourse debut, coming in 3rd at 20–1 in the Freshman's Hurdle at Newbury.

1955 Racecourse Association PRO GRAHAM ORANGE born.

1956 Amateur jockey RORY LAWTHER born.

1982 Former trainer GEOFFREY SCUDAMORE, grandfather of Peter, died aged 76.

1988 An extraordinary plunge on a horse called ZUSRAB saw her odds plummet from 100–1 to 6–1 throughout Australia as she started in the Savoir Handicap at Moonee Valley, Melbourne. Layers at the course were facing an AUS$1 million payout, while Sydney bookies had $600,000 more riding on the outcome and in Brisbane the projected payout was $400,000. Zusrab finished 2nd, beaten by inches.

1991 Bravefoot, Norwich and Flying Diva, victims of the 1990 doping scandal, were finally officially disqualified from their races by the Jockey Club. All 3 were proved to have been doped with a prohibited tranquillising drug. Norwich had finished 4th at Doncaster on September 13; Flying Diva finished last of 3 and Bravefoot last of 5 to Bog Trotter (both at Yarmouth on September 20).

1992 German trainer JURGEN ALBRECHT, aged 32, who had been sentenced to ten years' imprisonment for cocaine smuggling, was reported to have escaped from jail. Yorkshire-born jockey Nick Woodall, also jailed as a result of the same case, was not involved in the escape.

11 DECEMBER

1849   LESTER PIGGOTT'S great-uncle, JOE CANNON, born. He rode Regal to win the 1876 Grand National then turned to training and landed the 1878 1,000 Guineas and 2,000 Guineas double with Pilgrimage.

1928   Carlisle and Cartmel clerk of the course MAJOR TIM RILEY born. After an incident at Cartmel when Chrissie Kent, an over-exuberant female fan of jockey Phil Tuck, demonstrated her affection by taking a nip at his rear end, Major Riley commented: 'As a general rule we cannot have people going into the winners' enclosure and biting the jockeys' arses.'

1936   Champion Hurdler VICTOR NORMAN carried 12st 7lbs to win the Annual Handicap Hurdle at Sandown, ridden by Frenchie Nicholson.

1940   Epsom trainer DAVID WILSON born. First licence 1980. Best horses trained include Gambler's Dream, Durandal.

1947   Trainer NEIL DRYSDALE, who moved to USA, born. Best horses trained include Princess Rooney, Prized.

1953   DICK FRANCIS, who went on to become Champion Jump Jockey with 76 successes, won the Oxfordshire Chase on Mr Dick Wilkins' Owen o'Cork at Newbury.

1965   Newmarket jockey ADAM SHOULTS born. First winner 1984. Best horses ridden include Berry's Dream.

1982   COLIN HAWKINS rode his first treble, at odds of 828-1, when Quay Man, Sparkie's Choice and Mulata all won at Catterick.

12 DECEMBER

1911 Owner-breeder of Brigadier Gerard JOHN HISLOP born. Leading amateur rider on flat from 1946 to 1955; finished 3rd in Grand National on Kami (33-1) in 1947.

1921 Trainer ERIC COUSINS born. Sent out winner of Kempton Park Jubilee Handicap 4 years in succession (1961 to 1964) and won the Lincolnshire with John's Court (1961) and Hill Royal (1962).

1922 Australian jockey BILL 'WEARY WILLIE' WILLIAMSON born. Rode first winner at Flemington in 1937 and came to England in 1960. Won the 1,000 Guineas on Abermaid in 1962 and Night Off in 1965, and the 1972 Irish Sweeps Derby on Steel Pulse.

1933 Jockey GERARD THIBOUEF born.

1939 Desert Orchid's trainer, DAVID ELSWORTH, born. Jump jockey from 1957 to 1972. Trained Rhyme 'n' Reason to win the Grand National in 1988; Dessie to win the Gold Cup in 1989.

1942 Former jockey turned TV commentator, editorial director of the *Racing Post* and author (JOHN) BROUGH SCOTT born.

1945 Jockey FRED FOX died in a car accident. In 1930 he beat Gordon Richards to become Champion Jockey and in 1935 won the 2,000 Guineas and Derby on Bahram.

1948 First female Champion Flat jockey (1972) MERIEL TUFNELL born.

1958 Jockey NIALL MADDEN born.

1964 Not a good day at the office for LORD OAKSEY, at that time known as John Lawrence. In the Whaddon Amateurs' Handicap Chase at Cheltenham he and Pioneer Spirit had jumped clear at the 2nd last when the Noble Lord decided that he must have taken the wrong course. He turned his horse around, only to find French Cottage, ridden by Bill Tellwright, coming towards him, passing him and going on to win! Lawrence was fined £25 and later reportedly went home, ran a bath, answered the phone, and forgot about the bath until the water overflowed through the ceiling.

1990 Trainer MOHAMMED MOUBARAK was fined £8,000 by the Jockey Club disciplinary committee over the administration of anabolic steroids to 6 of his horses.

1991 Self-styled king of the professional punters ALEX BIRD died aged 75. His life story, *The Life and Secrets of a Professional Punter*, was published in 1985.

1992 History was made when Pennsylvanian BRUCE MILLER sent out Lonesome Glory, ridden by his daughter, Blythe, to win the Chris Coley Sport of Kings Hurdle at Cheltenham, thus becoming the first US-trained winner of a British jump race.

13 DECEMBER

1930 Breeder MARTYN MCENERY, who bred Red Rum, born.

1933 Exning trainer PETER FIELDEN born.

1936 Shergar's owner, Prince Karim, the AGA KHAN, born. Also owned Derby winners Shahrastani (1986, 11–2) and Kahyasi (1988, 11–1).

1945 The French trainer of Dunette, EMMANUEL CHEVALIER DU FAU, born.

1948 Newmarket jockey JOHN HIGGINS born. Rode three Trinidad Derby winners. First winner 1965. Best horses ridden include Raffingora.

1950 Somerset trainer JOHN ROBERTS born. Best horses trained Bickleigh Bridge, Atataho.

1952 Former Champion Jump Jockey turned TV commentator JOHN FRANCOME born. Champion 7 times, sharing 1 season with Peter Scudamore, who was leading when he was injured, allowing Francome to equal his total then retire for the season. Won Gold Cup on Midnight Court in 1978; Champion Hurdle in 1981 on Sea Pigeon.

1962 Jockey LESLIE BLOOMFIELD born. First winner 1981. Best horses ridden include Mr Peacock.

1988 JENNY PITMAN trained 4 winners at Plumpton. 'I nearly took all 4 out at the overnight stage, fearing the ground would be too firm,' she said.

1990 It was announced that JULIE CECIL had been officially granted a training licence.

1991 Former jockey LEN 'TITCH' GRANTHAM died at the age of 82.

1992 The Peter O'Sullevan-owned 1974 Daily Express Triumph Hurdle winner, Attivo, was put down at the age of 22.

1992 C. V. 'SONNY' WHITNEY, one of America's leading owners for over 50 years, died aged 93. His Counterpoint was 1951 Horse of the Year.

14 DECEMBER

1870   LORD POULETT, owner of chaser The Lamb, dreamed that his horse won the Grand National ridden by Tommy Pickernell. Upon waking he set about engaging Pickernell to ride the horse. He won the big race in 1871.

1895   The first Indian Grand National was run at Tollygunge and won by the Maharajah of Patiala's PRINCE IMPERIAL, ridden by J. D. Scott.

1922   Jump jockey JOHNNY BEASLY born.

1927   Aussie jockey RON (ROBERT) HUTCHINSON born. Rode his first winner at Mentone, Victoria, in 1943. Came to Britain in 1960 and rode Martial to win the 2,000 Guineas in the same year for Irish trainer P. J. Prendergast. Won the 1,000 Guineas (Full Dress II for Harry Wragg) and St Leger (Intermezzo, also Wragg-trained) in 1969. Retired in 1977.

1929   Ascot clerk of the course NICKY BEAUMONT born.

1936   Twenty-one-year-old RON SMYTH landed a double at Plumpton on Jocund, trained by his brother Willie, and Blue Shirt, trained by his father, Herbert.

1939   Welshman SIRRELL GRIFFITHS, owner-trainer of the 1990 100-1 Gold Cup winner, Norton's Coin, born.

1962   Jockey HILARY HANDEL of Taunton born. Best horses ridden include Daddy's Special, Hinter City.

1966   ARKLE won for the 27th and final time in the three-mile SGB Handicap Chase at Ascot, ridden by Pat Taaffe, carrying 12st 7lbs and starting at 1-3.

1967   Former trainer HENRY GOLIGHTLY died aged 85. His biggest triumph was Dropitin's 1925 Carlisle Bell success.

1989   Jockey TIM MOLONY, 5 times Champion Jump Jockey between 1949 and 1955, died aged 70. Rode 726 British winners. Won Gold Cup on Knock Hard (1953) and the Champion Hurdle 4 consecutive times on Hatton's Grace (1951) and Sir Ken (1952, 1953 and 1954). Began training in 1960.

1989   Jump trainer MARTIN PIPE lopped fifteen days off his own record when he became the first trainer to send out 100 winners before Christmas. King's Rank, ridden by Peter Scudamore, brought up the record at Haydock.

1990   The debt-ridden Macau Jockey Club, responsible for racing there which had started fifteen months earlier, was put in the hands of the receiver.

15 DECEMBER

1918 Grand National-obsessed rider DUQUE D'ALBERQUERQUE born. Having seen a film about the race he vowed to win it and first competed in 1952, when he fell on his horse Brown Jack III, cracking his vertebra. Eleven years later he returned and fell at the 21st. In 1965 he came down at the 9th and broke a leg. He made it to the 26th in 1966. In 1973 he pulled up on Nereo and in 1974 he prepared for the National by having 16 screws inserted in his leg and breaking his collarbone; but, aged 55, he completed the course, finishing 8th on Nereo. In 1976 he fell at the 13th and was unconscious for 2 days. Still he insisted he would compete again – until the Jockey Club stepped in and banned him for his own good.

1933 Newmarket trainer CLIVE BRITTAIN born. His Pebbles won the 1984 1,000 Guineas and 1985 Breeders' Cup Turf. In 1978 his Julio Mariner won the St Leger. First licence 1972.

1936 Waterford trainer HARRY DE BROMHEAD born. First licence 1960.

1938 Trainer ALAN JARVIS born. First licence 1969.

1945 Jockey GEORGE (ELFRED) CADWALADR born. Won the Wokingham (My Audrey) and King's Stand Stakes (Roughlyn) in 1966.

1946 Lockinge trainer HENRIETTA KNIGHT born. First licence 1989.

1946 Trainer DICK ALLAN born. First licence 1976–77.

1969 ARTHUR SMITH, who won the 1920 St Leger on 100-6 chance Caligula, died aged 71. The dual purpose rider set a record when riding 5 winners at Royal Ascot in 1919 – as an apprentice.

1970 Jockey FRANKIE DETTORI born. Champion apprentice 1989. First winner 1986. Son of Classic winning jockey Gianfranco.

1988 PETER SCUDAMORE completed the fastest century of jump winners in a season. However, since one of his winners was later disqualified, the ton was actually achieved on December 20.

1988 ARUM LILY was beaten at Haydock – having started at 1-14.

1991 Gypsies staged a Sunday race meeting along the A168 near Thirsk under cover of fog and protected by a line of parked cars and lorries. But just as the race was about to get underway police intervened and a 'stewards' inquiry' resulted.

1991 South Carolina trainer HENRY L. CARROLL born.

1992 Prominent owner-breeder VERA HUE-WILLIAMS died in her 90th year. She was born in Kiev and escaped from Russia during the Bolshevik Revolution. She owned the inaugural (1951) King George VI and Queen Elizabeth Stakes winner, Supreme Court.

1992 CHILD OF THE MIST carried 13st in a selling hurdle at Folkestone and – unsurprisingly – finished unplaced.

16 DECEMBER

1851 Racing took place for the first time at Canterbury, New Zealand, with a programme of 4 races at Hagley Park.

1915 Trainer SANDY CARLOS CLARKE born.

1931 Berwickshire permit trainer DAWN GOODFELLOW born. Best horses include Larry Hill.

1954 Lightweight jockey COMPTON RODRIGUES born.

1955 Cricket-loving Worcestershire trainer NEIL PAINTING born. First licence 1985.

1969 JACK BERRY trained his first winner when Camasco, ridden by Tony Potts, won over hurdles at Kelso.

1974 CHRIS MCCARRON, in his first season, rode Ohmylove at Laurel, USA, for his 516th win of the season, beating the previous record, set by Sandy Hawley the previous year.

1989 LESTER PIGGOTT became a grandfather for the first time when daughter Maureen, 29, gave birth to a 9lb girl, Marianne. Her husband is Newmarket trainer William Haggas.

1990 The first Sunday meeting was run in Western Australia. In an effort to please outspoken critics a non-denominational church service was staged in front of the grandstand before the first race.

1990 The first Sunday meeting took place at Clonmel where, to the disappointment of many of the 5,000 who turned up, the bar was dry.

1991 It was announced that a record entry of 634 yearlings had been entered for the 1993 Derby.

1991 Northern Dancer's trainer HORATIO LURO died in Miami aged 90.

17 DECEMBER

1892 Outsider Covert Side (20-1) managed to win the 3-runner Oving-dean Chase at Plumpton, despite being returned to the paddock after refusing to race a mile into the contest. After the other 2 runners fell and refused, jockey Mr Thompson took his horse back on to the course, where it jumped round to win.

1905 Jockey (JAMES HENRY) 'TIM' HAMEY born. Partnered Koko, on which he won the 1926 Gold Cup, and Forbra to win the 1932 Grand National.

1911 Newmarket trainer ARTHUR 'FIDDLER' GOODWILL born. First licence 1945. Best horses trained include Woolley, Peg's Fancy, Pee Mai, Captain John.

1912 COMMON, winner of the 1891 Triple Crown (he won the 2,000 Guineas on his debut), died at Boyce Burrow's stud near Chelmsford.

1932 Trainer CYRIL ALEXANDER born. First licence 1956. Best horses include Subaltern, Zebo.

1934 KEITH PIGGOTT on Crafty Captain and FULKE WALWYN on Dusky Troubadour rode a dead-heat finish in the £73 Ashbourne Hurdle at Derby.

1937 Media tycoon, racehorse owner and mega-punter KERRY PACKER born.

1937 Racing writer TONY JAKOBSON born.

1940 Racing writer GEORGE ENNOR born.

1959 Owner of Sub Rosa, winner of 7 chases, CHARLES GORDON-WATSON born. Colours: white; gold cuffs; quartered cap.

1960 WAYNE HARRIS, jockey for Kevin Prendergast, born.

1965 Owner-breeder MAJOR LIONEL HOLLIDAY died in his 85th year. Owned 3 Classic winners: Night Off (1,000 Guineas, 1965), Neasham Belle (Oaks, 1951) and Hethersett (St Leger, 1962). He had 28 horses in training when he died and once observed of his trainers: 'They all come to me on bicycles and leave in Bentleys.'

1966 Jockey DON MORRIS, 28, was killed in a car crash.

1975 Nineteen-year-old PHIL TUCK rode his first winner, Persian King, at Catterick.

1989 LESTER PIGGOTT, returning to the saddle after three years, rode 2 horses (Rochi, Soy Boucle) into last place at Monterrico, Lima, Peru. He had finished 3rd on Sulieman the previous day, winning $20 dollars' prize-money!

1992 Jockey HUGH MCMAHON, who had ridden in Britain, Belgium and the USA, rode his first winner in Italy for new employer, trainer Luigi Camici, Hallo Miss at Naples.

18 DECEMBER

1846 A race meeting announced in the *China Mail* is believed to have been the first held at Happy Valley, Hong Kong.

1926 Ex-jockey CHARLIE MAIDMENT died at the age of 82. Won the Derby twice (on Cremorne and Kisber), was twice joint Champion Jockey (1870 and 1871). On Hannah he won the 1871 1,000 Guineas, Oaks and St Leger.

1934 Owner of 1979 Grand National winner Rubstic JOHN DOUGLAS born. Colours: light blue; green cross of Lorraine.

1941 Racing took place for the first time at Pineda, Seville, Spain. The first race, the Premio Guadalquivir, went to CANICHON, ridden by Alvaro Diaz and trained by Juan Ponce de Leon.

1956 Jockey CHRIS KINANE born. At 6ft 2^1/$_2$ins he is one of the tallest in the business. Best horses ridden include Ross du Vin.

1964 Jockey DAVID LEADBITTER born.

1968 Trainer SIR JOHN 'JACK' JARVIS, who received a knighthood for services to racing in the 1967 Birthday Honours, died in his 81st year. He trained 9 Classic winners, including Blue Peter, which won the 2,000 Guineas and Derby in 1939, but was denied his Triple Crown attempt by the war. One of his owners was Sir John Jarvis, a Tory MP who went into ownership when he received by accident an account from a bookmaker intended for the trainer!

1991 Owner LEONARD SEALE was in the winners' enclosure at Lingfield waiting to hear whether his horse Super Sally (11–4) had won the 3-way photo-finish for the European Gold Patrons Handicap. Before the official announcement that his horse had indeed prevailed, Mr Seale collapsed and died of a heart attack.

1991 Fifty-year-old jockey TAKEMI SASAKI, whose first winner was recorded in 1960, rode 2 successes in Japan to take his overall total of winners to a record-breaking 6,500.

1991 Vintage Crop won at Fairyhouse by 4^1/$_2$ lengths, the first horse to triumph by that newly introduced 'official' distance.

1991 For the first time in a training career of over 30 years 77-year-old KEN OLIVER visited Bangor and duly saddled a winner, Kinlet Vision.

19 DECEMBER

1931   Wiltshire trainer PETER HAYWARD born. First licence 1979.

1946   Jockey DENNIS MCKAY born. Rode his first winner in 1968.

1946   Former jump jockey JIMMY O'GRADY born. First winner 1963. Best horses ridden include Waterloo Prince.

1961   Amateur rider ALEX FIGG born.

1963   Former Champion Lady Jockey GAY KELLEWAY, daughter of trainer Paul, born. She was the first female jockey to ride in the Oaks, in 1986.

1989   Actor and jockey EDWARD UNDERDOWN died aged 81. Dead-heated with John Hislop as leading amateur rider on flat in 1938; also rode over jumps. Appeared with Humphrey Bogart in the comedy film *Beat the Devil.*

1991   MARY REVELEY became the first woman to train 100 winners in a calendar year when 20–1 shot Festival Fancy won at Kelso.

20 DECEMBER

1605 KING JAMES I paid £154 for an Arabian horse purchased from a certain Gervase Markham, presumably with dreams of future glory. Sadly for the King, not even Royal patronage can guarantee success. The Duke of Newcastle reported: 'When he came to run, every horse beat him.'

1923 Trainer of 1887 Derby winner Merry Hampton MARTIN GURRY died aged 82. He built Newmarket's Abington Place stable, later occupied by Geoff Wragg. Gurry also handled The Bard, which won 16 times as a two-year-old in 1885, and his La Sagesse won the 1895 Oaks.

1925 New Orleans-based owner JAMES STONE born. Best horses include Ardross, Cajun.

1943 Trainer of the first Scottish winner of the Grand National (Rubstic, 1979) JOHN LEADBETTER born. Also handled Lordel, Paddy Hayton.

1945 Trainer DAVID BARRON born. Best horses trained include Vallymills, Miss Import.

1948 Newmarket jockey turned Malton trainer CHRIS DWYER born. Rider of Gunner B. and Decoy Boy.

1948 Dual purpose Newbury trainer PETER CUNDELL born. President of the National Trainers' Federation. Best horses trained include King of Spain, Bachelor's Hall, Celtic Ryde.

1982 DAWN RUN (4–6, ridden by A. Mullins) won over hurdles for the first time, in the Blackhills Maiden Hurdle at Navan.

1988 SAYFAR'S LAD was the horse that eventually gave Peter Scudamore the fastest 100 NH winners in a season when it won at Ludlow. The disqualification of one of his earlier winners, Norman Invader, had lopped one off his total.

1989 PETER SCUDAMORE rode his 100th winner of the season on the same date as last year. This time Redgrave Devil at Bangor was his 100th from 242 rides – the previous year it had taken 291.

1989 TARNYA DAVIS became the first lady jockey to ride a jumps winner on the all-weather track at Southwell. Olympus Reef succeeded in the Wensleydale Novice Handicap Hurdle.

1992 Goffs announced the withdrawal of their sponsorship of the Irish 1,000 Guineas.

21 DECEMBER

1925   Trainer JEREMY TREE, real name Andrew, born. His Only for Life (1963) and Known Fact (1980) both won the 2,000 Guineas and Juliette Marny (1975) and Scintillate (1979) were Oaks winners. Rainbow Quest won the 1985 Arc de Triomphe for him. He received his first training licence in 1952 and Jimmy Lindley was, for a long time, his stable jockey. Died March 6 1993.

1935   Mill Reef's 1971 Derby winning jockey GEOFF LEWIS born near Brecon, into a family of 13 children. His first job was as a hotel pageboy. First winner 1953; first Classic winner Right Tack (2,000 Guineas, 1969). Also won the Arc de Triomphe on the great Mill Reef. As an Epsom trainer he has specialised in backing himself to reach a certain number of winners each season – and he has collected best part of £200,000 from various bookies as a result.

1936   Prolific Puerto Rican horse GALGO JR died. He won a record 137 of his 159 starts.

1939   Jockey GREVILLE STARKEY born in Lichfield. Rode 110-1 German-trained Star Appeal to win the 1975 Arc de Triomphe. His first Classic winner was Homeward Bound in the 1964 Oaks. He won the Derby on Shirley Heights in 1978 but was heavily criticised for *not* winning it on Dancing Brave, runner-up in 1986 to Shahrastani.

1946   North Yorkshire trainer GEOFF OLDROYD born. As a jockey he partnered Roman Warrior.

1949   Newmarket jockey WALLY HOOD born.

1972   Jockey PAUL BARTON rode his first winner, Indigo Jones, at Folkestone.

1985   No one fancied the runner who finished 4th in the 2.15 race at Lingfield: YANKEE was a greyhound, who had escaped from owner Mrs Violet Cohen and overtook all but 3 of the 17-strong field!

22 DECEMBER

1900 Owner of Dunkirk and Barona, the latter twice winner of the Scottish National, COLONEL BILL WHITBREAD born. Colours: chocolate; yellow collar, cuffs and cap.

1931 Jockey SAMMY MILLBANKS born. Partnered Predominate, Hollyhock. First winner 1951.

1939 Trainer PETER HEDGER born. Rode 16 winners as a jockey but broke his neck at Kempton in 1965. Best horses trained include Jimmy Lorenzo, Al Asoof, Manston Marauder.

1941 Owner of Sexton Blake TIM MOTLEY born. Colours: yellow; red and blue checked collar, cuffs and cap.

1942 Irish trainer JOHN BRYCE-SMITH born. Best horses trained include Mwanadike, Rathinree, Spittin' Image.

1946 Owner–rider MAJOR VICTOR MCCALMONT (a Jockey Club and Irish Club member) partnered his Bluetit, trained by Neville Crump, to win the Killerby Handicap Hurdle at Catterick.

1957 Jockey RANDY ROMERO born.

1961 Jockey STEVE YOULDEN born. First winner 1981. Best horses ridden include Amber Rambler. Married Sarah on his birthday in 1989.

1962 UK racing abandoned because of the frozen weather. There would be just one more day's sport – on January 5 at Ayr – before March 8, when racing resumed at Newbury.

1964 Newmarket flat jockey WILLIE RYAN born. On his 28th birthday he became one of the select band to ride 100 winners in a season when he landed a 236-1 4-timer at Lingfield, every one of which won by a short head. Best horses ridden include Diminuendo, Old Vic, Snow Bride, Queen Midas.

1966 Jump jockey ANTHONY TORY, the butt of many corny political puns, born. Best horses ridden include Docklands Express, Cool Ground, Man o' Magic, King's Fountain.

1975 Ladbrokes announced a deal with BILL DAVIES, owner of Aintree, under which they would pay an annual fee for the right to manage the Grand National for seven years.

1982 Jockey GERRY GRACEY was forced to retire, having been out of action since falling at Ludlow in September. His first winner was in 1969. Best horses ridden include Colonel Christy.

23 DECEMBER

1921 Owner NOEL HETHERTON, also a steward at Ripon, Redcar and Wetherby, born. Best horses owned include 1983 Yorkshire Cup winner Line Slinger, St Leger 3rd Cold Storage and 1990 Champion Hurdle 3rd Past Glories. Colours: pink; navy blue collar, cuffs and quartered cap.

1947 Racing manager to Fahd Salman ANTHONY PENFOLD born.

1953 Trainer BRUCE JACKSON born.

1982 Irish jockey TOMMY CARBERRY announced that injury was forcing him to give up riding to commence training at Ratoath, Co. Dublin. He rode L'Escargot to win the Gold Cup and Grand National.

1992 Vaal race meeting from South Africa was shown live on SIS and broadcast into British betting shops, the first time South African racing alone had been featured on a particular day with no British racing at all in opposition. Commented Berjis Daver of Ladbrokes: 'We have got close to 50 per cent of what we would expect for a run-of-the-mill turf fixture in Britain.'

24 DECEMBER

1909   Racing journalist LIONEL CURETON, formerly Templegate of the *Sun*, born.

1924   Former Gosforth Park trainer RONALD ROBSON born. Best horses trained include 16-times winner Charlie Proper and 15-times winners King-Eider and Why Tell. First licence 1945.

1932   Former England cricketer, husband of trainer Lady Herries, and owner COLIN COWDREY born.

1932   Official starter NICK CROSSLEY born.

1943   Newmarket trainer (JOHN) JEREMY HINDLEY born. Trained over 600 winners between 1971 and 1987. Rode first winner in 1966. Began training in 1971. Best horses trained include The Go-Between, Huntingdale, Crash Course, Lockton, Star Pastures.

1944   Owner–trainer JOHN DOCKER born. Best horses include Lone Soldier.

1945   Owner JEFF SMITH born. Best horses include 1981 William Hill Lincoln winner Saher, Chief Singer, Dashing Blade. Colours: purple; light blue chevron; light blue cap.

1946   DAVE 'SHIPPY' ELLIS, jockeys' agent, born.

1956   Partner of Triptych and Fijar Tango TONY CRUZ born.

1986   Students from Widnes Sixth Form College were blamed for damaging the stuffed remains of great racehorse Brown Jack, which stood at the Stable Grill restaurant, Widnes. It was found lying on the ground minus an ear.

25 DECEMBER

1753 THE GODOLPHIN, one of the 3 horses from which all of today's thoroughbreds are originally descended, died and was buried at Gog Magog, Cambridgeshire.

1833 JOHN 'TINY' WELLS born at Sutton Coldfield, Warwickshire. In 1857 he won 20 times on Fisherman. He died in 1873, having won 8 Classics, including the Derby in 1858, 1859 and 1868. Something of a dandy, he once turned up to ride a horse at exercise sporting an Alpine hat with feathers in it, a suit in Gordon tartan and a pair of red Morocco slippers.

1907 Owner and Jockey Club member SONNY RICHMOND-WATSON born. Best horses owned include Blast, Night Appeal. Colours: bottle green; lime green and white checked cap.

1907 Trainer GEORGE OWEN born. Rode Brendon's Cottage to win the 1939 Cheltenham Gold Cup. As a trainer he sent out 1949 Grand National winner Russian Hero. Three Champion Jockeys started their careers in Owen's Tiverton stable as amateurs: Dick Francis, Tim Brookshaw and Stan Mellor.

1917 Dual purpose Hambleton trainer JACK CALVERT born. Best horses included 17-times winner Dieppe, 14-race winners Mannion and Crosby Don, Dondeen and Move Off.

1922 NOEL WHITCOMB, founder of the *Daily Mirror* Punters' Club, born. Owner of Even Up, the winner of 14 races. Colours: black; white sash and striped sleeves; flame cap.

1934 Racing began at Santa Anita, California. LAS PALMAS won the first race, the 7-furlong California Bred Handicap.

1939 Builder–permit-holder SIR CHRISTOPHER WATES born.

1941 Irish trainer JAMES BOLGER born. Trainer of 1992 Irish Derby winner St Jovite and 1991 Oaks winner Jet Ski Lady. As a rider he scored 3 winners from 12 mounts. Hobbies: Gaelic football and hurling.

1984 Yorkshire jockey MICHAEL WOOD celebrated Christmas by riding 3 winners in Madras, India.

1991 Great Australian champion VAIN died aged 25. One of the best-ever sprinter-milers. Won the 1969 Golden Slipper Stakes.

26 DECEMBER

1899 The day when a grand old chestnut was born: the day when GOOD FRIDAY literally fell on Boxing Day – the horse of that name capsized in the Thorneycroft Chase at Wolverhampton.

1936 Jockey BRUCE HOBBS rode for the last time as an amateur, completing a double on Circourt and Abbot's Glance at Wincanton. The very next day he rode his first two mounts as a professional, winning on both Baccharis and Eliza at Wolverhampton, and also celebrating his sixteenth birthday.

1953 LESTER PIGGOTT rode evens favourite Eldoret to victory at Wincanton, scoring his first win over hurdles.

1965 Former Melbourne Champion Jockey DARREN GAUCI born.

1970 Jockey PAT TAAFFE rode his final winner, Straight Fort, trained by Tom Dreaper, in the Paddock Handicap at Fairyhouse.

1972 The first Australian Derby was run at Ascot, Perth.

1973 At the age of fifteen NIGEL TINKLER rode his first winner, Nimble Joe, at Sedgefield. Before his next birthday he had ridden a winner on the flat, over hurdles and in a chase.

1983 ANGEL CORDERO rode Jacksboro to win at Aqueduct, New York, becoming the first rider to reach $10 million in prize-money.

1987 NUPSALA, trained by Francis Doumen, became the first French chaser to win in Britain in some 25 years as he took the King George VI Chase at Kempton.

1989 Trainer JENNY PITMAN sent out 7 winners from 14 runners.

1990 DESERT ORCHID won a record 4th King George VI Chase at Kempton, returning odds of 9–4.

1990 Newton Abbot became the first British course to use horse catchers.

1991 Trainer DERMOT WELD equalled JIM BOLGER's record of 148 Irish winners in a year, set in 1990, when Fortune and Fame and General Idea won at Down Royal.

1991 For the 3rd time in the season PETER NIVEN rode a 5-timer, on this occasion at Sedgefield at accumulative odds of 168–1.

1991 THE FELLOW (10–1), watched by a record crowd of 29,178, won the King George VI Chase at Kempton in a record time of 5 minutes 46.4 seconds under Polish-born jockey Adam Kondrat. Desert Orchid fell at the 3rd last in his final race, having won record prize-money of £652,802.

1992 The only horse ever disqualified as winner of the Kentucky Derby, Dancer's Image, died in Japan aged 27. Finished 1st in 1968 but was later thrown out after the discovery in his system of the then forbidden Butazolidin. Years of litigation followed but the race was finally awarded to runner-up Forward Pass.

27 DECEMBER

1825   Trainer JOSEPH DAWSON born. He trained 5 Classic winners and was one of the first to spend time building up yearlings, giving his two-year-olds a great advantage over their rivals. He died in 1880.

1910   Trainer CAPTAIN NEVILLE CRUMP born. Won the Grand National in 1948, 1952 and 1960; the Welsh National twice, Scottish 5 times. Best horses trained include Teal, Merryman II, Shining Gold.

1920   Jockey BRUCE HOBBS born in America. The youngest rider to win the Grand National, scoring aged seventeen on Battleship in 1938. During the Second World War he won the Military Cross (and the Palestine Grand National!).

1923   CAPTAIN TUPPY BENNETT, who won the Grand National earlier in the year on Sergeant Murphy, fell from Ardeen in the Oteley Handicap Chase at Wolverhampton. He was kicked on the head as he lay on the ground and died 17 days later.

1966   ARKLE ran his final race, fracturing a bone in his hoof. He still managed to finish 2nd in the King George VI Chase at Kempton, behind Dormant.

1971   1975 Gold Cup winner TEN UP won a bumper on his racecourse debut at Leopardstown, ridden by Jim Dreaper, who five days later became his trainer.

1982   MICHAEL DICKINSON sent out an amazing 12 winners from 21 runners, a world record: Marnik, Thornacre (Huntingdon); W. Six Times, Fearless Imp (Market Rasen); Londolozi, B. Jaski (Sedgefield); Wayward Lad (King George VI, Kempton); Delius, Happy Voyage (Wetherby); Brunton Park, Prominent Artist, Slieve Bracken (Wolverhampton).

1990   At 45 MARTIN PIPE became the youngest trainer to send out 1,000 winners when Catch the Cross (Martin Foster) won the Quicksilver Handicap Hurdle at Kempton.

1991   Jockey PHILIP BARNARD, 24, died in Bristol hospital from serious head injuries after falling from Sayyure at Wincanton the day before.

1991   Ambulanceman BOB CORFIELD, 55, died after falling out of his vehicle while it was tracking the runners in the first race at Wolverhampton.

1991   DERMOT WELD broke Jim Bolger's record of 148 Irish winners in a year when Vintage Crop became his 149th at Leopardstown, ridden by Brendan Sheridan.

1991   RICHARD QUINN rode his 99th winner of the year on (7–2 chance) Courtenay Bee at Lingfield's all-weather flat meeting.

28 DECEMBER

1787 COLONEL DENNIS O'KELLY, owner of the great Eclipse, died at Piccadilly, leaving the horse to his brother Philip.

1921 The last NH meeting took place at Newmarket.

1932 Trainer turned senior starter in Ireland STEPHEN QUIRKE born. As a trainer handled Atherstone Wood, Mistigo, Parnell.

1937 Chairman of Redcar racecourse LORD ZETLAND born. Owner of Major Owen, Foggy Buoy, Mister Ketchup. Colours: white; red spots and cap.

1941 Owner CAPTAIN GERALD MAITLAND-CAREW born. Best horses include Zonda, Moin Na Realtan, Tudor Ann. Jockey Club member. Colours: orange; brown sleeves; blue cap.

1945 Newmarket trainer CLAUD CHARLET born. Best horses trained include French Flutter. He moved to Macau.

1946 Panama-born New York jockey JORGE LUIS VELASQUEZ born. Rode Pleasant Colony to win the 1981 Kentucky Derby and Preakness Stakes. Leading US rider in 1967 with 438 victories. Won the 1989 Arlington Handicap on Unknown Quantity for the Queen.

1951 Trainer STEVE TAYLOR born. Moved to USA.

1955 LESTER PIGGOTT managed his only victory from 15 mounts during the 1955-56 jump season when he won on 3-1 favourite Dessin in the Walsall Handicap Hurdle at Wolverhampton.

1970 PAT TAAFFE announced his retirement as a jockey after a fall from Proud Tarquin in the Christmas Handicap at Fairyhouse.

1981 The highest odds in Irish Tote history, £289.64 for a 10p unit on Gene's Rogue, recorded at Limerick.

1987 ARTHUR BALDING, who until his retirement on January 1 1987 was Britain's oldest trainer, died aged 81. Best horses trained included Fortlin, Red Won, Tailor Don, Portia, Profile. As a jockey he rode Cresta Run (10-1) to win the 1927 1,000 Guineas.

1991 RICHARD QUINN was winnerless at the final flat meeting of the year, at the all-weather track at Southwell, finishing the season 1 short of his maiden century.

1992 MARTIN PIPE saddled 1, 2, 3 and 4 in the Coral Welsh National at Chepstow. Run For Free (11-4 joint favourite) won from Riverside Boy (50-1), Miinehoma (11-4 joint favourite) and Bonanza Boy. Pipe had also won this race in 1988, 1989 and 1991.

1992 Mighty Mogul won the Bonusprint Christmas Hurdle at Kempton, the 12th consecutive winner for owners BILL and SHIRLEY ROBINS with that horse, Wonder Man and Baydon Star, all of which had been relocated from Jenny Pitman to David Nicholson.

29 DECEMBER

1924   Owner JOE ALLBRITTON born. Best horses include He Loves Me, Firm Landing. Colours: emerald green; yellow chevrons.

1934   Trainer JIMMY ETHERINGTON born. Best horses trained include Fearnaught, Tesoro Mio, Brave Bambino.

1946   Jockey LAFFIT PINCAY JR, former US Champion, born in Panama City.

1950   Trainer–jockey STEVE HOLLAND born. Best horses ridden include Glanford Brig, Ben More, Primerello. First winner 1968.

1951   Trainer VINCENT O'BRIEN married Jacqueline Wittenoom. They have 5 children: David, Charles, Elizabeth, Susan and Jane.

1982   Grand National winner-to-be WEST TIP made his debut, winning at 50–1 in a novice hurdle at Warwick for trainer Michael Oliver and jockey Philip Hobbs.

1988   MARTIN PIPE saddled Mareth Line to win at Taunton, setting the fastest time for training 100 winners in a season.

1988   Former jockey and trainer TOMMY CROSS died aged 75, having trained over 300 winners, mostly over jumps. Best horses included Siren Light, Gorse.

1989   Brother and sister Marcus (Major Match) and Gee (Bold King's Hussar) Armytage both rode a winner at Warwick, although Gee was suspended for four days for her use of the whip on her mount.

1990   Jockey ALEX GREAVES rode the 50th winner of her career at Southwell on Andrew's First – the horse on which she had ridden the first winner of her career a year and four weeks earlier.

1990   Former barrister, jockey and trainer JOHN HARTY died in Armagh, Northern Ireland. He had suffered from motor neurone disease. Rode Daletta to win the 1980 Irish Grand National.

30 DECEMBER

1905   KING GEORGE V, then Prince of Wales, attended racing at Calcutta for the first time.

1942   Jockey JOHNNY HAINE born. Rode 30 winners on the flat before switching to jumps, where he won the 1966 Champion Hurdle on Salmon Spray. Retired in 1977 and began training.

1942   Former Champion Lady point-to-point jockey SCARLETT KNIPE born.

1945   CHARLES 'HELLFIRE JACK' TRIGG died in his 62nd year. The jockey won 843 races over 17 seasons from 7,221 mounts and was runner-up to Champion Jockey Frank Wootton in 1911, in which year he won the Lincoln on Mercutio.

1946   Former apprentice jockey turned 1960s pop star with the Monkees DAVY JONES born. He declared it was his ambition to ride in the Grand National. He must have been a Daydream Believer . . .

1946   Newmarket trainer COLIN WILLIAMS born.

1981   Former jockey PERRY HARDING died. He was one of only two amateurs to win the Champion Hurdle (1938 on Our Hope).

1982   Trainer FULKE WALWYN was awarded a CVO (Commander of the Victorian Order) 'for personal services' in the New Year's Honours List, while Willie Carson received an OBE for 'services to racing'.

1987   GEE ARMYTAGE won on her final mount as an amateur, Silent Echo, at Warwick. She was riding for Alan Blackmore in a race named after his son Michael, who was killed in a racing accident in May 1986.

1989   ROSS CARSON, son of Willie, had his first mount in public at the age of 21 when he partnered Pointer Man at Leicester.

1991   JOHN 'JACKIE' POWER, a leading Irish jockey for 30 years from the early 1940s, died aged 72. He rode two Irish Classic winners: Solferino, a first Classic winner for trainer John Oxx in the 1943 St Leger, and Valoris for Vincent O'Brien in the 1966 1,000 Guineas.

1992   Reigning Champion Hurdler ROYAL GAIT collapsed and died after a race at Leopardstown.

1992   China, which only a few weeks previously had permitted racing to recommence, suddenly announced a renewed ban on the sport and a strengthening of its anti-gambling laws.

1992   American jockey ALEX SOLIS was not best pleased when a spectator at Santa Anita accused him of riding a bad race – he broke the racegoer's nose! 'He was yelling and cussing at me and telling me I had ridden a bad race,' said the 37-year-old rider. 'When he took his hands out of his pockets I just swung at him with my left hand.'

31 DECEMBER

1935   Newark trainer OWEN BRENNAN born. First licence 1965.

1941   BOB WHEATLEY, owner of 1981 Triumph Hurdle winner Baron Blakeney, born. Also owned 13-times winner Up the Swanee. Colours: yellow; red striped sleeves. Listed as his recreation 'talking on the telephone to my trainer'.

1942   Owner of Artifice and Arctic Beau PAUL BARBER born. Colours: dark green; white V; light green sleeves; dark green and white checked cap.

1944   *Racing Post* columnist PAUL HAIGH born.

1954   Jockey JOHNNY KENNEALLY rode his first winner, Evening Paradise, at Manchester.

1967   Trainer CECIL BOYD-ROCHFORT was elevated to the status of Knight Commander of the Victorian Order in the New Year's Honours.

1967   BOBBY CARR, whose son Harry was stable jockey to Cecil Boyd-Rochfort, died aged 80. He was travelling head lad to Bob and Sam Armstrong.

1969   Owner of Vagador AMANDA HARWOOD born.

1987   Jockey GEE ARMYTAGE rode her first winner as a professional, on Nodalotte at Leicester.

1989   STAN CLARKE, 56, the Midlands businessman who saved Uttoxeter racecourse when his company bought it, was awarded the CBE in the New Year's Honours List. HAROLD NEWTON, for 20 years associated with the administration of Epsom's racing and training facilities, became an MBE.

1990   MICHAEL STOUTE announced that he would not be renewing his retainer with Walter Swinburn. They had originally teamed up in September 1980.

1990   Plumpton and Cheltenham both ran races named in honour of Bryan Robinson, former clerk of the course at Plumpton and director of the company that ran Cheltenham. Plumpton staged the Bryan Robinson Handicap Chase and Cheltenham the Robinson Handicap Hurdle.

1991   RAYMOND GUEST, the only man to own a Derby winner (Larkspur 1962 and Sir Ivor 1968), a Grand National winner (L'Escargot 1975) and a Gold Cup winner (L'Escargot 1970 and 1971), died in Virginia, USA, aged 84. Once US ambassador to the Republic of Ireland. Racing colours: chocolate; pale blue hoops and cap.

1992   The QUEEN's Abbey Strand won at Lingfield in the Any Post Maiden Stakes to crown her most successful year as an owner, taking her final score to 26.

INDEX OF PEOPLE ASSOCIATED
WITH PARTICULAR DATES

Demetriou, Harry 59
De Moraville, John 277
Dempsey, Eddie 38
Dempster, Nigel 87
Denaro, Michael 47
Denis, Rev. 242
Dennis, Paul 18
Dennis, Richard 48, 226
Dent, Neville 334
Dent, Tommy 105
Depalmas, Marcel 320
De Pass, Richard 75
Derby, Lord 112
Desaint, Jean-Claude 224
Desormeaux, Kent 22, 58, 335
Destasio, Richard 233
Dettori, Gianfranco 4, 67, 89, 108, 116, 159, 257, 271, 307, 308, 314, 350
Dettori, Lanfranco 240
De Trafford, Humphrey 335
Dever, Peter 192
Devonshire, Duke of 2
Dick, Dave 68
Dickens, Rodney 98
Dickin, Robin 93
Dickinson, Michael 34, 52, 66, 68, 77, 88, 177, 182, 154, 362
Dickinson, Monica 151, 263
Dickinson, Tony 66, 148, 177, 218
Dillon, Dennis 33
Dillon, Joe 198
Di Mauro, Steve 334
Dimmock, Peter 341
Dimsdale, Jonathan 18
Dineley, David 194, 316
Dingwall, Louie 236, 251
Dittfach, Hugo 331
Dittman, Mick 68
Dixon, John 335
Dixon, Mark 118
Dixon, Willie 322
Docker, John 359
Dolesji, Josef 194
Doleuze, George 35
Donoghue, Pat 97
Donoghue, Steve 83, 116, 158, 176, 313
Doolan, Kevin 210
Dooler, Jim 180, 210

Doughty, Neale 294
Douglas, A. J. 86
Douglas, Lady James 31, 156
Douglas, John 353
Douglas-Home, Jamie 137
Douieb, Olivier 174
Doumen, Francois 163
Dow, Simon 45, 165
Dowdeswell, Jack 148
Dowling, Bruce 50, 95
Dowling, John 251
Doyle, Jack 150
Doyle, Jim 15
Doyle, John 180
Dreaper, Jim 24, 30
Dreaper, Tom 48
Drew, Clive 182
Drysdale, Neil 346
Dudgeon, Ian 23
Dudgeon, Sandy 290
Duffey, Louis 327
Duffield, George 99, 158, 167, 193, 231, 232, 262, 294, 335
Dufosee, Peter 109
Duggan, Jimmy 222
Dun, Geordie 292
Dun, Robin 4
Dundas, Hugh 204
Dunlop, John 118, 192, 207, 289
Dunn, Allan 281
Dunraven, Lord 301
Dunster, Stephen 261
Dunwoody, Richard 18, 34, 89, 90, 125, 151, 284, 312, 314, 328
Durant, Yvonne 158
Durr, Frank 315
Dutrow, Dick 68
Dutton, David 131
Duval, Claude 158
Dwyer, Chris 355
Dwyer, Mark 161, 222
Dwyer, Phil and Mike 161
Dye, Shane 202

Eades, Gavan 163
Earnshaw, Robert 134
East, David 65
East, Johnny 184
Easterby, Michael 90
Easterby, Miles 217

Easterby, Sarah 180
Eaton, Judy 273
Eccles, Steve Smith 94, 185
Eccleston, Clive 190, 240
Eddery, Carolyn 128, 191
Eddery, Jimmy 174, 238
Eddery, Michael 329
Eddery, Pat 71, 78, 90, 115, 122, 139, 172, 178, 181, 198, 204, 208, 248, 259, 284, 291, 297, 316, 232, 234, 235
Eddery, Paul 196
Ede, George 70
Eden, Grant 225
Edmondson, Robert 47
Edwards, John 104, 239
Edwards, Roy 150, 248
Edwards, Simon 87
Edwards-Heathcote, Bill 256
Egan, Jack 212
Egan, James 334
Egan, John 145
Egerton, Charlie 314
Eldin, Eric 213
Ellerby, Michael 327
Elliott, Charlie 82, 203
Elliott, Bill 142
Elliott, Bobby 80
Ellis, Dave 359
Elsey, Bill 161, 343
Elsey, Charles 45, 327
Elsey, William 46
Elsworth, David 83, 98, 127, 147, 212, 347
Elwell, Robert and Theresa 125
Embiricos, Alexandra 9
Embiricos, Nick 29
Ennis, Peter 285
Ennor, George 352
Enright, Gerry 186
Enright, John 38
Essman, David 164
Etherington, Jimmy 364
Etherington, Tim 25
Eustace, James 86
Evans, James 147
Evans, Richard 153
Evatt, David 333

Fabricius, Rod 116
Faggotter, Val 171

INDEX OF HORSES ASSOCIATED
WITH PARTICULAR DATES